THE WORKING CLASS IN AMERICAN HISTORY

A list of books in this series appears at the end of this book.

The New England Working Class
and the New Labor History

Winslow Homer's *New England Factory Life—"Bell Time." Harper's Weekly*, July 25, 1868.

Edited by
Herbert G. Gutman and Donald H. Bell

The New England Working Class and the New Labor History

UNIVERSITY OF ILLINOIS PRESS
Urbana and Chicago

©1987 by the Board of Trustees of the University of Illinois
Manufactured in the United States of America
1 2 3 4 5 C P 5 4 3 2 1

This book is printed on acid-free paper.

Library of Congress Cataloging-in-Publication Data

Main entry under title:

The New England working class and the new labor history.

  (The Working class in American history)
  Papers presented at a conference held March 1979
at Smith College.
    1. Labor and laboring classes—New England—History—
Congresses. I. Gutman, Herbert George, 1928–1985.
II. Bell, Donald H., 1943–   . III. Smith College.
IV. Series.
HD8083.A11N48   1987   305.5′62′0974   85-27095
ISBN 0–252–01300–X (cloth; alk. paper)
ISBN 0–252–01301–8 (paper; alk. paper)

Contents

Preface

The publication of the papers presented at Smith College at the conference "The New Labor History and the New England Working Class" represents a realization of a dream. When we planned the conference, we hoped to honor three distinguished women pioneers in the study of the history of the American working class—Hannah Josephson, Caroline Ware, and Vera Shlakman—and to establish the continuity between the work of a new generation of scholars whose work was attracting attention in the decade of the 1970s with their trailblazing studies from the 1930s onward. When we planned the conference, we knew the breadth and quality of the scholarly work being done, but the papers presented surpassed in quality and in richness of material our fondest expectations.

Herbert G. Gutman, as the presiding genius of the field and the mentor of an extended network of young scholars, helped us to plan a program that would focus attention on the work of young and promising historians and also on the fresh and stimulating insights emerging from a study of working-class history in the decade of the 1970s. We also wished to direct attention to the study of New England history and culture, since the history of the region during the nineteenth century presents the student of industrialization with a working social laboratory. The range of records and archival materials is rich, and their creative use is brilliantly demonstrated in the essays presented in this volume.

A further objective of the conference was to highlight Smith's link to earlier scholarship in the study of industrialization and the emergence of the American working class through Smith's Council of Industrial Studies. This council, active in a variety of endeavors, attempted to coordinate and systematize efforts to preserve and study archival materials relating to the history of industrialization in the Connecticut Valley. As we watch the nineteenth-century mill towns become gentrified or reshaped by high technology, it seems even more important to capture and preserve the history of an earlier stage of industrialization. Thus, we hope to continue the efforts and concerns of Smith's earlier Council of Industrial Studies through the development of curricular materials and research efforts concerned with New England's nineteenth-century history.

Our debt to Herbert G. Gutman and Donald H. Bell, planners of the conference and joint editors of this volume, is very great indeed. Their contagious enthusiasm and unbounded curiosity about the details of our past and their drive to advance our understanding of this field produced a conference and a set of scholarly papers that are a fitting tribute to the earlier work of Hannah Josephson, Caroline Ware, and Vera Shlakman. I am delighted that Smith College could be the setting for a tribute to their work and for the support of scholarship in an important historical field. Our debt to the Rockefeller Foundation for enabling us to plan a conference of this scope and ambition is equally great; the foundation's support made the conference and the plans for publication possible. We are grateful to Joel Colton for being the program officer we all dream about, one who knows in advance the kind of impetus that such a conference can provide to youthful scholarly careers and the development of the research enterprise.

JILL KER CONWAY
Past President
Smith College

Introduction

The essays published in this volume deal with diverse and often little-known aspects of the New England working-class historical experience. Of course, much is known about that class and especially its trade union history and the nineteenth- and twentieth-century strikes and lockouts that have punctuated its history. Wage labor, after all, has a longer and a deeper history there than in any other part of the United States. And many fine historical monographs and essays detail the lives of its laboring men, women, and children. We need only think of what has been written about the textile workers of Lowell, Massachusetts, the shoemakers of Lynn, Massachusetts, and the gun and tool makers whose skills so enhanced the reputation of Connecticut metal goods. But a regionwide history of the New England working class does not exist. We do not have a book that sweeps that region's historical development, examining the changing relationship between the social and class structure, capitalist development and transformation, the constantly redefined labor process, and the changing composition of the wage-earning population. No single work about New England labor carries us from the time when the wage supplemented a family's income from the land to our time, when the numbers of workers earning wages in manufacturing industries with long and significant histories are dwindling rapidly.

This book of essays is not that badly needed regionwide history of the New England working class. But it moves us in that direction. Its emphasis is regionwide. The themes explored include the trade union but go beyond that subject in exploring working-class life and behavior. The volume brings together eleven essays on very different aspects of the New England working-class experience. The essays stretch in time from the Revolutionary War to the New Deal. They were prepared for (and read and discussed) at a conference at Smith College in early March 1979. Entitled "The New Labor History and the New England Working Class," the conference served several distinct but related purposes.

First, Smith College and especially its then president, Jill Ker Conway, saw such a conference as the long overdue occasion to honor an earlier generation of women historians. These were not colleagues whose contribution to American history had been marginal. The late Hannah Josephson, Vera Shlakman, and Caroline Ware had extended the boundaries of American working-class history beyond those fixed by John R. Commons and others described as this subject's founding fathers. Their books did more than record new information about working men and women; they also offered new ways to *think* about working-class history. Their works appeared between 1930 and 1950 and focused on the New England textile industry and its workers. Their perspectives differed, but all asked new questions about the early history of New England capitalism and wage labor. Theirs were works that dealt primarily with the formation of the first New England proletariat in rich conceptual and empirical ways.

Vera Shlakman and Caroline Ware attended the 1979 Smith College conference and were honored by the college in a formal ceremony. They, in turn, honored the college by participating fully in the conference deliberations, engaging in discussions of papers written by men and women young enough to be their grandchildren. Their comments were sharp and incisive—pushing, always pushing for the younger historian to tease fuller meaning out of this or that body of evidence. It often is asserted that the so-called new labor history—historical studies that examine the full life experience of working men and women—started in the 1960s. It also is often argued that such work involved little more than an American adaptation of British Marxist and neo-Marxist social and labor history, particularly E. P. Thompson's influential *The Making of the English Working Class* (1963). But the publication of *The Early New England Cotton Manufacture: A Study of Industrial Beginnings* (1931), *Economic History of a Factory Town: A Study of Chicopee, Massachusetts* (1935), and *Golden Threads: New England Mill Girls and Magnates* (1949) by Ware, Shlakman, and Josephson, respectively, belies such simplistic historiographic explanations. Those younger historians who read papers at the Smith College conference had among their critics elderly historians whose own youthful works remain central to what now is described as the *new* labor history.

The Smith conference had a second objective closely connected to the first. Its organizers did not merely want to discuss as yet unpublished works. Recent publications deserved attention, too. It was decided therefore to examine critically historical writings about nonelite New Englanders that made explicit use of the conceptual and/or methodological tools associated with either recent Britist Marxist and neo-Marxist labor history or the French social history loosely connected with the Annales school. A session each therefore was devoted to discussing Alan Dawley's book *Class and Community: The Industrial Revolution in Lynn,* published in 1976, and James Henretta's essay "Families and Farms, Mentalité in Pre-Industrial America," published in the *William and Mary Quarterly* in 1978.

These very different works struck the conference organizers as ideal for such a discussion. Both probed mentalité—among other matters—but used quite different methods. A panel of historians—only one (by design) a specialist in American working-class history—prepared formal comments on each work. The authors responded, and a general discussion followed. Robert Bezucha and Paul Faler analyzed the Dawley book. Stephen Nissenbaum and Joan Wallach Scott examined the Henretta essay. Each discussion lasted a full morning. The exchanges were friendly but sharp and probing. Not surprisingly, different conceptual approaches were debated. A lively exchange explored the problems associated with using quantitative data to infer mentalite. The presence of Bezucha and Scott assured thoughtful, comparative considerations.

We tape-recorded these two sessions, hoping to include them in this volume. But costs made that impossible. Instead, unedited copies of the tapes have been deposited in the Smith College library for use by students and scholars. The passage of a few years since these exchanges occurred has not diminished the importance of either Dawley's book or Henretta's essay. Instead, their significance has been enhanced. Discussing them in such public detail in 1979 was not fanciful. The conference organizers express their thanks to Bezucha, Faler, Nissenbaum, and Scott and especially to Dawley and Henretta for making this exchange possible in so stimulating a format.

The eleven essays of this book were all read and discussed at the Smith College conference; indeed, they served as the core of the three-day meeting. Not much needs to be written about them, as they speak for themselves. Their general high quality is indicated by the fact that some already have appeared in highly regarded journals. Other contributors have published revisions of their conference papers in well-received monographs. There is nevertheless a very good reason to publish these conference essays as a group: a thematically diverse single volume of essays on New England working-class history is made available to students and teachers in this format. No such work as yet exists. The essays also belong together in a single volume because with one exception they represent the work of younger labor and social historians trained in the 1960s and

1970s in institutions as diverse as Brown University (Gary Kulik and Judith Smith), Columbia University (David Bensman), Harvard University (Alexander Keyssar, Carol Lasser, Jonathan Prude, and Roy Rosenzweig), the University of Pittsburgh (Cecelia Bucki), the University of Rochester (Leon Fink), and the University of Wisconsin (Paul Buhle). The exception, of course, is Alfred F. Young, a distinguished scholar on late eighteenth- and early nineteenth-century U. S. History.

The conference brought together a group of historians whose works range thematically and chronologically over the entire New England working-class experience. Of course, not all aspects of that experience are covered, but in planning a conference entitled "The New Labor History and the New England Working Class," the conference organizers solicited papers dealing with *themes* central in the writing of recent American working-class history. Four themes were selected and papers prepared relating to these themes: *personality, biography, and family* (Young, Lasser, and Smith); *work* (Prude, Bensman, and Bucki); *culture* (Kulik and Rosenzweig), and *politics* (Fink, Keyssar, and Buhle). Because New England working-class history divides over time into an old (Yankee) and a new (immigrant and ethnic) working class, it was decided that these thematic essays should involve diverse groups over time. This is not a collection of essays about Yankee workers, nor is it a collection of essays about immigrant workers. These are essays examining the changing class relationships, experiences, behavior, and beliefs of New England working men and women. The volume includes essays on eighteenth- and nineteenth-century Yankee artisans, servants, and mill women and children as well as twentieth-century immigrant kinship networks and political radicalism.

A single theme, we believe, gives coherence to this volume. It is far more than the fact that its subject is the New England working class. The essays vary from each other in subject matter and in mode of analysis. But throughout the volume, working men and women are not viewed simply as the objects of historical process. They become the subjects of history. They are not romanticized. Their importance is not exaggerated. No one is arguing that exploited and subordinate men and women make history, but they regularly participate in and help shape significant historical processes. We learn in these pages how they protect skills and redefine workplace rights. Their presence helps transform the town meeting as a political institution. They struggle to discard deference in a republican society. They debate with manufacturers over water rights. They dispute their betters over the uses of public park space. They adapt kinship functions to strengthen class solidarities. They transform European political radicalism into a language appropriate to early twentieth-century corporate capitalism. These pages are filled with the thoughts and behavior of ordinary New England men and women experiencing changing patterns of inequality in the world of John Winthrop's descendants. The authors of these essays have reshaped old contexts and created new ones to bring these men and women to life and to tell us something new and important about New England history, not merely its laboring men, women, and children.

HERBERT G. GUTMAN
DONALD H. BELL

In Memoriam, Herbert G. Gutman (1928–85)

This volume serves as a kind of memorial to Herbert G. Gutman, who died on July 21, 1985, and it bears witness to several of Herb's particular interests and concerns. Indeed, its origins in an academic conference attest to Herb's unquenchable appetite for the sharing of scholarly insights (and differences) at meetings and symposia. As one of Herb's eulogists has remarked, Herb did not just attend conferences: he himself often presided over a kind of ongoing conference, and he continued the proceedings at any hour and wherever he might be—in his room, at dinner with colleagues, in hotel lobbies and halls.

At the 1979 Smith College conference (which he had largely organized), Herb was everywhere—checking on logistics and on the agenda, introducing participants to one another, and stimulating debate with well-directed questions of the sort that he himself might have labeled "very smart." At this meeting (and elsewhere), Herb acted as an interlocutor for the members of several scholarly generations, from the youngest graduate students to the most senior and respected emeriti. Herb had a knack for facilitating this sort of interchange as he had a knack for provoking curiosity into the unanswered (and even previously unasked) questions of labor and social history, and for stirring excitement in the possibilities of future research and the breakthroughs that lay just ahead.

The present collection provides evidence, as well, for the manner in which Herb especially supported the research of younger scholars. Most of the papers given at Smith College (and collected herein) are the work of a generation of social and labor historians just emerging into maturity, a generation much influenced by Herb and by his concern for the role of labor culture and for the connection between larger political questions and the actual lives of workers and artisans, black slaves, and immigrants to America. Herb introduced prospective historians to this field (which he himself had done much to shape and to reinvigorate); he helped them to focus on new questions and new ways to think about sources and evidence; he infused younger colleagues with his own enthusiasm; he followed and promoted their careers; he befriended them and devoted endless time and energy to their concerns. "He gave us the feeling," one contributor to this book has noted, "that the field was wide open and that there was always more to do. He brought many of us into this area of research in the first place, and he convinced us that we were all engaged in the work of American labor and social history together."

Although this volume focuses on discrete aspects of working-class life in a single geographic region, it reflects Herb's concern with larger issues and, indeed, with the task of formulating a new synthesis of American labor and social history (as part of a general process of rethinking the American past).* In concentrating upon New England, this volume considers the virtual crucible not only of American labor but also of American industry, and in treating the experience of New England labor from the colonial era into the twentieth century, this study provides an indication of how such a synthesis might proceed.

It is more than unfortunate that Herbert Gutman did not live to see the completion of that project of scholarly integration. In both his teaching and research, however, as well as in his participation in such endeavors as the American Working Class History Project, Herb provided guidelines as to how the last decade's outpouring of scholarly work might eventually provide a new awareness of our national past. It is a loss beyond measure that Herb is no longer here to help speed that undertaking and to employ his own formidable skills as a scholar and as a facilitator of research. In the last analysis, Herb was a great historian who was arguably at his best while engaged in collective effort with his colleagues. He lived the history about which he wrote: the history of the collective attempt of American men and women to build a better life and a better country. Herb—to borrow one of his favorite words—was a splendid person. He will be sorely missed.

D.H.B.

*See MARHO, *Visions of History* (New York, 1984), pp. 203ff.

PART ONE

PERSONALITY
Life Histories and Artisan
Culture and Behavior

Winslow Homer's *Ship-Building, Gloucester Harbor. Harper's Weekly,*
October 11, 1873.

CHAPTER 1

George Robert Twelves Hewes (1742–1840): A Boston Shoemaker and the Memory of the American Revolution

ALFRED F. YOUNG

Late in 1762 or early in 1763, George Robert Twelves Hewes, a Boston shoemaker in the last year or so of his apprenticeship, repaired a shoe for John Hancock and delivered it to him at his uncle Thomas Hancock's store in Dock Square. Hancock was pleased and invited the young man to "come and see him on New Year's day, and bid him a happy New-Year," according to the custom of the day, a ritual of noblesse oblige on the part of the gentry. We know of the episode through Benjamin Bussey Thatcher, who interviewed Hewes and wrote it up for his *Memoir* of Hewes in 1835. On New Year's Day, as Thatcher tells the story, after some urging by his master,

> George washed his face, and put his best jacket on, and proceeded straightaway to the Hancock House (as it is still called). His heart was in his mouth, but assuming a cheerful courage, he knocked at the front door, and took his hat off. The servant came:
>
> "Is 'Squire Hancock at home, Sir?" enquired Hewes, making a bow.
>
> He was introduced directly to the *kitchen*, and requested to seat himself, while report should be made above stairs. The man came down directly, with a new varnish of civility suddenly spread over his face. He ushered him into the 'Squire's sitting-room, and left him to make his obeisance. Hancock remembered him, and addressed him kindly. George was anxious to get through, and he commenced a desperate speech—"as pretty a one," he says, "as he any way knew how,"—intended to announce the purpose of his visit, and to accomplish it, in the same breath.
>
> "Very well, my lad," said the 'Squire—now take a chair, my lad."

3

He sat down, scared all the while (as he now confesses) "almost to death," while Hancock put his hand into his breeches-pocket and pulled out a crown-piece, which he placed softly in his hand, thanking him at the same time for his punctual attendance, and his compliments. He then invited his young friend to drink his health—called for wine—poured it out for him—and ticked glasses with him,—a feat in which Hewes, though he had never seen it performed before, having acquitted himself with a creditable dexterity, hastened to make his bow again, and secure his retreat, through not till the 'Squire had extorted a sort of half promise from him to come the next New-Year's—which, for a rarity, he never discharged.[1]

The episode is a demonstration of what the eighteenth century called deference.

Another episode catches the point at which Hewes had arrived a decade and a half later. In 1778 or 1779, after one stint in the war on board a privateer and another in the militia, he was ready to ship out again, from Boston. As Thatcher tells the story: "Here he enlisted, or engaged to enlist, on board the Hancock, a twenty-gun ship, but not liking the manners of the Lieutenant very well, who ordered him one day in the streets to take his hat off to him—which he refused to do for any man,—he went aboard the 'Defence,' Captain Smedley, of Fairfield Connecticut."[2] This, with a vengeance, is the casting off of deference.

What had happened in the intervening years? What had turned the young shoemaker tongue-tied in the face of his betters into the defiant person who would not take his hat off for any man? And why should stories like this have stayed in his memory sixty and seventy years later?

George Robert Twelves Hewes was born in Boston in 1742 and died in Richfield Springs, New York, in 1840. He participated in several of the principal political events of the American Revolution in Boston, among them the Massacre and the Tea Party, and during the war he served as a privateersman and militiaman. A shoemaker all his life, and intermittently or concurrently a fisherman, sailor, and farmer, he remained a poor man. He never made it, not before the war in Boston, not at sea, not after the war in Wrentham and Attleborough, Massachusetts, not in Otsego County, New York. He was a nobody who briefly became somebody in the Revolution and, for a moment near the end of his life, a hero.

Hewes might have been unknown to posterity save for his longevity and a shift in the historical mood that rekindled the "spirit of '76." To Americans of the 1830s the Boston Tea Party had become a leading symbol of the Revolution, and Hewes lived long enough to be thought of as one of the last surviving participants, perhaps the very last. In 1833, when James Hawkes "discovered" him in the "obscurity" of upstate New York, Hewes was ninety-one but thought he was ninety-eight, a claim Hawkes accepted when he published the first memoir of Hewes that year.[3] Thus in 1835 when Hewes was invited to Boston, people thought that this survivor of one of the greatest moments of the Revolution was approaching his one hundredth birthday and on "the verge of eternity," as a Fourth of July orator put it.[4] He became a celebrity, the guest of honor on Independence Day, the subject of a second biography by Thatcher and of an oil portrait by Joseph Cole, which hangs today in Boston's Old State House.

To Thatcher, Hewes was one of the "humble classes" that made the success of the Revolution possible. How typical he was we can only suggest at this point in our limited knowledge of the "humble classes." Probably he was as representative a member of the "lower trades" of the cities and as much a rank-and-file participant in the political events and the war as historians have found. The two biographies, which come close to being oral histories (and give us clues to track down Hewes in other ways), provide an unusually rich cumulative record, over a very long period of time, of his thoughts, attitudes, and values. Consequently, we can answer, with varying degrees of satisfaction, a number of questions about one man of the "humble classes." About the "lower trades": why did a boy enter a craft with such bleak prospects as shoemaking? what was the life of an apprentice? what did it mean to be a shoemaker and a poor man in Boston? About the Revolution: what moved such a rank-and-file person to action? what action did he take? may we speak of his "ideology"? does the evidence of his loss of deference permit us to speak of change in his consciousness? About the war: how did a poor man, an older man, a man with a family exercise his patriotism? what choices did he make? About the results of the Revolution: how did the war affect him? to what extent did he achieve his life goals? why did he go west? what did it mean to be an aged veteran of the Revolution? What, in sum, after more than half a century had passed, was the meaning of the Revolution to someone still in the "humble classes"?

I

A wide variety of sources can be used to check Hewes's recollections, fill in what is missing in the biographies, and supply context. But to get at Hewes, the historian has essentially a major double task: separating him from his biographers and sifting the memories of a man in his nineties to recover actions and feelings from sixty to eighty years before. The problem is familiar to scholars who have used the rich body of W.P.A. narratives of former slaves taken down by interviewers in the 1930s and who have had to ask: who recorded these recollections, under what circumstances, and with what degree of skill? how does memory function in the aged? what is remembered best and least? how do subsequent emotions and values color or overlie the memory of events in the distant past?[5]

The two biographies of Hewes were part of "a spate" of narratives of the Revolution by ordinary soldiers and sailors that appeared in print, especially from the 1820s on.[6] Together with the autobiographies, diaries, and journals, unpublished at the time, we know of at least 500 such first-person accounts of men who saw military service.[7] Much of this remembering was stimulated by the pension laws of 1818 and especially of 1832 that required veterans to submit, in lieu of written records, "a very full account" of their military service. These laws produced no less than 80,000 personal narratives—Hewes's among them—which are finally coming under the scrutiny of historians.[8]

Hawkes and Thatcher had different strengths and weaknesses. We know hardly anything about James Hawkes; he took the pseudonym "A New Yorker" and published in New York City. He may have been a journalist.[9] He discovered Hewes by an "accidental concurrence of events" and interviewed him in his familiar surroundings in Richfield Springs over several days in 1833 around the Fourth of July. Hawkes's virtue was that he tried to take down Hewes in the first person, although more often than not he lapsed into the third person or interrupted Hewes's narrative with long digressions, padding the story. He did not know enough about either the Revolution or Boston to question Hewes or follow up his leads, and he had a tendency to use Hewes as an exemplar of the virtues of Benjamin Franklin and selfless patriotism. But in his ignorance he allowed Hewes to structure his own story and convey his own feelings. Thus the book at times has an "as told to" flavor, and when Hawkes allows Hewes to speak, we can agree that "his language is remarkable for its grammatical simplicity and correctness."[10]

Benjamin Bussey Thatcher, on the other hand, intruded, as the language of his account of the visit to John Hancock suggests. He could not resist embellishing Hewes's stories or inventing dialogue. He brought to Hewes the same compassion for the lowly and sense of the uses of history that he brought to other historical subjects. A Boston gentleman, reformer, abolitionist, Bowdoin graduate, and lawyer, at the age of twenty-six he had written a short biography of Phillis Wheatley, Boston's black poet of the eighteenth century, a memoir of a Liberian missionary, and four volumes on American Indians, two of them collections of biographies.[11] Thatcher talked to Hewes on the latter's "triumphal" return to Boston in 1835, walked him around town, primed his memory. He lifted almost everything in Hawkes (without attribution) but also extracted a good many new anecdotes, especially about Hewes's youth, and expanded others about the Revolution. Occasionally he was skeptical; he read old newspapers and talked to other survivors to check the background. Thatcher thus added to the record, although in a form and tone that often seem more his own than Hewes's. And while his interests as a reformer led him to inquire, for example, about schools and slavery in Hewes's Boston, they also led him to dissociate Hewes from the "mob," probably with some distortion. Thus Thatcher's portrayal, while fuller than Hawkes's, is also more flawed.[12]

Hewes's remembering, once distinguished from the overlay of these biographies, also had strengths and weaknesses. He was, to begin with, in remarkable physical condition. In 1833 Hawkes found his "physical and intellectual" powers "of no ordinary character." "I have generally enjoyed sound health," Hewes said. He showed few signs of his advanced age. His hair was light brown, salted with gray, and he had most of it. He was not bent down by his years but was "so perfectly erect" and moved "with so much agility and firmness . . . that he might be taken for a man in all the vigour of youth." He regularly walked two or three miles each day, and for his sessions with Hawkes he walked five miles back and forth to Hawkes's lodgings. He was of such an "active disposition" that Hawkes found he would hardly stay put long enough to be interviewed. When Hewes became excited, his "dark blue eyes," which Hawkes called "an index to an intelligent and vigorous mind," would "sparkle with a glow of lustre."[13] Thatcher was impressed with "a strength and clearness in his faculties" often not present in men twenty years younger. "Both his mental and bodily faculties are wonderfully hale. He converses with almost the promptness of middle life." His mind did not wander. He answered questions directly, and "he can seldom be detected in any redundancy or deficiency of expression." He was not garrulous.[14]

Both men were amazed at Hewes's memory. Thatcher found it "so extraordinary" that at times it "absolutely astonished" him.[15] Hewes recounted details from many stages of his life: from his childhood,

George Robert Twelves Hewes (*The Centenarian* by Joseph G. Cole, Boston, 1835. Courtesy of The Bostonian Society, Old State House, Boston).

youth, and young adulthood, from the years leading up to the Revolution, from seven years of war. While he told next to nothing about the next half century of his life, his memory of recent events was clear. He graphically recalled a trip to Boston in 1821. He remembered names, a remarkable array of them that Thatcher checked.[16] He remembered how things looked; he even seemed to recall how things tasted. Most important, he remembered his own emotions, evoking them once again. He seems to have kept no diary or journal, and by his own claim, which Hawkes accepted, he had not read any accounts of the Tea Party or by implication any other events of the Revolution.[17]

His mind worked in ways that are familiar to students of the processes of memory.[18] Thus he remembered more for Thatcher in Boston in 1835 than for Hawkes in Richfield Springs in 1833. This is not surprising; he was warmed up and was responding to cues as he returned to familiar scenes and Thatcher asked him pointed questions. Having told many episodes of his life before—to his children and grandchildren, and to children and adults in Richfield Springs—he thus had rehearsed them and they came out as adventure stories.

His memory also displayed common weaknesses. He had trouble with his age, which may not have been unusual at a time when birthdays were not much celebrated and birth certificates not issued.[19] He had trouble with sequences of events and with the intervals of time between events. He was somewhat confused, for example, about his military tours of duty, something common in other veterans' narratives.[20] He also got political events in Boston somewhat out of order, telescoping what for him had become one emotionally. Or he told his good stories first, following up with the less interesting ones. All this is harmless enough. He remembered, understandably, experiences that were pleasant, and while he did well with painful experiences that had been seared into him—like childhood punishments and the Boston Massacre—he "forgot" other experiences that were humiliating. There are also many silences in his life story, and where these cannot be attributed to his biographers' lack of interest (as in his humdrum life from 1783 to 1833), because his memory is so good we are tempted to see significance in these silences.

All in all, we are the beneficiaries in Hewes of a phenomenon psychologists recognize in "the final stage of memory" as "life review," characterized by "sudden emergence of memories and a desire to remember, and a special candour which goes with a feeling that active life is over, achievement is completed." A British historian who has taken oral history from the aged notes that "in this final stage there is a major compensation for the longer interval and the selectivity of the memory process, in an increased willingness to remember, and commonly too a diminished concern for fitting the story to the social norms of the audience. Thus bias from both repression and distortion becomes a less inhibiting difficulty, for both teller and historian."[21]

On balance, Hewes's memory was strong, yet what he remembered, as well as the meaning he attached to it, inevitably was shaped by his values, attitudes, and temperament. There was an overlay from Hewes as well as his biographers. First, he had a stake, both monetary and psychic, in his contribution to the Revolution. He had applied for a pension in October 1832; by the summer of 1833, when he talked to Hawkes, it had been granted. He had also become a personage of sorts in his own locale, at least on the Fourth of July. And when he talked with Thatcher he was bathed in Boston's recognition. Thus though he did not have to prove himself (as did thousands of other veterans waiting for action on their applications), he had spent many years trying to do just that. Moreover, he had to live up to his reputation and had the possibility of enhancing it.

Secondly, he may have imposed an overlay of his current religious values on the younger man. He had generally been "of a cheerful mind," he told Hawkes, and Thatcher spoke of the "cheerfulness and evenness of his temper."[22] There is evidence for such traits earlier in his life. In his old age, however, he became a practicing Methodist—composed in the assurance of his own salvation, confident of his record of good deeds, and forgiving to his enemies. As a consequence he may well have blotted out some contrary feelings he had once held. One suspects he had been a much more angry and aggressive younger man than he or his biographers convey.

Finally, in the 1830s he lived in a society that no longer bestowed the deference once reserved for old age and had never granted much respect to poor old shoemakers.[23] In the Revolution for a time it had been different; the shoemaker won recognition as a citizen; his betters sought his support and seemingly deferred to him. This contributed to a tendency, as he remembered the Revolution, not so much to exaggerate what he had done—he was consistently modest in his claims for himself—as to place himself closer to some of the great men of the time than is susceptible to proof. For a moment he was on a level with his betters. So he thought at the time, and so it grew in his memory as it disappeared in his life. And in this memory of an awakening to citizenship and recognition from his betters—a memory with both substance and shadow—we shall argue lay the meaning of the Revolution to George Hewes.

II

In 1756, when Hewes was fourteen, he was apprenticed to a shoe-maker. Why did a boy become a shoemaker in mid-eighteenth-century Boston? The town's shoemakers were generally poor and their prospects were worsening. From 1756 to 1775, eight out of thirteen shoemakers who died and left wills at probate did not even own their own homes.[24] In 1790 shoemakers ranked thirty-eighth among forty-four occupations in mean tax assessments.[25]

It was not a trade in which boys were eager to be apprentices. Few sons continued in their father's footsteps, as they did, for example, in prosperous trades like silversmithing or shipbuilding.[26] Leather-workers, after mariners, headed the list of artisans who got their apprentices from the orphans, illegitimate children, and boys put out to apprenticeship by Boston's Overseers of the Poor.[27] In England, shoemaking was a trade with proud traditions, symbolized by St. Crispin's Day, a shoemakers' holiday, a trade with a reputation for producing poets, philosophers, and politicians, celebrated by Elizabethan playwrights as "the gentle craft."[28] But there were few signs of a flourishing shoemaker culture in Boston before the Revolution. In children's lore shoemakers were proverbially poor, like the cobbler in a Boston chapbook who "labored hard and took a great deal of pains for a small livelihood."[29] Shoemakers, moreover, were low in status. John Adams spoke of shoemaking as "too mean and dimi[nu]tive an Occupation" to hold a client of his who wanted to "rise in the World."[30]

Where one ended up in life depended very much on where one started out. George was born under the sign of the Bulls Head and Horns on Water Street near the docks in the South End. His father—also named George—was a tallow chandler and erstwhile tanner. Hewes drew the connections between his class origins and his life chances as he began his narrative for Hawkes:

> My father, said he, was born in Wrentham in the state of Massachusetts, about twenty-eight miles from Boston. My grandfather having made no provision for his support, and being unable to give him an education, apprenticed him at Boston to learn a mechanical trade. . . .
> In my childhood, my advantages for education were very limited, much more so than children enjoy at the present time in my native state. My whole education which my opportunities permitted me to acquire, consisted only of a moderate knowledge of reading and writing; my father's circumstances being confined to such humble means as he was enabled to acquire by

his mechanical employment, I was kept running of errands, and exposed of course to all the mischiefs to which children are liable in populous cities.[31]

Hewes's family on his father's side was "no better off than what is called in New England *moderate,* and probably not as good."[32] The American progenitor of the line seems to have come from Wales and was in Salisbury, near Newburyport, in 1677, doing what we do not know. Solomon Hewes, George Robert's grandfather, was born in Portsmouth, New Hampshire, in 1674, became a joiner, and moved with collateral members of his family to Wrentham, originally part of Dedham, near Rhode Island. There he became a landholder; most of his brothers were farmers; two became doctors, one of whom prospered in nearby Providence. His son—our George's father—was born in 1701.[33] On the side of his mother, Abigail Seaver, Hewes's family was a shade different. They had lived for four generations in Roxbury, a small farming town immediately south of Boston across the neck. Abigail's ancestors seem to have been farmers, but one was a minister.[34] Her father, Shubael, was a country cordwainer who owned a house, barn, and two acres. She was born in 1711 and married in 1728.[35]

George Robert Twelves Hewes, born August 25, 1742, was the sixth of nine children, the fourth of seven sons. Five of the nine survived childhood—his three older brothers, Samuel, Shubael, and Solomon, and a younger brother, Daniel. He was named George after his father, Robert after a paternal uncle, and the unlikely Twelves, he thought, for his mother's great uncle, "whose Christian name was Twelve, for whom she appeared to have great admiration. Why he was called by that singular name I never knew." More likely, his mother was honoring her own mother, also Abigail, whose maiden name was Twelves.[36]

The family heritage to George, it might be argued, was more genetic than economic. He inherited a chance to live long: the men in the Seaver line were all long-lived. And he inherited his size. He was unusually short—five feet, one inch. "I have never acquired the ordinary weight or size of other men," Hewes told Hawkes, who wrote that "his whole person is of a slight and slender texture." In old age he was known as "the little old man."[37] Anatomy is not destiny, but Hewes's short size and long name helped shape his personality. It was a big name for a small boy to carry. He was the butt of endless teasing jibes—George Robert what?—that Thatcher turned into anecdotes the humor of which may have masked the pain Hewes may have felt.[38]

"Moderate" as it was, Hewes had a sense of family. Wrentham, town of his grandfather and uncles, was a place he would be sent as a boy, a place of refuge in the war, and after the war his home. He would receive an inheritance three times in his life, each one a reminder of the importance or potential importance of relatives. And he was quite aware of any relative of status, like Dr. Joseph Warren, a distant kinsman on his mother's side.[39]

His father's life in Boston had been an endless, futile struggle to succeed as a tanner. Capital was the problem. In 1729 he brought a one-third ownership in a tannery for £600 in bills of credit. Two years later, he sold half of his third to his brother Robert, who became a working partner. The two brothers turned to a rich merchant, Nathaniel Cunningham, who put up £3500 in return for half the profits. The investment was huge: pits, a yard, workshops, hides, bark, two horses, four slaves, journeymen. For a time the tannery flourished. Then there was a disastrous falling out with Cunningham: furious fights, a raid on the yards, debtors' jail twice for George, suits and countersuits that dragged on in the courts for years. The Hewes brothers saw themselves as "very laborious" artisans who "managed their trade with good skill," only to be ruined by a wealthy, arrogant merchant. To Cunningham, they were incompetent and defaulters. Several years before George Robert was born, his father had fallen back to "butchering, tallow chandlering, hog killing, soap boiling &c."[40]

The family was not impoverished. George had a memory as a little boy of boarding a ship with his mother to buy a small slave girl "at the rate of two dollars a pound."[41] And there was enough money to pay the fees for his early schooling. But beginning in 1748, when he was six, there was a series of family tragedies. In 1748 an infant brother, Joseph, died, followed later in the year by his sister Abigail, age thirteen, and brother Ebenezer, age two. In 1749 his father died suddenly of a stroke, leaving the family nothing it would seem, his estate tangled in debt and litigation.[42] George's mother would have joined the more than one thousand widows in Boston, most of whom were on poor relief.[43] Sometime before 1755 she died. In 1756 Grandfather Seaver died, leaving less than £15 to be divided among George and his four surviving brothers. Thus in 1756, at the age of fourteen, when boys were customarily put out to apprenticeship, George was an orphan, the ward of his uncle Robert, as was his brother Daniel, age twelve, each with a legacy of £2 17s. 4d. Uncle Robert, though warmly recollected by Hewes, could not do much to help him: a gluemaker, he was struggling to set up his own manufactory.[44] Nor could George's three older brothers, whom he also remembered fondly. In 1756 they were all in the "lower" trades. Samuel, age twenty-six, and Solomon, twenty-two, were fishermen; Shubael, twenty-four, was a butcher.

The reason why George was put to shoemaking becomes clearer: no one in the family had the indenture fee to enable him to enter one of the more lucrative "higher" trades. Josiah Franklin, also a tallow chandler, could not make his son Benjamin a cutler because he lacked the fee.[45] But in shoemaking the prospects were so poor that some masters would pay to get an apprentice. In addition, George was too small to enter trades that demanded brawn; he could hardly have become a ropewalk worker, a housewright, or a shipwright. Ebenezer McIntosh, the Boston shoemaker who led the annual Pope's Day festivities and the Stamp Act demonstrations, was a small man.[46] The trade was a sort of dumping ground for poor boys who could not handle heavy work. Boston's Overseers of the Poor acted on this assumption in 1770;[47] so did recruiting officers for the American navy forty years later.[48] The same was true in Europe.[49] Getting into a good trade required "connections"; the family connections were in the leather trades, through Uncle Robert, the gluemaker, or brother Shubael, the butcher. Finally, there was a family tradition. Grandfather Shubael had been a cordwainer, and on his death in 1756 there might even have been a prospect of acquiring his tools and lasts. In any case, the capital that would be needed to set up a shop of one's own was relatively small. And so the boy became a shoemaker—because he had very little choice.

III

Josiah Franklin had known how important it was to place a boy in a trade that was to his liking. Otherwise there was the threat that Benjamin made explicit: he would run away to sea. Hawkes saw the same thrust in Hewes's life: shoemaking "was never an occupation of his choice," he "being inclined to more active pursuits."[50] George was the wrong boy to put in a sedentary trade that was not to his liking. He was what Bostonians called "saucy"; he was always in Dutch. The memories of his childhood and youth that Thatcher elicited were almost all of defying authority—his mother, his teachers at dame school, his schoolmaster, his aunt, his shoemaker master, a farmer, a doctor.

Hewes spoke of his mother only as a figure who inflicted punishment for disobedience. The earliest incident he remembered could have happened only to a poor family living near the waterfront. When George was about six, Abigail Hewes sent him off to the nearby shipyards with a basket to gather chips for the fire. At the water's edge George put the basket aside, straddled some floating planks to watch the fish, fell in, and sank to the bottom. He was saved only when some ship carpenters saw the basket without the boy, "found him motionless on the bottom, hooked him out with a boat hook, and rolled him on a tar barrel until signs of life were discovered." His mother nursed him back to health. Then she flogged him.[51]

The lesson did not take, nor did others in school. First there was a dame school with Miss Tinkum, wife of the town crier. He ran away. She put him in a dark closet. He dug his way out. The next day she put him in again. This time he discovered a jar of quince marmalade and devoured it. A new dame school with "mother McLeod" followed. Then school with "our famous Master Holyoke," which Hewes remembered as "little more than a series of escapes made or attempted from the reign of the birch."[52]

Abigail Hewes must have been desperate to control George. She sent him back after one truancy with a note requesting Holyoke to give him a good whipping. Uncle Robert took pity and sent a substitute note. Abigail threatened, "If you run away again I shall go to school with you myself."[53] When George was about ten, she took the final step: she sent him to Wrentham to live with one of his paternal uncles. Here, George recalled, "he spent several years of his boyhood . . . in the monotonous routine of his Uncle's farm." The only incident he recounted was of defying his aunt. His five-year-old cousin hit him in the face with a stick "without any provocation." George cursed the boy out, for which his aunt whipped him, and when she refused to do the same with her son, George undertook to "chastise" him himself. "I caught my cousin at the barn" and applied the rod. The aunt locked him up but his uncle let him go, responsive to his plea for "equal justice."[54]

Thus when George entered his apprenticeship, if he was not quite the young whig his biographers made him out to be, he was not a youth who would suffer arbitrary authority easily. His master, Downing, had an irascible side and was willing to use a cowhide. Hewes lived in Downing's attic with a fellow apprentice, John Gilbert. All the incidents Hewes recalled from this period had two motifs: petty defiance and a quest for food. There was an escapade on a Saturday night when the two apprentices made off for Gilbert's house and bought a loaf of bread, a pound of butter, and some coffee. They returned after curfew to encounter an enraged Downing, whom they foiled by setting pans and tubs for him to trip over when he came to the door. There was an excursion to Roxbury on

Training Day, the traditional apprentices' holiday in Boston, with fellow apprentices and his younger brother. Caught stealing apples, they were taken before the farmer, who was also justice of the peace and who laughed uproariously at Hewes's name and let him go. There was an incident with a doctor who inoculated Hewes and a fellow worker for smallpox and warned them to abstain from food. Sick, fearful of death, Hewes and his friend consumed a dish of venison in melted butter and a mug of flip—and lived to tell the tale.[55]

These memories of youthful defiance and youthful hunger lingered on for seventy years: a loaf of bread and a pound of butter, a parcel of apples, a dish of venison. This shoemaker's apprentice could hardly have been well fed or treated with affection.

The proof is that Hewes tried to end his apprenticeship by the only way he saw possible: escape to the military. "After finding that my depressed condition would probably render it impracticable for me to acquire that education requisite for civil employments," he told Hawkes, "I had resolved to engage in the military service of my country, should an opportunity present." Late in the 1750s, possibly in 1760, as the fourth and last of England's great colonial wars with France ground on and his majesty's army recruiters beat their drums through Boston's streets, Hewes and Gilbert tried to enlist. Gilbert was accepted, but Hewes was not. Recruiting captains were under orders to "enlist no Roman-Catholic, nor any under five feet two inches high without their shoes." "I could not pass muster," Hewes told Hawkes, "because I was not tall enough."[56] As Thatcher embroiders Hawkes's story, Hewes then "went to the shoe shop of several of his acquaintances and heightened his heels by several taps [;] then stuffing his stocking with paper and rags," he returned. The examining captain saw through the trick and rejected him again. Frustrated, humiliated, vowing he would never return to Downing, he took an even more desperate step: he went down to the wharf and tried to enlist on a British ship of war. "His brothers, however, soon heard of it and interfered," and, in Thatcher's words, "he was compelled to abandon that plan." Bostonians like Solomon and Samuel Hewes, who made their living on the waterfront, did not need long memories to remember the city's massive resistance to the impressment sweeps of 1747 and to know that the British navy would be, not escape, but another prison.[57]

About this time, shoemaker Downing failed after fire swept his shop (possibly the great fire of 1760).[58] This would have freed Hewes of his indenture, but he was not qualified to be a shoemaker until he had completed apprenticeship. As Hewes told it, he therefore apprenticed himself "for the remainder of his minority," that is, until he turned twenty-one, to Harry Rhoades, who paid him $40. In 1835 he could tell Thatcher how much time he then had left to serve, down to the month and day. Of the rest of his "time" he had no bad memories.[59]

Apprenticeship had a lighter side. Hewes's anecdotes give tantalizing glimpses into an embryonic apprentice culture in Boston to which other sources attest—glimpses of pranks played on masters, or revelry after curfew, of Training Day, when the militia displayed its maneuvers and there was drink, food, and "frolicking" on the Common. One may speculate that George also took part in the annual Pope's Day festival, November 5, when apprentices, servants, artisans in the lower trades, and young people of all classes took over the town, parading effigies of Pope, Devil, and Pretender, exacting tribute from the better sort, and engaging in a battle royal between North End and South End Pope's Day "companies."[60]

Hewes's stories of his youth, strained as they are through Thatcher's condescension, hint at his winning a place for himself as the small schoolboy who got the better of his elders, the apprentice who defied his master, perhaps even a leader among his peers. There are also hints of the adult personality. Hewes was punished often, but if childhood punishment inured some to pain, it made Hewes reluctant to inflict pain on others. He developed a generous streak that led him to reach out to others in trouble. When Downing, a broken man, was on the verge of leaving for Nova Scotia to start anew, Hewes went down to his ship and gave him half of the $40 fee Rhoades had paid him. Downing broke into tears. The story smacks of the Good Samaritan, of the Methodist of the 1830s counting his good deeds; and yet the memory was so vivid, wrote Thatcher, that "his features light up even now with a gleam of rejoicing pride." Hewes spoke later of the "tender sympathies of my nature."[61] He did not want to be, but he was a fit candidate for the "gentle craft" he was about to enter.

IV

In Boston from 1763, when he entered his majority, until 1775, when he went off to war, Hewes never made a go of it as a shoemaker. He remembered these years more fondly than he had lived them. As Hawkes took down his story, shifting from the third to the first person:

Hewes said he cheerfully submitted to the course of life to which his destinies directed.

He built him a shop and pursued the private avocation of his trade for a considerable length of time, until on the application of his brother he was induced to go with him on two fishing voyages to the banks of New Foundland, which occupied his time for two years.

After the conclusion of the French war . . . he continued at Boston, except the two years absence with his brother.

During that period, said Hewes, when I was at the age of twenty-six, I married the daughter of Benjamin Sumner, of Boston. At the time of our intermarriage, the age of my wife was seventeen. We lived together very happily seventy years. She died at the age of eighty-seven.

At the time when the British troops were first stationed at Boston, we had several children, the exact number I do not recollect. By our industry and mutual efforts we were improving our condition.[62]

Thatcher added a few bits to this narrative, some illuminating. The "little shop was at the head of Griffin's Wharf," later the site of the Tea Party. Benjamin Sumner, "if we mistake not," was a "sexton of one of the principal churches in town." His wife was a "washerwoman" near the Mill Pond, assisted by her five daughters. Hewes courted one of the girls when he "used to go to the house regularly every Saturday night to pay Sally for the week's washing." The father was stern, the swain persistent, and after a couple of years George and Sally were married. "The business was good, and growing better," Thatcher wrote, "especially as it became more and more fashionable to encourage our own manufactures."[63]

The reality was more harsh. What kind of shoemaker was Hewes? He had his own shop—this much is clear, but the rest is surmise. There were at that time in Boston about sixty to seventy shoemakers, most of whom seem to have catered to the local market.[64] If Hewes was typical, he would have made shoes to order, "bespoke" work; this would have made him a cordwainer. And he would have repaired shoes; this would have made him a cobbler. Who were his customers? No business records survive. A shoemaker probably drew his customers from his immediate neighborhood. Located as he was near the waterfront and the ropewalks, Hewes might well have had customers of the "meaner" sort. In a ward inhabited by the "middling" sort he may also have drawn on them. When the British troops occupied Boston, he did some work for them. Nothing suggests that he catered to the "carriage trade."[65]

Was his business "improving" or "growing better"? Probably it was never very good and grew worse. From his own words we know that he took off two years on fishing voyages with his brothers. He did not mention that during this period he lived for a short time in Roxbury.[66] His prospects were thus not good enough to keep him in Boston. His marriage is another clue to his low fortune. Sally (or Sarah) Sumner's father was a sexton so poor that his wife and daughters had to take in washing. The couple was married by the Reverend Samuel Stillman of the First Baptist Church, which suggests that this was the church that Benjamin Sumner served.[67] Though Stillman was respected, First Baptist was not "one of the principal churches in town," as Thatcher guessed, but one of the poorest and smallest, with a congregation heavy with laboring people, sailors, and blacks.[68] Marriage, one of the few potential sources of capital for an aspiring tradesman, as Benjamin Franklin made clear in his autobiography, did not lift Hewes up.

Other sources fill in what Hewes forgot. He married in January 1768. In September 1770 he landed in debtors' prison. In 1767 he had contracted a debt of £6 8s. 3d. to Thomas Courtney, a merchant tailor, for "making a sappled coat & breeches of fine cloth." The shoemaker bought this extravagant outfit when he was courting. What other way was there to persuade Sally's parents that he had good prospects? Over the three years since, he had neither earned enough to pay the debt nor accumulated £9 property that might be confiscated to satisfy it. "For want of Goods or Estate of the within named George Robt Twelve Hewes, I have taken his bodey & committed him to his majesty's goal [sic] in Boston," wrote Constable Thomas Rice on the back of the writ. There may have been a touch of political vindictiveness in the action: Courtney was a rich tory later banished by the state.[69] Who got Hewes out of jail? Perhaps his uncle Robert, perhaps a brother.

Once out of jail, Hewes stayed poor. The Boston tax records of 1771, the only ones that survived for these years, show him living as a lodger in the house of Christopher Ranks, a watchmaker, in the old North End. He was not taxed for any property.[70] In 1773 he and his family, which now included three children, were apparently living with his uncle Robert in the South End; at some time during these years before the war they also lived with a brother.[71] After almost a decade on his own, Hewes could not afford his own place. In January 1774 he inadvertently summed up his condition and reputation in the course of a violent street encounter. Damned as "a rascal" and "a vagabond" who had no right to "speak to a gentleman in the street," Hewes retorted that he was neither "and though a poor man, in as good credit in town" as his well-to-do antagonist.[72]

The economic odds were against a Boston shoemaker thriving these years. Even the movement "to encourage our manufactures"

may have worked against him, contrary to Thatcher. The patriot
boycott would have raised his hopes; the Boston town meeting of
1767 put men's and women's shoes on the list of items Bostonians
were encouraged to buy from American craftsmen.[73] But if this
meant shoes made in Lynn—the manufacturing town ten miles to
the north that produced 80,000 shoes in 1767 alone—it might well
have put Hewes at a competitive disadvantage, certainly for the ladies' shoes for which Lynn already had a reputation. And if Hewes
was caught up in the system whereby Lynn masters were already
"putting out" shoes in Boston, he would have made even less.[74]
Whatever the reason, the early 1770s were hard times for shoemakers; Ebenezer McIntosh also landed in debtors' jail in 1770.[75]

As a struggling shoemaker, what would have been Hewes's aspi-
rations? He does not tell us in so many words, but "the course of his
life," Hawkes was convinced, was marked "by habits of industry, in-
tegrity, temperance and economy"; in other words, he practiced the
virtues set down by "another soap boiler and tallow chandler's son"
(Thatcher's phrase for Benjamin Franklin). "From childhood,"
Hewes told Hawkes, "he has been accustomed to rise very early and
expose himself to the morning air; that his father compelled him to
do this from his infancy." ("Early to bed, Early to rise, makes a man
healthy, wealthy and wise.") "I was often . . . admonished," said
Hewes, "of the importance of faithfulness in executing the commands of my parents, or others who had a right to my services."
Thatcher also reported that "he makes it a rule to rise from the table
with an appetite, and another to partake of but a single dish at a
meal." ("A Fat kitchen makes a lean will, as Poor Richard says.")[76]

Poor Richard spoke to and for artisans at every level—masters,
journeymen, and apprentices—whose goal was "independence" or
"a competency" in their trade. What he advocated, we need remind
ourselves, "was not unlimited acquisition but rather prosperity,
which was the mid-point between the ruin of extravagance and the
want of poverty. The living he envisaged was a decent middling
wealth, which could only be attained through unremitting labor and
self-control."[77] Hewes's likely goal, then, was to keep his shop so that
his shop would keep him.

But he could no more live by Poor Richard's precepts than could
Franklin. "Industry" must have come hard. He was in an occupation
"never of his choice." How could he "stick to his last" when he was
"inclined towards more active pursuits"? "Avoid, above all else,
debt," counselled Poor Richard, warning that "fond pride of dress is
sure a very curse; E'er Fancy you consult, consult your purse." But
Hewes surrendered to pride and as a consequence to the warden of

the debtors' jail. "Economy"—that is, saving—produced no surplus. And so he would succumb, when war presented the opportunity, to the gamble for sudden wealth. He was as much the object as the exemplar of Poor Richard's advice, as indeed was Franklin himself.

If Hewes's memories softened such realities, in other ways his silences spoke. He said nothing about being part of any of Boston's traditional institutions—church, town meeting, or private associations. He was baptized in Old South, a Congregational church, and married by the minister of the First Baptist Church; there is no evidence that he took part in either.[78] In his old age a convert to Methodism, a churchgoer, and Bible reader, he reminisced to neither biographer about the religion of youth.

Nor does he seem to have taken part in town government. He was not a taxpayer in 1771. He probably did not own enough property to qualify as a voter for either provincial offices (£40 sterling) or town offices (£20 sterling).[79] Recollecting the political events of the Revolution, he did not speak of attending town meetings until they became what patriots called meetings of "the whole body of the people," without regard to property. The town had to fill some 200 minor positions; it was customary to stick artisans with the menial jobs. Hewes's father was hogreeve and measurer of boards. Harry Rhoades held town offices. McIntosh was made a sealer of leather. Hewes was appointed to nothing.[80]

He does not seem to have belonged to any associations. McIntosh was in a fire company. So was Hewes's brother Shubael. Hewes was not. Shubael and a handful of prosperous artisans became Masons. Hewes did not.[81] It was not that he was a loner. There was simply not much for a poor artisan to belong to.[82] There was no shoemakers' society or general society of mechanics. Shoemakers had a long tradition of taking ad hoc collective action, as did other Boston craftsmen, and Hewes may have participated in such occasional informal activities of the trade.[83] Very likely he drilled in the militia with other artisans on Training Day (size would not have barred him). He seems to have known many artisans and recalled their names in describing events. So it is not hard to imagine him at a South End tavern enjoying a mug of flip with Adam Colson, leatherworker, or Patrick Carr, breechesmaker. Nor is it difficult to imagine him in the streets on November 5, in the South End Pope's Day company captained by McIntosh. After all what else was there in respectable Boston for him to belong to? All this is conjecture, but it is clear that though he lived in Boston proper, he was not part of proper Boston—not until the events of the Revolution.

V

Between 1768 and 1775, the shoemaker became a citizen—an active participant in the events that led to the Revolution, an angry, assertive man who won recognition as a patriot. What explains the transformation? We have enough evidence to take stock of Hewes's role in three major events of the decade: the Massacre (1770), the Tea Party (1773), and the tarring and feathering of John Malcolm (1774).

Thatcher began the story of Hewes in the Revolution at the Stamp Act but based his account on other sources and even then claimed no more than that Hewes was a bystander at the famous effigy-hanging at the Liberty Tree, August 14, 1765, that launched Boston's protest. "The town's-people left their work—and Hewes, his hammer among the rest—to swell the multitude." The only episode for which Thatcher seems to have drawn on Hewes's personal recollection was the celebration of the repeal of the act in May 1766, at which Hewes remembered drinking from the pipe of madeira that John Hancock set out on the Common. "Such a day has not been seen in Boston before or since," wrote Thatcher.[84]

It is possible that Thatcher's bias against mobs led him to draw a curtain over Hewes's role. It is reasonable to suppose that if Hewes was a member of the South End Pope's Day company, he followed McIntosh who was a major leader of the crowd actions of August 14 and 26, the massive processions of the united North and South End companies on November 1 and 5, and the forced resignation of stampmaster Andrew Oliver in December. But it is not likely; in fact, he may well have been off on fishing voyages in 1765. Perhaps the proof is negative: when Hewes told Hawkes the story of his role in the Revolution, he began not at the Stamp Act but at the Massacre, five years later. On the night of the Massacre, March 5, Hewes was in the thick of the action. What he tells us about what brought him to King Street, what brought others there, and what he did during and after this tumultuous event gives us the perspective of a man in the street.

The presence of British troops in Boston beginning in the summer of 1768—4,000 soldiers in a town of fewer than 16,000 inhabitants—touched Hewes personally. Anecdotes about soldiers flowed from him. He had seen them march off the transports at the Long Wharf; he had seen them every day occupying civilian buildings on Griffin's Wharf near his shop. He knew how irritating it was to be challenged by British sentries after curfew (his solution was to offer a swig of rum from the bottle he carried).

More important, he was personally cheated by a soldier. Sergeant Mark Burk ordered shoes allegedly for Captain Thomas Preston, picked them up, but never paid for them. Hewes complained to Preston, who made good and suggested he bring a complaint. A military hearing ensued, at which Hewes testified. The soldier, to Hewes's horror, was sentenced to 350 lashes. He "remarked to the court that if he had thought the fellow was to be punished so severely for such an offense, bad as he was, he would have said nothing about it." And he saw others victimized by soldiers. He witnessed an incident in which a soldier sneaked up behind a woman, felled her with his fist, and "stripped her of her bonnet, cardinal muff and tippet." He followed the man to his barracks, identified him (Hewes remembered him as Private Kilroy, who would appear later at the Massacre), and got him to give up the stolen goods, but decided this time not to press charges.[85] Hewes was also keenly aware of grievances felt by the laboring men and youths who formed the bulk of the crowd—and the principal victims—at the Massacre.[86] From Hawkes and Thatcher three causes can be pieced together.

First in time, and vividly recalled by Hewes, was the murder of eleven-year-old Christopher Seider on February 23, ten days before the Massacre. Seider was one of a large crowd of schoolboys and apprentices picketing the shop of Theophilus Lilly, a merchant violating the anti-import resolutions. Ebenezer Richardson, a paid customs informer, shot into the throng and killed Seider. Richardson would have been tarred and feathered, or worse, had not whig leaders intervened to hustle him off to jail. At Seider's funeral, only a week before the Massacre, 500 boys marched two by two behind the coffin, followed by 2,000 or more adults, "the largest [funeral] perhaps ever known in America," Thomas Hutchinson thought.[87]

Second, Hewes emphasized the bitter fight two days before the Massacre between soldiers and workers at Gray's ropewalk down the block from Hewes's shop. Off-duty soldiers were allowed to moonlight, taking work from civilians. On Friday, March 3, when one of them asked for work at Gray's, a battle ensued between a few score soldiers and ropewalk workers joined by others in the maritime trades. The soldiers were beaten and sought revenge. Consequently, in Thatcher's words, "quite a number of soldiers, in a word, were determined to have a row on the night of the 5th."[88]

Third, the precipitating events on the night of the Massacre, by Hewes's account, were an attempt by a barber's apprentice to collect an overdue bill from a British officer, the sentry's abuse of the boy, and the subsequent harassment of the sentry by a small band of boys that led to the calling of the guard commanded by Captain Preston.

Thatcher found this hard to swallow—"a dun from a greasy barber's boy is rather an extraordinary explanation of the origin, or one of the occasions, of the massacre of the 5th of March"—but at the trial the lawyers did not. They battled over defining "boys" and over the age, size, and degree of aggressiveness of the numerous apprentices on the scene.[89]

Hewes viewed the civilians as essentially defensive. On the evening of the Massacre he appeared early on the scene at King Street, attracted by the clamor over the apprentice. "I was soon on the ground among them," he said, as if it were only natural that he should turn out in defense of fellow townsmen against what was assumed to be the danger of aggressive action by soldiers. He was not part of a conspiracy; neither was he there out of curiosity. He was unarmed, carrying neither club nor stave as some others did. He saw snow, ice, and "missiles" thrown at the soldiers. When the main guard rushed out in support of the sentry, Private Kilroy dealt Hewes a blow on his shoulder with his gun. Preston ordered the townspeople to disperse. Hewes believed they had a legal basis to refuse: "they were in the king's highway, and had as good a right to be there" as Preston.[90]

The five men killed were all workingmen. Hewes claimed to know four: Samuel Gray, a ropewalk worker; Samuel Maverick, age seventeen, an apprentice to an ivory turner; Patrick Carr, an apprentice to a leather breeches worker; and James Caldwell, second mate on a ship—all but Christopher Attucks. Caldwell, "who was shot in the back was standing by the side of Hewes, and the latter caught him in his arms as he fell," helped carry him to Dr. Thomas Young in Prison Lane, then ran to Caldwell's ship captain on Cold Lane.[91]

More than horror was burned into Hewes's memory. He remembered the political confrontation that followed the slaughter, when thousands of angry townspeople faced hundreds of British troops massed with ready rifles. "The people," Hewes recounted, "then immediately chose a committee to report to the governor the result of Captain Preston's conduct, and to demand of him satisfaction."[92] Actually the "people" did not choose a committee "immediately." In the dark hours after the Massacre a self-appointed group of patriot leaders met with officials and forced Hutchinson to commit Preston and the soldiers to jail. Hewes was remembering the town meeting the next day, so huge that it had to adjourn from Fanueil Hall, the traditional meeting place that held only 1,200, to Old South Church, which had room for 5 to 6,000. This meeting approved a committee to wait on the officials and then adjourned, but met again the same day, received and voted down an offer to remove one regiment, then accepted another to remove two. This was one of the meetings at which property bars were let down.[93]

What Hewes did not recount, but what he had promptly put down in a deposition the next day, was how militant he was after the Massacre. At 1:00 A.M., like many other enraged Bostonians, he went home to arm himself. On his way back to the Town House with a cane he had a defiant exchange with Sergeant Chambers of the 29th Regiment and eight or nine soldiers, "all with very large clubs or cutlasses." A soldier, Dobson, "ask'd him how he far'd; he told him very badly to see his townsmen shot in such a manner, and asked him if he did not think it was a dreadful thing." Dobson swore "it was a fine thing" and "you shall see more of it." Chambers "seized and forced" the cane from Hewes, "saying I had no right to carry it. I told him I had as good a right to carry a cane as they had to carry clubs."[94]

The Massacre had stirred Hewes to political action. He was one of ninety-nine Bostonians who gave depositions for the prosecution that were published by the town in a pamphlet. Undoubtedly, he marched in the great funeral procession for the victims that brought the city to a standstill. He attended the tempestuous trial of Ebenezer Richardson, Seider's slayer, which was linked politically with the Massacre. ("He remembers to this moment, even the precise words of the Judge's sentence," wrote Thatcher.)[95] He seems to have attended the trial of the soldiers or Preston or both.

It was in this context that he remembered something for which there is no corroborating evidence, namely, testifying at Preston's trial on a crucial point. He told Hawkes:

> When Preston, their captain, was tried, I was called as one of the witnesses, on the part of the government, and testified, that I believed it was the same man, Captain Preston, that ordered his soldiers to make ready, who also ordered them to fire. Mr. John Adams, former president of the United States, was advocate for the prisoners, and denied the fact, that Captain Preston gave orders to his men to fire; and on his cross examination of me asked whether my position was such, that I could see the captain's lips in motion when the order to fire was given; to which I answered, that I could not.[96]

Perhaps so: Hewes's account is particular and precise, and there are many lacunae in the record of the trial (we have no verbatim transcript) that modern editors have assiduously assembled. Perhaps not: Hewes may have "remembered" his brother Shubael on the stand at the trial of the soldiers (although Shubael was a defense witness) or his uncle Robert testifying at Richardson's trial. Or he may have given pre-trial testimony but was not called to the stand.[97]

In one sense, it does not matter. What he was remembering was that he had become involved. He turned out because of a sense of kinship with "his townsmen" in danger; he stood his ground in defense of his "rights"; he was among the "people" who delegated a committee to act on their behalf; he took part in the legal process by giving a deposition, by attending the trials, and, as he remembered it, by testifying. In sum, he had become a citizen, a political man.

Four years later, at the Tea Party on the night of December 16, 1773, the citizen "volunteered" and became the kind of leader for whom most historians have never found a place. The Tea Party, unlike the Massacre, was organized by the radical whig leaders of Boston. They mapped the strategy, organized the public meetings, appointed the companies to guard the tea ships at Griffin's Wharf (among them Daniel Hewes, George's brother), and planned the official boarding parties. As in 1770, they converted the town meetings into meetings of "the whole body of the people," one of which Hutchinson found "consisted principally of the Lower ranks of the People & even Journeymen Tradesmen were brought in to increase the number & the Rabble were not excluded yet there were divers Gentlemen of Good Fortunes among them."[98]

The boarding parties showed this same combination of "ranks." Hawkes wrote:

> On my inquiring of Hewes if he knew who first proposed the project of destroying the tea, to prevent its being landed, he replied that he did not; neither did he know who or what number were to volunteer their services for that purpose. But from the significant allusion of some persons in whom I had confidence, together with the knowledge I had of the spirit of those times, I had no doubt but that a sufficient number of associates would accompany me in that enterprise.[99]

The recollection of Joshua Wyeth, a journeyman blacksmith, verified Hewes's story in explicit detail: "It was proposed that young men, not much known in town and not liable to be easily recognized should lead in the business." Wyeth believed that "most of the persons selected for the occasion were apprentices and journeymen, as was the case with myself, living with tory masters." Wyeth "had but a few hours warning of what was intended to be done."[100] Those in the officially designated parties, about thirty men better known, appeared in well-prepared Indian disguises. As nobodies, the volunteers—anywhere from fifty to 100 men—could get away with hastily improvised disguises. Hewes said he got himself up as an Indian and daubed his "face and hands with coal dust in the shop of black-smith." In the streets "I fell in with many who were dressed, equipped and painted as I was, and who fell in with me and marched in order to the place of our destination."

At Griffin's Wharf the volunteers were orderly, self-disciplined, and ready to accept leadership.

> When we arrived at the wharf, there were three of our number who assumed an authority to direct our operations, to which we readily submitted. They divided us into three parties, for the purpose of boarding the three ships which contained the tea at the same time. The name of him who commanded the division to which I was assigned was Leonard Pitt [Lendell Pitts]. The names of the other commanders I never knew. We were imme-diately ordered by the respective commanders to board all the ships at the same time, which we promptly obeyed.

But for Hewes there was something new: he was singled out of the rank and file and made an officer in the field.

> The commander of the division to which I belonged, as soon as we were on board the ship, appointed me boatswain, and or-dered me to go to the captain and demand of him the keys to the hatches and a dozen candles. I made the demand accord-ingly, and the captain promptly replied, and delivered the arti-cles; but requested me at the same time to do no damage to the ship or rigging. We then were ordered by our commander to open the hatches, and take out all the chests of tea and throw them overboard, and we immediately proceeded to execute his orders; first cutting and splitting the chests with our tomahawks, so as thoroughly to expose them to the effects of the water. In about three hours from the time we went on board, we had thus broken and thrown overboard every tea chest to be found in the ship; while those in the other ships were disposing of the tea in the same way, at the same time. We were surrounded by British armed ships, but no attempt was made to resist us. We then quietly retired to our several places of residence, without having any conversation with each other, or taking any measures to dis-cover who were our associates.[101]

This was Hewes's story, via Hawkes. Thatcher, who knew a good deal more about the Tea Party from other sources, accepted it in its essentials as an accurate account. He also reported a new anecdote which he treated with skepticism, namely, that Hewes worked along-side John Hancock throwing tea overboard. And he added that Hewes, "whose whistling talent was a matter of public notoriety, acted as a boatswain," that is, as the officer whose duty it was to summon men with a whistle. That Hewes was a leader is confirmed by the reminiscence of Thompson Maxwell, a teamster from a neighboring town who was making a delivery to Hancock the day of the event. Hancock asked him to go to Griffin's Wharf. "I went accordingly, joined the band under one Captain Hewes; we mounted the ships and made tea in a trice; this done I took my team and went home as any honest man should."[102] "Captain" Hewes—it was not impossible.

As the Tea Party ended, Hewes was stirred to further action on his own initiative, just as he had been in the hours after the Massacre. While the crews were throwing the tea overboard, a few other men tried to smuggle off some of the tea scattered on the decks. "One Captain O'Connor whom I well knew," said Hewes, "came on board for that purpose, and when he supposed he was not noticed, filled his pockets, and also the lining of his coat. But I had detected him, and gave information to the captain of what he was doing. We were ordered to take him into custody, and just as he was stepping from the vessel, I seized him by the skirt of his coat, and in attempting to pull him back, I tore it off." They scuffled. O'Connor recognized him and "threatened to 'complain to the Governor.' 'You had better make your will first,' quoth Hewes, doubling his fist expressively," and O'Connor escaped, running the gauntlet of the crowd on the wharf. "The next day we nailed the skirt of his coat, which I had pulled off, to the whipping post in Charlestown, the place of his residence, with a label upon it," to shame O'Connor by "popular indignation."[103]

A month later, at the third event for which we have full evidence, Hewes won public recognition for an act of courage that almost cost his life and precipitated the most publicized tarring and feathering of the Revolution. The incident that set it off would have been trivial at any other time. On Tuesday, January 25, 1774, at about two in the afternoon, the shoemaker was making his way back to his shop after his dinner. According to the very full account in the *Massachusetts Gazette,*

> Mr. George-Robert-Twelves Hewes was coming along Fore-Street, near Captain Ridgway's, and found the redoubted John Malcolm, standing over a small boy, who was pushing a little sled before him, cursing, damning, threatening and shaking a very large cane with a very heavy ferril on it over his head. The boy at that time was perfectly quiet, notwithstanding which Malcolm continued his threats of striking him, which Mr. Hewes conceiving if he struck him with that weapon he must have killed him out-right, came up to him, and said to him, Mr. Malcolm I hope you are not going to strike this boy with that stick.[104]

Malcolm had already acquired an odious reputation with patriots of the lower sort. A Bostonian, he had been a sea captain, an army officer, and recently an employee of the customs service. He was so strong a supporter of royal authority that he had traveled to North Carolina to fight the Regulators and boasted of having a horse shot out from under him. He had a fiery temper. As a customs informer he was known to have turned in a vessel to punish sailors for petty smuggling, a custom of the sea. In November 1773, near Portsmouth, New Hampshire, a crowd of thirty sailors had "genteely tarr'd and feather'd" him, as the *Boston Gazette* put it: they did the job over his clothes. Back in Boston he made "frequent complaints" to Hutchinson of "being hooted at in the streets" for this by "tradesmen"; and the lieutenant governor cautioned him, "being a passionate man," not to reply in kind.[105]

The exchange between Malcolm and Hewes resonated with class as well as political differences:

> Malcolm returned, you are an impertinent rascal, it is none of your business. Mr. Hewes then asked him, what had the child done to him. Malcolm damned him and asked him if he was going to take his part? Mr. Hewes answered no further than this, that he thought it was a shame for him to strike the child with such a club as that, if he intended to strike him. Malcolm on that damned Mr. Hewes, called him a vagabond, and said he would let him know he should not speak to a gentleman in the street. Mr. Hewes returned to that, he was neither a rascal nor vagabond, and though a poor man was in as good credit in town as he was. Malcolm called him a liar, and said he was not, nor ever would be. Mr. Hewes retorted, be that as it will, I never was tarred nor feathered any how. On this Malcolm struck him, and wounded him deeply on the forehead, so that Mr. Hewes for some time lost his senses. Capt. Godfrey, then present, interposed, and after some altercation, Malcolm went home.[106]

Hewes was rushed to Joseph Warren, the patriot doctor, his distant relative. Malcolm's cane had almost penetrated his skull. Thatcher found "the indentation as plainly perceptible as it was sixty years ago." So did Hawkes. Warren dressed the wound, and Hewes was able to make his way to a magistrate to swear out a warrant for Malcolm's arrest "which he carried to a constable named Justice Hale."[107] Malcolm, meanwhile, had retreated to his house, where he responded in white heat to taunts about the half-way tarring and feathering in Portsmouth with "damn you let me see the man that dare do it better."

In the evening a crowd took Malcolm from his house and dragged

him on a sled into King Street "amidst the huzzas of thousands." At
this point "several gentlemen endeavoured to divert the populace
from their intention." The ensuing dialogue laid bare the clash of
conceptions of justice between the sailors and laboring people head-
ing the action and Sons of Liberty leaders. The "gentlemen" argued
that Malcolm was "open to the laws of the land which would undoubtedly award a reasonable satisfaction to the parties he had
abused," that is, the child and Hewes. The answer was political. Malcolm "had been an old impudent and mischievious offender—he
had joined in the murders at North Carolina—he had seized vessels
on account of sailors having a bottle or two of gin on board—he had
in other words behaved in the most capricious, insulting and dar-
ingly abusive manner." He could not be trusted to justice. "When
they were told the law would have its course with him, they asked
what course had the law taken with Preston or his soldiers, with
Capt. Wilson or Richardson? And for their parts they had seen so
much partiality to the soldiers and customhouse officers by the present Judges, that while things remained as they were, they would, on
all such occasions, take satisfaction their own way, and let them take
it off."[108] The references were to Captain Preston who had been
tried and found innocent of the Massacre, the soldiers who had
been let off with token punishment, Captain John Wilson, who had
been indicted for inciting slaves to murder their masters but never
tried,[109] and Ebenezer Richardson, who had been tried and found
guilty of killing Seider, sentenced, and then pardoned by the crown.

The crowd won and proceeded to a ritualized tarring and feathering, the purpose of which was to punish Malcolm, force a recan-
tation, and ostracize him.

With these and such like arguments, together with a gentle
crouding of persons not of their way of thinking out of the ring
they proceeded to elevate Mr. Malcolm from his sled into a cart,
and stripping him to buff and breeches, gave him a modern
jacket [a coat of tar and feathers] and hied him away to liberty-
tree, where they proposed to him to renounce his present
commission, and swear that he would never hold another inconsistent with the liberties of his country; but this he obstinately
refusing, they then carted him to the gallows, passed a rope
round his neck, and threw the other end over the beam as if
they intended to hang him: But this manoeuver he set at defiance. They then basted him for some time with a rope's end,
and threatened to cut his ears off, and on this he complied, and
they then brought him home.[110]

Hewes had precipitated an electrifying event. It was part of the upsurge of spontaneous action in the wake of the Tea Party that prompted the whig leaders to promote a "Committee for Tarring and Feathering" as an instrument of crowd control. The "Committee" made its appearance in broadsides signed by "Captain Joyce, Jun.," a sobriquet meant to invoke the bold cornet who had captured King Charles in 1647.[111] The event was reported in the English newspapers, popularized in three or four satirical prints, and dramatized still further when Malcolm went to England, where he campaigned for a pension and ran for Parliament (without success) against John Wilkes, the leading champion of America. The event confirmed the British ministry in its punitive effort to bring rebellious Boston to heel.[112]

What was lost to the public was that Hewes was at odds with the crowd. He wanted justice from the courts, not a mob; after all, he had sworn out a warrant against Malcolm. And he could not bear to see cruel punishment inflicted on a man, any more than on a boy. As he told the story to Thatcher, when he returned and saw Malcolm being carted away in tar and feathers, "his instant impulse was to push after the procession as fast as he could, with a blanket to put over his shoulders. He overtook them [the crowd] at his brother's [Shubael's] house and made an effort to relieve him; but the ruffians who now had the charge of him about the cart, pushed him aside, and warned him to keep off." This may have been the Good Samaritan of 1835, but the story rings true. While "the very excitement which the affront must have wrought upon him began to rekindle," Hewes conveyed no hatred for Malcolm.[113]

The denouement of the affair was an incident several weeks later. "Malcolm recovered from his wounds and went about as usual. 'How do you do, Mr. Malcolm?' said Hewes, very civilly, the next time he met him. 'Your humble servant, Mr. George Robert Twelves Hewes,' quoth he,—touching his hat genteely as he passed by. 'Thank ye,' thought Hewes, 'and I am glad you have learned *better manners at last.*' "[114] Hewes's mood was one of triumph. Malcolm had been taught a lesson. The issue was respect for Hewes, a patriot, a poor man, an honest citizen, a decent man standing up for a child against an unspeakably arrogant "gentleman" who was an enemy of his country.

Hewes's role in these three events fits few of the categories that historians have applied to the participation of ordinary men in the Revolution. He was not a member of any organized committee, caucus, or club. He did not attend the expensive public dinners of the Sons of Liberty. He was capable of acting on his own volition without being summoned by any leaders (as in the Massacre). He could volunteer and assume leadership (as in the Tea Party). He was at home on the streets in crowds but he could also reject a crowd (as in the tarring and feathering of Malcolm). He was at home in the other places where ordinary Bostonians turned out to express their convictions: at funeral processions, at meetings of the "whole body of the people," in courtrooms at public trials. He recoiled from violence to persons if not to property. The man who could remember the whippings of his own boyhood did not want to be the source of pain to others, whether Sergeant Burk, who tried to cheat him over a pair of shoes, or John Malcolm, who almost killed him. It is in keeping with his character that he should have come to the aid of a little boy facing a beating.

Nevertheless, Hewes was more of a militant than he conveyed or his biographers recognized in 1833 and 1835. He was capable of acting on his own initiative in the wake of collective action at both the Massacre and the Tea Party. He had "public notoriety," Thatcher tells us, for his "whistling talent"; whistling was the customary way of assembling a crowd.[115] According to Malcolm, Hewes was among the "tradesmen" who had "several times before affronted him" by "hooting" at him in the streets.[116] And the patriots whose names stayed with him included Dr. Thomas Young and William Molineaux, the two Sons of Liberty who replaced Ebenezer McIntosh as "mob" leaders.[117]

What moved Hewes to action? It was not the written word; indeed there is no sign he was much of a reader until old age, and then it was the Bible he read. "My whole education," he told Hawkes, "consisted of only a moderate knowledge of reading and writing."[118] He seems to have read one of the most sensational pamphlets of 1773, which he prized enough to hold onto for more than fifty years, but he was certainly not like Harbottle Dorr, the Boston shopkeeper who pored over every issue of every Boston newspaper, annotating Britain's crimes for posterity.[119]

Hewes was moved to act by personal experiences that he shared with large numbers of other plebeian Bostonians. He seems to have been politicized, not by the Stamp Act, but by the coming of the troops after 1768, and then by things that happened to him, that he saw, or that happened to people he knew. Once aroused, he took action with others of his own rank and condition—the laboring classes who formed the bulk of the actors at the Massacre, the Tea Party, and the Malcolm affair—and with other members of his family: his uncle Robert, "known for a staunch Liberty Boy," and his brother Daniel, a guard at the tea ship. Shubael, alone among his brothers, became a tory.[120] These shared experiences were interpreted and focused more likely by the spoken than the written word and as much by his peers at taverns and crowd actions as by leaders in huge public meetings.

As he became active politically he may have had a growing awareness of his worth as a shoemaker. McIntosh was clearly the man of the year in 1765; indeed, whigs were no less fearful than loyalists that "the Captain General of the Liberty Tree" might become the Masaniello of Boston.[121] After a shoemaker made the boot to hang in the Liberty Tree as an effigy of Lord Bute, "Jack Cobler" served notice that "whenever the Public Good requires my services, I shall be ready to distinguish myself." In 1772 "Crispin" began an anti-loyalist diatribe by saying, "I am a shoemaker, a citizen, a free man and a freeholder." The editor added a postscript justifying "Crispin's performance" and explaining that "it should be known what common people, even *coblers* think and feel under the present administration."[122] In city after city, "cobblers" were singled out for derision by conservatives for leaving their lasts to engage in the body politic.[123] Hewes could not have been unaware of all this; he was part of it.

He may also have responded to the rising demand among artisans for support of American manufacturers, whether or not it brought him immediate benefit. He most certainly subscribed to the secularized Puritan ethic—self-denial, industry, frugality—that made artisans take to the nonimportation agreement with its crusade against foreign luxury and its vision of American manufactures. And he could easily have identified with the appeal of the Massachusetts Provincial Congress of 1774 that equated the political need "to encourage agriculture, manufacturers and economy so as to render this state as independent of every other state as the nature of our country will admit" with the "happiness of particular families" in being "independent."[124]

But what ideas did Hewes articulate? He spoke of what he did but very little of what he thought. In the brief statement he offered Hawkes about why he went off to war in 1776, he expressed a commitment to general principles as they had been brought home to him by his experiences. "I was continually reflecting upon the unwarrantable sufferings inflicted on the citizens of Boston by the usurpation and tyranny of Great Britain, and my mind was excited with an unextinguishable desire to aid in chastising them." When Hawkes expressed a doubt "as to the correctness of his conduct in absenting himself from his family," Hewes "emphatically reiterated" the same phrases, adding to a "desire to aid in chastising them" the phrase "and securing our independence."[125] This was clearly not an afterthought; it probably reflected the way many others moved toward the goal of Independence, not as a matter of original intent, but as a step made necessary when all other resorts failed. Ideology thus did not set George Hewes apart from Samuel Adams or John Hancock. The difference lies in what the Revolution did to him as a person. His experiences transformed him, giving him a sense of citizenship and personal worth. Adams and Hancock began with both; Hewes had to arrive there, and in arriving he cast off the constraints of deference.

The two incidents with which we introduced Hewes's life measure the distance he had come: from the young man tongue-tied in the presence of John Hancock to the man who would not take his hat off to the officer of the ship named *Hancock*. Did he cast off his deference to Hancock? Hewes's affirmation of his worth as a human being was a form of class consciousness. Implicit in the idea, "I am as good as any man regardless of rank or wealth," was the idea that any poor man might be as good as any rich man. This did not mean that all rich men were bad. On the contrary, in Boston, more than any other major colonial seaport, a majority of the merchants were part of the patriot coalition; "divers Gentelmen of Good Fortunes," as Hutchinson put it, were with the "Rabble." This blunted class consciousness. Boston's mechanics, unlike New York's or Philadelphia's, did not develop mechanic committees or a mechanic consciousness before the Revolution. Yet in Boston the rich were forced to defer to the people in order to obtain or retain their support. Indeed, the entire public career of Hancock from 1765 on—distributing largesse, buying uniforms for Pope's Day marchers, building ships to employ artisans—can be understood as an exercise of this kind of deference, proving his civic virtue and patriotism.[126]

This gives meaning to Hewes's tale of working beside Hancock at the Tea Party—"a curious reminiscence," Thatcher called it, "but we believe it a mistake."

> Mr. Hewes, however, positively affirms, as of his own observation, that *Samuel Adams and John Hancock were both actively engaged in the process of destruction.* Of the latter he speaks more particularly, being entirely confident that he was himself at one time engaged with him not only by his *ruffles* making their appearance in the heat of the work, from under the disguise which pretty thoroughly covered him,—and by his figure, and gait;—but by his features, which neither his paint nor his loosened club of hair behind wholly concealed from a close view;—and by his voice also, for he exchanged with him an Indian *grunt,* and the expression *"me know you,"* which was a good deal used on that occasion for a countersign.[127]

Thatcher was justifiably skeptical; it is very unlikely that Hancock was there. Participants swore themselves to secrecy; their identity was one of the best-kept secrets of the Revolution. In fact, in 1835 Thatcher published in an appendix the first list of those "more or less actively engaged" in the Tea Party as furnished by "an aged Bostonian," clearly not Hewes.[128] Hancock was not named. More important, it was not part of the patriot plan for the well-known leaders to be present. When the all-day meeting that sanctioned the action adjourned, the leaders, including Hancock, stayed behind conspicuously in Old South.[129] Still, there can be little question that Hewes was convinced at the time that Hancock was on the ship: some gentlemen were indeed present; it was reasonable to assume that Hancock, who had been so conspicuous on the tea issue, was there; Hewes knew what Hancock looked like; he was too insistent about details for his testimony to be dismissed as made up. And the way he recorded it in his mind at the time was the way he stored it in his memory.

Hewes in effect had brought Hancock down to his own level. The poor shoemaker had not toppled the wealthy merchant; he was no "leveller." But the rich and powerful—the men in "ruffles"—had become, in his revealing word, his "associates." John Hancock and George Hewes breaking open the same chest at the Tea Party remained for Hewes a symbol of a moment of equality. To the shoemaker, one suspects, this above all was what the Revolutionary events of Boston meant, as did the war that followed.

VI

Hewes's decisions from 1775 to 1783—his choice of services and the timing and sequence of his military activities—suggest a pattern of patriotism mingled with a hope to strike it rich and a pressing need to provide for his family.

After the outbreak of hostilities at Lexington and Concord in April 1775, Boston became a garrison town; patriot civilians streamed out—perhaps 10,000 of them—Tory refugees moved in, and the number of British troops grew to 13,500 by July. Hewes sent his wife and children to Wrentham—his father's native town—where they would be safe with relatives. His brother Daniel did the same; Solomon went elsewhere; Shubael alone stayed with the British, as butcher-general to General Gage. George himself remained—"imprisoned," as he remembered it—prevented like other able-bodied men from leaving the city. He made a living as a fisherman; the British allowed him to pass in and out of the harbor in exchange for the pick of the day's catch. He was in Boston nine weeks, was harassed by soldiers on the street, witnessed the Battle of Bunker Hill from a neck of land far out in the bay (he "saw [Joseph Warren] fall"), and saw the corpses of British soldiers "chucked" into an open pit at one end of the Common. One morning he bade good-bye to Shubael, hid his shoemaker's tools under the deck of a small boat borrowed from a tory, and, after a narrow scrape with British guards, made good an escape with two friends to nearby Lynn. The Committee of Safety took him to Cambridge, where General Washington plied him with questions about conditions in Boston—an interview we shall return to. Then he made his way south to Wrentham.[130]

Hewes's record of service thereafter can be reconstructed with reasonable accuracy by matching what he claimed in his pension application in 1832 and told his biographers against information from official records and other contemporary sources.[131] After some months, very likely in the fall of 1776, he enlisted on a privateer at Providence on a voyage north that lasted about three months. He returned to Wrentham and a year later, in the fall of 1777, served in the militia from one to three months. In late August 1778 he served again, most likely for one month. In February 1779 he made a second privateering voyage, this time out of Boston, an eventful seven-and-a-half-month trip to the South and the West Indies. In 1780 he very likely was in the militia again from late July to late October, and in 1781 he definitely was in the militia at the same time of year. That was his final tour of duty: in the closing years of the war, to avoid the Massachusetts draft, he hired a substitute. All these enlistments were out of Attleborough, the town immediately south of Wrentham.[132] All were as a private; he did not rise in the ranks.

Several things stand out in this record. Hewes did not go at once, not until he provided for his family. He remembered that he did not make his first enlistment until "about two years after the battle of Bunker Hill," although actually it was closer to a year or fifteen months.[133] He served often, twice at sea, at least four and possibly five times in the militia, but not at all in the Continental army, which would have meant longer periods away from home. For almost all of these stints he volunteered; once he was drafted; once he sent a substitute; he drew these distinctions carefully.[134]

This record, put alongside what we know about other Massachusetts men in the war, places Hewes a good cut above the average. He served at least nine months in the militia and ten-and-a-half months at sea—about twenty months in all. In Concord, most men "were credited with under a half a year's time";[135] in Peterborough, New

Hampshire, only a third did "extensive service" of over a year.[136] Hewes served less than the thirty-three months of the average man in the Continental army.[137] He was not one of the men whom John Shy has called the "hard core" of Revolutionary fighters, like the shoemaker "Long Bill" Scott of Peterborough. But neither was he one of the sunshine patriots Robert Gross found in Concord who came out for no more than a few militia stints early in the war. He served over the length of the fighting. Like others who put in this much time, he was poor; even in Concord after 1778, soldiers in the militia as well as the army "were men with little or nothing to lose."[138] Hewes was in his mid-thirties; he and Sarah had four children by 1776, six by 1781. He spent most of the years of war at home providing for them, doing what, he did not say, but possibly making shoes for the army like other country cordwainers.[139] His patriotism was thus tempered by the need for survival.

Going to war was a wrenching experience. When Hewes told his wife he intended to "take a privateering cruise," she "was greatly afflicted at the prospect of our separation, and my absence from a numerous family of children, who needed a father's parental care." Taught from boyhood to repress his emotions ("I cannot cry," Thatcher reported him saying when punishment loomed), Hewes cut the pain of parting by a ruse.

> On the day which I had appointed to take my departure, I came into the room where my wife was, and inquired if all was ready? She pointed in silence to my knapsack. I observed, that I would put it on and walk with it a few rods, to see if it was rightly fitted to carry with ease. I went out, to return no more until the end of my cruise. The manly fortitude which becomes the soldier, could not overcome the tender sympathies of my nature. I had not courage to encounter the trial of taking a formal leave. When I had arrived at a solitary place on my way, I sat down for a few moments, and sought to allay the keenness of my grief by giving vent to a profusion of tears.[140]

Why was privateering Hewes's first choice? Privateering, as Jesse Lemisch has put it, was legalized piracy with a share of the booty for each pirate.[141] Under a state or Continental letter of marque, a privately owned ship was authorized to take enemy vessels as prizes. The government received a share, as did the owners and crew, prorated by rank. During the seven years of war, the United States commissioned 2,000 privateers, 626 in Massachusetts alone, which itself issued 1,524 commissions. In 1776, when Hewes made his decision, Abigail Adams spoke of "the rage for privateering" in Boston, and James Warren told Samuel Adams that "a whole country" was "privateering mad."[142]

War for Hewes meant opportunity: a chance to escape from a humdrum occupation never to his liking; to be at thirty-five what had been denied at sixteen—a fighting man; above all, a chance to accumulate the capital that could mean a house, a new shop, apprentices and journeymen, perhaps a start in something altogether new. He was following a path trod by tens of thousands of poor New Englanders ever since the wars against the French in the 1740s and 1750s.[143] As an economic flyer, however, privateering ultimately proved disastrous for Hewes.

His first voyage went well. He sailed on the *Diamond* out of Providence, attracted possibly by an advertisement that promised fortune and adventure. They captured three vessels, the last of which Hewes brought back to Providence as a member of the prize crew. He said nothing about his share; by inference he got enough to whet his appetite but not enough to boast about. He also nearly drowned off Newfoundland when a line he and two shipmates were standing on broke.[144]

His second voyage was shattering. He went on the Connecticut ship of war *Defence,* commanded by Captain Samuel Smedley and sailing from Boston with the *Oliver Cromwell.* The *Defence* and the *Cromwell* captured two richly laden vessels and later, after a layover in Charleston, South Carolina, two British privateers; on the way home, the *Defence* stopped a ship and relieved the tory passengers of their money. The prize money from the two privateers alone was $80,000.[145] But Hewes got nothing. His share was supposed to be $250, "but some pretext was always offered for withholding my share from me; so that I have never received one cent of it." When he asked for his wages, Captain Smedley "told me he was about fitting out an expedition to the West Indies, and could not, without great inconvenience, spare the money then; but said he would call on his way to Providence . . . and would pay me; but I never saw him afterwards. Neither have I, at any time since, received a farthing, either of my share of prize money or wages."[146]

There was an adventurous side to privateering. His stories stress the thrill of the chase, the intrepid maneuvering of his ship in battle, the excitement of a boarding party. They also deal with the prosaic. He remembered manning the pumps on the leaking *Defence* "for eight days and eight nights to keep us from sinking." He remembered before battle that "we sat up all night . . . we made bandages, scraped lint, so that we might be prepared to dress wounds as we expected to have a hard time of it."[147] The man of tender sympathies did not become a bloodthirsty buccaneer.

Most important of all was the memory that at sea he had partici-

pated in making decisions and that the captains had shown deference to their crews. On his first voyage, the initial agreement was for
a cruise of seven weeks. "When that term had expired," said Hewes,
"and we had seen no enemy during the time, we were discouraged,
and threatened to mutiny, unless he would return." Captain Stacey
asked for one more week, after which he promised to sail home if
they saw nothing, "to which we assented." On the second voyage,
when the *Defence* sighted enemy ships and Captain Smedley "asked
us if we were willing to give chase to them, we assented, we were all
ready to go and risk our lives with him." In Charleston, their tour
of duty legally over, Smedley proposed a five-day extension when
the British privateers were sighted. "Our Captain put it to a vote,
and it was found we were unanimously agreed to make the
cruise."[148] One hesitates to call this process democratic: even the
captain of a private ship could not function without the support of
his crew. What Hewes remembered was that the captains deferred
to him and his mates, not the other way around.

This is the motif of his encounter with George Washington in
1775. When Hewes and his fellow escapees from Boston were taken
to Washington's headquarters at Craigie House in Cambridge, the
Reverend Peter Thatcher recognized him as the nephew of the
"staunch Liberty Man" Robert Hewes. Washington invited Hewes
into his parlor—"with him, alone. There he told him his story, every
word of it, from beginning to end, and answered all his questions
besides." Washington, in Hewes's words, "didn't *laugh*, to be sure,
but *looked amazing good-natured* you may depend." Washington then
treated him and his companions to punch and invited them and
Thatcher to a meal. All this is entirely possible. Washington was considering an invasion of Boston; he would have welcomed intelligence
from a street-wise man just out of the town, and as a Virginia
planter he knew the importance of the gesture of hospitality. Hewes
also claimed that "Madam Washington waited upon them at table all
dinner-time," but this is improbable, and Thatcher the biographer
erred in stating that she was "known to have been with her husband
at the date of the adventure."[149]

In military duty on land there was no recognition of this sort from
his betters, though he was in the militia, by reputation the most democratic branch of service. Even his adventures were humdrum. The
"general destination" of his units, he told Hawkes, was "to guard the
coasts." He saw action at the Battle of Newport Island in August
1778 under General John Sullivan. He remembered "an engagement" at Cobblehill, "in which we beat them with a considerable
slaughter of their men." He remembered rowing through the dark-

ness in silence in an attack on a British fort that had to be aborted
when one of the rowers talked. He remembered the grim retreat
from Newport Island, crossing the waters at Howland's Ferry. On
duty at West Point in 1781 he went out on forays against the "cowboys," lawless bands pillaging Westchester County. In all this activity
he claimed no moment of glory; there was a lot of marching; a lot
of sentry duty; much drudgery.[150] If he mended shoes for soldiers,
as did other shoemakers in the ranks, he did not speak of it. And
military service did not kindle in him an ambition to rise, as it did in
a number of other shoemakers who became officers.[151]

After all this service it hurt to be subjected to an inequitable draft.
As Hewes explained to Hawkes with considerable accuracy, Massachusetts required all men of military age to serve "or to form themselves into classes of nine men, and each class to hire an able bodied
man, on such terms as they could, and pay him for his services, while
they were to receive their pay of the state." Attleborough instituted
such a procedure early in 1781. Why did Hewes refuse to go? He
was frank with Hawkes: the "extreme exigencies" of his family and
the "pressure of his circumstances" forced him to "withdraw his services from the army." The decision was painful, and it was costly.
Hewes's substitute "demanded . . . specie while we received nothing
of the government but paper money, of very little value, and continually depreciating."[152]

Thatcher was right: his service was "poorly rewarded." Hewes was
one of "the mass of people, at large; such as had little property to
fight for, or to lose, on one hand, and could reasonably expect to
gain still less, either in the way of emolument or distinction on the
other."[153] Instead, the inequities of civilian life were repeated on an
even crasser scale. The rich could easily afford a substitute; the men
who had already fought paid through the nose for one. The ship's
officers got their share of the prize; the poor sailor got neither prize
money nor wages.

But the war meant more than this to Hewes. It left a memory of
rights asserted (by a threat of mutiny) and rights respected by captains who put decisions to a vote of the crew, and of the crew giving
assent. It was a memory, above all, of respect from his betters: from
General Washington at Cambridge, from captains Stacey and Smedley at sea, as from John Hancock in Boston. For a moment, it had
been a world that marched to the tune of the old English nursery
rhyme supposedly played at Cornwallis's surrender, "The World
Turned Upside Down." Then "in a trice" Hewes's world came right
side up—but little, if any, better than before.

VII

For thirty-three years, from 1783 to about 1815, George Hewes almost eludes us. We know that at the end of the war he did not return to Boston but stayed in Wrentham; that he produced a large family; that after the War of 1812 he moved to Otsego County, New York. But we hardly know what he did these years. His biographers were uninterested. Hawkes said he was in "laborious pursuits either in some agricultural or mechanical employment." Later lore had it that he returned to the sea and "for many years" was "a mate on merchant vessels in the West Indies trade," lore that has been impossible to verify.[154] Legal documents refer to him in 1796–97 as a "yeoman" and in 1810 as a "cordwainer."[155] These clues are not inconsistent. Wrentham in those years was a small inland farming town of about 2,000 people, no more than a good day's walk to the port of Providence.[156] If Hewes was a cordwainer, he would have had to be a farmer too, as were most country shoemakers. If he went to sea, he would have had to fall back on landlubber pursuits, especially in his later years. There were few "old salts" in their fifties or sixties.

All we may say with certainty is that he came out of the war poor and stayed poor. By 1783, he had turned forty, and had very little to show for it. That he did not go back to Boston, that he did not visit there more than a few times until 1821, tells us how small a stake he had in his native city. In this he was like at least a thousand other Bostonians—for the most part "the poorest and least successful"—who migrated elsewhere.[157] "The shop which I had built in Boston, I lost," he told Hawkes. British troops "appropriated it for the purpose of a wash and lumber house, and eventually pulled it down and burnt it up."[158] He owned no real estate. After seven years of war he could hardly count on customers waiting at his door. There was really nothing to go back to. Uncle Robert had died. His brothers were still there: Solomon was a fisherman and Daniel a mason, but Shubael could list himself as gentleman. Hewes bore his loyalist brother no ill will; he named a son Shubael in 1781. But his own low estate, compared to his brother's success, must have rankled.

There is no evidence that he acquired land in Wrentham. The census names him; the records of real estate bought and sold do not.[159] The town's tax records of the 1790s list him only as a "poll rateable," owning neither real nor personal taxable property. In 1796, at the age of fifty-four, he was assessed thirty-three cents for his Massachusetts poll tax, seven cents for his county tax, fifty cents for his town tax.[160] He may possibly have been joint owner of property listed in someone else's name; more likely he rented or lived on a relative's land.[161] His uncle Joseph, a Providence physician who died in 1796, willed George and Sarah one thirty-sixth share of the estate—$580.25. The windfall helped keep him going. In 1810 he finally became a property holder in Attleborough: a co-owner, with eighteen others, of "a burying yard."[162]

That Hewes stayed poor is also suggested by what little we know about his children. Sarah Hewes gave birth to fifteen, it would seem, of whom we have the names of eleven, three girls and eight boys, possibly all who survived birth. Six were born by 1781, the rest by 1796 at the latest. The naming pattern suggests the strength of family attachments: Sally for her mother; Mary and Elizabeth for aunts, Hewes's father's sisters; Solomon, Daniel, and Shubael after his brothers (and Solomon also for his grandfather, Shubael also for Sally's relative). One son was named Eleven, and the last-born, George Robert Twelves Fifteen.[163] What can we make of this? A mischievous sense of humor? His own long name, the subject of teasing in his youth, after all had been a way of getting attention. Perhaps the only inheritance a poor shoemaker-farmer-seaman could guarantee—especially to his eleventh and fifteenth children—was a name that would be a badge of distinction as his had been.

Hewes could do little for this brood. Solomon, the first-born, became a shoemaker—undoubtedly trained by his father. Robert became a blacksmith. For the other sons we know no occupations. Of the daughters, two of the three married late—Elizabeth at twenty-two but Sarah (also Sally) in her mid-thirties and Mary at thirty-two—understandable when a father could not provide a suitor with dowry, position, or a sought-after craft skill.[164]

For a while the Heweses lived in Attleborough, but the only trace they left is the share of the "burying yard."[165] Attleborough was not much different from Wrentham; a farming town closer to Providence, it also had a few of the mills that dotted southern New England these years. For opportunity the family would have to move much farther away. And so they did, like tens of thousands of families who left New England in the 1790s and early 1800s, and like a large number of New England veterans.[166] Robert, Sally who married William Morrison, and Elizabeth who married Preserved Whipple moved to Otsego County, New York. George Fifteen went first to Connecticut, then to Richfield Springs, finally to Michigan. Solomon also moved to Otsego County for a while, then went down east to Union, Maine, where he acquired twenty-eight acres. Eleven went to Kentucky.[167]

What had become these years of George Hewes, the citizen? We have only one thing to go on. According to family tradition, during the War of 1812 he tried to enlist in the navy as a boatswain but was turned down; tried to ship out on the frigate *Constitution;* then tried to join Commodore Perry's fleet on Lake Erie. There is even a story that he walked to Braintree to enlist ex-President John Adams's support.[168] Two sons we know saw service, Eleven in the Kentucky militia, under General Henry Clay, and George Fifteen in Connecticut. Such patriotism in Wrentham, where there was "no rush of men" to arms, would have been extraordinary.[169] It meant that the War of 1812 was a second War of Independence to Hewes; and to have sons who responded meant that the father had passed on well the heritage of the Revolution.

At the end of the war, perhaps before, George and Sarah Hewes went west to Richfield Springs. George was seventy-four, Sarah sixty-five. His family was dispersed, but three or four children were already in Otsego County or accompanied him there. Did he mean to spend his declining years in retirement with his family? He was still vigorous. One suspects he went in search of the "living," the "independence," that had eluded the artisan and the recognition that had eluded the citizen. He had gone from city to sea to small town; now he would try again in a place where at the least he would be with sons and daughters. And so he left Wrentham about 1815, as he had left Boston in 1775, probably with not much more than the tools of his trade. Only this time he had an old soldier's uniform as well.

VIII

In New York, Hewes did not find independence either for himself or through his children. For the last decade of his life he did not even have the haven of family. He did find recognition.

Richfield Springs, sixty-five miles west of Albany and eighteen north of Cooperstown, was no longer frontier country after 1815. Otsego County had been opened up in the 1790s by Judge William Cooper, the novelist's father, who boasted of settling 50,000 families. The pioneers were already moving away to find more fertile land on better terms in western New York or the Old Northwest. Richfield Springs was located in a beautiful area of rolling hills and low mountain peaks, of streams and lakes. In the 1820s, after mineral waters were discovered, it became a resort town. But its prosperity was uneven. It did not get a post office until 1829.[170]

What did Hewes do these years? We have more to go on for the last twenty-five years of his life than for the three decades before:

Hawkes's account is supplemented by some fascinating reminiscences by Hewes's comtemporaries collected in 1896 by the historian
James Grant Wilson. According to "an old jesting rhyme attributed
to James Fenimore Cooper who knew honest Hewes,"

> Old Father Hewes, he makes good shoes,
> And sews them well together
> It has no heels but those he steals
> And begs his upper leather.[171]

Hewes, then, was once again a shoemaker.

He and Sally lived in "a small house which his son Robert had
built for him" on Robert's land.[172] Sarah Morrison was nine miles
away in German Flats and Elizabeth Whipple was also in the area,
each with a large and growing family. Fifteen lived nearby for a
time, a property holder; so did Solomon. As before, their father had
no house or land of his own.[173]

He can hardly have prospered. The clue is that when Daniel, his
last surviving brother, died in 1821, Hewes traveled with Robert to
Boston for five days in a one-horse wagon to secure their legacy. For
the third time in his life a will loomed—Grampa Shubael left £2 17s.
6d. in 1756, and Uncle Joseph, $580.25 in 1796—a windfall so im-
portant when there were no other prospects of accumulation.
George's brother Solomon had died in 1816, Shubael in 1813. Daniel left an estate that came to $2,900 after expenses; he willed a third
to Hewes and his children. Hewes considered his share "a considerable sum," but it could not have stretched very far. "For some years,"
Hawkes wrote in 1833, Robert had "contributed what was necessary"
to support his father and mother.[174]

Sarah died in 1828, age 87 years and 9 months, the tombstone
said. Actually she was 77. It is difficult to bring Sarah out from her
husband's shadow. He spoke of her with affection: "we lived together very happily," he told Hawkes; he expected to see her in
heaven. He had hardly married her for money; he had courted her
for two years. He was grief-stricken when he left her in wartime. He
called her Sally, not Sarah, certainly not Mrs. Hewes. What was her
role? A washerwoman before she was married, she labored a lifetime
as a housewife, without servants. She bore, it seems, fifteen children
and raised eleven of them. She was illiterate; unlike her husband,
she signed her name with a mark. A daughter of a sexton, she may
well have been religious. Certainly, she was apolitical; had she been
a "Daughter of Liberty," Thatcher, who dwelt on the subject, would
have caught it. When George got home from the Tea Party and told
her his story, " 'Well George,' said she, at the end of it, *did you bring*

me home a lot of it?' " "We shouldn't wonder," Thatcher added, "if
Mrs. Hewes was more of a tea-drinker than a Whig." Or, we might
add, more of a woman struggling to make ends meet on a shoemaker's income.[175]

After she died, it was all downhill. George moved from one child
to another, each so poor they could not long provide for him. At
first, he lived with Robert, who soon after, "having met with some
misfortune, was obliged to sell his house" and move farther west.
For a while he was "a sojourner among friends." Then he moved in
with his daughter and son-in-law, the Morrisons, but stayed only a
year. "Morrison and his wife had several children," wrote Hawkes,
"and were, as they are now very poor . . . Morrison not being able
by his manuel [*sic*] services to provide for his family but a mere subsistence." Hewes had a "severe sickness." Next he took up "a short
residence with a son who resides near Richfield Springs," very likely
George, Jr. Soon after, he "fell down a stairway on some iron ware,"
severely lacerating both legs. He healed with remarkable speed for
a man his age, but a son with eight children to feed could not provide "for his comfortable support." Finally, a "worthy gentleman" in
the neighborhood took the old man in, and it was there that Hawkes
found him in 1833, "pressed down by the iron hand of poverty" and
"supported by the charity of his friends." His children had failed
and, in the classic style of poor pioneers, were moving on to greener
fields. They and his grandchildren would scatter, most to the Midwest, some to California, some still in mechanic trades in Boston.[176]

In the fall of 1832 Hewes applied successfully for a veteran's pension. He may have applied earlier, for Hawkes spoke of a "long and
expensive process" begun about fifteen or twenty years before. If
true, Hewes must have been frustrated: he would not have been
eligible until the 1832 law required no more than six months' service
in any branch.[177] Hewes's application, in the hand of the county
clerk to which a local judge and county official attested, gives minute
details of his service. A clerk in Washington disallowed three of the
months he claimed at sea, listing him for seven months', fifteen days'
service as a seaman and nine months in the militia. It added up to
sixteen months, fifteen days, or less than the two years required for
a full pension; he was therefore prorated down to $60 a year, with
$150 in arrears retroactive to 1831. It was, Hawkes thought, a "mis-
erable pittance of a soldier's pension."[178]

Meanwhile, Hewes was winning recognition of a sort. A "venerable lady" whom James Grant Wilson spoke to in 1896 said she first
met Hewes in 1820 at a "house raising" where she saw "an alert and
little old man with the cocked hat and faded uniform of a continen-

tal soldier, who charmed the young people with the account of the destruction of the tea in Boston in December 1773, and his stories of battles on land and sea." Another woman, who attended school in Richfield Springs with one of Hewes's granddaughters, said she was always delighted to listen to the old soldier's stories and to see him on the Fourth of July, "when he would put on his ancient uniform, shoulder his crutch, like Goldsmith's veteran, and show how fields were won."[179] By the late 1820s, possibly earlier, Hewes had become a figure at Fourth of July observances. In 1829 the local paper reported that he "walked three miles on foot to join in the festivities," and "after mingling in the enjoyments of the occasion, with a fine flow of spirits returned in the same manner thro' the wet to home." In 1833 the celebrants toasted him as "the last survivor of the tea party," and he toasted them in turn.[180]

The "venerable lady" also claimed to have seen "the old soldier in conversation with James Fenimore Cooper who invited Hewes to his home in Cooperstown where he was quite a lion at the author's table." This is entirely possible. The novelist, who returned to his family home at intervals, was always mining old timers for the lore of the sea and the Revolution. Later he would invite Ned Meyers, an old salt, to spend five months at Cooperstown while he took down his life. Hewes's tales of the "cowboys and skinners" of Westchester could have added to Cooper's store of information for *The Spy;* his adventures at sea would have confirmed Cooper in his idealization of American privateersmen, a theme in several of his sea novels and his naval history.[181]

This recognition, it can be argued, had a price. The old man had to dress up in his uniform and tell stories. He was trotted out once a year on Independence Day. He had to play a role; perhaps this may have contributed to his "remembering" himself almost ten years older than he was. And the already-quoted "jesting rhyme," whether Cooper's or not, suggests that if children sat at his feet to hear his tales, they also poked fun at "Old Father Hewes."

Hawkes captured a mood in Hewes that bordered on alienation, especially as he talked about his reactions to Boston in 1821, when he went there to receive his legacy. Hewes spoke of the experience in haunting, poetic language. As he walked around town, he looked for old friends.

> But, alas! I looked in vain. They were gone. Neither were those who once knew them as I did, to be found. The place where I drew my first breath and formed my most endearing attachments, had to me become a land of strangers.

He looked for familiar places.

> Not only had my former companions and friends disappeared, but the places of their habitations were occupied by those who could give no account of them. The house in which I was born was not to be found, and the spot where it stood could not be ascertained by any visible object.

The physical city of 1775 was gone.

> The whole scenery about me seemed like the work of enchantment. Beacon hill was levelled, and a pond on which had stood three mills, was filled up with its contents; over which two spacious streets had been laid and many elegant fabrics erected. The whole street, from Boston Neck to the Long Wharf, had been built up. It was to me almost as a new town, a strange city; I could hardly realize that I was in the place of my nativity.

As he stood in the market, an "aged man" stared at him, then asked,

> Was you not a citizen of Boston at the time the British tea was destroyed in Boston harbour? I replied that I was, and was one of those who aided in throwing it into the water. He then inquired who commanded the division to which I belonged in that affair; I told him one Leonard Pitt. So he did mine, said he; and I had believed there was a man by the name of Hewes aboard the same ship with me, and I think you must be that man.[182]

They had a "social glass," reminisced, parted. "I found he as well as myself had outlived the associates of his youthful days." Hewes did his legal business, saw his nephews and nieces, and after three days headed home.[183]

Sometime in his declining years Hewes became a Methodist. He was known to the children of the village as "The Old Saturday Man," Wilson reported, because "every Saturday for several years he walked into Richfield Springs for the purpose of being present at the services of the Methodist Church of which he was a member."[184] This lore seems trustworthy. He had become a Bible reader ("he can still read his Bible without glasses," a grandson wrote in 1836), and Hawkes found that he "often expresses his gratitude to a kind providence, for the many favours with which he has been indulged." He was also known for his temperance, a badge of Methodists. It stuck in the memory of the "venerable lady" that at the house-raising Hewes was "perhaps the only man present who did not drink the blackstrap (a mixture of whiskey and molasses) provided for the occasion."[185]

Hewes had not been a member of any other church in Richfield

Springs and could hardly have been a Methodist before moving there.[186] But it is not surprising that he became one. Methodism had a growing appeal to poor, hard-working people low in status, whether among shoemakers in Lynn, Massachusetts (a center of Methodist missionaries), textile workers in Samuel Slater's mill in Webster, Massachusetts, or rural folk in the west.[187] Richfield Springs had no fewer than three Methodist chapels scattered around the township, none of which could sustain a minister; circuit riders or laymen served them. Many things about the Methodists would have attracted Hewes: a warm atmosphere of Christian fellowship; a stress on sobriety and industriousness, the Franklinian virtues he had been raised on; the promise of salvation without regard to rank or wealth.[188] This was also a church that stressed lay leadership; shoemakers could serve as stewards, "class" leaders, and lay preachers. Hewes's Methodism seems late blooming; he may have found in the fellowship of the chapel the wholehearted acceptance of himself as a person that was missing in the Fourth of July kind of recognition from the village.

                              IX

For Hewes, the publication of James Hawkes's *Retrospect* in 1834 led to recognition in New England. There is no sign that the book caused a ripple in Richfield Springs or Otsego County, but in Boston it paved the way for the return of one of the "last surviving members" of the Tea Party. Hewes's attraction was his age, supposedly almost 100, combined with his role in a symbolic moment of the Revolution. In 1821 Hewes had been ignored. By 1835 a change in historical mood made Boston ready for him. Angry veterans forced from the pension list in the 1820s helped bring old soldiers into the public eye, leading to the more liberal act of 1832. At the laying of the cornerstone of the Bunker Hill Monument in 1825, Daniel Webster and Lafayette shared the honors with forty veterans of the battle and 200 other veterans of the Revolution. In the 1830s Ralph Waldo Emerson interviewed survivors of the fight at Concord Bridge, and in 1831 Oliver Wendell Holmes wrote "The Last Leaf," a poem about an aged survivor of the Tea Party.[189]

    Workingmen demonstrated a special identification with the artisan republicanism of the Revolution. The Massachusetts Charitable Mechanics Association—masters all—toasted "our revolutionary mechanics" in 1825. On the Fourth of July, 1826, a shoemaker offered a toast to "the *Shoemakers* of *the Revolution*—they risked their little *all* upon the great *end* and gave *short quarters* to the foe, in 'the times that tried men's soles.' " Meanwhile Seth Luther, asserting the right of journeymen and factory operatives to combine against masters, asked, "Was there no *combination* when Bostonians . . . made a dish of tea . . . using Boston harbor for a tea pot?" In May 1835, when Boston journeymen house carpenters, masons, and stone cutters went on strike, they claimed "by the blood of our fathers shed on our battle fields on the War of the Revolution, the rights of American Freeman."[190]

In 1835 Hewes returned to New England on a triumphal tour of sorts accompanied by his youngest son, Fifteen. At Providence he was interviewed by the local newspaper, and the merchant patriarch Moses Brown called on him. On the way to Boston he stopped at Wrentham, perhaps to visit, perhaps to crow a bit. In Boston the papers noted his arrival, printing an excerpt from Hawkes's book. He was a celebrity. He stayed with his nephew Richard Brooke Hewes, Shubael's son, a politician who doubtless made the arrangements for his uncle's visit. Thatcher interviewed him for his biography, reliving his life in Boston. He sat for a portrait by Joseph G. Cole, Boston's rising young painter, which within a month would be on display at the Athenaeum Gallery, entitled *The Centenarian*. A group of ladies presented him with a snuff box.[191]

The highlight, of course, was the Fourth of July. He was the featured guest at South Boston's observance. "In a conspicuous part of the procession," according to the newspaper, "was the venerable Mr. Hewes, in a barouche, drawn by four splendid greys," accompanied by the lieutenant governor and his entourage. There was a church service and a dinner. When the orator of the day reached the Tea Party and "alluded to the venerable patriot," Hewes "arose and received the united and enthusiastic congratulations of the audience." He was supported on one side by Major Benjamin Russell, for forty years a leader of the mechanic interest as printer and publisher, and on the other by Colonel Henry Purkitt, who had been a cooper's apprentice and, like Hewes, a Tea Party volunteer. The orator was fulsome in his tribute to Hewes, "formerly a citizen of Boston," now "on the verge of eternity": "Though you come to the land of your childhood, leaning upon a staff and feeling your dependence on the charities of a selfish world, you are surrounded by friends who feel that their prosperity is referable to the privations sacrifices and personal labors of you and your brave associates in arms." At the dinner after the toasts it was Hewes's turn. "Under the influence of strong emotion he gave the following toast, 'Those I leave behind me, May God Bless them.' "[192]

When the celebrations ended, Hewes made his way to Augusta, Maine. Solomon, his eldest, had died there the year before, and his wife had just died, but there were grandchildren to visit. He also went to Portland, perhaps for more family. From Maine, back to Boston, and thence home to Richfield Springs.

Several things struck those who saw Hewes. The first, of course, was his age. Not surprisingly, people came forward from all around—Wrentham, Attleborough, Boston, Maine—to testify, as they had in Richfield Springs, that he was indeed 100, if not more. The second was his remarkable physical condition. Third was his wonderful mood. A correspondent of the *Boston Courier* who rode the stagecoach to Augusta was astonished that "he bore the ride of fifty-eight miles with very little apparent fatigue, amusing himself and his fellow passengers occasionally upon the route, with snatches of revolutionary songs, and by the recital of anecdotes of the days which tried mens souls." He was in his glory. And lastly, there was his demeanor. Hewes's Providence interviewer found him "even at this age, a brave, high spirited, warm hearted man, whose tongue was never controlled by ceremony, and whose manners have not been moulded by the fashion of any day. His etiquette may be tea party etiquette, but it was not acquired at tea parties in Beacon Street or Broadway."[193] Hewes, in short, was still not taking his hat off for any man.

The remaining five years in Richfield Springs were no different than the previous twenty. Thatcher's biography appeared late in 1835, but there is no sign that it was read any more than Hawkes's. "The Old Saturday Man" continued to walk to church. The veteran continued to be a guest on the Fourth of July. His family was dispersed; there were more than fifty grandchildren, and occasionally one visited him. In 1836 George Whipple, Elizabeth's son, found him "pretty well, and very jovial. He sang for me many old songs and told over all the incidents of the 'scrape' in Boston Harbor. His memory is uncommonly good for one of his age. He jumped about so when I made myself known to him he liked to have lost his drumsticks." The old man clearly was starved for company. A visit from a grandchild only underscored his isolation. In 1836 he sat for a portrait by a local artist, commissioned by a grandson. He looked smaller, shrunken.[194]

On July 4, 1840, as Hewes was getting into a carriage to go to the annual observance, the horses bolted and he was seriously injured. He died on November 5, Pope's Day, once the "grand gala day" of Boston's apprentices. He was buried in what became the Presbyterian cemetery, where his wife already lay. There seem to have been no obituary notices, no public memorial services.

From mid-century on, Hewes began to make an occasional appearance in histories of the nation, the Revolution, Boston, or the Tea Party.[195] Descendants also kept his memory alive. Children and grandchildren named sons after him; one great-grandson bore the distinctive George Twelves Hewes (1861–1921). The generation that matured late in the nineteenth century rediscovered him as some compiled a mammoth genealogy and others applied to patriotic societies.[196] In 1896 his remains were exhumed and reinterred ceremoniously in the Grand Army of the Republic plot in Lakeview Cemetery, Richfield Springs. The inscription on the tombstone reads "George R. T. Hewes, one who helped drown the tea in Boston, 1770, died November 5, 1840, aged 109 years 2 months."[197] If anyone in town knew the truth, no one wanted to destroy the myth. The next year James Grant Wilson published the first article devoted to Hewes, perpetuating the notion that Hewes was the last survivor of the Tea Party.[198]

In 1885 a great-grandson gave the Cole painting to the Bostonian Society, which has displayed it ever since at the Old State House. In the opinion of contemporaries, it was "an admirable likeness."[199] It shows a happy man of ninety-three in his moment of triumph in Boston. He wears Sunday clothes, nineteenth-century style, and leans forward in a chair, his hands firmly gripping a cane. His face is wrinkled but not ravaged; his features are full, his eyes alert. He has most of his hair. There is a twinkle in his eyes, a slightly bemused smile on his lips. The mood is one of pride. It is not a picture of a man as a shoemaker, but we can understand it only if we know the man was a shoemaker. It shows the pride of a man the world had counted as a nobody at a moment in his life when he was a somebody, when he had won recognition from a town that had never granted it before. It is the pride of a citizen, of one who "would not take his hat off to any man." The apprentice who had once deferred to John Hancock lived with the memory that Hancock had toiled side by side with him, throwing tea chests into Boston harbor. The man who had to defer to British officers, royal officials, and colonial gentry had lived to see General Washington, ship captains, and now lieutenant governors, educated lawyers, and writers defer to him.

It is the pride of a survivor. His enemies had all passed on. His "associates," the patriots, had all gone to their graves. He had outlived them all. Fortified by his religion, the old man could rejoice that he would soon join them, but as their equal. "May we meet hereafter," he told his Independence Day well-wishers, "where the wicked will cease from troubling and the true sons of Liberty be forever at rest."[200]

NOTES

This article was originally published in the *William and Mary Quarterly*, 3d Ser., 38 (Oct. 1981), 561–623. This essay would not have been possible without the help of a large number of scholars, librarians, and descendants and friends of the Hewes family. I acknowledge each of these at the relevant point. I wish to express my special appreciation to three scholars who read and commented on the essay in several drafts: Jesse Lemisch, Gary Nash, and Lawrence W. Towner. Michael Kammen and James Henretta also offered valuable reactions to an early draft. My debt to Jesse Lemisch is large; he helped me to work out problems too numerous to mention and provided a pioneering example of a biography of an ordinary person in "The American Revolution and the American Dream: A Life of Andrew Sherburne, a Pensioner of the Navy of the Revolution" (Columbia University Seminar on Early American History and Culture, 1975) to be published in his *The American Revolution and the American Dream*. I have also profited from the criticism of colleagues at the Conference on the "New" Labor History and the New England Working Class, Smith College; the Graduate Colloquium, Northern Illinois University; and the Newberry Library Seminar in Early American History. Research for the paper was completed on a Newberry Library– National Endowment for the Humanities Fellowship. © by author.

1. A Bostonian [Benjamin Bussey Thatcher], *Traits of the Tea Party; Being a Memoir of George R. T. Hewes, One of Its Survivors; With a History of That Transaction; Reminiscences of the Massacre, and the Siege, and Other Stories of Old Times.* (New York: Harper & Brothers, 1835), pp. 52–55, hereafter cited as Thatcher, *Memoir of Hewes*.

2. Ibid., pp. 226–27.

3. A Citizen of New York [James Hawkes], *A Retrospect of the Boston Tea-Party, with a Memoir of George R. T. Hewes, a Survivor of the Little Band of Patriots Who Drowned the Tea in Boston Harbour in 1773* (New York: S. Bliss, printer, 1834), hereafter cited as Hawkes, *Retrospect*.

4. *Evening Mercantile Journal* (Boston), July 6, 1835.

5. C. Vann Woodward, "History from Slave Sources," *American Historical Review*, 79 (1974), 470–81. For the related problems in slave memoirs, see John W. Blassingame, *The Slave Community: Plantation Life in the Antebellum South*, rev. ed. (New York, 1979), pp. 369–78.

6. Michael Kammen, *A Season of Youth: The American Revolution and the Historical Imagination* (New York, 1978), p. 26; Richard M. Dorson, ed., *America Rebels: Narratives of the Patriots*, 2d ed. rev. (New York, 1966), p. 17. Dorson, defining "narrative" somewhat loosely, counted over 200 entries in

the Library of Congress catalog; in his appendix he lists thirty-seven, eleven of which appeared between 1822 and 1833.

7. J. Todd White and Charles H. Lesser, eds., *Fighters for Independence: A Guide to Sources of Biographical Information on Soldiers and Sailors of the American Revolution* (Chicago, 1977), lists under "Diaries, Journals and Autobiographies" 538 entries, both published and in manuscript. Walter Wallace's " 'Oh, Liberty! Oh, Virtue! Oh, My Country!' An Exploration of the Minds of New England Soldiers during the American Revolution" (M.A. thesis, Northern Illinois University, 1974) is based on 164 published diaries. Also relevant is Jesse Lemisch, "The American Revolution Bicentennial and the Papers of Great White Men," American Historical Association, *Newsletter,* 9 (Nov. 1971), 7–21, as well as "The Papers of Great White Men," *Maryland Historian,* 6 (1975), 43–50, and "The Papers of a Few Great Black Men and a Few Great White Women," ibid., 60–66.

8. John C. Dann, ed., *The Revolution Remembered: Eyewitness Accounts of the War for Independence* (Chicago, 1980), introduction. For other scholars who have made use of the pension applications, see the works cited in sec. VI below. John Shy and Dann are directing a project, "Data Bank for American Revolutionary Generation," William L. Clements Library, University of Michigan, Ann Arbor, based on samples from the 1818 and 1832 pension applications.

9. Cataloguers attribute the book to James Hawkes on the basis of the copyright entry on the overleaf of the title page. I am indebted to Walter Wallace for searching for Hawkes in the New York Public Library, unfortunately without success.

10. The body of Hawkes's book with the memoir runs 115 pages, about 27,000 words; a lengthy preface and an appendix bring it to 206 pages.

11. *Dictionary of American Biography,* s.v. "Thatcher, Benjamin Bussey." See also Nehemiah Cleaveland, *History of Bowdoin College. With Biographical Sketches of its Graduates . . .* , ed. Alpheus Spring Packard (Boston, 1882), pp. 356–58.

12. Thatcher's book has 242 pages, about 49,000 words, plus a short appendix.

13. Hawkes, *Retrospect,* pp. 13–16, 85–93.

14. Thatcher, *Memoir of Hewes,* pp. iv, 250–53.

15. Ibid., p. 250, and examples at pp. 52, 89, 95, 112.

16. For example, Hewes gave Hawkes, who had no way of prompting or correcting him, the more or less correct names and occupations of the five victims of the Boston Massacre, five leading loyalist officials, and half-a-dozen relatives he visited in 1821. A typical error was "Leonard Pitt" for Lendell Pitts as his "Captain" at the Tea Party.

17. Hawkes, *Retrospect,* p. 28.

18. See Ian M. L. Hunter, *Memory* (London, 1957), esp. ch. 6.

19. According to John R. Sellers, "Many [veterans who applied for pensions under the 1818 act] did not know how old they were" ("The Origins and Careers of New England Soldiers, Non-Commissioned Officers, and Privates in the Massachusetts Continental Line" [paper, American Historical

Association, 1972], pp. 4–5, cited with the author's permission). Sellers was able to compute the ages of 396 men in a sample of 546.

20. Dann, ed., *Revolution Remembered.* p. xx. For examples in which narratives faulty in some respects still checked out as essentially credible, see ibid., pp. 204–11, 240–50, 268–74.

21. Paul Thompson, *The Voice of the Past: Oral History* (Oxford, 1978), p. 113 and ch. 4. For a remarkable example of this in a black sharecropper interviewed in his eighty-fifth year, see Theodore Rosengarten, *All God's Dangers: The Life of Nate Shaw* (New York, 1974). See also John Neuenschwander, "Remembrance of Things Past: Oral Historians and Long-Term Memory," *Oral History Review,* 6 (1978), 45–53.

22. Hawkes, *Retrospect,* p. 93; Thatcher, *Memoir of Hewes,* p. 251.

23. See David Hackett Fischer, *Growing Old in America,* expanded ed. (New York, 1978), esp. ch. 2.

24. Based on a computer print-out of all wills at probate entered at Suffolk County Court, kindly loaned to me by Gary B. Nash. For analysis of the context see his "Urban Wealth and Poverty in Pre-Revolutionary America," *Journal of Interdisciplinary History,* 6 (1976), 545–84, and *The Urban Crucible: Social Change, Political Consciousness, and the Origins of the American Revolution* (Cambridge, Mass., 1979), ch. 7. Before 1735, eight shoemakers on the probate list ended up in the top 10 percent of wealthholders (albeit most at the bottom of that bracket), but from 1736 to 1775 only one did.

25. Allan Kulikoff, "The Progress of Inequality in Revolutionary Boston," *William and Mary Quarterly,* 3d Ser., 28 (1971), 375–412; James A. Henretta, "Economic Development and Social Structure in Colonial Boston," ibid., 22 (1965), 75–92. The 1771 tax assessment does not list occupations; the 1780 assessment, which does, is incomplete; the 1790 list is the first point at which occupations can be measured for wealth.

26. In Nash's list of sixty-one shoemakers, 1685–1775, seven names are repeated, appearing twice; after 1752, no name is repeated (see above, n. 24). For examples of trades passed down within families, see Esther Forbes, *Paul Revere & the World He Lived In* (Boston, 1942). For a family engaged in shipbuilding over six generations, see Bernard Farber, *Guardians of Virtue: Salem Families in 1800* (New York, 1972), pp. 104–8.

27. Lawrence W. Towner, "The Indentures of Boston's Poor Apprentices: 1734–1805," Colonial Society of Massachusetts, *Transactions,* 43 (1966), 417–68. The maritime, shipbuilding, and leather trades each accounted for about 8 percent of the boys; about 40 percent went into husbandry. From 1751 to 1776, twenty-six boys were put out to cordwainers, six in Boston, twenty in country towns.

28. Eric Hobsbawm and Joan Scott, "Political Shoemakers," *Past and Present,* no. 89 (1980), 86–114, which the authors kindly allowed me to see in MS. See also Peter Burke, *Popular Culture in Early Modern Europe* (London, 1978), pp. 38–39.

29. *The Most Delightful History of the King and the Cobler . . .* ([Boston, 1774]), reprinted from an English chapbook, and also printed in *Crispin*

Anecdotes; Comprising Interesting Notices of Shoemakers . . . (Sheffield, Eng., 1827).

30. John Adams, June 17, 1760, in L. H. Butterfield et al., eds., *Diary and Autobiography of John Adams*, I (Cambridge, Mass., 1961), p. 135.

31. Hawkes, *Retrospect*, pp. 17–18.

32. Thatcher, *Memoir of Hewes*, p. 11.

33. For a very full genealogy and family history of the several branches of the Hewes family, see Eben Putnam, comp., *Lieutenant Joshua Hewes: A New England Pioneer and Some of his Descendants* . . . (New York, 1913).

34. William B. Trask, "The Seaver Family," *New-England Historical and Genealogical Register*, 26 (1872), 303–23.

35. Will of Shubael Seaver, Suffolk Co. Probate Court, LII. 20–21, a copy of which was provided by Gary Nash.

36. Trask, "Seaver Family," p. 306; Putnam, comp., *Joshua Hewes*, p. 318.

37. Hawkes, *Retrospect*, pp. 18, 86.

38. Thatcher, *Memoir of Hewes*, pp. 26–33. Hewes did not volunteer these anecdotes to Hawkes.

39. Ibid., pp. 129, 132. Warren was his grandmother's sister's son.

40. Petitions by Nathaniel Cunningham and George and Robert Hewes, 1740–43, MS, Massachusetts Archives, Manufactures, LIX, 316–19, 321–24, 334–37, 342–45, State House, Boston. I am indebted to Ruth Kennedy for running down Hewes and his family in a variety of legal and other sources in Boston, and to Gary Nash for his help in interpreting the sources.

41. Thatcher, *Memior of Hewes*, p. 38.

42. Letter of Administration, Estate of George Hewes, Suffolk Co. Probate Court, 1766, Docket No. 13906.

43. Alexander Keyssar, "Widowhood in Eighteenth-Century Massachusetts: A Problem in the History of the Family," *Perspectives in American History*, 8 (1974), 98, 116–19. A census of 1742 showed 1,200 widows, "one thousand whereof are in low circumstances," in a population of 16,382 (Nash, *Urban Crucible*, p. 172).

44. Petition of Robert Hewes, Nov. 1752, MS, Mass. Archs., Manufactures, LIX, 372–74. He is not to be confused with Robert Hewes (1751–1830) of Boston, a highly successful glassmaker (*DAB*, s.v. "Hewes, Robert"), or the father of this man, also Robert, who migrated from England ca. 1751. See petitions of Robert Hewes to the General Court, May 25 and June 8, 1757 (in a different hand from that of Uncle Robert), Mass. Archs., Manufactures, LIX, 434–35.

45. Benjamin Franklin, *The Autobiography of Benjamin Franklin*, ed. Leonard W. Labaree et al. (New Haven, 1964), 57.

46. George P. Anderson, "Ebenezer McIntosh: Stamp Act Rioter and Patriot," Colonial Society of Massachusetts, *Transactions*, 26 (1927), 15–64, and "A Note on Ebenezer McIntosh," ibid., 348–61.

47. The Overseers of the Poor first put out Thomas Banks, age eight, to a farmer, William Williams. In 1770 Williams informed the overseers that Thomas "is now seventeen years . . . old and about as big as an ordinary

Country boy of thirteen . . . and scarcely able to perform the service of one of our boys at that age," and so he placed him with a cordwainer. Williams to Royal Tyler, Jan. 23, 1770, in Towner, "Boston's Poor Apprentices," pp. 430–31.

48. James Biddle to David Conner, Aug. 9, 1813, Fourth Auditor Accounts Numerical Series, 1141, Record Group 217, National Archives, Washington, D.C., kindly brought to my attention by Christopher McKee.

49. Hobsbawm and Scott write that "there is a good deal of evidence that small, weak or physically handicapped boys were habitually put to this trade" ("Political Shoemakers," pp. 96–97).

50. Hawkes, *Retrospect*, pp. 23–24; Franklin, *Autobiography*, ed. Labaree et al., p. 57. For a boy whose threats forced his parents to allow him to go to sea, see Lemisch, "Life of Andrew Sherburne," sec. III.

51. Thatcher, *Memoir of Hewes*, pp. 17–18. For a boy in the laboring classes who fell into a cistern of rain water and was rescued from drowning, see Isaiah Thomas, *Three Autobiographical Fragments* . . . (Worcester, Mass., 1962), p. 7.

52. Thatcher, *Memoir of Hewes*, pp. 18–26.

53. Ibid., p. 25.

54. Hawkes, *Retrospect*, pp. 21–22.

55. Thatcher, *Memoir of Hewes*, pp. 29–47. Thatcher presented this story as occurring shortly after Hewes became twenty-one, which might make it 1764, the year of a massive smallpox inoculation campaign in Boston.

56. Hawkes, *Retrospect*, pp. 23–25. See also *By His Excellency William Shirley, Esq.* . . . (Boston, Apr. 17, 1755), with the eligibility requirement, and *By His Excellency Thomas Pownall* . . . (Boston, Apr. 10, 1758, and Mar. 14, 1760), broadsides, Library of Congress, Washington, D.C.

57. Thatcher, *Memoir of Hewes*, pp. 47–49. For the anti-impressment riots of 1747, see Jesse Lemisch, "Jack Tar in the Streets: Merchant Seamen in the Politics of Revolutionary America," *William and Mary Quarterly*, 3d Ser., 25 (1968), 371–407, and John Lax and William Pencak, "The Knowles Riot and the Crisis of the 1740's in Massachusetts," *Perspectives in American History*, 10 (1976), 163–214.

58. This may have been the great fire of 1760. I find no record of a Downing in the claims filed by 365 sufferers in "Records Relating to the Early History of Boston," *Report of the Record Commissioners of the City of Boston* (Boston, 1876–1909), vol. 29, hereafter cited as *Record Commissioners' Reports*, but the published records are incomplete.

59. Thatcher spelled his name Rhoades (*Memoir of Hewes*, pp. 49–50). Henry Roads is listed as a cordwainer assigned an apprentice Oct. 30, 1752, in Towner, "Boston's Poor Apprentices," Table, p. 441. If the apprenticeship ran the customary seven years, Rhoades (or Roads) would have needed another one in 1760, which would fit Hewes's story.

60. Alfred Young, "Pope's Day, Tar and Feathers, and Cornet Joyce, Jun: From Ritual to Rebellion in Boston" (MS, Anglo-American Labor Historians' Conference, 1973). See also Thomas, *Three Autobiographical Fragments*, pp. 22–25, for one apprentice's near-fatal participation.

61. Thatcher, *Memoir of Hewes*, pp. 50–52. For another anecdote about a gift of food during the siege of Boston see ibid., p. 204.

62. Hawkes, *Retrospect*, pp. 26–27.

63. Thatcher, *Memoir of Hewes*, pp. 58–64.

64. My estimate. There were seventy-eight shoemakers in Boston in 1790, when there were 2,995 people on the assessment rolls in a population of 18,000 (Kulikoff, "Progress of Inequality," p. 412). I count twenty-six shoemakers in 1780, when there were 2,225 on the assessment rolls in a population of less than 15,000 and at a time when poorer men were apt to be at war (Boston Assessing Department, *Assessors' "Taking Books" of the Town of Boston 1780* [Boston, 1912]). If the population of Boston was 20 percent smaller in 1774 than in 1790, with a proportional loss of shoemakers, it would have included sixty-three shoemakers. For comparisons of occupational breakdowns, see Jacob Price, "Economic Function and the Growth of American Port Towns in the Eighteenth Century," *Perspectives in American History*, 8 (1974), 176, 181.

65. See Thatcher, *Memoir of Hewes*, pp. 39–40, 85, for evidence that he made and repaired shoes. Griffin's Wharf was in the area of the tenth and eleventh wards where in 1771 the mean tax assessment was £193 and £254, twice as high as the mean in the crowded North End wards but considerably below the mean of £695 in the center of town (see Kulikoff, "Progress of Inequality," p. 395, map).

66. Putnam, comp., *Joshua Hewes.* p. 335.

67. "Boston Town Records," in *Record Commissioners' Reports*, III, 65; "Boston Marriages, 1752–1809," ibid., XXX, 65; and Samuel Stillman, "Record of Marriages from the Year 1761," indicate marriage by Stillman. The records of the First Baptist Church, including the Minutes, List of Adult Baptisms, and Pew Proprietors Record Book, do not show the names of either the Sumners or the Heweses as members or of Sumner (or anyone else) as sexton (MS, Andover Newton Theological Seminary, Andover, Mass.). Researched by Elaine W. Pascu.

68. The First Baptist Church had "not 70 members" before 1769 and about eighty more during the next three years (Isaac Backus, *History of New England, with Particular Reference to the . . . Baptists*, III [Boston, 1796], pp. 125–26). See also Nathan Eusebius Wood, *The History of the First Baptist Church of Boston (1665–1899)* (Philadelphia, 1899), pp. 266–67. After the great fire of 1760 the church gave £143 to charity compared, for example, to £1862 from Old South and £418 from Old North. See Franklin Bowditch Dexter, ed., *Extracts from the Itineraries and Other Miscellanies of Ezra Stiles . . .* (New Haven, 1916), p. 120.

69. Writ of Attachment on George Robert Twelves Hewes, including Hewes's note of indebtedness to Courtney, Sept. 3, 1770, Suffolk Co. Court, Case 89862. Ruth Kennedy discovered this document. For Courtney see E. Alfred Jones, *The Loyalists of Massachusetts: Their Memorials, Petitions and Claims* (London 1930), p. 103.

70. Bettye Hobbs Pruitt, ed., *The Massachusetts Tax Valuation List of 1771*

(Boston, 1978), pp. 14–15. Hewes is listed only for one "Polls Rateable." Christopher Ranks is listed as the owner. Stephanie G. Wolf brought this publication to my attention. Ranks is listed in the Thwing File, Massachusetts Historical Society, Boston, as a shopkeeper in 1750, a clockmaker in 1751, and a watchmaker in 1788.

71. Thatcher, *Memoir of Hewes*, pp. 84, 204.

72. *Massachusetts Gazette and Boston Weekly News-Letter*, Jan. 27, 1774, discussed below, sec. V.

73. See *At a meeting of the Freeholders . . . the 28th of October, 1767* (Boston, 1767), broadside, Massachusetts Historical Society.

74. Blanche Evans Hazard, *The Organizations of the Boot and Shoe Industry in Massachusetts before 1875* (Cambridge, Mass., 1921), p. 128, ch. 6, and appendices on pp. 256–64. Lynn shoes were being sold in Boston at public auctions by the hundred pair, dozen pair, or single pair. Moreover, there were several hundred petty retailers, predominantly women, who would have been driven to the wall by the boycott and eager to sell such items. See Thatcher, *Memoir of Hewes*, pp. 139–40, for a reprint of a newspaper notice, Feb. 14, 1770, from Isaac Vibert implying a putting-out system.

75. *Peter Oliver's Origin & Progress of the American Rebellion: A Tory View*, ed. Douglass Adair and John A. Schutz (San Marino, Calif., 1961), pp. 54–55. Similarly in 1771, one in six Philadelphia shoemakers was on poor relief (see Billy G. Smith, "Material Lives of Laboring Philadelphians, 1750 to 1800," *William and Mary Quarterly*, 3d Ser., 38 [1981], 163–202).

76. Hawkes, *Retrospect*, pp. 20, 89, 92; Thatcher, *Memoir of Hewes*, pp. 251–52; Richard Saunders, *Poor Richard Improved: Being an Almanac and Ephemeris . . . for the Year of Our Lord 1758 . . .* (Philadelphia, 1758), also appearing as *Father Abraham's Speech . . .* (Boston, n.d. [1758, 1760]), a compilation of aphorisms from the previous twenty-six almanacs. See Leonard W. Labaree et al., eds., *The Papers of Benjamin Franklin*, VII (New Haven, Conn., 1963), pp. 326–55.

77. J. E. Crowley, *This Sheba, Self: The Conceptualization of Economic Life in Eighteenth-Century America*, The Johns Hopkins University Studies in Historical and Political Science, 92 (Baltimore, 1974), p. 84. See especially James A. Henretta, "The Study of Social Mobility: Ideological Assumptions and Conceptual Bias," *Labor History*, 18 (1977), 165–78.

78. Hewes is listed in the baptismal records of Old South as having been christened on Sept. 26, 1742 (O.S.). See Thatcher, *Memoir of Hewes*, p. 255. There is no other trace of Hewes in Old South records, searched by Elaine W. Pascu. I am indebted to Charles W. Akers for help in identifying and locating Boston church records.

79. Chilton Williamson, *American Suffrage: From Property to Democracy, 1760–1860* (Princeton, N.J., 1960), pp. 13, 16. See *Notification to Voters, William Cooper, Town Clerk, May 1, 1769*, publicizing the property requirement, and *Notification, Mar. 17, 1768*, warning that "a strict scrutiny will be made as to the qualification of voters" (broadsides, Library of Congress). The average total vote in annual elections at official town meetings from

1763 to 1774 was 555; the high was 1,089 in 1763 (see Alan and Catherine Day, "Another Look at the Boston Caucus," *Journal of American Studies,* 5 [1971], 27–28).

80. For the father, see Putnam, comp., *Joshua Hewes,* p. 321, and for McIntosh see Anderson, "Ebenezer McIntosh," pp. 26–28. I find no record of Hewes in "Records Relating to the Early History of Boston," in *Record Commissioners' Reports,* XIV–XX. For the wealth of leaders of the town meeting, see Edward M. Cook, Jr., *The Fathers of the Towns: Leadership and Community Structure in Eighteenth-Century New England,* The Johns Hopkins University Studies in Historical and Political Science, 94 (Baltimore, 1976), chs. 2, 3.

81. For Shubael see Putnam, comp., *Joshua Hewes,* p. 332, and for McIntosh see Anderson, "Ebenezer McIntosh," p. 25.

82. For the low level of associations, see Richard D. Brown, "Emergence of Voluntary Associations in Massachusetts, 1760–1830," *Journal of Voluntary Action Research,* 2 (1973), 64–73.

83. Mary Roys Baker, "Anglo-Massachusetts Trade Union Roots, 1130–1790," *Labor History,* 14 (1973), 335, 362, 365–67, 371, 381–83, 388, 394.

84. Thatcher, *Memoir of Hewes,* pp. 68, 72. For crowd events in Boston the most reliable guide is Dirk Hoerder, *Crowd Action in Revolutionary Massachusetts, 1765–1780* (New York, 1977). Hoerder has generously shared with me his detailed knowledge. I also draw on my forthcoming book on the laboring classes in Boston in the Revolutionary era.

85. Thatcher, *Memoir of Hewes,* pp. 84–87. Bostonians were "shocked by the frequency and severity of corporal punishment in the army" (John Shy, *Toward Lexington: The Role of the British Army in the Coming of the American Revolution* [Princeton, 1965], p. 308).

86. Hawkes, *Retrospect,* pp. 31–32. My statement on the composition of the crowd is based on my analysis of participants, witnesses, and victims identified in the trial record, depositions, etc., and is supported by Hoerder, *Crowd Action,* pp. 223–34, and James Barton Hunt, "The Crowd and the American Revolution: A Study of Urban Political Violence in Boston and Philadelphia, 1763–1776" (Ph.D. dissertation, University of Washington, 1973), pp. 471–79.

87. Hawkes, *Retrospect,* p. 43; Thatcher, *Memoir of Hewes,* pp. 88–95. Hewes told about the event after he recounted the Massacre. He correctly remembered Seider, reported as "Snider" by Thomas Hutchinson and other contemporaries. His recollection is borne out in essentials by Hoerder, *Crowd Action,* pp. 216–23. See Hutchinson to Thomas Hood, Feb. 23, 1770, to Gen. Gage, Feb. 25, 1770, and to Lord Hillsborough, Feb. 28, 1770, Hutchinson Transcripts, Houghton Library, Harvard University, Cambridge, Mass.

88. Hawkes, *Retrospect,* pp. 31–32; Thatcher, *Memoir of Hewes,* pp. 96–99. For verification by another contemporary see "Recollections of a Bostonian," from the *Boston Centinel.* 1821–22, reprinted in Hezekiah Niles, *Principles and Acts of the Revolution in America . . .* (Baltimore, 1822), pp. 430–31.

For the fray at the ropewalk, accepted as a precipitating cause by contemporaries on both sides, see Richard B. Morris, *Government and Labor in Early America* (New York, 1946), pp. 190–92.

89. Hawkes, *Retrospect*, pp. 30–31; Thatcher, *Memoir of Hewes*, pp. 118–19. For the trial see L. Kinvin Wroth and Hiller B. Zobel, eds., *Legal Papers of John Adams* (Cambridge, Mass. 1965), III, 50, 52, 56, 93–94, 108.

90. Hawkes, *Retrospect*, p. 29. For the event itself see Hiller B. Zobel, *The Boston Massacre* (New York, 1970), in conjunction with Jesse Lemisch, "Radical Plot in Boston (1770): A Study in the Use of Evidence," *Harvard Law Review*, 84 (1970), 485–504, and Pauline Maier, "Revolutionary Violence and the Relevance of History," *JIH*, 2 (1971), 119–35.

91. Hawkes, *Retrospect*, pp. 29–32; Thatcher, *Memoir of Hewes*, pp. 110–12.

92. Hawkes, *Retrospect*, p. 30.

93. Zobel, *Boston Massacre*, pp. 206–9; Hoerder, *Crowd Action*, p. 232.

94. Deposition No. 75, in *A Short Narrative of the Horrid Massacre in Boston . . . To Which is Added an Appendix . . .* (Boston, 1770), p. 61. Thatcher reprinted this in *Memoir of Hewes*, pp. 116–18. Hewes's deposition testified to the soldiers' threats to kill more civilians and to someone entering the Custom House at the time of the Massacre, both themes emphasized by whig leaders.

95. Thatcher, *Memoir of Hewes*, p. 95. Thatcher did not give the words. I suspect that what Hewes remembered was the verdict brought in by the jury after a dramatic trial repeatedly interrupted by what Peter Oliver called "a vast concourse of rabble." The verdict was "Guilty of Murder," at which "the Court Room resounded with Expressions of Pleasure" (*Oliver's Origin & Progress*, ed. Adair and Schutz, p. 86). The judges delayed the sentence until the crown granted a pardon. The case aroused a furor. See Wroth and Zobel, eds., *Legal Papers of Adams*, II, 396–430, and Zobel, *Boston Massacre*, ch. 15 and pp. 423–26. For the way in which the killing of Seider and the killings of the Boston Massacre were linked politically, see *A Monumental Inscription in the Fifth of March Together with a few lines on the Enlargement of Ebenezer Richardson Convicted of Murder* [1772], broadside, Massachusetts Historical Society.

96. Hawkes, *Retrospect*, p. 32. Thatcher does not even mention this claim of Hewes, possibly because he was skeptical.

97. Wroth and Zobel, eds. *Legal Papers of Adams*, III, has no record of Hewes at the trial, but see L. H. Butterfield's "Descriptive List of Sources and Documents": "This operation has been a good deal like that of an archeological team reconstructing a temple from a tumbled mass of architectural members, some missing, many mutilated, and most of them strewn over a wide area" (ibid., p. 34). For Shubael Hewes see ibid., pp. 176–77, 224–75, and for Robert Hewes ibid., II, 405, 418.

98. Hutchinson to Lord Dartmouth, Dec. 3, 1773, Hutchinson Transcripts. For Daniel Hewes see Francis S. Drake, *Tea Leaves: Being a Collection of Letters and Documents Relating to the Shipment of Tea . . .* (Boston, 1884), p. xlvi.

99. Hawkes, *Retrospect*, pp. 36–37. Hewes's account is verified in its essen-

tials by Hoerder, *Crowd Action,* pp. 257–64, and is not inconsistent with the less detailed account in Benjamin Woods Labaree, *The Boston Tea Party* (New York, 1964), ch. 7. For analysis of the participants see Hoerder, *Crowd Action,* pp. 263–64, and Hunt, "The Crowd and the American Revolution," pp. 481, 485.

100. Joshua Wyeth, "Revolutionary Reminiscence," *North American,* 1 (1827), 195, brought to my attention by Richard Twomey.

101. Hawkes, *Retrospect,* pp. 38–39.

102. Thatcher, *Memoir of Hewes,* pp. 180–81, 261. Maxwell's reminiscence is in *NEHGR,* 22 (1868), 58.

103. Hawkes, *Retrospect,* pp. 40–41; Thatcher, *Memoir of Hewes,* pp. 182–83.

104. *Mass. Gaz. and Boston Wkly. News-Letter,* Jan. 27, Feb. 3, 1774. Hewes told this story to Hawkes essentially as reported in this paper but with only some of the dialogue. He may have kept the clipping. Thatcher added dialogue based on the account in the paper but also extracted additional details from Hewes not in either the *Gazette* or Hawkes.

105. Frank W. C. Hersey, "Tar and Feathers: The Adventures of Captain John Malcolm," Colonial Society of Massachusetts, *Transactions,* 34 (1941), 429–73, which also reprints the documents. The full letter, Hutchinson to Lord Dartmouth, Jan. 28, 1774, is in K. G. Davis, ed., *Documents of the American Revolution, 1770–1783,* VIII (Shannon, Ireland, 1972), pp. 25–27.

106. *Mass. Gaz. and Boston Wkly. News-Letter,* Jan. 27, 1774.

107. Thatcher, *Memoir of Hewes,* p. 132; Hawkes, *Retrospect,* pp. 33–35.

108. *Mass. Gaz. and Boston Wkly. News-Letter,* Jan. 27, 1774. For other comments from the crowd, see *Boston-Gazette, and Country Journal,* Jan. 31, 1774.

109. Hawkes, *Retrospect,* p. 44; Zobel, *Boston Massacre,* p. 102.

110. *Mass. Gaz. and Boston Wkly. News-Letter,* Jan. 27, 1774.

111. See Albert Matthews, "Joyce, Jun," Colonial Society of Massachusetts, *Publications,* 8 (1903), 89–104, and Young, "Pope's Day, Tar and Feathers," sec. VI.

112. For the newspaper accounts and prints see R. T. H. Halsey, *The Boston Port Bill as Pictured by a Contemporary London Cartoonist* (New York, 1904), pp. 82–94, 121n, 132–33; Mary Dorothy George, comp., *Catalogue of Political and Personal Satires . . . in the British Museum,* V (London, 1935), no. 5232, 168–69; and Donald Creswell, comp., *The American Revolution in Drawings and Prints; A Checklist of 1765–1790 Graphics in the Library of Congress* (Washington, D.C., 1975), nos. 668–70. For the impact on the king and his ministers see Peter Orlando Hutchinson, comp., *The Diary and Letters of His Excellency Thomas Hutchinson . . . ,* I (London, 1883), p. 164.

113. Thatcher, *Memoir of Hewes,* p. 132.

114. Ibid., p. 133.

115. Ibid., pp. 181, 263; *Oliver's Origin & Progress,* ed. Adair and Schutz, pp. 74–75.

116. Hutchinson to Lord Dartmouth, Jan. 28, 1774, in Davis, ed., *Documents of the Revolution,* pp. 25–27.

117. Hawkes, *Retrospect,* pp. 42–44.

118. Ibid., pp. 18–19.

119. Ibid., p. 87. Hewes made an allusion to having brought with him what could only have been *Copy of Letters Sent to Great Britain, by His Excellency Thomas Hutchinson, the Hon. Andrew Oliver, and Several Other Persons* . . . (Boston, 1773). See Bernard Bailyn, *The Ordeal of Thomas Hutchinson* (Cambridge, Mass., 1974), pp. 222–24. For Dorr, see Bailyn, "The Index and Commentaries of Harbottle Dorr," Massachusetts Historical Society, *Proceedings,* 85 (1973), 21–35, and Barbara Wilhelm, *The American Revolution as a Leadership Crisis: The View of a Hardware Store Owner,* West Georgia College Studies in the Social Sciences, 15 (Carrollton, Ga., 1976), pp. 43–54.

120. Robert Hewes attended the 1769 dinner commemorating the Stamp Act action of 1765 (see "An Alphabetical List of the Sons of Liberty who Dined at Liberty Tree, Dorchester, August 14, 1769," MS, Massachusetts Historical Society). "Parson Thatcher" called Robert "a great Liberty Man" in 1775 (see Thatcher, *Memoir of Hewes,* p. 217). Daniel Hewes was a guard at the tea ships, Nov. 30, 1773 (see Drake, *Tea Leaves,* p. xlvi). For Shubael Hewes, who testified for the defense at the Massacre trial, see Putnam, comp., *Joshua Hewes,* p. 331.

121. See Alfred Young, "The Rapid Rise and Decline of Ebenezer McIntosh" (MS, Shelby Cullum Davis Center, Princeton University, Jan. 1976).

122. "Jack Cobler," *Massachusetts Gazette* (Boston), Feb. 20, 1776; "Crispin," *Massachusetts Spy* (Boston), Jan. 16, 1772.

123. For derogatory references in New York, Baltimore, and Savannah, see Philip S. Foner, *Labor and the American Revolution* (Westport, Conn., 1976), pp. 120, 197, 151, and for Charleston, see Richard Walsh, *Charleston's Sons of Liberty: A Study of the Artisans, 1763–1789* (Columbia, S.C., 1959), p. 70.

124. Edmund S. Morgan, "The Puritan Ethic and the American Revolution," *William and Mary Quarterly,* 3d Ser., 24 (1967), 3–43, esp. sec. II; "Declaration of the Massachusetts Provincial Congress, Dec. 8, 1774," in Merrill Jensen, ed., *English Historical Documents: American Colonial Documents to 1776* (New York, 1955), pp. 823–25. Thatcher dwelled on the patriot promotion of American manufactures without, however, attributing such ideas to Hewes (*Memoir of Hewes,* pp. 58–60).

125. Hawkes, *Retrospect,* pp. 62, 64.

126. Charles W. Akers, "John Hancock: Notes for a Reassessment" (paper, University of Michigan–Flint Conference, Oct. 1976), which the author kindly allowed me to read.

127. Thatcher, *Memoir of Hewes,* pp. 192–93.

128. Ibid., pp. 261–62.

129. L. F. S. Upton, "Proceedings of Ye Body Respecting the Tea," *William and Mary Quarterly,* 3d Ser., 22 (1965), 298. The standard sources are dubious. See Edward L. Pierce, "Recollections as a Source of History," Massachusetts Historical Society, *Proceedings,* 2d Ser., 10 (1896), 473–90, and Labaree, *Boston Tea Party,* p. 144, and ch. 7.

130. Hawkes, *Retrospect*, pp. 59–62; Thatcher, *Memoir of Hewes*, pp. 198–220. For verification of the context, see Richard Frothingham, *History of the Siege of Boston* . . . (Boston, 1849), and Justin Winsor, ed., *The Memorial History of Boston, Including Suffolk County Massachusetts* . . . , III (Boston, 1881). ch. 2. The Hewes family was not listed among the 5,000 or more Boston families who received charity from the Friends, although over a score of shoemakers were (see Henry J. Cadbury, "Quaker Relief during the Siege of Boston," Colonial Society of Massachusetts, *Transactions*, 34 [1943], 39–179).

131. Hewes claimed five separate stints, two as a privateersman and three in the militia, in his Pension Application and Statement of Service, Military Service Records, MS, No. 14748, National Archives, hereafter cited as Pension Application. The two privateering expeditions can be verified from corroborative evidence (see below, nn. 144, 145). Of his three claims for militia service, two are verified in Massachusetts Secretary of the Commonwealth, *Massachusetts Soldiers and Sailors in the Revolutionary War* (Boston, 1896–1908), VII, 792–93, s.v. "Hewes, George," and "Hewes, George R. T.," hereafter cited as *Mass. Soldiers*. This compilation attests to one of the three months he claimed for 1777 (Sept. 25–Oct. 30) and more than the three months he claimed for 1781 (July 23–Nov. 8). Using unnamed "official records" that could only have been the as-yet-unpublished MS records in the Massachusetts Archives, Putnam found evidence for four separate enlistments, one more than Hewes claimed, two of which (1777 and 1781) are printed in *Mass. Soldiers*, VII, and two of which (Aug. 17–Sept. 9, 1778, and July 28–Oct. 21, 1780) are not (see Putnam, comp., *Joshua Hewes*, pp. 335–36). Putnam's 1778 finding verifies Hewes's pension claim for three months in 1778 for dates he did not specify (but which place him at the Battle of Newport Island at the right period). Hewes did not claim the 1780 stint Putnam found. There is corroboration for his pension claims in the Attleborough records (see below, n. 132). There is thus good evidence for his two privateering claims, direct verification for two of his militia claims, and evidence for two more he did not claim.

132. George Hewes's name is not on the militia musters for Attleborough reprinted in John Daggett, *Sketch of the History of Attleborough from its Settlement to the Present Time* (Boston, 1894 [orig. publ. Dedham, Mass., 1834]), pp. 134–45. In his petition of 1832 Hewes indicated several times that he returned to his family at Wrentham but enlisted at Attleborough. The explanation may be that "these lists comprise all the *town* enlistments, not individual enlistments of certain citizens elsewhere in which the town would have no monetary interest" (Daggett, *Sketch of Attleborough*, p. 143n). The Attleborough evidence, however, corroborates Hewes's claims: (1) The town's units were in the three campaigns Hewes claimed in 1777, 1778, and 1781. (2) Caleb Richardson, the officer Hewes listed twice as his captain, served in the Attleborough militia. He is listed as captain for six tours of duty, the dates of two of which (1778 and 1780) coincide with Hewes's claims (*Mass. Soldiers*, XIII, 230). (3) Luke Drury is listed as Lt. Col. Com-

mandant for the service at West Point that Hewes claimed under "Col. Drury" in 1781 (ibid., IV, 987).

133. In his Pension Application Hewes said he went on board the privateer *Diamond* "about two years after the battle of Bunker Hill," adding, "sometime in the month of April." This would have made it in 1777. But the two vessels whose names he remembered as prizes were taken in Oct. and Dec. 1776. If it was a three months' voyage, as Hewes remembered, this would have meant the *Diamond* sailed about Sept. 1776. See below, n. 144.

134. The clerk wrote that Hewes "enlisted as a volunteer on board of a privateer"; he "volunteered into a company of militia"; "he again volunteered into a company of militia"; but finally, "he enlisted . . . into a company of militia" (Pension Application). Hewes also told Hawkes that in "a hot press for men to go and recapture Penobscot" from the British, "I volunteered to go with a Mr. Saltonstall, who was to be the commander of the expedition, which for some cause, however, failed" (*Retrospect*, p. 72). This was the naval expedition of July–Aug. 1779, led by Capt. Dudley Saltonstall, which ended in disaster.

135. Robert A. Gross, *The Minutemen and Their World* (New York, 1976), p. 149.

136. John Shy, *A People Numerous and Armed: Reflections on the Military Struggle for American Independence* (New York, 1976), p. 171.

137. John Resch to author, May 29, 1980, based on research cited in n. 166 below.

138. Gross, *Minutemen*, p. 151.

139. For example, see the petition of Sylvanus Wood of Woburn, Mass., in Dann, ed., *Revolution Remembered*, p. 8.

140. Hawkes, *Retrospect*, pp. 62–63.

141. The phrase and analysis are from Lemisch, "Jack Tar Goes A'Privateering" (MS). I am indebted to Christopher McKee for sharing his unrivaled knowledge of naval sources.

142. Gardner Weld Allen, *Massachusetts Privateers of the Revolution* (Massachusetts Historical Society, *Collections*, 77 [Boston, 1927]), pp. 716–17; James Warren to Samuel Adams, Aug. 15, 1776, in Henry Steele Commager and Richard B. Morris, eds., *The Spirit of 'Seventy-Six: The Story of the American Revolution as Told by Participants*, II (New York, 1958), p. 965; Abigail Adams to John Adams, Sept. 29, 1776, in L. H. Butterfield et al., eds., *Adams Family Correspondence*, II (Cambridge, Mass., 1963), p. 135.

143. Nash, *Urban Crucible*, chs. 3, 7.

144. Hawkes, *Retrospect*, pp. 64–67; Thatcher, *Memoir of Hewes*, pp. 220–26. William P. Sheffield verifies Hewes's recollections of the vessel, commander (Thomas Stacey), owner (John Brown), and the names of the captured prizes: the *Live Oak*, listed as taken in Dec. 1776, and the *Mary and Joseph*, listed as taken Oct. 1776 (but by the *Montgomery* under Stacey) (*Privateersmen of Newport* [Newport, R.I., 1883], p. 64).

145. Hawkes, *Retrospect*, pp. 67–72; Thatcher, *Memoir of Hewes*, pp. 227–37. Hewes's recollections of the details of this voyage are verified in Louis F. Middlebrook, *History of Maritime Connecticut during the American Revolution*

(Salem, Mass., 1925), I, 44, 51–52, 65; II, 285–86, 303–4, 306–10, 313–16. Hewes is not on the crew list, I conclude, because Capt. Smedley, who did not give him his wages, eliminated his name (ibid., I, 70–73). For other vivid details of the encounters of the *Defence* verifying Hewes, see the diary of a sailor on the accompanying ship *Cromwell* in Samuel W. Boardman [ed.], *Log-Book of Timothy Boardman. Kept on Board the Privateer Oliver Cromwell . . .* (Albany, N.Y., 1885), entries Apr. 7–30, 1778. For additional verification, see the petition of Abel Woodworth, also on the *Cromwell*, in Dann, ed., *Revolution Remembered*, pp. 319–20. See also Gardner W. Allen, *A Naval History of the American Revolution*, I (New York, 1913), pp. 321–23.

146. Hawkes, *Retrospect*, pp. 71–72. Ira Dye has very kindly checked for Hewes in the computerized naval records of the Continental Congress, 1774–89, National Archives, but without success.

147. Hawkes, *Retrospect*, p. 68.

148. Ibid., pp. 65, 68.

149. Thatcher, *Memoir of Hewes*, pp. 216–20. Hewes did not tell this story to Hawkes, who reported Hewes as saying, "I went on shore at a safe place, and repaired straitway to my family at Wrentham" (*Retrospect*, p. 61). Thatcher elicited the story as he did several others about famous people. For the Washingtons at Cambridge, see Douglas Southall Freeman, *George Washington: A Biography*, III (New York, 1951), pp. 405, 477, 580–81. Hewes spoke of being in Boston nine weeks, which means his escape would have been late August or early September, about the time Washington was considering an attack on Boston. Martha Washington did not arrive until Dec. 11, 1775. Thatcher reported one other encounter with a famous man during the war, an episode at the Newport Island action, August 1778, in which Hewes claimed he rescued James Otis, who was "roaming about the lines in one of his unhappy spells of derangement" (*Memoir of Hewes*, p. 238). I have not been able to prove or disprove this incident.

150. Hawkes, *Retrospect*, pp. 73–74; Thatcher, *Memoir of Hewes*, pp. 237–40.

151. For shoemakers as officers, see Don Higginbotham, *The American War of Independence: Military Attitudes, Policies, and Practice, 1763–1789* (New York, 1971), p. 400, and Shy, *People Numerous and Armed*, pp. 163–79. For shoemaker officers mending shoes, see the Baroness von Riedesel's comments cited in Forbes, *Paul Revere*, p. 336.

152. Hawkes, *Retrospect*, pp. 74–75; Daggett, *Sketch of Attleborough*, p. 128; Jonathan Smith, "How Massachusetts Raised Her Troops in the Revolution," Massachusetts Historical Society, *Proceedings*, 55 (1921), 345–70.

153. Thatcher, *Memoir of Hewes*, pp. 242–43. How much Hewes made can only be guessed: in privateering, very little on his first voyage, nothing on his second. For militia duty in 1777 Attleborough paid £3 a month plus a £2 bounty; in 1778, £2 8s. a month and £5 a month bonus (Daggett, *Sketch of Attleborough*, pp. 124, 126). Thus if Hewes served nine months, he might have earned £27 in pay and perhaps the same as a bounty. As a resident of Wrentham, he might have been attracted to Attleborough by extra pay for nonresidents. Had he wanted to make money from land service he could

have enlisted in the Continental army; in 1778 Attleborough was offering £30 a month plus a bounty of £30 for army enlistment.

154. Hawkes, *Retrospect*, pp. 74–75; James G. Wilson, "The Last Survivor of the Boston Tea Party," *American Historical Register*, N.S., 1 (1897), 5, hereafter cited as Wilson, "Last Survivor." See Ira Dye, "Early American Merchant Seafarers," American Philosophical Society, *Proceedings*, 120 (1976), 331–60. After 1796 the federal government issued protection certificates to merchant seamen who requested them. Dye has generously checked for Hewes in abstracts of the surviving certificates, but without success. Providence, however, was not checked.

155. See a will of Joseph Hewes [1796] summarized in Putnam, comp., *Joshua Hewes*, pp. 327–38, and in Bristol County Northern District Registry of Deeds Record Book, two conveyances dated Mar. 18, 1797, in Book 76, p. 126, and Sept. 10, 1810, in Book 91, p. 453, copies of which were kindly provided by Alfred Florence, assistant register of deeds, Bristol County, Taunton, Mass.

156. Jordan D. Fiore, *Wrentham, 1673–1973: A History* (Wrentham, Mass., 1973), pp. 136–40.

157. Kulikoff, "Progress of Inequality," p. 402. "By 1790, 45 per cent of the taxpayers in town in 1780 had disappeared from tax lists." Of 2,225 individuals on the assessors' books in 1780, 1,000 were missing in 1790. The rate of persistence was only 42 percent for those paying no rent, and 52 percent for those paying from £1 to £20, but 66 percent for those paying from £100 to £199, and 74 percent for those paying over £200 (401–2).

158. Hawkes, *Retrospect*, p. 72.

159. U.S. Bureau of the Census, *Heads of Families at the First Census of the United States Taken in the Year 1790: Massachusetts* (Washington, D.C., 1908), Wrentham, p. 210, lists a George Hewes; Laraine Welch, comp., *Massachusetts 1800 Census* (Bountiful, Utah, 1973), Norfolk County, p. 174, lists George R. L. Hewes; Ronald Jackson et al., *Massachusetts 1810 Census Index* (Bountiful, Utah, 1976), does not list Hewes. Anne Lehane Howard, a title examiner, of Quincy, Mass., finds no record of Hewes buying or selling real estate in Suffolk or Norfolk counties in the Suffolk Co. Registry of Deeds, 1695–1899.

160. The Wrentham tax records, incomplete and in disarray, were examined at the Assessor's Office, Wrentham, with the cooperation of Lois McKennson, assessor, by Gregory Kaster and Patricia Reeve. Hewes is listed only as a poll rateable for 1791, 1792, 1794, 1796, and 1797; he does not appear in the other available tax lists for 1780, 1798, 1799, and 1817. Daniel Scott Smith helped interpret these data. Kaster did not find Hewes in "Massachusetts Direct Tax of 1798," MS, New England Historic Genealogical Society, Boston. This was a dwelling tax.

161. One list, for 1793, lists Solomon Hewes for £1 4s. under commonwealth real estate assessment and £5 4s. 5d. town tax. He is listed immediately above George R. T. Hewes. This possibly is Solomon his eldest son (1771–1834), who entered his majority in 1792 and would marry in Wrentham in 1794. However, Anne Lehane Howard finds no record of a Solo-

mon Hewes buying or selling property in the Suffolk Co. Registry of Deeds after the death of grandfather Solomon Hewes (1674?–1756).

162. See Bristol County Conveyance, n. 155 above.

163. Putnam, comp., *Joshua Hewes*, pp. 334–35, 353–57, lists nine children, leaving space between Robert and Eleven for three unnamed children, and between Eleven and Fifteen for three more. A relative sent in the names of two "missing" children as Asa and Walter (ibid., Addendum, pp. 601–2). Fifteen was identified as the fifteenth child in a newspaper account (*Providence Journal*, reprinted in *Columbian Centinel* [Boston], July 1, 1835). For the significance of child-naming practices, see Daniel Scott Smith, "Child-Naming Patterns and Family Structure Change: Hingham, Massachusetts, 1640–1880" (Newberry Papers in Family and Community History, No. 76-5, Jan. 1977), and Herbert G. Gutman, *The Black Family in Slavery and Freedom, 1750–1925* (New York, 1976), ch. 5.

164. *Vital Records of Wrentham, Massachusetts to the Year 1850*, II (Boston, 1910), p. 321, lists Sarah Hewes, born about 1769, marrying William Morason *(sic)*, Nov. 27, 1806. *Vital Records of Attleboro, Massachusetts . . . to 1849* (Salem, Mass., 1934), p. 456, lists Eliza *(sic)* Hewes, born 1773, marrying Preserved Whipple, "both of Attleboro," Mar. 19, 1795, and Mary Hewes "of Wrentham," born 1777, marrying Able Jillison of Attleborough, Jan. 21, 1809.

165. The clerk put down that Hewes "resided in Wrentham and Attlebury [*sic*] since the Revolution" (Pension Application, Oct. 16, 1832). The only evidence for Hewes's residence at Attleborough is Elizabeth's marriage record of 1795 (see above, n. 164). The conveyance of the "burying yard," Mar. 18, 1797 (see above, n. 155), lists Hewes as a "cordwainer *of Wrentham.*" I have not conducted a search of the tax records of Attleborough.

166. For the migration from Attleborough, see Daggett, *Sketch of Attleborough*, pp. 664–65. John Resch found in a sample of applications under the 1818 pension law that "a third of the total no longer lived in the regions where their units originated and another 20 per cent appeared to have moved to a different state within the same region" ("Poverty, the Elderly and Federal Welfare: The 1818 Revolutionary War Pension Act" [paper, Organization of American Historians, 1980], 9). For another veteran who went west, see Lemisch, "Life of Andrew Sherburne," sec. XII.

167. Putnam, comp., *Joshua Hewes*, pp. 353–57.

168. Ibid., p. 339; Wilson, "Last Survivor," p. 5. Wilson heard the story of the walk out in Otsego County. There S. Crippin, the clerk who endorsed Hewes's pension application at Richfield Springs in 1832, wrote on it: "He was a soldier in the Late War as well as in the Revolution." Hewes himself made no such claim to Hawkes or Thatcher. Hewes's name does not appear on any of the checking lists in the Adams Papers, Massachusetts Historical Society, for either John or John Quincy Adams, kindly checked for me by Malcolm Freiberg.

169. Fiore, *Wrentham*, p. 100. The War of 1812 pension applications of Eleven and George Fifteen are reported in Putnam, comp., *Joshua Hewes*, pp. 357–58.

170. Duane Hamilton Hurd, *History of Otsego County, New York* (Philadelphia, 1878), pp. 298–306 passim, W. T. Bailey, *Richfield Springs and Vicinity* . . . (New York, 1874), passim. I am indebted to Ethylyn Morse Hawkins, local historian, for sharing her knowledge with me, and the following friends of the Hewes family for answering inquiries: Vern Steele of Las Vegas, Nev., and Harry B. Carson of Golden, Colo.

171. Wilson, "Last Survivor," p. 5.

172. Hawkes, *Retrospect*, p. 94. "New York State Census for 1820: Otsego County," the handwritten takers' book, p. 163, lists George R. T. Hewes as living with his wife, and Robert Hewes below him with his family, and, p. 160, George R. T. F. Hewes, that is, Fifteen. The 1830 census lists only Robert Hewes but with one free white male "of ninety and under one hundred" living with him, confirming Hawkes.

173. For running Hewes down assiduously in the property records, vital records, and newspapers of Otsego County, I am especially indebted to Marion Brophy, special collections librarian, New York State Historical Association, Cooperstown, as well as to Wendell Tripp, chief of Library Services, and Wayne Wright, Edith R. Empey, and Susan Filupeit of the library staff. Marion Brophy found no record of Hewes's owning property but found Fifteen owning land in Richfield Springs, corroborating Hawkes.

174. Hawkes, *Retrospect*, pp. 77–78, 94; will of Daniel Hewes, recorded July 16, 1821, Suffolk Co. Probate Court, and Aug. 5, 1822, Record Book 120, p. 129, for the final sum, $2,904.79, located by Ruth Kennedy.

175. Tombstone, Lakeview Cemetery, Richfield Springs. For Sarah's signature as a mark, see the 1797 conveyances above, n. 155. For the Tea Party, see Thatcher, *Memoir of Hewes*, p. 186, and for Hewes on her age, see Hawkes, *Retrospect*, p. 27.

176. Hawkes, *Retrospect*, pp. 94–97. See also Putnam, comp., *Joshua Hewes*, pp. 353–57. I am grateful to Catherine Wilson of Des Moines, Ia., a descendant via Solomon, for copies of letters by Virgil Hammond Hewes, George's grandson.

177. Hawkes, *Retrospect*, pp. 94–96, 114. See also Putnam, comp., *Joshua Hewes*, for a story from "a near relative" that Hewes walked 10 miles to visit ex-President John Quincy Adams to ask for help on his pension, possibly a variant of the story about Hewes's walk to ex-President John Adams to get into the navy. For the laws, see Resch, "Poverty, the Elderly and Federal Welfare," pp. 1–7. Resch clarified a number of points for me. See also Robert George Bodenger, "Soldiers' Bonuses: A History of Veterans' Benefits in the United States, 1776–1967" (Ph.D. dissertation, Pennsylvania State University, 1971), pp. 26–42, and Lemisch, "Life of Andrew Sherburne," secs. XII, XIII, for one veteran's long, bitter battle for his pension.

178. Hawkes, *Retrospect*, p. 114; Pension Application. The clerk disallowed the three months on the *Diamond*, probably because it was a privateer, but allowed the seven months and fifteen days on the *Defence*, also a privateer but officially a ship of war in the Connecticut navy, under a naval officer.

179. Wilson, "Last Survivor," pp. 5–6.

180. *Freeman's Journal* (Cooperstown, N.Y.), July 13, 1829; Hawkes, *Retrospect*, p. 90.

181. Cooper's occasional residence in Cooperstown, 1816–40, may be established from James F. Beard, *Letters and Journals of James Fenimore Cooper* (Cambridge, Mass., 1960–64), I–IV, passim. Beard kindly answered my inquiry about Cooper's sources. See Cooper, *The Spy: A Tale of the Neutral Ground* (New York, 1821), and *Ned Meyers; or, a Life Before the Mast* (Philadelphia, 1843); and Thomas Philbrick, *James Fenimore Cooper and the Development of American Sea Fiction* (Cambridge, Mass., 1961), chs. 2, 4.

182. Hawkes, *Retrospect*, pp. 77–80.

183. Wilson repeated a tale that Hewes had attended the laying of the cornerstone of the Bunker Hill Monument in Boston in 1825 ("Last Survior," p. 6). Hewes said nothing of this to Hawkes or Thatcher, and Hawkes said he "had made but one visit," that of 1821 (*Retrospect*, p. 76). Wilson's tale mixed images of the 1821 and 1835 trips. *Freeman's Journal*, May 30, June 27, July 11, 1825, and *Cherry Valley Gazette* (N.Y.), June 28, Aug. 9, 1825, say nothing of Hewes in reports of the observance. Benson J. Lossing garbled the story further by claiming that Hewes was at the ceremony for the *completion* of the monument, June 17, 1843, three years after his death (*Pictorial Field-Book of the Revolution; or, Illustrations by Pen and Pencil . . .* , I [New York, 1851], pp. 501–2).

184. Wilson, "Last Survivor," p. 6. Marion Brophy reports that "there are no Methodist church records for the 1830s or 1840s in Richfield unless they are hidden in an attic somewhere. The local officials instituted a search and found nothing" (letter to the author, July 17, 1978).

185. Wilson, "Last Survivor," p. 6; Hawkes, *Retrospect*, pp. 93–94. He was not a total abstainer; Hawkes indicated that he used "stimulating liquors" when needed.

186. The clerk wrote on Hewes's petition for a pension that there was "no clergyman residing in his neighborhood whose testimony he can obtain pursuant to the instructions from the War department"(see above, n. 178).

187. See Paul Gustaf Faler, "Workingmen, Mechanics and Social Change: Lynn, Massachusetts, 1800–1860" (Ph.D. dissertation, University of Wisconsin, 1971), ch. 2; Barbara M. Tucker, "Our Good Methodists: The Church, the Factory, and the Working Class in Ante-Bellum Webster, Massachusetts," *Maryland Historian*, 8 (1977), 26–37; and Charles G. Steffen, "The Mechanic Community in Transition: The Skilled Workers of Baltimore, 1788–1812" (MS), ch. 6.

188. Bailey, *Richfield Springs*, p. 148. For the character of early western Methodism, see Frank Baker, *From Wesley to Asbury: Studies in Early American Methodism* (Durham, N.C., 1976), ch. 11, esp. pp. 195–97, and George Peck, *Early Methodism within the Bounds of the Old Genesee Conference from 1788 to 1828 . . .* (New York, 1860), passim.

189. Auguste Levasseur, *Lafayette in America in 1824 and 1825*, II (Philadelphia, 1829), pp. 202–6; Kammen, *Season of Youth*, pp. 21, 26, 120; Oliver Wendell Holmes, *Complete Poems* (Boston, 1836).

190. Joseph Buckingham, *Annals of the Massachusetts Charitable Mechanics Association* (Boston, 1853), p. 202, reporting a toast at a dinner for Lafayette in 1825; shoemaker toast, 1826, in Kammen, *Season of Youth*, pp. 44–45; Seth Luther, *An Address to the Working-Men of New-England . . . Delivered in Boston . . .* (Boston, 1832), p. 27. For documents of Boston labor organizations, 1825–35, see John R. Commons et al., eds., *A Documentary History of American Industrial Society*, 6 (Cleveland, 1910), pp. 98, 73–100.

191. *Columbian Centinel*, July 1, 9, 1835; *Evening Mercantile Journal*, July 1, 8, 1835; *American Traveller* (Boston), July 28, 1835. I am indebted to Helen Callahan for making a search of the Boston newspapers for July 1835.

192. *Evening Mercantile Journal*, July 8, 1835; *American Traveller*, July 7, 1835.

193. *Boston Courier*, July 22, 1835; *Providence Journal*, reprinted in *Columbian Centinel*, July 1, 1835.

194. Putnam, comp., *Joshua Hewes*, pp. 362–63, 439, reported this as an oil by Charles Palmer of Richfield Springs, done Jan. 1836 on a board 2'1" × 2'6", in the possession of David Hewes, Robert Hewes's son. Wilson reprints this, "redrawn from a photograph by Mr. Sidney Waldman" ("Last Survivor," p. 3). I have been unable to locate painting, photograph, or drawing. Hawkes's *Retrospect* has a drawing in the frontispiece, which could have been made from life, and Thatcher's *Memoir of Hewes* has still another drawing, most likely copied from the Cole portrait. Sometime after Hewes's death there was a second printing of Hawkes's *Retrospect* with a new frontispiece drawing of Hewes and sixteen illustrations of events of the Revolution, copied from other engravings.

195. Lossing, *Pictorial Field-Book*, pp. 499n, 501–2; with numerous inaccuracies repeated in *Appletons' Cyclopedia of American Biography*, ed. James Grant Wilson and John Fiske, III (New York, 1887), p. 190; William Cullen Bryant and Sidney Howard Gay, *A Popular History of the United States*, III (New York, 1883), p. 374; Henry C. Watson, *The Yankee Tea Party* (Philadelphia, 1851); F. Drake, *Tea Leaves*, p. cxv; Samuel Adams Drake, *Old Landmarks and Historic Personages of Boston* (Boston, 1873); pp. 269–70, 282–83; Bailey, *Richfield Springs*, pp. 98–99. Esther Forbes is the only modern historian to have used the memoirs extensively.

196. Putnam, comp., *Joshua Hewes*, pp. 353–58, 601–2. I am indebted to the registrar general of the Daughters of the American Revolution for providing me with copies of five applications by Hewes's descendents.

197. The end of the century had "an obsession with transplanting Revolutionary heroes to more suitable graves" (Kammen, *Season of Youth*, p. 65).

198. David Kinneson, who died in Chicago in 1848, seemingly was the last survivor (see Lossing, *Pictorial Field-Book*, pp. 501–2).

199. *American Traveller*, July 28, 1835, wrote of the portrait that "it is an admirable likeness—everything about it—the coloring, expression &c. even to the cane, are true to life." The Bostonian Society acquired the portrait in 1885, according to an article by D. T. V. Hustoon, its secretary (*Boston Weekly Transcript*, Jan. 26, 1886). For Cole (1803–58) see William Dunlap, *History of the Rise and Progress of the Arts of Design in the United States*, III

(New York, 1834), p. 136, who said that the Hewes portrait was "among the best of his portraits." The dating of the portrait is confirmed by Mary Leen, librarian, Bostonian Society (letter to the author, Aug. 16, 1977).

200. Hawkes, *Retrospect*, p. 91, citing a toast of July 4, 1833.

CHAPTER 2

"The World's Dread Laugh": Singlehood and Service in Nineteenth-Century Boston

CAROL LASSER

I

Mary Morton was born in Duxbury, Massachusetts, in 1810. She was the fifth child and oldest girl of the eleven children born to sail-maker Josiah Morton and his wife Abby. During her youth in her hometown, the young woman witnessed the marriages of most of her eight surviving siblings, while she herself remained unwed. When her father died in June 1842, she moved to Boston. There, as a thirty-two-year-old single woman alone in the city, she turned to domestic service to support herself. Thirteen years later, she moved west, living in Ohio for five years, probably in the home of a married sister. On the eve of the Civil War, she returned to Boston, where for a decade she worked again as a domestic. Finally, at the age of sixty, increasingly troubled by a severe varicose vein, she sought an escape from her labors. She took the $100 she had on deposit in a savings bank account and applied for admission to the Boston Home for Aged Women.[1]

Morton never captured the attention of famous contemporaries, and she and other women like her have been ignored by historians as well. According to standard historical accounts, she should not have existed at all. Native-born women were not supposed to spend a lifetime in domestic service in Victorian America; if they entered service at all, they were to do so as youths and to leave upon maturation into marriage and matronhood. Moreover, by 1870, Yankee women had supposedly been completely displaced by the influx of Irish domestics. Thus Morton seems to have been a quaint, anachronistic relic: an elderly, native-born, Protestant single woman who performed housework for pay from people to whom she was not related.[2]

Yet whatever the assumptions of society and historians, demography suggests that Morton's case was not unique. Throughout the early nineteenth century, the proportion of native-born New England women who never married rose, hovering around 20 percent in the earlier decades and rising to over one-quarter of all women who survived beyond the age of twenty in the later part of the century.[3] While many such single women made lives for themselves within their families of birth, others pursued more independent courses, sometimes from choice and other times from necessity. For wealthy women, the role of maiden aunt provided a comfortable perch from which to pursue a variety of interests; and a few talented single souls like Lucy Larcom and Louisa May Alcott became the "scribbling women" about whom so much has been written. But for working-class women, independence was far more problematic; it meant confronting the difficulties of self-support in a society that was indifferent, if not hostile, to the needs of wage-earning women. How then did the growing number of single women like Morton survive?[4]

The records of the Boston Home for Aged Women shed welcome light on this question. Opened in 1850, the home provided a refuge for native-born Protestant women whom the world seemed to have forgotten or overlooked. Indeed, Morton and her kind had a special benefactor, an elusive woman named Mary Q. Townsend about whom little is known save that she herself was single, had substantial means, and left a precise bequest to the home when she died in 1861. She specified in her will that $60,000 was to be used to endow a fund to be "applied to the support of those females who, in the legal phraseology are called spinsters or single women. . . . The virtuous poor of this description who, from choice or necessity remain on the single list, will always be large." Poignantly, Townsend explained her sympathy for the plight of the older woman who had never married: "As I belong to the sisterhood, I am duty bound to procure for them a shelter from the 'world's dread laugh,' and a quiet home." Thus, not surprisingly, a disproportionate number of single women found their way to the home.[5]

Descriptions of the life strategies of these single women (and those of their married sisters as well) were preserved by the Admissions Committee, which collected information on the 377 women who were accepted for residence in the home in the first three and one-half decades of its existence. As the committee members listened to respectable old women detail their arduous lives, they recorded on long blue printed sheets information about the place and date of birth, parentage, residences, marital partners and children (if any), and occupations of the applicants (past and present). These case records, later bound into imposing volumes, chronicle the vital events in the lives of the 158 single women who made up over 40 percent of all residents of the home. The records underscore the importance of work to single women, for over 96 percent of the single women who were admitted to the home had been employed at some point in their lives. The range of jobs they had pursued included sewing, nursing, boardinghouse keeping, teaching, and even shopkeeping. The most important occupation, however, was domestic service. Never-married domestic servants like Morton were the largest group of residents in the home (see Table 1).

Table 1. Occupations by Marital Status Reported by Inmates of the Boston Home for Aged Women, 1850–85

| | Number | |
Occupation	Single	Married
Domestic service	78	61
Needle trades	63	66
Nursing	34	59
Boardinghouse keeping	1	15
Teachers and proprietors	13	16

Source: Compiled from the Admissions Records, Volume I, Boston Home for Aged Women.
aBecause women frequently reported more than one occupation, individual occupations add up to more than total number of workers.
Note: Of the workers surveyed, 150 were single, 177 married. Of the total number of inmates at the home during these years, 158 were single, 219 were married.

What was it about domestic service that gave it a special relationship to singlehood in nineteenth-century New England? Traditionally, domestic service, like singlehood, had been viewed as a stage in the life cycle of young women from all ranks of society, much as apprenticeship was seen to serve as a bridge between childhood and maturity for young men. To a certain extent, a "golden age" of service had existed in the colonial era, when a prominent person like Roger Williams had sent his daughter to the home of a social equal to learn the mysteries of the craft of housewifery. In the seventeenth century, intimacy and reciprocity tied together "help" and mistress in bonds of affection and mutuality.[6]

But by the beginning of the nineteenth century, service was no longer the same classless rite of passage. Wealthy and middle-class girls now disdained working in others' homes. Instead, they spent their adolescence in school, in prolonged visits to their relatives, or in their own homes where their mothers taught them to *supervise* the household labor of others.[7] Two groups of adolescents, however, continued to go into service: poor girls and farmers' daughters. They were attracted both by the promise of money and the hope of enhancing marital prospects at the same time. Yet their expectations reflected a fundamental shift in the service relation. From a general life-cycle stage common to young women of all social strata, it had become a class-specific mode of earning wages, paralleling larger changes in the structure and regional balance of the New England economy.[8]

In the light of this shift came other changes; during the early nineteenth century native-born women in service found themselves increasingly isolated. Irish immigration to New England rose rapidly in the 1840s, and by 1850 Irish women comprised the vast majority of domestic servants in Boston. Morton and some other native-born women, however, had not completely disappeared. Instead of being displaced from service either by marriage or by immigrant workers, they had learned to adapt the service relation to their requirements as independent single adults.[9]

In the remainder of this article I explore the content and meaning of the lives of the ever-single former domestic servants who retired into the Boston Home for Aged Women. The ability of this significant minority of the nineteenth-century population to survive, much less to mature or succeed, runs counter to most of the current orthodoxy in history, which ignores their existence or assumes that single women could not exist outside the confines of a family economy.[10] Although the lives of single women did not have the same guideposts as those of married women, all women progressed through a series of distinct life stages. It is useful to think of three crucial periods in their lives: first, an early period characterized by the rootedness of an individual in her family, town, and social network of birth; second, a middle period in which she achieved adulthood through marriage and/or geographic, occupational, and social mobility; and finally, a later period in which the social and/or economic productivity of the individual declined.[11]

I discuss first how these women made the transition from youth to maturity and then from adult to elder. I then compare the lives of single women to those of their married sisters. Finally, I assess the relative situations of married and single women who spent their last days in the Boston Home for Aged Women.

II

According to tradition, the first important transition—from youth to maturity—occurred when a young woman left the home of her employer to enter upon comfortable, if not luxurious housekeeping as a matron and mother in a home of her own. But for over half of the domestics who were to take refuge in the Boston Home for Aged Women, maturity arrived without marriage. For many, their mature careers represented a prolongation of their adolescent situations.

Take, for example, Sally Hyler, who began but did not complete a traditional path. Born in Boston in 1796, she came to the attention of the Boston Female Asylum in July 1803. Her mother had died the previous year, and her father, a caulker, was "so dangerously sick from a fall that his physician thought his recovery quite impossible." His relatives felt unable to bear the financial burden of raising his daughter, so, "sensible of his dying state, he solicited a place in the Asylum for his destitute child." From ages seven through ten, the child remained in residence, after which she was indentured to service. In the ideal plan, Hyler next should have become a wife and mother, using the household skills acquired during her indenture in her own home. But Sally Hyler never married. She remained single and employed, accumulating nothing but "a little furniture" over the ninty-six years of her life.[12]

Similarly, Susan Allen spent her youth in the home of Eleazar Jones, a lawyer in Barre, Massachusetts, where her mother worked as a domestic to escape from life with her intemperate husband. Presumably, young Susan assisted her mother and, in effect, apprenticed under her tutelage. Then, while still young, Allen went out to service herself; she continued in this work, never marrying, until, at the age of seventy, she sought to retire. Thus, for Allen, as for Hyler and seventy-six other former domestics in the Boston home, service undertaken as a youthful domestic apprentice offered training for survival but did not guarantee married respectability.[13]

Marriage, the customary mode by which women moved from the social identity of youth to that of adulthood, was often combined with another significant event: geographic movement. For ever-single women, relocation alone became a key guidepost marking their maturity. Most of the domestics in the home—82 percent of both those who had married and those who remained single for life— came to the city from the country. In part, the propensity of domestics to be country-bred was a result of the ways in which rural areas lagged behind the city. On farms and in small towns, the traditional beliefs in the efficacy of service as a life-cycle stage survived far longer than in Boston itself, where commercialization hastened the transition of the occupation to simple wage labor.[14]

It is noteworthy that single women were more likely to migrate later in life than those domestics who were to marry. Over 75 percent of the never-married domestics on whom the data are complete migrated when they were twenty-six or older; significantly, the same twenty-six years marked the average age of marriage among the former domestics in the home who had taken spouses.[15] It is possible that later migration circumscribed opportunities for marriage, but the evidence suggests another interpretation as well. For many single women, migration, even when not accompanied by marriage, offered a route to social maturity. Sara Hibra, for example, began her life in Swansea, New Hampshire, and at the age of twenty-eight came to Boston, where she spent the rest of her life in service. Mary Ellsworth moved from Strong, Maine, to become a domestic in Boston at the age of thirty-six. She, too, stayed single and in service for the remainder of her productive years. Yet both young women had at least physically distanced themselves from their childhood homes. Similarly, if Harriet Bayley perhaps felt suspended in time, reporting that after sixty-eight years of her life, she was "*still* a domestic," she nonetheless could look to her movement from Portsmouth, New Hampshire, to Boston to mark her transition to adulthood.[16]

For an important group of single women, the passage to adulthood combined geographic relocation with occupational change. When Ruth Pierce, a New Hampshire farmer's daughter, moved to Boston at the age of thirty-eight, she left behind both her childhood home and her former occupation as a general domestic to become a children's nurse. A number of women used the move to enhance their status within the hierarchy of service, especially by becoming cooks. Others, however, made even more dramatic transitions. Ruth Stratton left Holden, Massachusetts, for Boston at age thirty-two and ceased doing housework to become a skilled seamstress. Similarly, Pamela Brown from Tewksbury learned tailoring in the city, becoming a skilled female artisan. Esther Day Kuhn used her experience in service to help her manage a boardinghouse in her later years.[17]

With its greater options for women's employment, Boston undoubtedly served as a magnet for those who sought to mark adulthood with new residences and new types of employment. This important group of women did not use the skills they had learned as domestic apprentices to secure their vocations as wives and mothers. Rather, one-third of those who never married used the occupation of their youth to launch themselves into upwardly mobile female careers. Their transition to adulthood was hardly traditional, but it was, in its own way, quite successful.

The records of the home are curiously silent on the transition to adulthood made by a few of its residents. Perhaps these women had reason to suppress discussion of their passages from youth to maturity. There was, for example, the case of Maine-born Dorcas Hodges, who had reported her lifetime occupations as those of cook and shopkeeper. In 1861, shortly after she became the first single woman considered under the bequest of Mary Q. Townsend, the Board of Managers received a report "as to a peculiar circumstance in the early life of Miss Hodges which rendered doubtful the propriety of continuing her on the Townsend Fund." The board investigated the report but determined that the incident that made her "Christian character" suspect had happened "more than fifty years since, when she was a girl of 15 or 16 years of age." Forgetting neither the sin nor the life of respectability Hodges had led since, the committee compromised, striking Hodges's name from the list of Townsend beneficiaries but allowing her to remain in the home.[18]

Most single residents left no such colorful records. And none stated explicitly whether they "remained on the single list . . . from choice or necessity" as Townsend had put it. For some, the motives were probably too mixed to differentiate. None of the five former domestics whose fathers were highest in social and economic status—daughters of the two merchants and three civil servants—married. These women might have felt ambiguities and cross-pressures in choosing a mate, for they were both servants—a working-class occupation—*and* daughters of the middle class. Rather than "marry down," they may have preferred the status they enjoyed vicariously as servants in well-to-do households.

Others may have rejected marriage not on the basis of the occupational or personal qualifications of a spouse, but from a more basic disillusionment with the complexity of the institution itself. Esther Day Kuhn saw her mother marry twice, and her father three times, while watching her sister dispense with the formality of marriage until after the birth of her third child. Nancy Hawkins was born only three months after her parents married. Shortly thereafter, her mother died, and her father quickly remarried her mother's sister. Such family histories challenge common notions of the orderly Victorian household. These women probably regarded marriage as a nexus of the confusions of the world, not a haven from them.[19]

What emerges from this overview is a sense of the variety of transitions to adulthood made by women who did not marry. Their transitions between youth and adulthood were amply, if unconventionally, marked by migration and occupational mobility, sometimes singly and at other times combined. In this context domestic service served a variety of purposes. Some single women used it simply to survive, while others looked to it for the emotional security encompassed in its older notions of the reciprocity and mutuality. Most striking, however, is the significant minority of single women who built upon early experiences in service to find their way to better paying forms of women's work. Notwithstanding the obstacles of social convention, they found their way to personal and economic independence.

III

For single women, the transition in life from adult to elder was often more difficult than the transition to adulthood. With both the passage of time and the individual aging process, the appropriateness of employment in domestic service was questioned. Not only had the prestige of domestic work fallen since the days of their youth in the early nineteenth century, but also the work itself was physically demanding on bodies once younger and stronger. Yet service still offered a form of security for older single women. Thus, those who spent long years laboring in the same households expected a special status in their longtime adopted homes. The spinster who had not married but ministered to the needs of her mistress's family had traditionally been granted deference and support in the household in her later years. Visions of care and mutuality might induce some aging women to remain domestics, but more likely women who had not escaped into other work earlier were increasingly excluded from well-paying, alternative employment. They simply lacked more advantageous options.

The women who had left service, either in making the transition to adulthood or as mature single women, faced a slightly more happy prospect as they grew older. They found that the skills they had accumulated over several decades could often compensate for declining strength, at least for a time. Trained seamstresses and dressmakers were able to pursue careers without the interruptions of childbearing and household responsibilities. Their marketable talents provided them with a comfortable existence. Accustomed to adapting to the exigencies of the market to support themselves, they could view old age as simply another challenge.

Many of those who had remained within the hierarchy of domestic service reached its more lofty positions as housekeepers or hotel matrons. Some remained in its lower rungs, but were at least able to save their wages, providing for themselves a modicum of security in their old age even if their employers no longer took seriously responsibilities toward elderly domestics. For those with more dignified places in the domestic hierarchy, the higher wages they had received had given them even greater opportunities to prepare for retirement. The accumulation of skill and savings, then, aided single women as they made this transition. Their actions reflected economic rationality. They entered old age as they had always been, alone; but they had acquired both a knowledge of the means by which a woman cares for herself and some material proof that they had learned their lessons well.

That a substantial proportion of single women had learned to cope effectively with their circumstances is perhaps best illustrated by the relative financial positions of married and single former domestics when they applied for admission to the home. Never-married women were far more likely to possess property than their widowed sisters. While two-thirds of the widows with a background in service were propertyless, nearly half of the unmarried former domestics possessed resources worth over $25. Although the amount was usually modest, it represented a margin of safety and an achievement of at least some measure of autonomy. Moreover, this differential in property existed *despite* the provisions of the Townsend Fund, which encouraged the home to recruit truly destitute single women.[20] This finding suggests that, contrary to common assumptions, mid–nineteenth-century women could survive, if not really thrive, outside the family economy. Some of the domestics studied here obviously learned the rules of a changing game over the course of their lives. Beginning their employment in service, they were able to capitalize on this training, turning to careers unbroken by marriage or childrearing responsibilities. Their accumulation of material possessions was part of a strategy to avoid both destitution and the social ridicule of "the world's dread laugh." Though "old maids," they arrived at the home with dignity, not in a spirit of capitulation.[21]

IV

An examination of the lives of the never-married women who retired to the Home for Aged Women clarifies some of the important differences in the stages and transitions for single and married women. Undoubtedly the widows who arrived in the home cannot be viewed as typical of working-class women in the nineteenth century. Married or widowed women with living children who could support them would most probably have chosen to reside with their kin; thus, the women whose stories are related here were undoubtedly a more destitute and dispirited group than random selection would have produced. Nonetheless, the contrast between their lives and the lives of single women still proves instructive, illustrating some of the pitfalls to which formerly married nineteenth-century working-class women might succumb.

For many, life began within the traditional pattern. They had undertaken domestic work in their girlhood and then left their employers' homes as young women to embark upon marriage and motherhood in families of their own. Eliza Wilder, for example, at the age of six moved from Portsmouth, New Hampshire, to Boston, where she spent her youth fulfilling domestic duties in the homes of two comfortable families. These years were a prelude to her marriage to a carpenter, and she completed her transition to traditional domesticity by bearing two children. Similarly, Maine-born Mary Ann Hosford moved to Boston, where she had a long career in service and then married a carpenter from her home state.[22]

Marriage, however, was not always prompted by the purest of motives. For example, Olive Pease, a Shrewsbury farmer's daughter, presented her farmer husband with his first son barely four months after their marriage. This union lasted only seven years, when Pease died, leaving a young widow with three children to support. Olive Pease found work as a housekeeper in the nearby Worcester Insane Asylum and later moved to Boston, where she became an agent of the New England Moral Reform Society.[23]

Pease's case suggests that early widowhood could force a woman back onto the labor market and often into service or closely related work. In a similar case, Lydia Reiney married an Irish mariner when she was sixteen. Her husband sailed to Manila one month after the marriage, and died. Without property or children, Reiney spent the rest of her life in service. And unlucky Isabella Hines married a shoemaker who proved to be a drunkard. She reported that they had "lived together but six months" when she left him for a lifetime career in service. She later received word that he had died in the Boston Almshouse. Charlotte Johnson moved from Maine to Boston at the age of twenty-three, then worked an additional fifteen years before marrying a Danish-born pilot. Apparently her husband's occupation required that he continue traveling the waterways. So two years after the marriage, she returned to service. When he died four years later, she was already settled into the family whom she would serve for another thirty-six years. Marriage had been a brief interlude. With ease she returned to singlehood and service. As with other women widowed or separated shortly after marriage, service provided the basis for continuity in the transition from youth to maturity; it was not simply a life-cycle stage.[24]

Women widowed late in life faced a particularly difficult set of problems. Probably now too weak to undertake the physically taxing work of service, they also lacked the training or skill of female artisans; they had no longtime employer, nor had they accumulated marketable skills during their years as wives and mothers. Nonetheless, they needed to compensate for the lost income of a spouse. Most commonly, they turned to simple sewing; it required little skill but also provided little income. Some widowed former domestics combined sewing with charity from a church, a one-time employer, or even the Overseers of the Poor to survive. Thus Ann Lane, who had been a domestic until her marriage but had retired from work after she made her own home, turned to "slop work" (i.e., unskilled sewing of ready-to-wear garments) to support herself late in life. Abby W. Clark, who had been by turns a domestic, wife of a "botanic physician," and a housekeeper, took up sewing to avoid the rigors of housework and the perils of poverty.[25]

Some widowed women, however, developed a special set of skills for which there was a market in nineteenth-century America. It seems that witnessing the death of a husband was the credential that proved that an older woman possessed the requisite skill to enter the field of nursing, an occupation that then required no formal training or licensing. Thus after Elizabeth DaCosta had seen her husband die, she became a nurse. Lydia Chamberlain began her work life as a domestic, married an intemperate stonemason who subsequently died, and then turned to nursing. Nursing was closely related to widowhood; in the Home for Aged Women, only one-third of the former nurses had never been married.[26]

To call the skills of nursing valuable in the nineteenth-century city would be to overstate the monetary worth and social prestige; but, like sewing, nursing could generate some income in years that were increasingly less productive and so help older women stave off total dependency somewhat longer. Yet life was still precarious for the widows who tried to survive on income from unskilled sewing or nursing.

Formerly married women who turned to their offspring for supplementary support were often disappointed. The children themselves might well be on the edge of destitution and could ill-afford to support yet one more person in their household. Isabella Mitchell, for example, reported that all five of her daughters would have liked to help, but were indigent themselves. Ruth Thompson's only son was described as "poor." Sarah Hodges's daughter had recently lost the struggle to support herself as a boardinghouse keeper, and her son was a whitewasher and church sexton; both were described as "generally poor" and could offer little assistance to their aging mother.[27]

Moreover, a typical sixty-year-old woman might well have outlived her children. In fact, barely more than one-third of the women who had been married reported children still alive when they entered the home; among all of the 219 formerly married inmates, only thirty sons and twenty-five daughters could have provided alternatives to institutionalization. Offspring were no insurance against old age, as Jane Blunt knew, having buried both of her daughters. Hannah Dodge "lost a promising son," apparently her only child; and Lydia Lord's only daughter died the year before she entered the home. Thus, even for those who had been married, the coming of old age often meant the coming of aloneness, as a result either of demography or poverty. The transition from adult to elder in many ways brought to the married woman the challenges of self-support and solitude faced much earlier by her single sisters.[28]

V

The inhabitants of the home—whether single or widowed, domestic, seamstress, nurse, shopkeeper, or teacher—probably did not anticipate a joyful old age in this institution. Although Margaret Mead has noted that in some cultures the old woman is a respected and powerful figure accorded special rights and privileges, these women in "decayed circumstances" were hardly deemed oracles or empress-dowagers. Ever-single and formerly married alike, they were, in fact, more in the position that David Hackett Fischer has described: "treated with a contempt which was deepened all the more by their womanhood."[29]

For both the widowed and the single, entry into the home meant recognizing their progressive loss of mental and/or physical faculties; it signaled the end of the wage-earning or self-supporting years. Many arrived at the home with symptoms of crippling rheumatism or diseases that required hospitalization or confinement. One old domestic with a failing memory proved too great a burden for the home, and she was sent to a mental hospital.[30]

The transition from adult to elder may have been less wrenching for single women than for widows. Not only did the never-married bring more property with them to the home, but they presumably felt less trauma at their aloneness, for they had coped with solitude throughout their lifetime. Impressionistic evidence suggests, for example, that widowed women, shocked by their loss of family, were more likely to take refuge in "gross intoxication." The twice-widowed Mary Grant was dismissed after only three days because of her fondness for alcohol. Perhaps it was not merely the loss of two husbands, but also her years as a cook that had contributed to her alcoholism. Two old widows seem to have caused the home's greatest disruption when they found sisterhood in drinking. Mrs. Webber and Mrs. Cobbell worked together to assure that visitors brought them quantities of liquor, constituting, in effect, an organized smuggling ring. An investigation identified these guilty inmates, and they were reprimanded; drink was not acceptable solace, even for old and lonely working-class women. The records of the home do not report such incidents of alcoholism among single women, perhaps suggesting by their silence the greater immunity of those who had always been alone to the bitterness of solitude in old age.[31]

Their married sisters found themselves, in old age, reexposed to the world that had changed so strikingly over their lifetimes. Increasingly stripped of family and other resources, they, too, now felt the shrillness of exposure to "the world's dread laugh." For single women, always buffetted about, the cruelty of the world was less surprising; they had come to expect it much earlier in life, and they had learned to adapt to it.

It is difficult to call the life histories of women in the home representative of the general experience of nineteenth-century working women, and great care must be taken in generalizing on the basis of the data presented here. Nonetheless, the patterns of these women's lives reveal the variety of adaptations they undertook as one New England city made the transition from mercantile to mature capitalist society. Clearly, we still need to know more about the lives of working-class women in general and the important minority of single women in particular. As we proceed with this task of historical recovery, we must not assume that all single women were losers in the difficult transitional process. Some learned the rules of a changing game effectively, finding within themselves a haven from "the world's dread laugh."

NOTES

Gary Kornblith has been an integral part of this project since it began in March 1979; I wish to acknowledge his invaluable assistance. I also thank Thomas Dublin and Margo Horn for their helpful comments.

1. Mary Morton is case 221 in Admissions Committee Records, vol. 1, box 11, Home for Aged Women Records, Schlesinger Library, Cambridge, Mass., 78-M126. The collection is cited hereafter as HAW; all case records are from vol. 1, box 11. Other information on Mary Morton was obtained from the U.S. Census Manuscript schedules for 1850 and *Vital Records of the Town of Duxbury, Massachusetts to 1850* (Boston, 1911).

2. Catharine Beecher is quite explicit about the value of service as apprenticeship. See her *Letters to Persons Engaged in Domestic Service* (New York, 1842). Lydia Maria Child expresses similar thoughts in *History of the Condition of Women* (Boston, 1839), pp. 266–67. Authors of fiction made similar points; see, for example, Catharine Sedgwick, *Home* (Boston, 1839), and her *Live and Let Live; or, Domestic Service Illustrated* (New York, 1837), Lucy Salmon's *Domestic Service* (New York, 1897) is the classic work; she describes life-cycle service and blames the Irish for the decline in quality of service. For the entrance of the Irish into service, see also Oscar Handlin, *Boston's Immigrants: A Study in Acculturation*, rev. ed. (New York, 1971). More recently, Faye E. Dudden has written a fine history of the transformation of domestic service in the nineteenth century: *Serving Women: Household Service in Nineteenth-Century America* (Middletown, Conn., 1983). My own work has looked closely at domestic service in Boston; see Carol Lasser, "Mistress, Maid and Market: The Transformation of Domestic Service in New England, 1790–1870" (Ph.D. dissertation, Harvard University, 1981). I am currently at work on a larger manuscript on this subject.

3. Peter R. Uhlenberg, "A Study of Cohort Life Cycles: Cohorts of Native-Born Massachusetts Women, 1830–1920," *Population Studies*, 23 (Nov. 1969), 411.

4. Catharine Sedgwick was, in many ways, an archetypal maiden aunt. For her relationship to her brothers' children, see Mary E. Dewey, ed., *Life and Letters of Catharine M. Sedgwick* (New York, 1871); and also Mary Kelley, "A Woman Alone: Catharine Maria Sedgwick's Spinsterhood in Nineteenth-Century America," *New England Quarterly*, 51 (June 1978), 209–25. Lee Chambers-Schiller, "The Single Woman Reformer: Conflicts between Family and Vocation, 1830–1860," *Frontiers*, 3 (1978), 41–48, explores both the freedom and the constraints on women who never married. Lucy Larcom presents her own story in *A New England Girlhood* (Boston, 1889). Ann Douglas reveals the large number of female authors who never married in *The Feminization of American Culture* (New York, 1977), Appendix B, pp. 402–9. Virginia Penny, *The Employments of Women: A Cyclopedia of Woman's Work* (Boston, 1863), pp. v–vi, displays a sympathy for the difficulties single working women faced.

5. The Boston Home for Aged Women was explicitly modeled on predecessors established in Philadelphia in 1817 and in New York in 1838. See Board of Managers Records, "Memorial to the City Government," Association for the Relief of Aged and Indigent Women, Box 8, HAW; this association undertook the founding of the home and remained its governing agency. Their records will be cited hereafter as HAW Board.

For an excellent study of the Philadelphia home, see Carole Haber, "The Old Folks at Home: The Development of Institutionalized Care for the Aged in Nineteenth-Century Philadelphia," *Pennsylvania Magazine of History and Biography*, 101 (1977), 240–57.

Relevant portions of Townsend's will are reproduced in the Bequest Book, Mar. 27, 1861. Box 10, HAW. Massachusetts Vital Records at the McCormick Building, Boston State House Annex, include an entry in vol.

149, no. 4, recording the death of Mary P. Townsend at age sixty-five on Jan. 7, 1861. Although the middle initial differs from that given in the HAW records, no other Mary Townsend of single marital status appears in the death records for either 1860 or 1861.

In all, 158 women or 42 percent of the residents of the home never married. See Table 1 for the occupational distribution of the single women.

6. For a full exposition of service as a life-cycle stage, see Peter Laslett, *Family Life and Illicit Love in Earlier Generations* (Cambridge, 1977), pp. 30–34, 41–45. Other work on life-cycle stages include Uhlenberg, "Cohort Life Cycles," and Joseph Kett, *Rites of Passage: Adolescence in America, 1790 to the Present* (New York, 1977), although Kett focuses almost exclusively on the male experience. I also drew upon John Modell, Frank J. Furstenberg, Jr., and Theodore Hershberg, "Social Change and Transitions to Adulthood in Historical Perspective," in Michael Gordon, ed., *The American Family in Social-Historical Perspective*, 2d ed. (New York, 1978), pp. 166–91.

Reference to Roger Williams is made by Albert Matthews, *The Terms Hired Man and Help* (Cambridge, 1900); see also the placement of Samuel Sewall's sister in service, in his *Diary* in *Collections of the Massachusetts Historical Society* (Boston, 1878–82), I, 34. I describe other examples in "Mistress, Maid and Market," ch. 1, passim.

7. On the rise of middle-class alternatives, see Nancy F. Cott, *The Bonds of Womanhood: "Woman's Sphere" in New England, 1780–1835* (New Haven, 1977), particularly ch. 3.

8. See Salmon, *Domestic Service*, ch. 4; for the training of poor girls in domestic service see Carol Lasser, "A 'Pleasingly Oppressive' Burden: The Transformation of Domestic Service and Female Charity in Salem, 1800–1840," *Essex Institute Historical Collections*, 116 (Apr. 1980), 156–75.

9. Handlin, *Boston's Immigrants*, p. 251; and Lasser, "Mistress, Maid and Market," ch. 7. David Katzman's *Seven Days a Week: Women and Domestic Service in Industrializing America* (New York, 1978) is a nice summary of the changes in the place of service in a somewhat later time period.

10. Louise A. Tilly and Joan W. Scott, *Women, Work, and Family* (New York, 1978), argue that European women worked almost entirely within the context of a family economy, but the applicability of their conclusions for the American setting has been disputed by Thomas Dublin in *Women at Work* (New York, 1979), ch. 3. Most historians simply assume that women will marry and overlook single women. See, for example, Robert A. Gross, *The Minutemen and Their World* (New York, 1976), and Daniel Scott Smith, "Parental Power and Marriage Patterns: An Analysis of the Historical Trends of Hingham, Massachusetts," *Journal of Marriage and the Family*, 35 (Aug. 1973).

11. I have found Modell, Furstenberg, and Hershberg, "Transitions to Adulthood," very helpful in conceptualizing the early stages of life.

12. Admissions Records, case 77, HAW. I thank Susan Porter, who shared her information on the girl's background in the Boston Female Asylum with me. She is currently working on a dissertation on the Boston Female Asylum at Boston University.

13. Admissions Records, case 148, HAW.

14. Figures compiled from the Admissions Records, HAW. See also Dudden, *Serving Women*, chs. 1, 2.

15. Age at migration was compiled from the Admissions Records, HAW; individual cases were traced to local vital records for marriage dates.

16. Admissions Records, cases 70, 94, and 215, HAW.

17. Admissions Records, cases 361, 129, 59, and 60, HAW.

18. Admissions Records, case 116, HAW. Board discussion of her case appears in HAW Board, Oct. 16, and Nov. 17, 1861.

19. Another of Kuhn's sisters also resided in the home. See Admissions Records, cases 60, 267, and 68, HAW.

20. Figures compiled from the Admissions Records, HAW. While it is undoubtedly true that the formerly married women who took refuge in the home were probably more destitute (both financially and in terms of living kin) than typical working-class widows, that the differential in property exists, even with the Townsend bequest, remains significant. It suggests that single women *could* accumulate property on their own, even if they were believed to be among the most needy of old women. Thus, the property differential is significant as an absolute indicator of the achievements of single women.

21. In one of the few discussions of old women that address the question of their differences by marital status, Peter Stearns argues that "the tendency of the industrial economy to withdraw women from productive labor left them cruelly exposed insofar as they outlived their earning spouses." He therefore suggests that widows were probably in a better financial position in pre-industrial France than their unmarried counterparts, but that widows encountered greater difficulties as industrialization proceeded. See Peter Stearns, "Old Women: Some Historical Observations," *Journal of Family History*, 5 (Spring 1980), 44–57, esp. 48–50. The women in the home were living through the transition from the pre-industrial to the industrial.

22. Admissions Records, cases 174 and 228, HAW.

23. Admissions Records, case 123, HAW.

24. Admissions Records, cases 210, 21, and 238, HAW.

25. For an excellent discussion of exploitation in the needle trades in New York City, see Christine Stansell, "The Origins of the Sweatshop: Women and Early Industrialization in New York City," in Michael H. Frisch and Daniel J. Walkowitz, eds., *Working-Class America: Essays on Labor, Community and American Society* (Urbana, Ill., 1983), pp. 78–103. I briefly discuss the needle trades in Boston in "Mistress, Maid and Market," ch. 3. See also Admissions Records, cases 57 and 163, HAW.

26. On nursing in this period, see Susan Reverby, "The Nursing Disorder: A Critical History of the Hospital-Nursing Relationship, 1861–1945" (Ph.D. dissertation, Boston University, 1982); she directly draws upon material from the Admissions Records of the home. See also Admissions Records, cases 39 and 48, HAW.

27. Admissions Records, cases 304, 45, and 157, HAW.

28. Admissions Records, cases 198, 101, and 126, HAW. On mortality,

see Maris Vinovskis, "Mortality Rates and Trends in Massachusetts before 1860," *Journal of Economic History*, 32 (1972), 184–213. Clearly, widows without living children were more likely to end up in the home than those whose children were still alive, thus biasing the figures on the number of children. Yet the facts of mortality and poverty are still quite striking.

29. Margaret Mead, *Blackberry Winter* (New York, 1975), p. 107; David Hackett Fischer, *Growing Old in America*, expanded ed. (New York, 1978), pp. 62–63. Fischer's discussion of old age is, however, primarily based on the male experience, as is W. Andrew Achenbaum's in his *Old Age in the New Land: The American Experience since 1790* (Baltimore, 1978).

30. Admissions Records, case 12, HAW; the home may have feared that she would commit suicide, as had case 159.

31. Admissions Records, case 40, HAW; HAW Board, Dec. 18, 1856, and Nov. 21, 1858.

PART TWO

WORK

Changing Patterns of Factory Life and Labor

Winslow Homer's ". . . *for those who throw the clanking shuttle to and fro*" from William Cullen Bryant's *The Song of the Sower* (1871).

CHAPTER 3

The Social System
of Early New England Textile Mills:
A Case Study, 1812–40

JONATHAN PRUDE

"A cotton factory is a school for the improvement of ingenuity
and industry. . . ."
—Samuel Ogden, 1815

"[Our employee] James Fenton ran away yesterday and Samuel
Greene has gone to day. . . . If it is suffered to pass another will
go tomorrow and so on until they are all gone. . . ."
—Samuel Slater to Almy and Brown, Mar. 20, 1797

I

In 1812, in the rural Massachusetts township of Dudley, fifty miles
southwest of Boston, five local entrepreneurs built a woolen mill,
several tenements, and a store. Initially titled Merino Village, this
manufacturing compound suffered reversals and in time even
passed on to other proprietors. But in one form or another it remained a presence in Dudley's history throughout the next two generations.[1] In 1813, Samuel Slater—the celebrated English immigrant
to Rhode Island who in 1793 had helped construct America's first
successful water-powered spinning mill—arrived in Oxford, abut-
ting Dudley to the east, and opened a cotton factory. Along with its
workshops, store, cottages, and boardinghouse, this establishment
was styled the East Village. By 1828, Slater had added the South
Village woolen mill and the North Village thread factory, both in
Dudley—his three enclaves lying north of the Merino Village in a
triangle roughly four miles around and all of them, like the Merino
Village, surviving downturns and setbacks to endure through the
succeeding decades.[2]

We remain curiously ignorant about such "manufactories." As

vanguard institutions of the American factory system, New England's antebellum textile mills have, of course, received abundant scholarly attention. But most writers have lavished their energies on the large, self-consciously famous "boardinghouse" establishments: the factories of Lowell, Waltham, and other urban or rapidly urbanizing manufacturing centers; the factories which, beginning with Waltham's prototype Boston Manufacturing Company in 1814, undertook a fully integrated production process encompassing machine-weaving as well as machine-spinning; and (perhaps their best-known feature) the mills which sought to recruit into their workrooms and carefully supervised boardinghouses single young women from the "virtuous rural homes" of middling yeomen.[3] The social and economic importance of these mills—even their reputation among contemporary European literati—cannot be disputed. But focusing so exclusively on their story has distorted our perception of early textile factories and thus, given the pioneering role of these factories, skewed our understanding of basic patterns in early American industrialization.

This is because scattered through the antebellum Northeast were also mills like the Slater and Merino factories. Usually small and moderately capitalized, these factories were not rooted in cities but "studded thickly along . . . wild and rapid streams" of rural communities—and so carried the phenomenon of textile industrialization far into the Yankee hinterland.[4] These were also factories which, for many years, commonly "put out" various tasks to farming households outside the mill villages: the task of picking clean the raw fibers used by early mills, for example, and the task of weaving mechanically spun yarn into cloth.[5] And finally, these were factories which followed the "Rhode Island" or "family" plan—inaugurated by Slater himself in the 1790s—of recruiting workers from across the social and economic spectrum and of hiring households as well as unattached individuals.[6]

The distinction between family and boardinghouse factories was, to be sure, neither permanent nor rigid. After 1840 pressures within the industry and the influx of immigrant operatives combined to meld the two types; and even in the 1820s and 1830s some mills combined traits of both genres. By all indications, however, rural family enterprises like the Slater and Merino villages comprised the typical format of textile manufactories throughout the early nineteenth century, and hence were the typical setting for America's earliest factory employees.[7] The scholarly inclination to overlook these country mills is thus an anomaly that needs to be corrected.

This is the most general and obvious rationale for the study that follows. But an equally pressing reason to explore the Slater and Merino villages concerns the relations between labor and management that developed within these compounds. To most scholars, the key indices of employer-employee interaction in early Yankee mills have been strikes or some other overt gestures of protest. Thus they have either stressed the relative absence of such incidents and concluded that "labor militancy was rare" because operatives "worked hard and for the most part without complaint"; or they have used the few upheavals that did transpire to argue that millworkers were militant in the orthodox labor historian's sense of the word: capable of mounting large, explicit confrontations.[8] The Slater and Merino villages suggest another perspective. On the one hand, only one insignificant turnout occurred in these factories before 1840; and exploring the history of these mills throws light on why large-scale confrontations were uncommon among antebellum operatives generally and family mill operatives particularly. On the other hand, Slater and Merino workers were not passive. Quite the contrary: there developed between employees and employers in these four compounds intricate patterns of give and take, of managerial demands evoking operatives' efforts to win greater earnings and (what was equally important) greater independence, of struggles and compromises. Reflecting relationships among workers as well as between workers, and their supervisors, expressing goals and strategies that never changed and others that evolved, these patterns defined the fundamental social system of the Slater and Merino villages.

And they do more besides. While the Slater and Merino villages were not the first American textile manufactories, employers and employees working in these enclaves still ranked among the earliest New World participants in factory labor. As a result, their complex choreography of friction and accommodation should actually be viewed as an early installment in a critically important educational process: a kind of learning which is unavoidable in industrializing societies; which initial generations of every American occupation affected by industrialization had to undergo; and which—in different ways and degrees—in fact often provided the prelude and backdrop to whatever overt militancy some American industrial workers achieved. Put briefly, what early textile employers and employees taught themselves was how to respond to one another. They deciphered—or, more accurately, they created—the rules of the game for being industrial employers and employees. And by doing so they implemented a pivotal lesson in the social meaning of industrial capitalism.

II

The size and structure of society in the Slater and Merino villages can be set out fairly easily. Available data suggest that between the early 1820s and the early 1830s the Merino labor force grew from around 60 to 108, of whom 40 percent were men, 50 percent were "women and girls," and 33 percent were attached to families. The aggregate roster of the three Slater compounds increased from 54 operatives in 1813 to around 260 in 1840, and in the East Village— requiring fewer skilled adult employees than a woolen factory—men accounted for 25 percent of the employees, women and children hovered around one-fifth and one-half, respectively, and two-thirds were attached to families living inside the compound. To these statistics we should add the ten to fifteen managerial officials—all adult, all male—resident in each village. And we should also add the various mill-village inhabitants—of both sexes, all ages, and totaling perhaps 20 percent of each compound's labor force—who coresided with working parents, siblings, or children but did not themselves hold berths.[9]

But how did this social structure function? What were its dynamics and lines of force? We may begin unraveling these issues by exploring management and the regimen it sought to impose. And the point of departure here is the highly personal character of the Slater and Merino administrative structure. For a striking fact disclosed by the records is that several Merino owners served supervisory stints at their mills, and that even in the early 1830s—after Boston investors had purchased stock—the entire proprietary retinue met regularly at the Dudley factory.[10] It is striking too that Samuel Slater, despite business interests scattered throughout New England, frequently visited his southern Massachusetts mills. Along with his sons, who began shouldering administrative duties around 1825 and who took control of the villages after their father's death in 1835, Slater intervened frequently: establishing wage guidelines, evaluating work turned out, setting requirements for "steady," punctual, "industrious and temperate" workers, providing favorite employees with cash gifts, scolding others for "unfaithfulness"—all enough to communicate a continuing personal involvement with the "hands."[11]

Below the proprietors were the agents, charged with overall daily supervision of the villages, and the room overseers, responsible for the "business" of each factory room. Hired mainly from mercantile positions or administrative posts in other mills, and working for the most part in secluded offices, the former officials were not intimate with the rank and file under their authority. But agents were suffi-

ciently involved in the ongoing operation of these mills to develop
ties with some operatives and to be at least known to all of them.
Overseers were even more familiar to the labor force. Typically recruited from experienced male operatives (one-third of Slater's East
Village overseers were drawn from the payroll of this compound)
these front-line supervisors were every day brought into direct, continuous contact with the hands under their charge.[12]

Coupled with this administrative inclination to personal contact—
providing an important animus for this tendency and legitimizing its
capacity to embrace both strictness and generosity—was management's claim of "interest" in employees. Antebellum mill masters (or
commentators writing on their behalf) commonly declared that efforts by managers to prevent tardiness and drinking, for example,
were merely "prudent and effectual" attacks "against disorderly and
immoral behavior"; and along with more obvious expressions of al-
truism—such as Slater's cash presents—these efforts disclosed the
industrialists' "kindly and paternal" concern in the workers' "welfare."[13]

Given the frequency with which such interest was proclaimed, it is
scarcely surprising that scholars have often described antebellum
factory management as paternalistic. In the hands of recent writers
the characterization can be used pejoratively (in the sense of overly
intrusive) as well as approvingly; and it is conventional scholarly wis-
dom that, whether judged positively or negatively, paternalism
faded after immigrants began entering the mills in the 1840s and
1850s. The rubric itself, however, remains firmly embedded in the
scholarship of early Yankee manufactories.[14]

This, in turn, has created difficulties. The administrative order
ramifying through mills like the Slater and Merino factories was
complex, and if it reflected personal involvement and interest it also
reflected an array of contrary themes. We can continue to call these
factories paternalistic: the term usefully underscores important dimensions of their regimen. But we need to establish precisely what
paternalism meant in these compounds. And this requires examining elements and trends generally ignored by both antebellum commentators and modern historians.

We should note, first, that management's rhetoric of paternalism,
while not necessarily hypocritical, was manifestly self-serving. By following the long line of Protestant moralizing that fused righteous-
ness with diligence, mill masters could simultaneously assert concern
for their workers' well-being and strive to inculcate values encouraging productivity. Even more important, factory managers used paternalistic slogans to counter the suspicions with which late eigh-

teenth- and early nineteenth-century New Englanders greeted manufactories. Yankees were not insensitive to the tax revenues and jobs textile mills represented. But from the outset there was worry that American factories would create a permanent, degraded proletariat (as they supposedly had in England), or would disrupt customary riparian privileges, or would find some way to avoid paying local taxes. And over time concern also grew that industrialists accustomed to "ruling . . . their mills" might "step out into the community with the same air. . . . What is this but tyranny?"[15]

Invoking paternalism could not forestall all these anxieties. But in an era when milldams blocking local streams were often met with lawsuits and occasionally with physical attacks, when tight labor markets (an issue even more fundamental and far more often confronted) left many manufacturers struggling to find hands—at such a time it made sense to assure New Englanders that factories gave operatives the same "moral protection of their character" as "virtuous rural homes." And some county mill masters (including Slater) pushed further. They offered what amounted to a counterimage of rustic New England in which factories offset the "ignorance, weakness, and barbarism" they saw as imminent in rural life. In part, it was said, mills effected this cure by providing markets for foodstuffs and thus galvanizing an otherwise "sluggish" farming population. But it was also argued that paternalistic managers provided relief from the "neglect" many children suffered in rural homes, and that "interested" employers helped poor and unskilled workers by providing both jobs and a "strict though mild and paternal scrutiny" to instill good habits.[16]

By every indication, the Slater and Merino mills rang the changes on paternalism in all these ways—and in one other way as well. In company with other country factories, the North, South, East, and Merino villages found particular utility in using assertions of paternalistic interest to justify intrusions into the operatives' family life. There can be little question that domestic relationships were vitally important in the Slater and Merino compounds. Often it was kinship that drew operatives into the mills: "My sister is coming ther to work this week," announced a prospective Merino employee, "and I will come in two weeks."[17] Once within the enclaves, moreover, workers attached to families usually coresided (sometimes with boarders) in small cottages provided by the factories. But more than a physical locus, the family provided a close-knit haven, a continuing refuge, from the pressures of factory discipline.[18] While mill supervisors apparently relied on parents to keep order over their children after working hours, there is no evidence families systematically coopera-

ted with management's efforts to produce industrious young employees. And while, over time, domestic ties were doubtless strained
by mill-village life, it is clear families persisted as significant institutions for many Slater and Merino operatives. But what the family
did not do—what it was not permitted to do—was work together.
Siblings sometimes labored in close proximity, but Slater and Merino
managers appear to have systematically separated parents and children during the working day.

Probably the mills feared that adults placed near their offspring
would challenge the overseers, or, if overseers themselves, would
cause friction by favoring their own youngsters. Their concern, coupled with the emerging pattern of awarding skilled "male" jobs to
unmarried men or to teenagers promoted from below, increasingly
forced fathers to remain idle, leave the villages for jobs elsewhere, find work on neighboring farms, or content themselves with
outdoor duties for the mills. Coupled with the antebellum prejudice
against wage-earning mothers, management's suspicion of parental
authority inside the mills led to complete exclusion of married women
from the Slater and Merino labor force in the years prior
to 1840.[19]

These were the developments establishments like the Slater and
Merino villages sought to justify with paternalism. Managers, it was
said, could undermine daytime parental authority because they were
themselves acting *in loco parentis*. Apprenticeship offered an obvious
precedent for this role, but, save for a few paupers and some train-
ees in management and cassimere weaving, Slater and Merino officials avoided "unfree" laborers.[20] Instead they took schoolmasters as
their model, arguing that mill families "delegated" temporary authority to their employers just as Yankee households surrendered
authority to teachers.[21] Again, the rationale by no means precluded
resentment, but it may well have dampened its intensity.

Such was the self-interest behind management's rhetoric. But we
must also consider structural limitations of paternalism in the Slater
and Merino villages—and the consequent distinction between the
form managerial interest took in these compounds and the pattern
existing in "Waltham" mills. Unlike the latter enterprises—with their
carefully monitored tenements, curfews, and mandatory church
attendance[22]—the four Slater and Merino compounds made little effort to control their employees' lives after quitting time. Because
these establishments were relatively isolated, most workers depended
upon company housing for residences and on company stores for
provisions. But it was rarely required that workers use only factory
retailers; boardinghouses (for unattached laborers) evidently posted

few rules; and because of their reliance on the after-hours authority of parents, family cottages were supervised not at all.

Reliance on family government may also explain the mills' relaxed attitude toward religious and secular instruction. Though often pious themselves, and though doubtless pleased to find operatives occasionally participating in local revivals and churches (most often those run by Methodists and Baptists), Slater and Merino managers built no chapels within the villages and left "devine services" entirely optional. And so with secular instruction: efforts were made to establish schools in or near the villages during the 1820s, but since attendance was not mandatory and since most operative households preferred wage earners to scholars, mill children generally escaped formal education.[23]

From another perspective, it was the market that limited paternalism. Whatever their claims to serve the workers' welfare, decisions to expand or trim the Slater and Merino rosters, for example, were dictated almost entirely by sales. Generally between 1810 and 1840, conditions permitted expansion. But the Slaters laid off employees during commercial downturns, and the Merino Village closed completely during the 1816 depression.[24] Moreover, as factories grew more numerous and competitive during the 1820s and 1830s, Slater and Merino managers began jettisoning less profitable elements of their payrolls even during good times. Most dramatically, they dismissed their part-time out-working employees during the 1820s, replacing them with more efficient full-time pickers (mainly children) laboring inside the factory villages, and full-time power loom operatives (mainly young women) posted in the mills. Indeed, by 1830 even the skilled woolen handloom weavers resident inside the South and Merino compounds had been largely supplanted by operatives "tending" water-driven weaving machines. And in the winter of 1828, feeling increasingly pressed by rival mills, Slater pointed out to his supervisors that "as days are now short and cold and much time is taken up by . . . [outdoor workers] . . . in thrashing their hands," agents should "discontinue [i.e., dismiss] all you can."[25]

Impersonal economic factors shaped the income as well as the number of Slater and Merino employees. Proprietors might occasionally distribute cash presents, but the formal bargains management offered were always confined by guidelines—increasingly rigid as time went on—designed to protect profit margins.[26] In themselves these formulas did not preclude comparatively high wages—a fact the mills naturally emphasized in their recruiting campaigns. While skilled men earned two to four times more than women and children, and while the presence of youngsters kept overall Slater and

Merino wages about 10 percent below comparable "boardinghouse" statistics, the average price of labor in these villages—fifty-one cents per day in 1832—encompassed rates surpassing most nonindustrial pay scales.[27] But this is misleading. Absenteeism and another economic factor—living expenses—quietly undermined operatives' earnings. Skilled machinists and mule spinners, especially those unattached to households, could earn $200-$300 above room and board. But members of families whose male heads were unemployed or held only outdoor jobs were sometimes rudely shocked to find that after a year's labor they were actually "owing the mill."[28]

The lack of involvement in nonworking hours and the force of economic pressures were two factors that significantly diluted management's personal interest. Technology was another. By 1830, perhaps 70 percent of the workers on the Slater and Merino payrolls tended machines driven "perpetually" or partially by water. For these employees (mainly women and children), the personal authority of the overseer was mediated through the unprecedented stricture of mechanically imposed work rhythms. It is likely children managed to play between their chores, and all "tenders" enjoyed some respite—daily for lunch, occasionally for repairs. We should also recall that operating machines was initially considered "not half so hard" as many agricultural chores.[29] But the demands of the pounding looms and spindles pressed with cumulative weight upon millworkers and, like a number of other pressures, became more intense with passing years. Again we may cite the shift from hand-looms to power looms. Beyond this, beginning around 1817, managers sought to improve their competitive position by increasing both the number and speed of machines assigned to operatives.[30]

Finally, there was the bureaucratic dimension of the mills: the established procedures and bylaws which, however freighted with moralism, inevitably introduced a flavor of formality and even distrust into employer-employee relations. Although "[R]ules and regulations" ran like stiff girders all through the industrial order, they were especially obvious in management's treatment of time. It was not, after all, the length of the factory schedule that was new; during harvests rural Yankees labored the same twelve-hour days, six-day weeks early textile mills required. Similarly, management's stress on punctuality expressed values long since put forward by Benjamin Franklin and countless Puritan divines. What was new in the mills was the rigidity with which the schedule and norms were promulgated. In factories, seventy-two-hour weeks were a constant requirement, even during winter months when the mills ran past dusk and had to rely on candlelight. Moreover, because they generally paid

employees by the hour, managers reckoned each worker's attendance with unprecedented care. Transcribed in coded shorthand
into an array of interlocking ledgers and Time Books, daily punctuality of Merino employees was measured to the nearest three
hours—twice as accurately as the attendance of most nonindustrial
employees. The Slater books were equally precise before 1817;
thereafter, as a further emblem of mounting stringency, the standard became the nearest ninety minutes.[31]

Such, then, was paternalism in the Slater and Merino villages: on
the one hand, interested and intimate; on the other hand, impersonal, self-serving, and bounded—in some respects increasingly
bounded—by technology, bureaucracy, and the vicissitudes of the
market. This complex, evolving alloy of attitudes and disciplines
comprised the stance management came to hold within these manufactories. This is what pressed upon the workers and, by pressing,
evoked reactions that shaped the social system of the North, South,
East, and Merino villages.

III

But to understand precisely how operatives learned to respond to
the industrial regimen we must first consider how they responded to
one another. The strength and scope of relationships among workers, the degree to which they felt isolated or bound into group loyalties—all this critically affected how they coped with factory life.
Often, as we have seen, employees were linked by kinship. But ca-
maradarie in the mills, if it existed at all, rested on ties stretching
beyond the household. It is the nature of extradomestic bonds that
requires attention here.

Such bonds obviously existed. In the glimpses of daily life provided by the Slater and Merino records we find millworkers standing
in for absent colleagues; and we find friendship leading on to something more—65 percent of East Village operatives who married during their stints took another village resident as mate.[32] But the critical question is whether these liaisons gave workers a continuing
sense of unity, and here glimpses are inadequate. The problem requires systematic investigation of factors which, though perhaps only
occasionally apparent to workers, constantly conditioned extrafamilial relations.

One such factor was the extraordinary heterogeneity of the labor
force: a pervasive lack of common denominators that weakened
links among nonrelatives. Some of this diversity has already been
signaled by the range of skills and income levels among the workers.

The lines between family and nonfamily operatives, and between operatives from different families, are also relevant here: even as they provided afterhours relief from managerial supervision, kinship ties tended to deflect energy from more inclusive alliances among workers. But beyond these were further divisions, less immediately obvious but in some ways deeper, sharper, and even more corrosive.

It is significant, for example, that workers lacked common geographic origins and so typically entered the villages as strangers. Most Slater and Merino employees in this period were native-born Americans, sharing both a common language and general traditions of republicanism and Protestantism. But drawn by advertisements and word of mouth ("I have heard you was in want of some one . . ."), operatives came from all over southern New England, sometimes from New York, and even from Delaware. Few were local. Less than 33 percent of Slater and Merino operatives can be definitely shown to have arrived from communities immediately surrounding these factories.[33]

To their varied geographic provenance, employees added a mixed sociological background. There was no "average" millworker in the Slater and Merino villages. Some operatives (exact numbers are not possible) entered the factories because they supposed—despite the tainted reputation of manufactories and the low net earnings befalling some employees—that millwork would provide an interesting and profitable interlude. Comprised principally of individuals rather than families, this relatively prosperous contingent included young adults waiting upon inheritances, property owners and craftsmen seeking funds to enlarge their estates, and women like those the boardinghouse mills claimed to employ before immigrants arrived: "respectable" women who became operatives to sample the independence of their own wage-earning jobs, to provide financial help to their families, to increase their dowries and find husbands, or perhaps simply to escape the endless round of chores on country homesteads.[34]

Unlike boardinghouse proprietors, however, family mill masters like the Slaters and the Merino owners acknowledged from the outset that they also employed "destitute . . . and very poor" workers who embraced factory berths out of economic necessity.[35] This, of course, dovetailed neatly with the orchestration of paternalistic rhetoric explored earlier: many mills guaranteed to preserve their workers' character; family factories also claimed to assist and reform New England's more needy citizens. So it was the Slater and Merino villages hired landless laborers, both rural and urban, often with their families and some with extra children "[made] up from the neighbors." And they engaged yeomen whose "small and poor farms" no longer provided support, artisans and small shopkeepers over- whelmed by debt, and teenagers from poor or middling households, expecting little or no patrimony and obliged to start out on their own.[36]

A third group was composed of veterans; employees who arrived already seasoned in millwork and who, by all indications, moved on to other factories after leaving the Slater and Merino compounds. In the earliest New England mills such operatives had been skilled Irish and English workers. At least by 1815, however, veterans also included native-born workers. These were skilled and unskilled Americans, single men and women (the latter especially after power looms were introduced), widows depending on wages earned by their children, whole families ("I can spine or weave and one boy that can spine one gerl that can wave on a pour loom . . .")—who were all convinced millwork offered the highest wages they could expect but who also, sometimes, were trapped on a treadmill of low net earnings and unable to move easily to other employment. Their extended commitment to factory work did not necessarily make these workers the permanent factory proletariat Americans feared; by all accounts, experienced employees moved not only between mills but also in and out of millwork, and few ended their working lives as factory hands.[37] Yet veterans deserve notice as people com- mitting many years to the mills.

Middling, poor, and veteran—combined with the other differen- tiations etched into the work force, such divisions, while doubtless overlapping, must have affected relations among the operatives. Ar- riving from widely scattered communities, their experience within the compounds varying according to job, income, and the presence of kin, Slater and Merino operatives could only have found the lack of common backgrounds and expectations a further hindrance to fellowship.

These were the consequences of the workers' heterogeneity. But there were also other barriers to camaraderie. Contact among oper- atives inside the mill buildings, for example, was constrained by the ceaseless attention required in tending machines, by the patrolling overseers, and by the deafening racket—"like frogs and Jewsharps all mixed together"—thrown up by the technology.[38] Then too, the characteristic transiency of Slater and Merino workers (both novices and veterans) further reduced opportunities to develop ties. Opera- tives did not commonly limit their engagements to a single season, but periodic managerial efforts to balance reduced sales with re- duced payrolls and—as we shall later have reason to stress—the workers' own restlessness combined to keep stints quite brief. Employment periods increased somewhat over time, but in 1830 only 10 percent of the East Village payroll remained at that enclave three or more years, most (51 percent) remained nine months or less, and about 6 percent (10 percent in the Merino Village) stayed less than half of any given month.[39]

A further critically divisive feature of life in these villages was the absence of settings where operatives could gather communally after factory hours. While the isolation of the Slater and Merino mills encouraged workers to use company housing, the fact that operatives were dispersed through both tenements and family cottages meant residences in these compounds never became the social centers into which Waltham-style boardinghouses—for all their tight supervision—commonly evolved.[40] Moreover, because the four villages were isolated, operatives found it difficult to tap facilities in surrounding communities. Indeed, coupled with residency requirements surrounding the franchise, the logistical problem of reaching town meetings discouraged adult men in the villages from participating even in local political activities. It is true (as earlier noted) that some workers trekked to nearby churches; and even without convenient meeting places some collective festivities—July 4th parties, for example—probably took place.[41] But unlike employees in urban factories, Slater and Merino operatives did not find the resources of broader community life ready at hand. As a consequence, these workers could neither draw on nor generate the clubs, societies, and voluntary associations that buoyed wage laborers in more developed milieus.

Thus engendered by the character of the work force and thus amplified by practical obstacles to unity, centrifugal pressures tugged continuously at Slater and Merino employees, limiting the intensity and range of their nonfamilial ties. There are signs, however, that over time the divisions following from the intrinsic variety of the labor force may have grown less pronounced. Though sketchy (and again resisting definitive quantification) the evidence suggests that between 1812 and 1840 veterans in the Slater and Merino villages increased sufficiently to become socially, and perhaps numerically, dominant. Certainly there are indications managers were increasingly determined to hire experienced employees to avoid the burden of training green hands, Slater stipulated after 1815 that operatives who had already "worked in a Mill would perferred."[42] It is also demonstrable that during the 1820s increasing numbers of incoming operatives of all skill levels were actually returning to mills they had previously quit: between 1820 and 1830 the proportion of

East Village employees who had logged earlier stints in this very mill rose from 4.5 percent to just under 33 percent. Together with references to experience at other establishments ("I have worked for the Pocasset Co. over 16 years and I think I should be able to suit you . . .") these clues indicate an expanding presence of workers thoroughly familiar with manufactories.[43]

This in turn evidently promoted a more dense and self-conscious occupational culture. By the 1820s Slater and Merino operatives were routinely manipulating a specialized jargon of "slubbing billys" and "dresser-warpers." Moreover (again despite the absence of convenient meeting places) workers had by this point probably appropriated the English operatives' custom of bracketing the months of candlelit work with "lighting up" and "blowing out" parties. This emerging array of arcane terms and ceremonies did not, of course, equal the heritage of older, established crafts. By 1830 the net consequence of an operative culture expanding amidst the divisive pressures of factory life was no more than limited camaraderie; a fraternalism that was most intense among small groups, that did not preclude broader collaborations but failed to encourage a "habit of solidarity" among nonrelatives.[44] Yet there had been change. Within the confines of limited fellowship, the enlarged corps of veterans and their growing web of common experience promoted a measure of increased mutuality. It was, in sum, a work force pushing toward at least somewhat greater unity that confronted—and slowly began learning how to counteract—the variegated but increasingly stiff, impersonal, and harsh regimen of the Slater and Merino villages.

IV

The relationship that gradually developed between employers and employees in these four compounds took various forms, some of which were devoid of any trace of friction. This was because one strategy Slater and Merino operatives adopted for coping with the industrial order was simply obedience. And this in turn, of course, was in large measure a consequence of the personal and "kindly" dimensions of management's authority and the resulting loyalty and sense of indebtedness some workers came to feel toward their employers.[45]

But workers also acceded to the formal, bureaucratic strictures of the regimen: time discipline, for example. During Slater's first years in Rhode Island, operatives had sometimes drifted away for a few hours or days to pick berries or to protest delayed wage payments. Others, accustomed to the pre-industrial convention of quitting work at sundown, had bridled when mill masters demanded they labor past dusk on winter evenings: "The first night I lit candles," Slater acknowledged in 1795, "[Benchley] sent for his children to come home" and it took "considerable and warm debate" to retrieve them. By 1812, however, a cultural accommodation had taken place. Attendance continued to dip slightly in autumn as operatives took off occasional hours to help harvest nearby fields. But working long days the year round no longer sparked debates, and, by 1830, the average Merino operative—even counting the 10 percent staying only a half a month—registered 77.9 percent perfect attendance. The comparable figure for the East Village was 91.3 percent, which included a steady 20-21 percent with no absenteeism at all.[46]

Such pliability and loyalty obviously raise the possibility that at least some operatives accepted the legitimacy of industrial rhythms and strictures. And the notion becomes all the more compelling when we remember that churchgoing residents of these villages inclined to worship among the discipline-minded Methodists and Baptists. In the end, however, docility is only a small part of the story. Throughout these years, in widely varying ways, Slater and Merino operatives blended obedience and deference with efforts to push back against the men and rules governing them. Prompted by the novel and increasingly intrusive pressures of factory life, prompted also by the unwillingness of post-Revolutionary Americans to submit entirely to a regimen so frequently labeled "tyranny," perhaps inspired by the hostility Yankees occasionally vented at milldams, or by the cocky independence of first-time wage earners—evoked and encouraged in all these ways, resistance emerged as a fundamental motif of the industrial social system.

Often the opposition was individualistic: the fact that even in the 1830s ties among workers remained limited tended to channel opposition into gestures essayed alone or in small groups. Often too it involved operatives' directly challenging fundamental managerial policies or threatening the mills' existence: the broadening accommodation of Yankees to elements of the industrial regimen did not prevent some employees from being thoroughly repulsed by factory life. And often these two themes intersected. Thus, we find parents protesting the daily separation from their children. Peter Mayo—acting alone, refusing to compromise, almost certainly knowing his resistance precluded continuing employment—was dismissed from the East Village in 1827 for trying to "controul his family whilst [it was] under charge of the Overseers."[47]

And thus we find hints of arson. Rumors abounded in antebellum New England that fires suffered by textile factories were often of "incendiary origin." As a result, while the Merino mill never burned, Slater was never certain the several conflagrations striking his properties were all accidental. His suspicions were never proved, nor were the precise issues that might have prompted such attacks ever explained.[48] But if it did occur, this expression of opposition would have closely resembled the uncompromising attacks on milldams Yankees living around factory villages occasionally mounted. And it would clearly disclose the presence of operatives on Slater's payroll committed only marginally to industrialization and deeply offended by its implications.

From the outset, however, many Slater and Merino employees also resisted in ways that accepted the continuing existence of the mills and their own continuing involvement as operatives. This was accommodation that avoided docility. Here workers—not just men, as was the case with the more aggressive opposition, but women and children too—pushed back, but in measured ways: to bolster their earnings or to assert the precious antebellum republican value of independence, and sometimes both at once. Absenteeism should be cited here, for even as punctuality increased, staying away from the mills remained a satisfying, relatively nondisruptive means of expressing autonomy from factory pressures. After all, the attendance rates quoted earlier suggest that Slater and Merino operatives in 1830 were still absenting themselves about 15 percent of working hours. Equally important, many millworkers—again acting alone—supplemented their incomes and demonstrated their independence by stealing raw materials and finished goods from their employers. The practice was evidently common among Slater's earliest Rhode Island employees and may well have looked back to the "almost traditional" thievery in the eighteenth-century English textile trade.[49] In southern Massachusetts in the early nineteenth century stealing did not threaten the solvency of Slater and Merino mills, but officials had "to rise sometime before the sun" if they hoped to prevent operatives from making off with management's property.[50]

This inventory of certain and probable resistance—seeking "controul" over their children, arson, absenteeism, stealing—persisted through the 1830s. As conditions changed, however, such continuity was bracketed by important shifts in the complexion of resistance. With the growing realization that textile mills would not soon fade away, and with the growing number of veterans dependent on these manufactories, tactics aimed at rejecting or destroying manufacturing establishments received less emphasis than efforts to achieve a *modus vivendi* with the industrial order. But at the same time, management's mounting stringency prompted new and more varied opposition. Thus by the 1820s there is reason to suppose Slater and Merino employees had begun sabotaging their machines—not to destroy the mills but simply to give themselves temporary respite from engines running "perpetually" at ever faster speeds. And by 1830, East Village residents had implemented another response to technology: women power-loom weavers were routinely pacing themselves so that, despite the looms' steady speed, they could pursue a psychologically more palatable slow-to-fast weekly work rhythm.[51]

While rooted (like all resistance) in attitudes shared by operatives, these emerging responses to machine discipline were still essentially individualistic gestures. The drift toward at least more fellowship among workers, however, produced a further evolution: by the 1820s we find hints of collaborative resistance. Admittedly the clues are elusive: collective opposition only once involved confrontation, and (like the workers' extrafamilial activities generally) never found institutional expression. Yet there are traces of whispering campaigns and slowdowns aimed at excessively demanding overseers. There are hints too of a strange choreography of funeral attendance, by which operatives took half-days off to bury their friends and relatives but declined to attend services for managers.[52] And we can detect—if only after the fact, from shifts in factory routine they induced—the goals and efficacy of these tactics.

In effect, operatives collaborated to fill a vacuum. Lacking established traditions specifying normal demands in factory work, operatives sought to create norms. Time discipline was once more a focus, for if workers balanced punctuality with persisting absenteeism, they also collectively appropriated management's seventy-two-hour week and turned it to their own purposes. Thus, whereas in 1814 Slater's Smithfield employees were "willing to work as long as they do to [i.e., in] Pawtucket," even if that meant a few minutes longer, by the 1830s in the Merino Village and as early as 1817 in the East Village, demands for work beyond seventy-two hours, even five minutes' worth, was "extra," to be purchased with "extra" pay.[53] The stringency with which the mills calculated punctuality was thus paralleled by the workers' invention of overtime.

Comparable boundaries appeared around production. In the years before machine-made cloth undercut their position, handloom woolen weavers in the Merino Village set output ceilings and demanded bonuses for added work. Similarly Slater's mule spinners and power-loom weavers did not reject assignments of more and faster machines during the 1820s, but they insisted the added output be accompanied by higher gross earnings. And women throstle spinners, who operated twice as many machines in 1835 as in 1817, received both more pay and pay at higher rates for "tending extra sides."[54]

Thus developed a kind of balance. The increased stress on opposition which countenanced continued employment in the mills, and especially the emergence of collaborative efforts to distinguish normal from extra demands, suggests that many operatives were coming to accept the industrial order but simultaneously modifying the regimen with their own requirements. Accepting factory life on these terms—giving and taking in ways which both employers and employees could more or less accept but which also underscored the differences between them—this was an established pattern in the Slater and Merino villages by 1820, and significantly colored life and work in the compounds over the next two decades. But once, in 1827, the balance collapsed, precipitating the single expression of overt militancy these villages experienced before 1840.

The incident arose out of Slater's handling of handloom weavers—not the part-time outworkers, for they were too scattered and for the most part insufficiently committed to weaving to protest when they were laid off. Rather, it was the skilled cassimere weavers inside the South Village who rose into action. Responding to competitive pressures, Slater had cut the piece rates of these men in the spring of 1827. While the size of the reduction is unknown, it was evidently too large to be offset with compromises, and the affected weavers quickly voiced a "determination not to weave unless at the old prices . . .": in other words, to strike.[55]

The 1827 turnout should be viewed in two ways. First: as the consequence of pressures playing across life and work in Slater's woolen village. The strike did not arise *ex nihilo*, or even simply as a reaction to a wage cut. The weavers' "determination" arose largely because they were skilled workers and hence particularly inclined to protest economic demotions. Doubtless, too, the weavers drew inspiration from the overall rise of labor militancy in this period; indeed, the operatives' transiency makes it possible that South Village employees had learned from events in other mills—the 1824 strike in Pawtucket, for example, which introduced turnouts to American manufactories.[56] But most of all, the 1827 confrontation arose from the long-building momentum of resistance—the tradition of individual gestures, the collaborative insistence on extra pay for extra work—brewing in the Slater and Merino villages. Here, in fact, is where the South Village incident illuminates a pattern common in overt labor confrontations. For throughout American industrialization, but perhaps particularly during its antebellum phase, strikes typically emerged from a background of employees and employers struggling to establish the lines and limits of their relationship. As in the South Village, so in other workplaces, strikes were usually conservative efforts to forestall changes—whether wage cuts or (sometimes seemingly trivial) amendments in work rules—that workers felt went too far too fast, as though a threshold had been reached that workers were unwilling to cross without a struggle. But as in the South Village also, such eruptions of militancy were usually shaped by—indeed, are often comprehensible only in light of—prior, more subtle histories of fencing between labor and management.[57]

But it is also true that the South Village turnout must be viewed in a second way—as a failure. Despite advancing bonds of common experience among Slater and Merino employees, countervailing factors—the acceptance of discipline, the personal loyalty to managers among some workers, and the various obstacles to unity we have recounted—all remained too strong. The weavers stood alone, and management won simply by replacing them with operatives tending power looms.[58] Nor did the strike even prove a helpful precedent. Despite further wage reductions, there was no significant rise in political activism among Slater and Merino operatives after 1827, no rush to participate in workingmen's conventions or the Ten-Hour Movement during the 1830s and 1840s, and no further strike among any local textile workers until 1858—and this second turnout was as fruitless as the first.[59]

Yet none of this should surprise us. If their turnouts followed patterns common in antebellum labor struggles, textile operatives as a group were still less militant than other workers of the era: skilled urban journeymen, for example, whose craft heritage provided both firmer standards to defend and greater unity with which to wage the defense. Those strikes and other public protests millworkers did mount before 1860, moreover, were concentrated among employees in large, urban factories. In cities operatives could draw support from surrounding social institutions and artisans. And urban boardinghouse mills provided even further inducement. By hiring mainly adult, single, middle-class women and housing them in a few dormitories, Waltham establishments ironically produced a labor force more homogeneous and unified, more uniformly quick to treat wage reductions and tighter disciplines as challenges to their status—in short, more prone to organized militancy than employees of small, rural mills. Yet it is just these hundreds of family factories we must bear in mind. Their record implies that turnouts and other large, overt protests, while not unknown, were not the notation in which most antebellum operatives tended to register resistance.[60]

As we have seen, other notations existed. But at this juncture we should pause to consider whether they succeeded in altering the basic character of the industrial regimen. After all, managerial vigilance in the Slater and Merino mills almost certainly confined, even if it did not prevent, whatever stealing, arson, and machine-breaking that went on. And the various other gestures of opposition had limited impact on daily operations. Even after securing their extra rewards, for example, the output of mule spinners and power-loom weavers increased more than their gross wages in this period by 33.9 percent and 49.2 percent respectively.[61] In an important sense, the operatives' response to industrialization which we have considered to this point, while far from inconsequential, appears to have left mill masters with the upper hand.

But there is more to say. A close reading of Slater and Merino records reveals one response that did force significant compromises from management. It is a response thus far glimpsed only in passing: leaving.

V

All that we know suggests employees throughout the early New England textile industry were transient. But so, of course, were most Americans. A host of investigations have disclosed significant patterns of geographic mobility beginning at least in the mid-eighteenth century and continuing on past the Civil War.[62] In itself the restlessness of Slater and Merino employees (a necessary corollary of their short work stints) is thus not surprising. Still, the level of movement is remarkable. As Figure 1 indicates, aggregate arrivals and departures of East Village operatives, while varying widely from year to year, dipped below 100 percent of the average annual work force only two times before 1840. Nor did this turnover merely register movement through the payrolls: for just as most employees traveled long distances to reach these compounds, so most—around 80 percent—moved beyond nearby communities after leaving the Slater and Merino rosters.[63]

For our purposes, however, the key rates disclosed by Figure 1 are voluntary departures. While only estimates, these data indicate that exits reflecting the workers' own decisions were numerous. Except for the 1816–20 depression, when operatives clung to jobs they had, at least 45 percent of the East Village average annual work force evidently chose to leave. Samplings from the Merino records yield even higher estimates: 116.4 percent in 1823, 108 percent in 1830.[64]

Besides its volume, other structural aspects of this mobility warrant attention. First, transiency varied somewhat with skill levels and

Figure 1

Aggregate Turnover and Estimated Voluntary Departure Rate,
Slater Employees, 1814-40

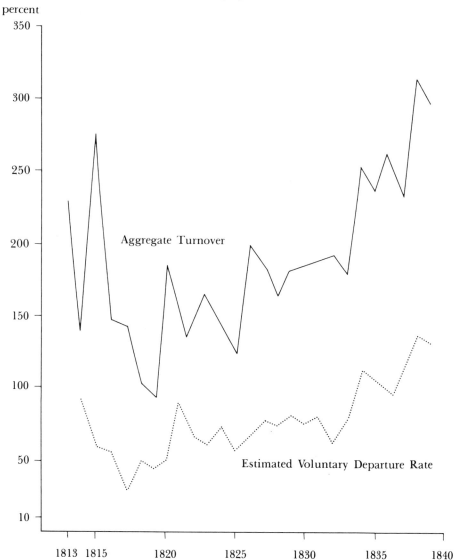

Source: Slater Collection: Slater and Tiffany, vols. 88-91; Union, vol. 144; Phoenix, vols. 24-25. (Data are for East Village alone, 1814-27; East Village and North Village, 1828-40. Data are unavailable for South Village.)

sex. Both skilled mule spinners and women power-loom weavers had below-average voluntary departure rates. The differences were not systematic, however, and were never greater than 20 percent.[65]

Second, transiency ranks among the operatives' more private reactions to industrialization. We have already suggested that movement could undercut ties within the villages; what requires notice here is that workers typically left by themselves or with just a few others. Even families rarely left together. A sampling of children (between eight and sixteen) and fathers showed half of the former and most (56 percent) of the latter left kin behind when they departed. And many arriving workers had left relatives in other factories.[66] This dispersal, of course, did not signal the breakdown of domestic relations any more than did the daily separation of parents and children within the villages. We find, after all, that compared to the unattached employees, workers with kin remained 50 percent longer in these mills, and upon leaving were 30 percent more likely to return; that some household members did travel together; and that scattered relatives often remained in contact and often journeyed to rejoin one another.[67] We should also bear in mind that antebellum Yankee youngsters commonly began a cycle of shifting to and from their homes—seeking schooling and sampling jobs—around twelve or thirteen. Nonetheless, the mobility of family operatives offers some structural indication that policies and pressures of the industrial regimen at least occasionally attenuated domestic bonds. For only among other hard-pressed wageworkers did fathers so frequently leave their families. And while less anomalous, departures of children always implicitly threatened terminal separation: "My daughter . . . about 12 . . . left the service of . . . the Cotton Factory at Waterford; since that time, no intelligence . . . has been received respecting her."[68]

But why did family members leave? Indeed, why did any operative leave? Those using millwork as a temporary expediency departed when their expectations matured. Others left simply because they were accustomed to movement. Or, in rare instances, they left because they had saved enough to buy a business or farm. Or, especially among fathers lacking regular berths and perhaps feeling ineffectual in the villages, they left because they found better work situations elsewhere. Or, especially among children who could expect neither training nor bequests from their parents if they stayed, they left because factory labor was intolerably tedious.[69]

Operatives had left factories for such reasons even in the 1790s, and Slater and Merino workers reflected these promptings right through 1840. Gradually, however, in a manner paralleling other developments we have cited, another motive developed. As mills grew more numerous across New England, as there emerged among Slater and Merino employees cadres of operatives committed to long stretches of factory work, and as these operatives were subjected to stiffer demands, some workers began using movement, not to leave textile work, but to improve their situation within it. Obviously, this was a strategy for prosperous times. Depressions, as already noted, reduced mobility of operatives; and those who did move during slumps generally accepted any available opening and even angled for multiyear contracts.[70] Yet against this we must contrast a mounting inclination of veterans to use good years as hunting seasons for better berths. Again there were precedents: Slater had lost skilled men to another mill as early as 1802. But by the 1820s and 1830s the pattern was commonplace, and had broadened to include women and youngsters. In the East Village in 1834: "[M]ore [power-loom weavers] have given their notice to Leave to go to . . . where they can do better . . ."; in the Merino Village in 1841: workers are "leaving our employ more wages wanted." Nor was maximizing income the operatives' only priority. They moved to secure better working facilities ("faster water"), more compatible supervisors, or more flexible "rules and regulations."[71] Indeed, among workers who rarely voted and whose other forms of resistance had only moderate effect, mobility may well have emerged as the principal means of rejecting "corrupt" dependency on management—of asserting independence and freedom.

But operatives did more than merely seize existing opportunities. They also used movement, or the threat of movement, to bid up the value of their services to create better jobs for themselves. They could do this because mobility presented difficulties for factory masters. While ideologues argued that turnover proved America had no permanent proletariat,[72] managers found the phenomenon burdensome. The task of assigning incoming workers to suitable jobs, preparing lodgings, and maintaining current records taxed administrative facilities. And the stream of demands for terminal wage payments created frequent shortages of cash. Most serious, however, was that transiency aggravated the labor shortage these managers confronted, for it meant rosters had to be repeatedly replenished. All early manufactories faced this challenge. But the greater fame of the Waltham factories, and the somewhat higher wages they offered their all-adult work force, appear to have given these establishments an edge over family mills in securing recruits at short notice. Thus, although rarely left short of help for long, Slater and Merino managers often had to scramble to fill empty positions: "I have sent out in various directions after weavers," moaned an East Village agent, "but have not as yet had the Good Luck to get any."[73]

Here was the workers' leverage. In good times, factories wishing to retain hands were frequently maneuvered into bidding against other establishments. So William Richmonds used an offer from the Merino Village to chivy his Southbridge employer into "paying him his price." By the same token, mills needing workers, and wishing to hire veterans, were often challenged to improve on bargains operatives already had: "I am [given] fair pay . . . where I am now," a prospective Slater employee wrote in 1827, "[and it] would not be an object for me to change places unless I can receive as pay one dollar pr. day and board."[74]

There were, of course, limits to what workers could win this way. Mills needed operatives. But since some workers continued to face low net incomes, it is clear that managers were too protective of profit margins to give all employees what (in Slater's words) "their unlimited consciences . . . dictate them to ask."[75] Similarly, the fact that the local mill regimen grew more demanding suggests that officials declined to dismantle disciplines they believed promoted productivity. Concessions gained through movement were thus confined to the margin, where proprietors thought compromise was at least potentially affordable. Yet even here the stakes were sufficiently high to create fierce struggles—the most dense and protracted to develop within these villages—as management sought to control the mobility of millworkers, and operatives sought to retain freedom of movement.

So it was that the mills introduced contracts. The Merino Village in 1813 and the Slater compounds around 1824 began systematically imposing twelve-month (April-to-April) work agreements and withholding wages "until the expiration of yr." Such agreements obviously served several purposes: the deferred payments simultaneously eased liquidity problems and effectively granted interest-free loans to the mills. But the basic goals were, first, to reduce movement (if workers traveled only in April, aggregate turnover could not surpass 100 percent) and, second, to funnel what movement there was into predictable, manageable periods each spring.[76]

The effort failed. This was partly because employers proved more interested in obliging workers to honor yearlong engagements than in honoring such arrangements themselves. The mills increased their April hirings; but layoffs continued to follow slumps, and between 1812 and 1840 sales did not slip only in the spring. The more critical resistance, however, came from workers. While springtime voluntary departures grew and while operatives increasingly spoke of yearlong factory "seasons," at least half the exits workers chose to make after contracts were introduced fell in the summer, fall, or winter quarters.[77] Unsettled accounts were no deterrent. Those in debt simply took "French leave . . . in the night." Those with net wages due them frequently denied the legitimacy of management's contracts (". . . I made no engagement . . . for any particular time I should not think any one could have any objections my leaving . . .") and persuaded their next employers to help them secure the money—and in one instance even the clothes—left behind.[78]

Faced with such resistance, the mills could only retreat. By 1830, despite occasional lingering threats to withhold wages from workers until their "time is up," payments in the Slater villages had apparently slipped to quarterly, monthly, and even bimonthly rhythms. Moreover, while operatives occasionally signed on for lengthy stints up through 1840, agreements after 1830 commonly stipulated less than twelve months and contained clauses permitting "either party [to] be released . . ." by giving one month's notice.[79]

Contracts, however, were only one front of the battle. Officials of family mills evidently often sought to lure employees with inflated bargains, aiming to "cut down" their wages after their rosters were filled—to which operatives responded by demanding guarantees of good faith with all offers.[80] More defensively, managers tried to protect their payrolls against other mills by establishing guidelines for wages and by threatening law suits against factories "enticing" employees already under contract. But this too proved useless. Mill masters were too numerous and varied to collaborate on wages, and too often desperate for workers to stop their "inveigling." (Indeed, Slater and the Merino proprietors were themselves accused of improperly approaching employees of brother manufacturers.) But again it was the workers' resistance that was most significant. Civil action against "enticements" usually required sworn statements by employees; since, however, such offers typically meant better jobs, operatives called on to testify would, as Slater's lawyer acknowledged glumly, as soon "cut our throats" as tell the truth.[81]

Finally, management stressed the ethical importance of workers staying put. Along with punctuality, rootedness was, in fact, what managers invoked when they set "steadiness" among the principal *desiderata* of textile operatives. As we have seen, Slater and Merino workers did become quite punctual, and even hoisted management on its own clocks with overtime. But their extraordinary transiency makes clear operatives never accepted the moral necessity of remaining in a manufactory longer than they wished. Even intense religious experiences did not prevent unsteady behavior: workers used mobility to assert their autonomy throughout the revivals that occasionally swept the four villages.[82]

In sum, efforts to coerce operatives into stability had little impact. As this approach faltered, however, the Slater and Merino mills began pursuing a different and more successful task. Once again the records are only suggestive, but what they imply is a campaign by management to give the villages a good reputation among employees. Part of this program, of course, involved the "kindly and paternal interest" earlier considered. But these factories went further. Unlike boardinghouse administrators, who used fines, firings, and blacklists to enforce discipline,[83] Slater and Merino officials (in company with other family mill managers) reacted to their more severe staffing difficulties by offering what amounted to a hidden contract: a tacit agreement to avoid such draconian measures.

Every social institution, of course, implicitly specifies which formal regulations will be stressed and which ignored. Indeed, there are signs Slater hesitated to mobilize harsh disciplinary techniques even in the 1790s.[84] But it is surely significant that despite the rising pressure for increased efficiency, the pattern of restraint both persisted and broadened out, becoming a distinctive characteristic of antebellum country factories. Thus, in the Slater and Merino villages between 1812 and 1840 sobriety was required, but drinking was tolerated and a Merino agent had no qualms recommending an operative who had been "the worse for Liquor but once during 12 months." Punctuality was stressed, but existing tardiness went unfined. Obedience was mandated, but only three workers were discharged for "misconduct," and "work badly done" met only sporadic sanctions. Finally, employees leaving before their times were up were neither pursued nor sued and their names were not "sen[t] around": "I shall make some inquiry after them [two runaways]," Slater informed son John in 1825, "tho' I shall not take much trouble to find them."[85]

We should not exaggerate this administrative slack. It did not raise wage levels, or countermand increased workloads, or alleviate the mounting precision with which work time was measured—in short it did not offset the increasing burden of the industrial order. Nor, as we have seen, did it remove the need many operatives felt to resist that order. Yet this pattern of informal leniency may well have represented the greatest victory Slater and Merino workers wrung from their employers, for it guaranteed a small but valuable addition in daily freedom. This is perhaps the final reason strikes were rare in mills like the Slater and Merino establishments. It is also why, from management's perspective, leniency was a successful policy: despite their constant worry about labor shortages, manufactories like the

Slater and Merino mills could usually rely on their good reputation to attract sufficient employees.

Here, then, was the final compromise: a bargain yielding advantage to both managers and workers. But the question remains how operatives discovered that certain mills tacitly avoided strict enforcement of rules and regulations. The answer can only be from one another. Circulating through smaller factories, especially in southern New England, veteran millworkers learned "the customs of all the villages roundabout."[86] And at least by the 1830s the same informal networks that communicated news of openings were also ranking managers. Thus a young man informed the South Village: "You may think [it] rather strange why I keep writing to you the reason is that your place has been recommended to me as . . . a good one."[87] We may suspect hypocrisy. It is equally likely, however, that such statements disclose that the transiency of experienced operatives was coming to rest on shared evaluations —and hence providing further reason for separated friends and relatives to remain in contact. While continuing to reflect and effect divisions within the labor force, movement may thus have grown gradually less atomizing, may to some degree have reflected the increased unity of textile workers. Even movement, that is, may ultimately have involved a kind of community.

VI

We have considered changes in the nature of work and work discipline and accompanying shifts in the structure of the Slater and Merino labor force. We have observed these strands interacting and moving forward to produce increasingly defined patterns of demands and resistance. But what, finally, do we make of these developments? How should we characterize the way employees and employers in the Slater and Merino villages came to deal with one another?

No single formula is entirely adequate. But it is difficult to ignore signs that what we are chronicling is, fundamentally, the emergence of class. It is significant in this context that during the 1820s and 1830s operatives were increasingly perceived from outside the factory villages as a separate, ominous social grouping. Despite industry's claim to protect and improve its employees, New Englanders became steadily more convinced that millworkers deviated sharply from Yankee norms. The very term "operative" achieved currency—probably by the 1830s—to distinguish these wage laborers from other workers. And outside the Slater and Merino mills we find local townspeople in the early 1830s concluding that, despite their own chronic mobility, the "floating and transient" character of textile operatives was most alarming.[88]

But the more significant indication of class was the social system developing within the mill compounds. By 1840 the net result of all the conflicts and compromises was a clear demarcation between the interest of employees and employers. One side wished to maximize output and minimize labor costs; the other side sought a regimen permitting the best price and the greatest independence possible. When every allowance is made for paternalism and concern on the one hand and deference and obedience on the other, this opposition is the axis around which the Slater and Merino mills came to revolve.

There was, to be sure, an imbalance in the consciousness of the competing groups. Managers acted with consistent forcefulness to achieve their goal. Operatives, by contrast, must be seen as comprising a class in itself that acted overtly for itself only to a limited extent. Yet workers quite obviously did find ways to resist between 1812 and 1840, and at least limited forms of cooperation—of community—increasingly underlay their opposition. All this denotes a considerable social achievement.

And one that lasted. Extant Merino records run only to 1845. The more extensive Slater materials suggest that after 1840 heightened competition among textile mills prompted further stiffenings in industrial discipline. The simultaneous influx of immigrants presented new obstacles to unity among the operatives and, as already noted, there was no upsurge of organized militancy. But in more discrete ways—in ways that reflect patterns explored in these pages, in ways that continued to be typical of many antebellum millworkers—operatives in the North, South, and East Villages succeeded in limiting the hegemony of their employers.[89]

NOTES

This essay was originally published in Michael H. Frisch and Daniel J. Walkowitz, eds., *Working-Class America: Essays on Labor, Community, and American Society* (Urbana: University of Illinois Press, 1983), pp. 1–36. Research for this essay was supported by the National Endowment for the Humanities, the American Antiquarian Society, and the Faculty Research Committee of Emory University. I gratefully acknowledge their assistance. I should also like to thank the consistently helpful comments and suggestions offered by Milton Cantor, Thomas Dublin, Steven Hahn, Alexander Keyssar, Michael Frisch, and Daniel Walkowitz.

118   Jonathan Prude

1. Holmes Ammidown, *Historical Collections*, 2 vols. (New York, 1874), I, 435–36. The principal manuscript collection available for the Merino mill is the "Merino and Dudley Wool Company Records, 1811–1845," at Old Sturbridge Village, Sturbridge, Mass. (hereafter Merino Records). The Merino proprietors dissolved their partnership in April 1818, and the Dudley Woolen Manufactory company took over the mill in August of that year. For convenience, however, I have continued to refer to the property as the Merino Village throughout the 1812–40 period.

2. George F. Daniels, *History of the Town of Oxford, Massachusetts* (Oxford, Mass., 1892), pp. 190–91; Jonathan Prude, *The Coming of Industrial Order: Town and Factory Life in Rural Massachusetts, 1810–1860* (New York, 1983), ch. 2. The principal manuscript sources for the Slater mills are: (1) the Slater Collection at Baker Library, Harvard University (hereafter Slater Collection) and (2) the Almy and Brown Papers at the Rhode Island Historical Society, Providence, R.I. (hereafter Almy and Brown Papers).

3. See, for example, Thomas Dublin, *Women at Work: The Transformation of Work and Community in Lowell, Massachusetts, 1826–1860* (New York, 1979); Hannah Josephson, *The Golden Threads: New England's Mill Girls and Magnates* (New York, 1949); and Howard Gitelman, *Working Men of Waltham: Mobility in American Urban Industrial Development, 1850–1898* (Baltimore, 1974).

4. John Carver, *Sketches of New England, or Memories of the Country* (New York, 1842), p. 10, As late as 1845, 82 percent of the cotton and woolen mills in Massachusetts and 54 percent of the operatives were located in townships of under 5,000 people. (Derived from the *Massachusetts State Census, 1845* ([Boston, 1846]).

5. Merino Records: Series IV, Part I, D, vols. 80-81, 84-86. Slater Collection: Slater and Tiffany Weave Books A-D: S. Slater and Sons, vol. 191. East Village outworkers initially included pickers, but they were replaced by full-time operatives by 1820. The handloom weavers increased from 135 weavers between 1813 and 1817 to around 280 by the mid-1820s. By the latter years, so-called commercial weavers, controlling their own networks, were acting as subcontractors for Slater, and some of the farming-weaving households were themselves becoming more dependent on weaving. But until the outwork system was disbanded in 1827 (see p. 97), most East Village weaving outworkers continued to regard their employment as peripheral. See Prude, *Coming of Industrial Order*, pp. 72–78, 122–23. Outwork is an important and curiously neglected aspect of industry's interaction with New England's society and economy. Since, however, the present essay focuses on relationships developing within the mill villages, the subject can here be treated only cursorily.

6. J. Brennan, *Social Conditions in Industrial Rhode Island: 1820–1860* (Washington, D.C., 1940), pp. 32–34, Caroline F. Ware, *The Early New England Cotton Manufacture, a Study in Industrial Beginnings* (Boston, 1931), pp. 22–23, 199.

7. See n. 4 above. Also Caroline Ware, *Early New England Cotton Manufacture*, p. 202. Elsewhere (p. 199) Ware suggests that "about half" of New

England's mills were family factories. But the overall tilt of her discussion would indicate this is simply a misstatement.

8. Barbara M. Tucker, "The Family and Industrial Discipline in Ante-Bellum New England," *Labor History*, 21 (1979–80), 55; Anthony F. C. Wallace, *Rockdale* (New York, 1978), p. 69. Compare Caroline Ware, *Early New England Cotton Manufacture*, pp. 272–76, with Thomas Dublin, "Women, Work, and Protest," *Labor History*, 16 (1975), 99–116.

9. Derived from: Louis McLane, *Report of the Secretary of the Treasury, 1832, Documents Relative to the Manufacturers in the United States* (Washington, D.C., 1833) (*House Executive Documents*, 22nd Cong., 1st Sess., Doc. No. 308), I, 484–85, 526–27, 576–77. Merino Records: Series IV, Part I, D, vol. 75. Slater Collection: Slater and Tiffany, vols. 84, 88–91; Union, vol. 144; Phoenix, vols. 24–25; Webster Woolen, vols. 45–46. The figures for family workers and, in the Slater mills, for women and children also, are estimates based on names, coresiding patterns, and wage rates. The Slater and Merino ventures were probably larger than most family mills (the average factory in Massachusetts employed only fifty-eight workers in 1845). But they were considerably smaller than mills in Lowell and Waltham. (See *Massachusetts State Census, 1845*.)

10. Merino Records: Series IV, Part 1, A, vol. 1, pp. 6, 28.

11. Prude, *Coming of Industrial Order*, pp. 79–80. Slater Collection: Slater and Tiffany, vol. 93; Samuel Slater and Sons, vol. 235, Samuel Slater to John Slater, Mar. 5, 1826; Mar. 30, 1826; Oct. 23, 1827; Nov. 11, 1827; July 15, 1828; Samuel Slater and Sons, vol. 109, S. Slater and Sons to D. W. Jones, Dec. 30, 1839; Samuel Slater and Sons, vol. 110, S. Slater and Sons to D. W. Jones, May 1, 1837.

12. Prude, *Coming of Industrial Order*, pp. 80–84. Merino Records: Series IV, Part I, A, vol. 1, pp. 9–11. Slater Collection: Slater and Kimball, vol. 111. The rank-and-file background of East Village overseers is derived from Slater Collection: Slater and Kimball, vol. 111, and Slater and Tiffany, vols. 88–90.

13. George White, *Memoir of Samuel Slater* (Philadelphia, 1836), p. 108; William R. Bagnall, *Samuel Slater and the Development of the Cotton Manufacture in the United States* (Middletown, Pa., 1890), pp. 68–69. For the assertion that paternalism persisted in the Slater mills after 1840, see Holmes Ammidown, *Historical Collections*, I, 502.

14. Scholarly evocations of paternalism include: J. Coolidge, *Mill and Mansion, a Study of Architecture and Society in Lowell, Massachusetts, 1820–1865* (New York, 1942), pp. 114–15, 164; George Rogers Taylor, *The Transportation Revolution 1815–1860* (New York, 1968), pp. 275–76; and (though he means the term critically) Norman Ware, *The Industrial Worker, 1840–1860* (New York, 1964), chs. VI–VIII.

15. For the controversy over water rights see Morton J. Horwitz, *The Transformation of American Law, 1780–1860* (Cambridge, Mass., 1977), pp. 35, 274 n. 5; J. Conrad, Jr., "The Evolution of Industrial Capitalism in Rhode Island, 1790–1830: Almy, the Browns, and the Slaters" (Ph.D. dissertation, University of Connecticut, 1973), pp. 90–91; J.D. Van Slyck, *Rep-*

resentatives of New England Manufacturers (Boston, 1879), p. 415; Merino Records: Series IV, Part II, E, Box 23, S. W. Babcock to Mr. Clemens, May 28, 1834. Fear that the mills degraded workers is recorded in Sui Generis: Alias Thomas Man, *Picture of a Factory Village* (Providence, R.I., 1832), pp. 8–9. And fear of losing taxes is cited in Thomas Steere, *History of the Town of Smithfield* (Providence, R.I., 1881), p. 65. "[T]yranny" is cited from the *Pawtucket Chronicle*, Aug. 29, 1829. See also Samuel Ogden, *Thoughts, What Probable Effect the Peace with Great Britain Will Have on the Cotton Manufacture of This Country* (Providence, R.I., 1815), pp. 6–7, 26. Such concerns directly affected the Slater and Merino factories: complicating their efforts to recruit workers, for example, and fueling community tensions that by 1832 led Slater to break completely with Dudley and Oxford and petition to have his villages set off into the new township of Webster. See Prude, *Coming of Industrial Order*, ch. 6.

16. H. A. Miles, *Lowell, as It Was, and as It Is* (Lowell, Mass., 1847), pp. 130–31. McLane, *Report of the Secretary of the Treasury*, I, 931. Ogden, *Thoughts, What Probable Effect*, pp. 6–7. White, *Memoir of Samuel Slater*, pp. 108, 207.

17. Merino Records: Series IV, Part II, E, Box 20, Phebe N. Larned to Mr. Permans (?) Feb. ?, 182?.

18. See Slater Collection: Map in Slater and Howard, Box 26. For indications of families maintaining control over children's wages and determining which household members would fill available berths, see Slater Collection: Slater and Tiffany, vols. 89–91. For a distinctly different interpretation see Barbara M. Tucker, "Family and Industrial Discipline in Ante-Bellum New England," pp. 55–74.

19. Some married women "washed towels," others turned out candle wicks in their living quarters, and widows frequently ran the boardinghouses. The point here is simply that married women and mothers did not hold berths. See Slater Collection: Slater and Tiffany, vols. 73, 88–91, 93; Slater and Kimball, vol. 111. Seven out of ten male household heads had berths in 1817; by 1830 the proportion was 35.3 percent. Out of eleven mule spinners and dressers in 1830, eight (72.7 percent) had been promoted or hired as unmarried men.

20. Slater made brief, unsatisfactory attempts to use apprentices in Rhode Island during the 1790s. See Conrad, "Evolution of Industrial Capitalism in Rhode Island," pp. 100–103. The records of Slater's Oxford and Dudley establishments contain only two indenture forms. (See Slater Collection: Slater and Howard, vol. 22.) For Slater's management trainee, see Prude, *Coming of Industrial Order*, p. 81. Apprenticeships in the Merino Village were confined to 1813–14. Merino Records: Series I, A, vol. 2.

21. *Manufacturers' and Farmers' Journal, Providence and Pawtucket Advertiser*, Sept. 22, 1823.

22. Miles, *Lowell, as It Was*, pp. 67–70, 128–33, 145–46.

23. For indications of religious involvement of workers and manufacturers see Ammidown, *Historical Collections*, I, 448; Daniels, *History of the Town of Oxford*, pp. 64–80 passim, 88–89; Slater Collection: H. N. Slater, vol. 33,

Alex Hedges to H. N. Slater, Sept. 12, 1837: ". . . [T]his being camp meeting week with our Good Methodists will be rather a broken one with the mills . . . ." On day schools see Prude, *Coming of Industrial Order*, pp. 124–26. In Rhode Island, during the 1790s and subsequently, Slater was somewhat more involved in educational and religious activities; and elsewhere some New England family mills provided such facilities into the 1820s and 1830s. On balance the laissez-faire attitude in the southern Massachusetts Slater and Merino villages was thus neither wholly anomalous nor wholly typical. See Conrad,"Evolution of Industrial Capitalism in Rhode Island," pp. 123, 262–64; Brennan, *Social Conditions in Industrial Rhode Island*, pp. 95–96. Peter J. Coleman, *The Transformation of Rhode Island, 1790–1860* (Providence, R.I., 1963), p. 231.

24. Slater Collection: Slater and Tiffany, vols. 84, 88–91; Union, vol. 144; Phoenix, vols. 24–25. There were lay-offs in 1816–19, 1834, and probably 1827. Breaks in the records suggest the possibility of brief shutdowns in 1816 and 1834–35. For the Merino mill see Merino Records: "A Checklist and Guide," p. 1. For an economic history of the textile industry in these years see Caroline Ware, *Early New England Cotton Manufacture*, pp. 79–104, and Arthur H. Cole, *The American Wool Manufacture* (Cambridge, Mass., 1926), I, chs. XI–XII.

25. Conrad, "Evolution of Industrial Capitalism in Rhode Island, " pp. 338–44; Prude, *Coming of Industrial Order*, pp. 120–24. Slater Collection: S. Slater and Sons, vol. 235, S. Slater to John Slater, Nov. 16, 1828. Compare this to the more generous attitude Slater showed during the 1790s when he discovered that operatives were inconvenienced by tardy wage payments and were "grieving" for lack of stoves in the mills. See Almy and Brown Papers: Box 1, No. 126, Samuel Slater to Almy and Brown, Nov. 23, 1794; Box 1, No. 101, S. Slater to Almy and Brown, Nov. 4, 1793; Box 2, No. 374, Slater to Almy and Brown, Oct. 17, 1796.

26. Slater Collection: Samuel Slater and Sons, vol. 110, S. Slater and Sons to Jones, May 1, 1837.

27. Ratio of wages for men, women, and children derived from Slater Collection: Slater and Kimball, vol. 111; Slater and Tiffany, vol. 73. Comparison to boardinghouse wages is derived from 1830 and 1835 data in Slater Collection: Slater and Tiffany, vols. 84–85, 91; Phoenix, vol. 84; and Robert Layer, *Earnings of Cotton Mill Operatives, 1825–1914* (Cambridge, Mass., 1955), p. 18. Daily rates in Slater and Merino mills are computed from McLane, *Report of the Secretary of the Treasury*, I, 484–85, 526–27, 576–77. Average annual wages for an operative who labored every day for a full working year in 1832 came to $154.20.

28. Slater Collection: Slater and Tiffany, vols. 89–90, 93–94; Slater and Howard, vol. 26, Joseph W. Collier to Slater and Howard, Mar. 26, 1829.

29. *New England Offering*, I, no. 1 (Apr. 1848), 5. Merino Records: Series IV, D, vols. 74–75. Slater Collection: Slater and Tiffany, vols. 84, 89–91; Slater and Kimball, vol. 111.

30. Slater Collection: Slater and Kimball, vol. 111; Slater and Tiffany, vols. 73, 93, 84; Union, vol. 84.

31. Merino Records: Series IV, Part I, D, vols. 74, 78. Slater Collection: Slater and Tiffany, vol. 88. See E. P. Thompson, "Time, Work-Discipline, and Industrial Capitalism," *Past and Present,* 38 (Dec. 1967), 66–97.

32. Slater Collection: Slater and Tiffany, vols. 84, 88–91. *Vital Records of Dudley and Oxford Massachusetts* (Worcester, Mass., 1908 and 1905.)

33. Slater Collection: Webster Woolen, vol. 110, Ashron Loring to D. W. Jones, Sept. 4, 1836. The proportion of locals entering the mills is derived from comparison of payrolls in Slater Collection: Slater and Tiffany, vols. 84, 88–90, and Merino Records: Series IV, Part I, D, vols. 74–75, with Dudley and Oxford enumerations, Fourth and Fifth Federal Censuses (1820 and 1830), Worcester County, Mass.

34. Derived from William R. Bagnall, "Contributions to American Economic History" (unpublished materials, Baker Library, Harvard University), II and III, passim; Van Slyck, *Representatives of New England Manufacturers,* passim; and analysis of local workers found in Daniels, *History of the Town of Oxford,* Genealogy, pp. 365–753. See also Dublin, *Women at Work,* ch. 3.

35. Almy and Brown Papers: Box 10, No. 1443, Sally Brown to Almy and Brown, Nov. 14, 1794.

36. John Slater Papers at the Rhode Island School of Design, Providence, R.I. (hereafter John Slater Papers): R. Rogerson to John Slater, Sept. 2, 1814. White, *Memoir of Samuel Slater,* p. 127. Daniels, *History of the Town of Oxford,* Genealogy, pp. 365–753.

37. Bagnall, "Contributions to American Economic History," II and III, passim; Slater Collection: Slater and Howard, vol. 26, passim, and John Brierly to Edward Howard, Mar. 5, 1829.

38. *Lowell Offering,* IV (June 1844), 170.

39. Derived from Merino Records: Series IV, Part I, D, vols. 74–75. Slater Collection: Slater and Tiffany, vols. 88–89. There may have been seasonality in the demand for textile goods, but most employers were evidently reluctant to release hands regularly and risk being short in busier periods. Certainly Slater and Merino records reveal no systematic seasonal payroll cuts between 1812 and 1840. These factories released workers only during slumps.

40. See Dublin, *Women at Work,* ch. 5.

41. Thomas Leavitt, ed., *The Hollingworth Letters: Technical Change in the Textile Industry, 1826–1837* (Cambridge, Mass., 1969), p. 30.

42. *Massachusetts Spy,* May 27, 1818.

43. Figures on returning workers are derived from Slater Collection: Slater and Tiffany, vols. 84, 88–89; Samuel Slater and Sons, vol. 234, P. Pond to H. N. Slater, July 31, 1839; see also Slater and Howard, vol. 26, passim. For evidence of experienced women see Slater Collection: Webster Woolen, vol. 110, Anne Smith to D. W. Jones, Jan. 15, 1838; Joanne Littlefield to D. W. Jones, Aug. 3, 1838.

44. See Slater Collection: Slater and Howard, vol. 26, passim. Josephson, *Golden Threads,* p. 83. Eric Hobsbawm, *Labouring Men: Studies in the History of Labour* (London, 1964), p. 9.

45. Two workers actually named sons after Samuel Slater (see *Vital Rec-*

ords of Dudley and Oxford) and when newly appointed agents and overseers arrived at the North Village in 1838, operatives evinced such loyalty to their former supervisors that one newcomer feared "some of the hands will rebell and refuse to do duty under me." Slater Collection: H. N. Slater, vol. 33, Hedges to H. N. Slater, Apr. 11, 1838.

46. Almy and Brown Papers: Box 3, No. 352, Slater to Almy and Brown, July 19, 1796; Box 2, No. 227, Slater to Almy and Brown, June 2, 1795; Box 2, No. 256, Slater to Almy and Brown, Sept. 25, 1795. Autumn slips in attendance and Slater attendance figures are derived from Slater Collection: Slater and Tiffany, vols. 88–91. Merino figures are derived from Merino Records: Series IV, Part I, D, vol. 75. It should be pointed out that the fall harvesting in which Slater's southern Massachusetts workers engaged may have been in fields owned by Slater and undertaken at his orders. And it should be noted further that punctuality increased even within the 1812–40 period: Slater employees were 2.5 percent more punctual in 1830 than in 1813; Merino workers "improved" 8.7 percent just between 1820 and 1830.

47. Slater Collection: Slater and Kimball, vol. 111.

48. Brennan, *Social Conditions in Industrial Rhode Island,* pp. 32–33. Slater acknowledged that "many are of the opinion" that an 1811 fire in a Providence mill with which he was associated "was set . . . willfully"; he personally could only "think and hope not." Almy and Brown Papers: Box 7, No. 944, Samuel Slater to Almy and Brown, Oct. 9, 1811. Fire struck his southern Massachusetts holdings in 1820 and 1834; see Daniels, *History of the Town of Oxford,* p. 191. Slater Collection: Samuel Slater and Sons, vol. 235, Samuel Slater to John Slater, Dec. 23, 1834. See also Gary Kulik, "Pawtucket Village and the Strike of 1824: The Origin of Class Conflict in Rhode Island," *Radical History Review,* 17 (Spring 1978), 23–25.

49. Conrad, "Evolution of Industrial Capitalism in Rhode Island," pp. 259–60, discusses stealing by Slater's operatives in the 1790s and the widespread fear among early mill masters that thieves would attack any goods shipped by land. For stealing among eighteenth-century English weavers see Neil J. Smelser, *Social Change in the Industrial Revolution: An Application of Theory to the British Cotton Industry* (Chicago, 1959), p. 66.

50. Slater Collection: Slater and Tiffany, vol. 101, Charles Waite to John Slater, Aug. 8, 1834.

51. "Work Diary," in Gordon Papers, Baker Library, Harvard University, 12 vols. (hereafter N. B. Gordon, "Diary"), vol. 5, June 8, 1831. The rhythm of power-loom weaving is derived from Slater Collection: Slater and Tiffany, vol. 89. See Prude, *Coming of Industrial Order,* pp. 138–39.

52. Slater Collection: Samuel Slater and Sons, vol. 235, Samuel Slater to John Slater, Apr. 4, 1820. Funeral attendance is noted in Slater Collection: Slater and Tiffany, vols. 88–91; Samuel Slater and Sons, vol. 235, Samuel Slater to John Slater, Aug. 6, 1834.

53. Old Slater Mill Collection at Providence, R.I.: Caleb Farnum to Samuel Slater, June 9, 1814. (Reference courtesy of Gary Kulik.) Merino Records: Series IV, Part I, D, vols. 74–78. Slater Collection: Slater and Tiffany, vols. 88, 91, 93. For an example of other mills starting to pay "something

extra" for work past normal quitting time see Caroline Ware, *Early New England Cotton Manufacture*, p. 69.

54. Merino Records: Series I, A, vol. 2; Contracts with William Taylor, Dec. 19, 1814, and Luther Hammond, May 2, 1815, Slater Collection: Slater and Tiffany, vols. 73, 89, 93; Slater and Kimball, vol. 111.

55. Merino Records: Series IV, Part II, E, Box 20, Slater and Howard to Major John Brown, Mar. 10, 1827.

56. Gary Kulik, "Pawtucket Village and the Strike of 1824," pp. 5–37.

57. For indications of this pattern elsewhere in the textile industry see Caroline Ware, *Early New England Cotton Manufacture*, p. 273; Philip Foner, *The History of the Labor Movement in the United States*, 4 vols. (New York, 1947), I, 105. For the context surrounding confrontations among antebellum shoemakers see Alan Dawley, *Class and Community: The Industrial Revolution in Lynn* (Cambridge, Mass., 1976).

58. Data on the 1827 strike are sparse, but it is clear that, while some hand weaving persisted in the South Village until 1830, this factory had stopped turning out cassimere by handlooms considerably before that. Slater Collection: Samuel Slater and Sons, vol. 191.

59. Slater Collection: Union, vol. 119. Voting data kindly supplied by Ronald P. Formisano. For failure to attend regional mechanics' meetings see *Providence Daily Journal*, Oct. 25, 1831.

60. Some brief confrontations doubtless escaped the public record, but the perspective argued here is generally substantiated by Carrol D. Wright, *Strikes in Massachusetts, 1830–1880*, from the *Eleventh Annual Report of the Massachusetts Bureau of Statistics of Labor for 1880* (1880; reprint ed. Boston, 1889). A general treatment of strikes and a suggestion they did not become important in antebellum America are found in David Montgomery, "Strikes in Nineteenth Century America," *Social Science History*, 4 (1980), 81–104.

61. Derived from Slater Collection: Slater and Tiffany, vols. 73, 84; Slater and Kimball, vol. 111.

62. Philip Greven, *Four Generations, Population, Land, and Family in Colonial Andover, Massachusetts* (Ithaca, N.Y., 1970); Kenneth Lockridge, *A New England Town: The First Hundred Years* (New York, 1970); Stephen Thernstrom, *Poverty and Progress, Social Mobility in a Nineteenth Century City* (Cambridge, Mass., 1964).

63. The number of arrivals and departures used to compute aggregate turnover was established by comparing payroll listings four times each year (April, July, October, and January). Names of departing workers were compared to 1820 and 1830 enumerations, Fourth and Fifth Federal Censuses, of Dudley, Oxford, Charlton, Ward, Millbury, Sutton, Woodstock, and Southbridge, Worcester County, Mass.

64. Voluntary exits were estimated by subtracting departures coinciding with net reductions in the work force from each year's total exits and computing the remainder as a percentage of the average annual work roster. (The rate of voluntary departure could exceed 100 percent of the average annual labor force because the calculations for this rate are derived from measurements of movement taken quarterly.) The assumption behind this

methodology is that net reductions reflected managerial decisions. This in turn assumes management succeeded in finding the number of workers it wanted during any given quarter. As will be indicated, Slater and Merino managers worried constantly about being left shorthanded and often had difficulty filling their berths. Nonetheless, available evidence indicates these mills were not left short often or long enough to distort the estimates revealed in Figure 1. The larger shifts in Figure 1 were probably caused by economic pressures. Turnover and voluntary rates trailed off in 1815 when sales began falling. But in 1816 the two rates moved in opposite directions as the East Village dropped fifty workers, while those with jobs chose to remain in place. Slow times continued into 1820, and only in 1821 was prosperity sufficient to permit those wishing to leave to do so. Movement then continued at a fairly even pace until 1826–27, when power-loom operatives were added, forcing up aggregate turnover rates. Both movement and the payroll contracted during the downturns of 1833–34; in 1837 turnover rose as workers were released, while voluntary departure rates declined. Overall, however, we see after 1830 a general rise in movement—a trend continuing through the 1840s and 1850s.

65. Slater Collection: Slater and Tiffany, vols. 73, 84.

66. Slater Collection: Slater and Tiffany, vols. 88–91; Slater and Kimball, vol. 111. "My family," wrote one incoming Merino father, "will remain in Millbury for the present." Merino Records: Series IV, Part II, E, Box 23, Tyler Chamberlain to Major John Brown, Mar. 11, 1831.

67. Slater Collection: Slater and Tiffany, vol. 88.

68. Joseph F. Kett, *Rites of Passage: Adolescence in America 1790 to the Present* (New York, 1977), pp. 15–29. *Massachusetts Spy*, Nov. 27, 1816.

69. Derived from Bagnall, "Contributions to American Economic History," and Daniels, *History of the Town of Oxford*, Genealogy, pp. 365–753. *Providence Daily Journal and Evening Bulletin*, Sept. 29, 1890.

70. See Slater Collection: Slater and Howard, vol. 26, passim, for letters of wool workers desperate for jobs during the 1828–29 downturn. There is no evidence, however, that workers generally traded longer contracts for lower rates.

71. Slater Collection: Samuel Slater and Sons, vol. 236, Hedges to John Slater, Aug. 18,1834. Merino Records: Series IV, Part I, A, vol. 5, Sept. 1, 1841. Desire for nonfinancial improvements is indicated in Slater Collection: Webster Woolen, vol. 110, Ashron Loring to D. W. Jones, Sept. 4, 1836; Slater and Howard, vol. 25, Thomas Haywood to Edward Howard, May 28, 1827. For Slater's earlier experience with intermill mobility see Conrad, "Evolution of Industrial Capitalism in Rhode Island," p. 292.

72. Miles, *Lowell, as It Was*, p. 129.

73. The relative ease Waltham mills had in securing workers is suggested in Caroline Ware, *Early New England Cotton Manufacture*, pp. 201, 214. For logistical inconveniences facing smaller mills, see Slater Collection: Dudley Thread, vol. 26, Phoenix Mill to Mr. James Cooke, June 30, 1831; Samuel Slater and Sons, vol. 236, Hedges to John Slater, Aug. 18, 1834.

74. Merino Records: Series IV, Part II, E, Box 23, S. A. Hitchcock to

John Brown, Feb. 26, 1831. Slater Collection: Webster Woolen, vol. 26, J. M. Gibbs to Edward Howard, Nov. 30, 1827.

75. John Slater Papers: Samuel Slater to John Slater, Dec. 23, 1808.

76. Slater may have occasionally used such agreements during the 1790s. See Almy and Brown Papers: Box 3, No. 398, Slater to Almy and Brown, Jan. ? [1796]. For contracts during the 1812–40 period see Merino Records: Series I, A, vol. 2, "Contracts." Slater Collection: Slater and Howard, vol. 22; Slater and Kimball, vol. 111. A variation on year-end payments was to dole out "expenses through the year" and the rest in April, or "15 percent on demand" and the remainder in April. All these approaches, however, differed significantly from the previous policy of paying workers their outstanding wages on demand. See Slater Collection: Slater and Tiffany, vol. 93.

77. Derived from: Merino Records: Series IV, Part I, D, vols. 74–75. Slater Collection: Slater and Tiffany, vols. 88–91. In the East Village the proportion of voluntary departures undertaken in the spring grew from 34.1 percent before 1824 to 50.3 percent between 1825 and 1830; the level never became higher. In the Merino Village, the proportion ranged from 14.0 percent (1823) to 34.1 percent (1830).

78. Almy and Brown Papers: Box 8, No. 1092, Slater to Almy and Brown, Mar. 3, 1814. Merino Records: Series IV, Part II, E, Box 23, Nancy Gossett to [Merino Factory], Mar. 26, 1831. Slater Collection: Slater and Howard, vol. 25, William Buckminster to Edward Howard, May 29, 1827.

79. For continuing threats not to pay workers who left precipitously see Slater Collection: Slater and Kimball, vol. 111. Wage payment schedules cannot be derived precisely from extant records, but see Slater Collection: Slater and Tiffany, vols. 89–91; and vol. 101, Samuel Slater to Sales and Hitchcock, Apr. 25, 1827. For an example of workers signing agreements with "time up" before April see Slater Collection: S. Slater and Sons, vol. 237, Joseph Gregory to John Slater, June 7, 1829. For contracts permitting giving "notice," see Slater Collection: Slater and Kimball, vol. 111. Even with these clauses, workers continued to leave "unexpectedly." See Slater Collection: Webster Woolen, vol. 114, Hedges to S. Slater and Sons, Oct. 25, 1838.

80. Slater Collection: Samuel Slater and Sons, vol. 236, Hedges to John Slater, Apr. 11, 1834; Webster Woolen, vol. 110, Christy Davis to D. W. Jones, Dec. 4, 1836. Merino Records: Series IV, Part II, E, Box 20, James Wolcott, Jr., to John Brown, Sept. 5, 1825.

81. On the failure of textile masters to establish wage agreements see James Montgomery, *A Practical Detail of the Cotton Manufacture of the United States of America* (Glasgow, 1840), pp. 39–40, and Paul F. McGouldrick, *New England Textiles in the Nineteenth Century* (Cambridge, Mass., 1968), pp. 35–38. Merino Records: Series IV, Part II, E, Box 20, James Wolcott to Perez B. Wolcott, Sept. 5, 1825. John Slater Papers: P. C. Bacon to John Slater, Mar. 20, 1831.

82. Philip Greven, *The Protestant Temperament: Patterns of Child-Rearing, Religious Experiences, and the Self in Early America* (New York, 1977), p. 25. Whitney R. Cross, *The Burned-Over District: The Social and Intellectual History*

of Enthusiastic Religion in Western New York, 1800–1850 (Ithaca, N.Y., 1950), p. 6. For a substantially different view of how revivals affected operatives see Wallace, *Rockdale,* Parts III–IV.

83. Miles, *Lowell, as It Was,* pp. 128–40. Carl Gersuny, " 'A Devil in Petticoats' and Just Cause: Patterns of Punishment in Two New England Textile Factories," *Business History Review,* 50 (1976), 131–52.

84. Prude, *Coming of Industrial Order,* pp. 45–46.

85. Merino Records: Series IV, Part II, E, Box 23, Edward Howard to Chester Clemons, July 8, 1830. Slater Collection: Slater and Tiffany, vol. 84; Samuel Slater and Sons, vol. 235, Samuel Slater to John Slater, Aug. 19, 1825. For comments on comparable situations among the other small mills of southern New England during the middle and late antebellum era, see Brennan, *Social Conditions in Industrial Rhode Island,* pp. 66–67, 86.

86. Brennan, *Social Conditions in Industrial Rhode Island,* pp. 66–67.

87. Slater Collection: Webster Woolen, vol. 114, John A. Wheelock to J. Wilson, Feb. 6, 1840.

88. Quoted in Prude, *Coming of Industrial Order,* p. 179.

89. Ibid., ch. 8.

CHAPTER 4

Workers' Control in the
Nineteenth-Century Hatting Industry

DAVID BENSMAN

I

The American hat industry grew and changed dramatically during the first three quarters of the nineteenth century. Production became concentrated in six cities in the Northeast: Danbury, South Norwalk, Orange, Newark, Brooklyn, and Philadelphia; wholesale jobbers distributed hats all over the country; production volume increased many times over; hat prices dropped; and labor was divided ever smaller. By 1880 the industry employed more than 10,000 men and 3,000 women in factories from Danbury, Connecticut, to Philadelphia, Pennsylvania. But the unit of production remained small—most factories employed only seventy-five hands and embodied only $20,000 in capital.

Competition among such small units was intense and merciless. Manipulated by the wholesale merchants, hat manufacturers strove desperately to cut production costs, and the workers' "inefficient" work practices were among the employers' prime targets.

Three thousand union hat finishers were heirs to a long artisan tradition, creators of a gradually maturing national union. An examination of these hatters' attempts to maintain their control of work in the late nineteenth century, despite their employers' repeated attacks, allows us to understand better how the work process became the ground on which key battles of the industrial revolution were fought.

II

Neither the individual finisher nor his employer controlled work in the hat finishing shops of the late nineteenth century. Instead, shop crews and the local trade union to which they belonged shared responsibility. The members of each shop elected a steward to collect union dues, to protect the interests of both the journeymen and their employer, and to supervise the hiring of new hands. Stewards had "great power."[1]

To make decisions about work rules and prices, journeymen broke off from work during most of the nineteenth century. Was the foreman behaving too rudely? Was the current batch of hat bodies harder to finish than previous ones? Was this a good time to ask for a wage increase?

Employers naturally resented their employees' interrupting work to discuss such matters, and to placate the manufacturers, in 1882 the Hat Finishers' National Trade Association (HFNTA) passed an amendment to the national bylaws, requiring shop crews to elect committees to handle grievances, so that the entire work force would not have to stop working.[2] Although many shops disregarded the bylaw,[3] resenting it as an unwarranted expropriation of their rights, shop committees came to bear the primary responsibility for resolving problems at the work place.

The shop committee was nevertheless not the key institution in the finishing trade. For one thing, many hatters changed jobs so often they could not form close ties to their shopmates.[4] More important, shop committees could not determine many of their own work rules, for no employer would long operate under stricter conditions than his competitors. To ensure uniformity among the factories within its district, the local committee became the legislator for work rules on such issues as how apprentices were taught, how many journeymen could work by the week, and what kind of machinery could be used.

In addition to setting policy, the local committee mediated disputes between shopmates and between shop crews; decided under what conditions men who had quit the union to work in unfair shops could rejoin; and made sure that owners, foremen, and craftsmen in all the shops obeyed local rules. Generally the local established a vigilance committee, composed of representatives of each shop crew, to handle such matters between local meetings.[5] But the local remained the hatters' primary institution for control of the trade.

III

Throughout the late nineteenth century, shop committees and the local union enforced trade rules whose collective impact was to make the finishers, rather than their bosses and foremen, masters of the work environment.

Rules limiting management's ability to hire and fire were of crucial importance. From the very beginning of American trade unionism, hatters had refused to allow their labor to be sold on the market as a commodity. Instead, they supervised hiring by a system called "going on turn," which in England and America had been "that one great principle which always distinguished [hatters] from all other trades."[6]

IV

The finishers limited the foreman's power further by requiring that he give all his crew an equal amount of work to do by the piece. This practice protected the finishers' independence by denying the foremen the means with which to reward pliable workers and to punish intransigents. Since finishers were often deeply in debt in depressed times, favoritism was a major problem. To strip the foreman of such power, the journeymen (in Brooklyn and Orange) devised a system called "running the buck." "In dull times, a piece of wood or paper (was) passed from one bench to another," to mark who was next in line to receive his batch of hat bodies to finish.[7] (Work-sharing—and the concept of equality that underlay it—was a practice shared by some other craftsmen, such as dock coopers; but many others, carpenters, for example, believed in equality.)

V

Labor economist David McCabe found that 65 percent of American trade unions worked for time wages in 1910, and eight more unions with a combined membership of more than 60,000 wished to eliminate piece work but could not. Only 314,000 workers, 20 percent of the total organized, preferred and received piece wages: boot and shoe workers, cigarmakers, coopers, iron and steel workers, textile workers, miners, some longshoremen, molders, lathers, printers, and, finally, hatters.

McCabe believed that it was not difficult to explain the varying preferences of different groups of journeymen; in some trades, piece work was not feasible because the labor was too varied; in others, it inevitably meant speed-ups and wage cuts. Workers desired piece rates only in those cases where they could ensure that manufacturers could not continually cut the rate to increase output.[8]

But the hatters knew that matters were not that simple. They maintained piece rates because they wanted the power to set their pace of work and to break off from their labor whenever they wished. But finishers knew they bought that freedom at a price—in forfeited wages, impaired relations with employers, and time lost in disputes.[9] Retaining piece rates required considerable effort on the finishers' part, for in the seasonal and unsteady hatting trade, employers preferred to hire men by the week. Not wanting to get caught short in periods of peak demand, they preferred the security of time contracts.

Moreover, preservation of piece rates in the finishing industry was difficult, for the operation of the system was extremely complicated. At the beginning of each season, the journeymen would draw up a "bill of prices," setting a remuneration schedule for finishing each style, shape, and grade of hat. Fixing piece rates was frustrating, for new styles appeared frequently, requiring new determinations of what prices would allow journeymen to earn a "fair" wage of approximately $2-$2.50 per day. Moreover, whenever a manufacturer changed his fur mixture, he would change the amount of time required to finish the hat, thereby raising the question of whether or not the price should be changed.

Journeymen and their employers spent countless hours arguing over what a fair price would be; strikes ensued frequently. Indeed, many employers went "foul" (i.e., hired nonunion labor) because they could not tolerate their crews' constant requests for adjustments. Since work methods, quality standards, and fur mixtures varied so much from factory to factory, comparability of prices was hard to achieve. Manufacturers often believed that their competitors were paying lower rates than they themselves, and it was difficult for the union men to prove them wrong.[10] Moreover, when shop crews set piece rates, there was always the danger that a particularly powerful or crafty employer could obtain lower rates than his competitors, who would themselves soon call for a price cut. But when locals tried to meet this threat by adopting uniform price lists, they found it impossible to satisfy their bosses that the prices were truly comparable.[11]

By the late nineteenth century, hatters had modified the piecework system to meet their employers' needs for a steady labor force. Like American printers' and English coopers' unions, each finishers' local allowed the manufacturers to employ a limited number of men by the week, primarily to operate machinery. Doing so helped the journeymen resist speeding up of new machines, but the hatters disliked the arrangement, fearing that weekly workers would become attached to their bosses and so act subserviently toward them.[12]

Their fear was not chimerical; among London coopers, the less skilled dry workers, who were paid by the week, were under much stricter discipline than their piece-working confreres. And at shop meetings held during work hours, they were so "apprehensive of the inevitable reprimand from the foreman cooper for being away from their benches" that they hovered "restlessly, eager to bring the matter to a vote in order to escape to their shop."[13]

It was precisely to prevent the development of such dependency that finishers preserved piece rates, along with the problems they generated, late into the nineteenth century.

VI

In order to make sure that journeymen did not break union rules to curry favor with the employer and foremen, the finishers' locals maintained their own disciplinary system. If a finisher took work out of turn, insulted a fellow worker, or failed to train his apprentice, one of his shopmates (usually the steward) would call a shop meeting or convene the shop committee to discuss the infraction and fine the guilty party.[14] When shops could not resolve such charges, or if an entire crew violated the rules by allowing too much week work, for example, the union local or its vigilance committee would hear the case and impose the fines.[15] The bylaws of Danbury's finishers' local (1885) made it the "duty of every journeyman who shall be cognizant of a palpable violation of these rules or the common rules of the trade by a member of this association to report the same to the president."[16] While we may doubt that every finisher eagerly informed on his brother, it seems clear nonetheless that hatters preferred to police themselves rather than have management enforce discipline.

Locals had authority over former members as well. A journeyman who had belonged to the HFNTA and then had gone foul, wherever he might be, had to apply for reinstatement at the local where he had committed his violation. Naturally, finishers who had seen their bread taken away by a former craftmate were not always quick to forgive. Fines levied against offenders often exceeded $100—two months' earnings—and could go as high as $500, although usually provisions were made for installment payments. In the mid-1870s the HFNTA's board of directors began to hear appeals from heavily fined journeymen for reductions in their penalties; the board often granted such requests, but locals retained the first right to punish.[17]

Perhaps there is no better measure of the finishers' dominance in the shops than the enforcement of the provision that foremen were not allowed to attend union meetings, because they were viewed as agents of management, but were required to be union members, subject to punishment by their locals' vigilance committee for any violation of union rules.[18] Such power over the foremen greatly enhanced the finishers' control over work in the shop. For example, the Brooklyn local fined a foreman and saw that he was fired in October 1887 because he had taken a $50 bribe from a journeyman who wanted help getting a job.[19] Foremen who abused their power by showing favoritism in dividing the work—a constant temptation—were similarly subject to the union's wrath.[20]

VII

Unlike the weavers of Manchester, England, American finishers were neither tied to their places nor constantly supervised by their foremen. And they considered it oppressive to work without breaks. When Brooklyn journeymen went to work in the nonunion bonnet shops of New York, they complained about having to work from 7:10 to 12:30 and from 1:00 to 6:00 without a stop and without leaving the shop.[21] Since the piece rates were very high in such seasonal ladies' shops, they put up with the obnoxious rules, but in the union men's hat factories, journeymen insisted upon controlling their work.

The men jealously guarded their right to drink, and they also interrupted their work for play. When times were dull, they turned their shops into recreation rooms and played card games, checkers, or quoits; indeed, "no finishing room would be complete without a checker board and a deck of cards."[22] Even in busy times, hatters broke up their work with frequent diversions. Salesmen regularly went through the shops selling jewelry or other wares, while job hunters from outside wandered about, renewing old acquaintances.[23] Meanwhile, the finishers themselves walked through the factories, from department to department, visiting with neighbors and friends.

Funerals and celebrations sometimes brought production to a halt. For example, in September 1885 Newark finishers went out for a picnic to honor Richard Dowdall, a former union officer, on his retirement. Two months later, all the factories shut down when Dowdall died. St. Patrick's Day, Fair Week, Columbus Day, Independence Day, and even the week before elections occasioned shop closings.[24]

When work was not piled up too high, hatters left their shops to play baseball or to go on a clambake. Danbury finishers found the lure of the great outdoors to be so strong that they left for picnics even without their bosses' permission during the summer of 1886. So passionate was the Orange men's love for baseball that they

played when they had ample work to do.[25] Even when their employers were rushing out orders, journeymen would break off from their
work to go out and tell their friends that the shops were hiring.[26]

Finishers even broke off from work to help journeymen from another trade. They insisted that they would work only on hat bodies
that had been "sized" by members of the makers' union. When Orange makers were conducting an organizing campaign in 1886, the
finishers' local enforced a system by which each dozen hats sized in
a fair shop received a voucher, and only hats with vouchers would
be finished. Despite their bosses' complaints that the practice
impeded production, [27] the journeymen insisted on asserting their
power to aid their fellow workers.

Thus American hat finishers in the late nineteenth century had
successfully resisted the imposition of industrial factory discipline.
To maintain their power, they made significant sacrifices in money
and had been involved in bitter disputes with their employers. But
the rewards were commensurate; hatters were able to remain masters in their shops and thereby to preserve their traditional culture.

Of course, the hatters' victory was neither complete nor permanent. As employers attempted to reduce labor costs in the highly
competitive hatting industry, the finishers had to give up their local-
istic orientation. By the mid-1880s the HFNTA had become highly
centralized, powerful enough to control its locals' ability to strike or
to make their own work rules. In the years betweeen 1885 and 1890
the HFNTA even signed a national trade agreement with hat manufacturers. It also inaugurated a union label campaign, which entailed much central control of the locals' conduct.

Hat finishers had to surrender more than craft autonomy; in 1896
they swallowed their craft pride and amalgamated with other, generally less skilled hat workers. The new United Hatters Union was
so successful in its use of union label campaigns to reinforce the
journeymen's shop-floor power that their employers were forced to
go to the Supreme Court, in *Loewe vs. Lawlor,* to gain relief.

The strategy of the HFNTA cannot be characterized as business
or reform unionism. Instead, its efforts were an extension of the
craft's long-lived struggle to preserve the autonomous status and traditional culture of the hat finishers. In this effort the association was
remarkably successful. Yet the hatters did not survive their struggles
unchanged. As the factories grew and specialized and as production
became less seasonal, the hatters themselves lost some of their autonomy, militancy, and preference for irregular work schedules. They
became less unique.

NOTES

1. Danbury Finishers' Association, *Constitution and Bylaws*, Article XIV, Section 12, reprinted in Connecticut Bureau of Labor, *Annual Report* (Hartford, 1890), p. 273, hereafter referred to as DFA, *Constitution*. Stewards kept 5 percent of the dues as compensation.

2. Hat Finishers' National Trade Association (HFNTA), "Proceedings of Special Convention, May, 1882," p. 431, located in the United Hatters' Collection, Wagner Archives, New York University.

3. This was an issue in the South Norwalk strike. See HFNTA, *Semi-Annual Report*, Nov. 1885, United Hatters' Collection. London coopers also held shop meetings, called "roll-ups," during work hours. The steward, known as the "collector," would stand up in the shop and call "roll-up." Everyone would drop his work to discuss piece rates, new materials, the cleanliness of the shops, victimization by the foreman, or employer treatment of "bad" work. Only journeymen could attend. After the meeting was over, the collector would discuss the crew's decision with the employer. The men stayed away from work until that discussion had been satisfactorily concluded. Bob Gilding, *The Journeymen Coopers of East London*, History Workshops Pamphlets, no. 4 (Oxford, 1971), pp. 84–85.

4. *Hatter and Furrier*, July 1881, p. 4.

5. Ibid., June 1892, p. 27; Dec. 1891, p. 48; Mar. 1891, p. 38; Oct. 1885, p. 11; Jan. 1887, p. 15.

6. *Rules and Regulations of the Journeymen Hat Finishers of the City and County of New York* (1845).

7. *Hatter and Furrier*, Apr. 1886, pp. 20, 31; Apr. 1889, p. 29. Dividing work equally also helped to maintain the finishers' solidarity. If the better or faster men had been given more work to do than the others, the craft could have become divided into high- and low-skill divisions. See also Lloyd Ulman, *The Rise of the National Union* (Cambridge, Mass., 1955), p. 553.

8. David McCabe, *The Standard Rate in American Trade Unions*, Johns Hopkins University Studies in Historical and Political Science, Series 30, no. 2 (Baltimore, 1912), pp. 187–99.

9. In his essay "Custom, Wages, and Work-Load," Eric Hobsbawm notes that skilled workers in the nineteenth century were often paid at below their market cost, "but demanded some of their extra price in terms of non-economic satisfactions, such as independence of supervision, dignified treatment, and solidarity." See his *Labouring Men* (Garden City, N.Y., 1967), p. 409.

10. Such was the case in Orange, N.J., on Mar. 21, 1877, when manufacturer John J. Perrine asked his finishers to accept a price cut on some grades of hats, claiming he was paying more for them than his competitors were. The journeymen turned down Perrine's request but called in an arbitration committee, composed of three manufacturers and three finishers, to effect a settlement. The committee proposed a compromise wage cut, but Perrine, believing he was entitled to a larger one, began negotiating with the town's

foul men. Alarmed, the Orange Finishers' Association agreed to a more substantial cut. But the matter did not end there: because Perrine had antagonized the foul men, they determined not to work for him in the future. Emboldened by the foul men's action, the fair hatters struck Perrine twice to regain their old prices. In this case, both sides lost: Perrine, his production; his men, their work. *Hatter and Furrier,* Apr. 1887, p. 8; July 1887, p. 19.

11. Ibid., June 1886, p. 43; Apr. 1888, p. 31; Dec. 1884, p. 30; May 1885, p. 8; Apr. 1891, p. 27; Apr. 1893, p. 25.

12. Ibid., Oct. 1885, p. 11; Ulman, *Rise of the National Union,* p. 549.

13. Gilding, *Journeymen Coopers,* p. 10.

14. DFA, *Constitution,* p. 276. American printers practiced a similar fining system to prevent infringement on the piece scale and other infractions. George Barnett, *The Printers* (Cambridge, Mass., 1909), pp. 292–95.

15. *Hatter and Furrier,* Jan. 1886, pp. 15, 29; July 1887, p. 31.

16. DFA, *Constitution,* p. 274.

17. HFNTA, *Proceedings of the Board of Directors,* 1875–85, passim, United Hatters' Collection.

18. *Hatter and Furrier,* Sept. 1892, p. 36; Apr. 1886, p. 23.

19. Ibid., Nov. 1887, p. 26; Mar. 1886, p. 50.

20. Ibid., Apr. 1886, pp. 23, 31.

21. Ibid., July 1889, p. 36.

22. Ibid., Apr. 1885, p. 30; Mar. 1886, p. 15.

23. Ibid., Sept. 1886, p. 20; Jan. 1888, p. 36; Aug. 1886, p. 24.

24. Ibid., Nov. 1885, p. 35; Sept. 1885, p. 11; Feb. 1886, p. 15; Sept. 1886, p. 21; Oct. 1887, p. 19; July 1890, p. 43; Apr. 1886, p. 32; Nov. 1886, p. 57.

25. Ibid., Aug. 1886, p. 30; Sept. 1886, pp. 28, 32; Oct. 1885, p. 35.

26. Ibid., Dec. 1887, p. 31.

27. Ibid., May 1891, p. 31.

CHAPTER 5

Dilution and Craft Tradition: Munitions Workers in Bridgeport, Connecticut, 1915–19

CECELIA BUCKI

Relations between workers and managers underwent a profound transformation in the early years of the twentieth century. Employers began a systematic attempt to control production and rationalize shop-floor processes through technological innovation, subdivision of tasks, and the application of the principles of scientific management (Taylorism). Their concern for a tractable labor force produced the profession of personnel management and corporate welfare systems. The all-round skilled craftsman, trained by union apprenticeship and able to work in any area of the trade without management instruction and supervision, gave way to the semiskilled machine operative, trained by the company to work on a few tasks using modified and specialized machinery.

At the same time, craftsmen accustomed to autonomy in their work and governed by a collective ethic felt their organized power threatened by this management offensive that debased skill, imposed new forms of discipline, and promoted individualism and competition. Craftsmen challenged management's encroachment upon the shop floor through militant union action, but in doing so they were forced, by the "dilution" of their trade (the British term for the destruction of skilled jobs), to rethink their traditional reliance on the exclusivity of craft knowledge. The key to any new strategy was the willingness of craftsmen to transcend old craft lines, join with the less skilled workers whose jobs were created by management reorganization, and formulate new demands. The metal trades were the industrial sector most affected by management reorganization, and during the World War I years the "new factory system" became a permanent feature in the United States and elsewhere. During the war the metal trades were the most strike-prone sector.[1]

Bridgeport, Connecticut, as a major metal-working center and the

137

foremost producer of war materials from 1915 to 1918, was the scene both of management experiments in work reorganization and of strikes by skilled craftsmen that wracked the city's munitions industry throughout the entire war period. Here, the International Association of Machinists (IAM), using the war boom conditions to expand organization and win concessions from employers, faced stiffening opposition from companies determined to increase war production and hold down labor costs. As manufacturers undercut skilled labor and increased the pace of production in Bridgeport plants, the local machinists, led by radical industrial union-minded craftsmen, began a broadly conceived effort to organize the entire munitions industry to counter employers' plans. Three factors affected the outcome of the unionists' efforts in Bridgeport: first, the nature of management's reorganization of production processes; second, the craftsmen's traditional methods of organization and the pressure for change because of dilution—change that offered the choice of either going beyond craft boundaries to organize together with workers of all skill levels or retreating into an ever-narrowing emphasis on defending the last vestiges of skill; third, the changing composition of the munitions work force, which included the introduction of less skilled men and women into new areas of production.

Bridgeport, located on the Connecticut shore some sixty miles from New York City, was the top-ranked manufacturing city in the state before 1915. The Park City's long history as a center for the production of machine tools, forgings, and brass products, diverse commodities like automobiles, submarines, sewing machines, phonographs, and ammunition, as well as an extensive garment industry, made it an ideal choice for the concentration of war-related production from 1915 to 1918. In the prewar years the labor movement in Bridgeport was weak, curtailed by the strong open-shop stance of the Bridgeport Manufacturers Association and further debilitated by the depressed economic conditions of 1914. A ten-hour day was standard in the city's shops. Lodge 30 of the IAM, led by reform-oriented members of the Bridgeport Socialist party, was small and ineffective, many of its members unemployed because of the economic slump.[2]

The year 1915 began auspiciously for Bridgeport, as the city's firms received war orders from the European belligerents. Older Bridgeport firms retooled for the mass production of military equipment, new firms set up operations in the city, and skilled workmen from around the country eagerly sought work there. The city's population soared from 120,000 to an estimated 170,000 during the four-year war period. The most significant industrial addition to the city in 1915 was an immense rifle factory of the Remington Arms Company, built in Bridgeport's East End next to the company's older Union Metallic Cartridge Company (UMC) plant. By mid-year, Bridgeport was producing two-thirds of all small arms and ammunition being shipped to the Allies from the United States. Remington-UMC alone had received $168 million worth of war orders.[3]

Remington-UMC quickly came to dominate the city's economy. It was the largest employer in Bridgeport, had the most European (and later American) contracts, provided subcontract work for the smaller machine shops to build specialized production machinery, and gave orders to larger Bridgeport firms for ammunition components. At the same time, Remington-UMC competed with all these shops for workers and set the pace for Bridgeport's handling of labor unrest.

The UMC had been established in Bridgeport in 1867 and acquired the Remington Arms Company of Ilion, New York, in 1888. The two concerns were formally merged in 1916. The UMC plant, which produced all of the composite parts for ammunition and assembled the final product, had been modernized in 1907, and production was routinized and performed on automatic machines. In January 1915, UMC's work force was 2,200; by the war's end it would reach 11,000. Sex segregation characterized the division of labor. Women were employed at tending cartridge-making machines and trimming machines and in the inspection and packing departments. In contrast, making shot and lead bullets was a man's job, as were working in the powder rooms and running the heavier stamping machines. Skilled male machinists set up the machines and replaced tools, while unskilled male laborers carried materials to and from the machines.[4]

The modern Remington Arms plant, a complex consisting of thirteen sectional buildings of five stories each, placed side by side and connected by service corridors, was completed in the fall of 1915. When in full operation, Remington expected to employ a work force of 16,000 to 18,000 men to produce rifles, handguns, and bayonets by mass-production methods. The trade journal *Iron Age* commented on the composition of the projected work force, "a large part of whom will not be specifically skilled, inasmuch as a few hours' instruction will suffice to acquaint a man with his particular task."[5] While most of the production work force would thus consist of machine operators, Remington planned a toolroom with a work force of 2,000 skilled machinists to manufacture and maintain the tools, jigs, and fixtures that were needed to allow partially skilled workers to run the production machinery. (While Remington's plans were on a large scale, the plant never reached full capacity during the war and the 1918 work force was 9,000, with 700 toolroom machinists.) Personnel matters for Remington-UMC were supervised by a model management system. Hiring and job training were done by a central employment office, not by department foremen, thereby providing more managerial control over the work force. A welfare department set up mutual aid and benefit clubs, administered an informal loan system for employees, and heard dismissal grievances from workers in an attempt to control turnover.[6]

The lucrative war contracts that prompted Remington-UMC's expansion also compelled the company constantly to increase production efficiency and rationalization. The Remington plant, designed to utilize the latest advances in machine production, was overcapitalized and under pressure to maintain a high profit margin. It was in financial trouble within a year of operation. In the summer of 1916 Remington, under the direction of a new management team, revamped and introduced a new Taylor management system and piecework wages. The aims of the new system, management stated, were to "weed out" the "inefficient" workers picked up in Remington's year of rapid expansion and to eliminate the high turnover of labor, a problem that plagued all Bridgeport plants during the war boom.[7]

This reorganization, however, was just the first step in Remington's experimentation in new production techniques—a project that continued for the duration of the war. In essence, this reorganization was the continued subdivision of production tasks and the remodeling and refining of production machinery, both to eliminate skilled labor in the production departments and to increase the pace of production. The workday was also steadily lengthened. The first result in the summer of 1916 was the replacement of some machinists in Remington's production departments by newly trained machine operatives.[8] By spring 1918 the company had perfected its training procedures and set up a "vestibule school" to teach operations to new workers before assigning them to the shop floor. Through 1918 Remington regularly laid off various production departments for a week or two in order to restructure departments and staff them with new workers.[9]

In January 1917, for example, the polishing department at Remington was reorganized. Management subdivided jobs, cut the wage rates of the skilled male polishers, and set up a separate department staffed by women to perform the rougher polishing jobs. This reorganization marked the first entrance of women into the Remington plant, a situation duplicated in war plants across the country. Women's introduction into new areas of the metal trades during the war was part of the general dilution of machine work. The need for more workers during the economic boom and the fact that the high volume of war production made subdivision of labor a profitable experiment were reasons behind management's search for women and unskilled men as workers. While these jobs represented new opportunities for women workers and caused shifts away from traditional women's industries, they were by no means skilled positions. Women received special training and paternalistic supervision and were often acclaimed by managers as docile and hardworking.[10] Most important, they, along with unskilled men, represented an unorganized wedge into traditional craft union–dominated areas. Nationally, the reactions of male unionists to women workers in these areas were mixed.[11]

Bridgeport's Remington-UMC works was the state's largest employer of women, with about 4,000 women working there by late 1916. The wartime female work force was mostly single, between the ages of eighteen and twenty-four, and equally divided between those who had previously worked in industry (most commonly corset-making) and those who had just entered the labor market. The Bridgeport works also attracted women from nonindustrial jobs from as far as New York City.[12] The rising cost of living, however, also resulted in increasing numbers of married women and school-age girls seeking work in munitions.[13]

The enlarged female work force did not alter the existing production process or the nature of women's jobs at UMC, but it did at the Remington rifle plant. Remington, which had been built for an all-male labor force, began hiring women in late 1916. As in the polishing department, the introduction of women workers was symptomatic of widespread job division and reorganization. In 1917 a Remington supervisor reported at a conference on women workers that "1300 girls and women had been very successfully employed in milling, drilling, polishing, filing and inspecting and all of the operations in the shop not requiring a man's strength." He felt that the women would be retained after the war, "for they were doing good work and work that was satisfactory to the management."[14] By 1918 women were employed in nearly all production rooms in the rifle plant, and it was not uncommon for women hired originally for the UMC plant to be shifted back and forth between Remington and UMC during their employment. The women workers were closely supervised, and a dress code was strictly enforced.[15]

The reorganization of work and the introduction of new workers severely affected craftsmen who had built their union organization upon their control over work processes. The turmoil engendered by technological change, division of labor, and scientific management had been reflected in IAM discussions during the previous two decades. The fierce and complex debates over the question of altering membership qualifications to admit less skilled workers reflected *both* an exclusivity on the part of the craftsmen and a deep fear that admitting less skilled workers would destroy the craft. By the turn of the century the IAM had been compelled to admit "specialists"— men who worked in one area of the craft (such as lathe work or milling) without full apprenticeship training. In the prewar years the union began admitting "handymen" (semiskilled machine operators who worked on certain designated machines); it admitted helpers to local (though not national) membership; and it explicitly reworded the constitution to authorize the admission of women machinists. In 1918 it allowed women machine operators within IAM jurisdiction to join at a lower rate of dues and lower level of benefits. The IAM opposed piecework wages and tried to uphold its one man–one machine rule in its losing battle against scientific management.[16]

The reorganization of production, while generally undermining the power of highly skilled workers, increased some craftsmen's power in the short term. Companies' reliance on a large pool of skilled machinists in toolrooms to keep the single-purpose production machinery running and to produce the jigs and fixtures for operatives to use, as at the Remington plant, made toolroom machinists essential to production in the entire plant. The temptation for craftsmen to act alone, rather than to embark on an industrial union campaign, was greatest here.

Lodge 30 of the IAM in Bridgeport reacted to the first wave of wartime economic prosperity in a traditional fashion. In July 1915, while the Remington plant was still under construction, Lodge 30 announced a drive for an eight-hour day for machinists and recognition of the union. IAM members at seventeen machine shops, including 500 men from Remington-UMC, struck. Remington-UMC, in order to avoid delays in production, broke ranks with the Bridgeport Manufacturers Association and agreed to the shorter hours. Other Bridgeport machine shops had little choice but to follow suit, and by August 1 most machinists were back at work.

This orderly assertion of craft union power contrasted sharply with events during the next month, as unskilled workers in virtually every Bridgeport workplace struck. Without benefit of union involvement, 1,600 women machine operators at the Warner Corset Company walked off the job, demanding an eight-hour day, a 20 percent wage increase, and the elimination of irksome disciplinary rules. They were quickly followed by unskilled men and women in other corset and garment shops, textile plants, foundries, laundries, and other service industries. Many strikers were foreign-born workers who conducted strike meetings in Italian, Hungarian, and Polish. Sympathy strikes spread, as employees in nonstriking shops refused to work on jobs transferred from the struck shops, and jitney drivers declined to carry nonstriking workers to their jobs. By the end of September, most strikes had been settled, and the eight-hour day had been gained in most workplaces. However, employers remained adamantly opposed to the recognition of union shop committees.[17]

The eight-hour movement in the summer of 1915 was two-tiered. While the eight-hour demand had first been raised by the IAM, most of the 2,500 striking machinists were back at work when strikes swept the rest of the city. The separate walkouts of over 11,000 unskilled laborers and operatives ultimately carried the movement and the drive to unionize the city. Indeed, when AFL organizer Mary Scully threatened a strike of UMC women workers because it appeared that the eight-hour agreement was not being honored by management, the IAM business agent stated that skilled machinists at UMC would not engage in any sympathy actions for the women.[18] The contrast between the craft unionists' aloofness and the mass strike movement among the unskilled indicated the considerable distance separating these groups of workers during the first year of war mobilization.

While organization among workers in the non-munitions industries subsided for the rest of the war, machinists planned an organizing campaign in the burgeoning war production plants. Though the union's power was greatest in the small specialty machine shops with highly skilled workers, the key to strength in the city lay in organizing the Remington-UMC complex. The IAM was also spurred on by the threat of the scientific management movement begun in summer 1916.[19]

Though the leadership of the local union remained in the hands of craft-oriented machinists, the 1916 organizing committee quickly became dominated by more radical-minded newcomers who espoused mass action and industrial unionism. Leading the campaign was Samuel Lavit, a machinist with six years' residence in the city. He was described by one IAM member as "a fine agitator . . . who would get up and speak at a meeting and put the stuff across. He understood Industrial Unionism and he wanted the Bridgeport workers to understand it."[20] The organizing committee broke with traditional craft structure (for example, Lodge 30 accepted as members all qualified machinists within the geographical area) by setting up a plant-based lodge, Remington Lodge 584, and two ethnic lodges, Scandinavian Lodge 826 and Polish Lodge 782. The four lodges formed a new District Lodge 55. Finally, because few women munitions workers had made moves toward organization, the machinists recruited a committee of active women from the Corset Workers Union to begin organizing the women at Remington-UMC.[21]

The great gap between skilled craftsmen and semi- and unskilled workers, though narrowed by management's steady destruction of the machinists' craft, proved difficult to close as the organizing campaign got underway. Tension at Remington between toolroom machinists and the specialists working in production departments caused a number of the all-round machinists to refuse to transfer membership from Lodge 30 to Remington Lodge 584, a dispute that continued until 1918. When Remington managers first introduced the new piece-rate plans in 1916, the toolmakers adopted an exclusivist stance and were unwilling to support the specialists in production departments who wanted to strike over the new rates (toolmakers remained on an hourly rate). When specialists were replaced by newly trained semiskilled workers, and Remington production departments were put back on a ten-hour schedule, toolmakers defended only the toolroom's eight-hour day. In other factories, however, where heavier artillery and equipment were produced, rationalization of production was less feasible and thus limited, with less tension between machine workers of different skill levels. There, IAM recruitment was more general.[22]

The first significant labor action over Remington's new production methods was taken, not by the machinists, but by the Polishers Union, which protested Remington's reorganization of the polishing department in the winter of 1917. They were supported by IAM members. The 370 Remington polishers protested the introduction of women because the women were accompanied by the subdivision of tasks and the consequent loss of craft power. The local, reflecting its position that it would be unpatriotic to call for the exclusion of women from war jobs, emphasized that women were being paid lower rates and forced to work longer hours. The union insisted that the women be paid the men's rates. A federal conciliator, however, dismissed the polishers' grievance and agreed with Remington on its need to restructure jobs for greater productivity. Besides, he stated, "the women are receiving as high as $4.00 to $4.50, to $4.75 to $5.00 a day—higher wages than a big majority of the male polishers were able to earn according to the stint of work they were in the habit of turning out."[23] By the end of 1917 the Remington rifle plant was producing 100,000 rifles a month and 10,000 bayonets a day.[24]

Thus, by 1917 alarmed machinists and other craftsmen faced employers intent upon eroding craft work and increasing the intensity of the production pace. The entry of the United States into the war gave patriotic sanction to managers' productivity efforts. At the same time, the IAM saw a new work force of increasingly unskilled operatives, some of them women, who were trained to perform only one or two production operations and who were far removed from the craftsmen's ethic and practice of work. The high turnover of both skilled and unskilled workers in war plants, a result of the economic boom, further complicated organizing attempts.

The failure of the old union leadership to combat the deteriorating shop-floor conditions or to deal effectively with the new munitions work force caused a shake-up within IAM ranks. In April 1917 Lavit was elected as District 55 business agent and other organizing committee members were voted in as local officers. Interpreting this stunning victory as a repudiation of exclusivist craft unionism and an endorsement for his industrial union position, Lavit embarked on a bold course. That August the IAM sent letters to all Bridgeport employers of machinists, stipulating new union rules under which IAM members would work. Besides such standard demands as wage increases, the eight-hour day with overtime pay, and union recognition, the union attempted to bring order to management reform by demanding a minimum wage rate for seven machine shop classifications encompassing the highest through the lowest levels of machine worker. The new classifications were: toolmaker, machinist, automatic and hand screw machine operator, toolsetter, specialist and operator, machinist's helper, and apprentice. Lavit also issued a special appeal to unskilled workers and women workers to join the IAM. The union, by transcending the old craft standard of one or two union-scale levels, recognized the changes in the machinists' trade that had been wrought by technological and managerial innovation and signaled the union's intention to include most machine workers under the IAM banner. Most important, the demands were intended to replace the myriad individual rates created by scientific management rationalization with a union-sanctioned plan.[25]

Lavit attempted to negotiate these demands with Bridgeport employers through the autumn with no success. Finally, as Remington laid off production workers to retool the plant for increased production of U.S. service rifles and revolvers, Remington toolroom machinists decided to break the stalemate. At a February 1918 meeting, called without Lavit's knowledge, the toolmakers and toolroom machinists formulated demands for an 80¢ hourly minimum rate for toolmakers and 75¢ for all toolroom machinists. These demands were ignored by Remington until Good Friday, when 700 toolmakers and machinists walked off the job in a dispute over holiday pay. With this action IAM concerns returned to protection of the status and wages of skilled machinists while ignoring the less skilled. When the Army Ordnance Department stepped into the conflict, Lavit regained his authority over the movement and presented the machinists' demands to the government. These demands were a minimum rate of 80¢ per hour for "toolmakers, die makers, gaugemakers, and men working on jigs or fixtures, and all specialized branches of the same" and a 70¢ minimum for "all machinists, specialists, operators and bench hands who are essential to the fitting and assembling of machines or parts thereof," plus demands for equal pay for women performing men's jobs (a demand adopted at the request of the Polishers Union), the right to union representation, and a thirty-day extension of draft deferments for war workers changing jobs.[26] These job descriptions and draft deferments clearly related only to skilled toolroom workers. Meanwhile, the Remington toolroom voted to reincorporate the ill-fated Remington lodge back into Lodge 30.[27]

Machinists engaged in a series of sporadic work stoppages designed to bring pressure on Washington while the War Department weighed the situation. When the War Department announced its decision in favor of the machinists, however, Bridgeport employers refused to accept it. Enraged by their employers' intransigence, over 7,000 machinists ignored appeals to patriotism and downed their tools. By the end of June, the stoppage included craftsmen from twenty-two machine shops, 700 men from Remington's toolroom, and 1,000 at each of the two other munitions plants, Liberty Ordnance and the American-British Company. The machinists returned to work as the newly created National War Labor Board (NWLB) assumed jurisdiction over the dispute. The NWLB announced that it would examine the wages and working conditions of *all* Bridgeport war workers.[28]

Hearings of the NWLB were held throughout July, with the machinists' case presented by a subdued Lavit flanked by two national IAM officials. Much of the testimony revolved around the Remington-UMC plant. Lavit now claimed jurisdiction over some 5,000 of the 18,000 workers at Remington-UMC, widening somewhat the Good Friday demands that had included only toolroom machinists but a far cry from the all-inclusive demands of the previous summer. According to the national IAM, this jurisdiction included operators on Jones & Lamson, Potter & Johnson, and Gisholt and automatic screw machines as well as machinists' helpers, but the union hesitated to include more routine machine operations. At the same time, however, the District 55 newspaper *Labor Leader*, with Lavit as editor, continued to exhort unskilled workers and women workers to join the IAM.[29] The union presented a variety of grievances, including the general practice of blacklisting union members, employers' stiff resistance to any form of workers' representation, and the use of military conscription to threaten workers.

The main point of contention in the hearings, however, was the dilution of the machinists' craft under the pressure of war production. Bridgeport employers admitted that there had been substantial changes in machinery and methods of production in every shop since the war's beginning. Indeed, they insisted that even toolroom machinists were only partially skilled and thus did not deserve full machinist pay. The Polishers Union, which had joined the IAM for the hearings, argued that the dilution of their trade had meant lower wages, a speedup in production, and the introduction of women, thereby "intimidat[ing] and terroriz[ing] men who had threatened to strike because of evil working conditions."[30] In response, employers insisted on the necessity of increasing productivity by the subdivision and rationalization of labor and resisted the demand for a minimum rate, stating that the thousands of individual wage rates in the city were an inducement to production. "A high minimum wage for each craft and a curtailment of the employer's freedom to classify and grade, would radically alter factory management . . . would prove impracticable, destroy efficiency, reduce production and stir up unrest."[31] The NWLB itself was deeply divided on the issue and appointed a mediator to settle the dispute.[32]

Massive strike meetings were held in August, with only Lavit's pleas preventing another machinist walkout. Even so, the Remington toolroom engaged in a one-day strike on August 15 to show its resolve. Rumors began circulating that Lavit had "sold out" the skilled workers. Bridgeport had taken on the appearance of a military camp; pacifist demonstrations had early been quashed, and speakers from the Connecticut Council of Defense staged war rallies on factory grounds. State militia units had been deployed and agents of the War Department Military Intelligence Bureau were engaged in plant surveillance in the city. A Navy submarine guarded the harbor, ostensibly against German attack. The Bridgeport City Council entered the fray, passing a "Work or Fight" ordinance that authorized city police to arrest unemployed males of draft age and turn them over to the draft board for induction. While the *Labor Leader* carefully avoided political or antiwar statements, IAM members showed their patriotism by selling war bonds all during the troubled summer. Many machinists were confident that the NWLB, in light of the previous War Department's decision and the classification schemes set up in U.S. shipyards and arsenals, would accede to the Bridgeport machinists' demands.[33]

Instead, the NWLB mediator focused his wage award on unskilled workers and refused to redress the machinists' grievances, exacerbating the tension between skilled and unskilled workers. In the August 28 decision, the NWLB rescinded the previous War Department statement and awarded a flat 15 percent increase to the lowest-paid munitions workers up to a *maximum* of 78¢ per hour (2¢ below the toolmakers' demanded minimum). A minimum wage of 42¢ for men over twenty-one years of age and 32¢ for women over eighteen, equal pay for equal work for women, and a mechanism for setting up representative shop committees (a favorite government plan) were also included in the decision. No alterations in craft classifications were allowed.[34]

The skilled workers, incensed at the award and dubbing their 5¢ increase a "Jitney Feast," voted another walkout. Five thousand machinists struck, calling on President Woodrow Wilson to take over the Bridgeport factories and stating: "After more than a year of patient appeal to government agencies to grant the workers of Bridgeport a measure of security and justice under which we could forge ahead with important war work confident that our own status as workers would not be slipped out from under us, leaving us to fall victims to the profiteering greed of employers, we find that as machinists, toolmakers, and specialists we were totally ignored."[35]

National IAM president Johnston, a member of the NWLB, initially supported the strikers but within the week bowed to government pressure and ordered the lodges back to work. The strikers voted to forfeit their lodge charters rather than obey the Grand Lodge. The stalemate lasted until September 13, when President Wilson issued a back-to-work order and threatened to rescind the men's military exemptions. The strikers quickly returned to work.[36]

The summer 1918 actions, while affecting all war production in Bridgeport, were clearly undertaken by skilled machinists. Few production workers or women workers from Remington-UMC were part of the strike activities. The impetus for the IAM's activities came from the toolroom at Remington. The retreat from the union's stated aims of minimum wage rates for all classes of machine workers began with the toolmakers' demands of March 1918. In asking for classification and wage increases for the toolroom only, skilled workers had abandoned the increasingly unskilled production areas in favor of using their craft knowledge and power to challenge employers. Their timing—striking just as Remington was conducting a massive retooling of the plant—revealed their strategic reliance on craft rather than industrial solidarity. The hostility between the toolroom and the production departments was hinted at by the *Bridgeport Sunday Herald*, which reported that a common complaint of the machinists was the situation where a production machine operator, though paid a low hourly wage, was able to earn $30-$42 a week with piece rates and bonus, while toolmakers and machinists, paid a straight hourly rate, averaged $24 a week.[37] The machinists' added demand for the extension of draft exemptions only widened the gap between toolroom machinists and production workers, since most production workers were not eligible for the exemptions.

Increased management pressures on craftsmen had fractured the tenuous alliance betweeen skilled and unskilled workers that Bridgeport IAM leaders were attempting to build. The IAM's changing classification demands, as well as the confusion evidenced by the union during the NWLB hearings concerning the proper machinists' jurisdiction, suggested the extent to which rapid dilution of the machinist craft was taking place at Remington, so rapid, in fact, that machinists had difficulty identifying production operations as part of their craft from one time to another. At the NWLB hearings the IAM solved its immediate problem of defining jurisdiction by classifying certain *machines,* rather than their *operators,* as being within IAM jurisdiction. This apparent split between toolroom and production departments was not a factor in Bridgeport's two smaller munitions plants (American-British Company and Liberty Ordnance), where most workers participated in the strike. Conditions differed in those plants, where dilution had been limited by the nature of heavy armaments production, where few women had been employed, and where the entire work force had been subjected to management harassment immediately prior to the walkouts. The machinists in small machine shops made up the rest of the strike movement. These shops had experienced the least amount of dilution, producing less tension between workers of different skill levels. The federal government, aware of the lack of unity among war workers, sided with employers in favor of scientific management reorganization.

Unskilled men and women machine operators at Remington were not attracted to the IAM. Though the hostility of some skilled machinists toward them played a role, other factors were also at play. Unskilled women, for example, sought work in munitions because it was a temporary opportunity for better wages than traditional women's industries, because of the rising cost of living, or because of the need to supplement family incomes when a male relative was drafted.[38] The heavy atmosphere of coercive patriotism that pervaded Bridgeport may also have contributed to many production workers' lack of union involvement. The events of 1915, where women machine operatives actively participated in and sometimes led the eight-hour strikes in traditional women's industries, contrasted sharply with the inactivity of women in munitions. The Remington-UMC work force undoubtedly included many women who had participated in those strikes and then switched to the munitions industry for the duration of the war. Women workers at Remington, introduced into the shop accompanied by a reorganization of the work process itself, with no union tradition in that setting and under stringent forms of managerial supervision, were not able to transfer their earlier style of union organization to munitions.

Labor activity after the denouement in September contrasted sharply with the exclusivist machinist activity during the summer, but also resulted in an open split among the machinists. Industrial strife by no means abated, since the three labor representatives chosen at a citywide conference of shop committee delegates (themselves elected at government-supervised voting at each work place) were Lavit and two other IAM leaders, who were to sit on the city labor representation board. Employers refused to deal with them, and the NWLB declined to force employers' participation.[39]

Ironically, the government award spurred significant union efforts among Remington-UMC women for the first time. The women, incensed that Remington-UMC was not abiding by the government award, which stipulated a minimum rate of 32¢ an hour for women workers, signed membership cards. Women workers noted the inadequacy of the equal pay provision and petitioned the local NWLB board for an extension of the award to women under eighteen years old. Growth of the women's organization was rapid enough that by the end of October, a Women's Lodge 1196 with 100 members was granted a charter. The acceptance of women into the union was not without its difficulties, however; at one union meeting Lavit was obliged to engage in a fistfight with an unruly IAM member who insisted on calling the women "scabs."[40]

The declaration of the Armistice, however, cut short developments in union organization among war workers. IAM activity after the end of the war focused on the consequences of demilitarization, especially unemployment. The petitions of manufacturers and unions alike succeeded in putting off cancellation of government contracts for a few months, and in the intervening period the IAM mounted large unemployment demonstrations and sought to retain the citywide shop committee structure. The Women's Lodge became active in the cause of women's suffrage, and four members, led by lodge president Elsie Ver Vane, were arrested during the Washington, D.C., watch fire demonstrations in January. By March 1919 all government contracts were cancelled, the wartime government apparatus was dismantled, and the Bridgeport office of the NWLB was closed. The government-sponsored system of shop committees, floundering as it was, ceased to operate.[41]

With the munitions factories closing and many other shops curtailing operations, workers in the non-munitions industries suddenly went on the offensive. The Corset Workers Union, dormant since 1916, struck the Warner Corset Company and four other corset shops in town, demanding a forty-four hour week and 20 percent wage increase (demands first formulated by the IAM at its unemployment demonstrations). Lavit announced an IAM drive for the forty-four hour week, a wage increase, and a minimum wage rate for all workers in the city's machine shops. This call to represent all machine shop workers, regardless of craft status, was answered as 10,000 skilled and unskilled workers at other shops, including Bryant Electric, Remington–Yost Typewriter, Hawthorne Manufacturing, and American Graphophone, joined the 3,000 corset workers on strike. The machine shopworkers asked for IAM sponsorship, and Lavit enrolled them as IAM members and wired the national office for strike benefits.[42]

At this point, factionalism within Lodge 30 broke open. At a rump session of the lodge in June, machinists displeased with Lavit's rule passed, by a slight margin, a resolution to abolish District 55 and reaffiliate the Bridgeport lodges with the New Haven District. This move would have deprived Lavit of his position as district business agent. The three other lodges had not had time to vote on the resolution when the national IAM acted. Refusing to sanction the ongoing strikes, the Grand Lodge secretary appeared at a meeting of Lodge 30 and announced Lavit's removal from office by order of the Grand Lodge. The charges against Lavit included his having called unauthorized strikes, his being a "Bolshevik" and "IWW," and (worst of all) his allowing non-machinists, such as clerks in the accounting department at American Graphophone, to become members in the IAM. The *Bridgeport Sunday Herald* characterized the dispute as a rebellion of the "old guard" of Lodge 30 against Lavit's rule, noting that Lavit's support came from "the temporary, the new members," many of whom were leaving town with the closing of the war industries.[43] Even when a full meeting of Lodge 30, including the strikers, responded with a vote of confidence in Lavit, the lodge's charter was revoked and a new Lodge 116 was chartered with "loyal" IAM members. Most of the strikes were settled on employers' terms. Lavit and a section of Lodge 30 continued their industrial union stance and in 1920 formed an independent Amalgamated Metal Workers of America. This union eventually drifted into obscurity with the economic downturn later that year.[44]

During the war years Bridgeport was the scene of militant, craft-based labor action on the part of an IAM determined to uphold its position in Bridgeport industry. But labor's activity in the munitions industry remained craft-based, and few significant inroads were made during the war years to break down the divisions between skilled machinists and less skilled men and women. Though Bridgeport's IAM leaders promoted industrial unionism and encouraged less skilled workers to join, this broadly conceived effort by a militant minority was handicapped from the start. First, a portion of Lodge 30's membership, which retained its craft outlook throughout the war, opposed the formation of the new lodges and provided the impetus and direction for the machinists' actions in 1918. Second, the influx of new workers, combined with employers' steadfast refusal to deal with the union, slowed labor's advance. Finally, the union was hampered by the reorganization of production induced by the war effort, resulting in the dilution of the machinists' craft to a wider extent than before. While wages and working conditions in general were always at issue, the concern of the machinists became the job itself—who would do it and how those workers would be classified and paid. The intensity of concern over dilution grew in Bridgeport during the war years and directly altered the primary goals of the IAM. Thus the strikes in the summer of 1918 focused almost exclusively on this question and involved only one sector of the workforce. The goal of organizing less skilled men and women was lost.

Machinists' strikes during the war, with their emphasis on the defense of craft, contrasted sharply with the activity of skilled and unskilled women and men workers in the non-munitions industries after the war. The dilution crisis was not evident in the older Bridgeport shops, and workers in those shops succeeded in overcoming the traditional distance between skilled and unskilled. It took the intervention of the IAM Grand Lodge and of conservative elements in the Bridgeport IAM to destroy this move toward union organization on an industrial basis after the war. The next generation of workers would face the task of meeting the challenge of modern capitalist management with new forms of union organization.

NOTES

An earlier version of this article appeared in *Social Science History*, 4 (Winter 1980), 105–24. I thank David Montgomery, Maurine Greenwald, Ronald Schatz, Steven Sapolsky, and Charles Stephenson for their valuable comments and criticisms on various drafts of this article.

1. On the new factory system, see Daniel Nelson, *Managers and Workers: Origins of the New Factory System in the United States, 1880–1920* (Madison, 1975); Frederick Winslow Taylor, *The Principles of Scientific Management* (1911; reprint, New York, 1967); Harry Braverman, *Labor and Monopoly Capitalism: The Degradation of Work in the Twentieth Century* (New York, 1974). On craftsmen and union activity, see David Montgomery, "Workers' Control of Machine Production in the Nineteenth Century," *Labor History*, 17 (Fall 1976), 485–509; Montgomery, "The 'New Unionism' and the Transformation of Workers' Consciousness in America, 1909–1920," *Journal of Social History*, 7 (Summer 1974), 509–29; Milton J. Nadworny, *Scientific Management and the Unions, 1900–1932* (Cambridge, Mass., 1955); James Hinton, *The First Shop Stewards' Movement* (London, 1973); Alexander Bing, *Wartime Strikes and Their Adjustment* (New York, 1921). David Montgomery, "Quels Standards? Les ouvriers et la réorganization de la production aux Etats-Unis 1900-1920," *Le Mouvement Social*, 108 (1978), 101–27, discusses the Bridgeport strikes, but overestimates the unity between skilled and unskilled workers during the war.

2. George C. Waldo, Jr., *History of Bridgeport and Vicinity*, 2 vols. (New York, 1917), I, 165–89; Bridgeport Socialist Party Minute Books, Dec. 21, 1914, July 26, 1915, McLevy-Schwartzkopf Papers, Bridgeport Public Library, Conn.; Thomas Banit, "The War Machine: Bridgeport, 1914–1918" (M.A. thesis, University of Bridgeport, 1973), p. 142; "Bridgeport during the World War," manuscript notes, Works Project Administration Federal Writers' Project–Connecticut Bureau (hereafter cited as WPA-CT), R.G. 33, Box 134, Connecticut State Library, Hartford.

3. *New York Times*, July 15, 1915; *Bridgeport Morning Telegram*, Jan. 12, 13, May 5, 1915; *Bridgeport Post*, Mar. 8, 24, Apr. 1, 1915.

4. Elsie Nicholas Danenberg, *The Story of Bridgeport* (Bridgeport, 1936), pp. 114–16; Alden Hatch, *Remington Arms in American History* (New York, 1972), pp. 203–14; Amy Hewes, *Women as Munitions Makers: A Study of Conditions in Bridgeport, Connecticut* (New York, 1917). See also E. A. Suverkrop, "Making One Hundred Thousand Cartridges in Ten Hours," *American Machinist*, 42 (Apr. 22, 1915), 203–4, for a description of the stages of ammunition manufacture.

5. "War Order Activity in New England," *Iron Age*, 96 (July 22, 1915), 201.

6. Hugh M. Wharton, "Plants of Remington Arms—I and II," *American Machinist*, 45 (Nov. 23, 30, 1916), 881–86, 925–29; "Huge Remington Small Arms Factory Represents Effective 'Preparedness,' " *Iron Trade Review*, 58

(Jan. 27, 1916), 246–49; "Remington Arms Plant," *Iron Age*, 97 (Feb. 3, 1916), 296–303.

7. "Teaching Efficiency," *Iron Trade Review*, 59 (July 20, 1916), 136.

8. "A. W. Reports," reports of an IAM informer to the Bridgeport Manufacturers Association, typewritten, Manufacturers Association of Southern Connecticut, Stratford, May 9, June 29, 1916.

9. "Training 150 Operators Per Week," *Automotive Industry*, 39 (Aug. 11, 1918), 277–80.

10. U.S. Department of Labor, Women's Bureau, *The New Position of Women in Industry*, bulletin no. 12 (Washington, D.C., 1920); National Industrial Conference Board, *Wartime Employment of Women in the Metal Trades*, research report no. 5 (Boston, 1918). Contemporary management literature was filled with reports of women's introduction into new areas. See, for example, C. B. Lord, "How to Deal Successfully with Women in Industry," *Industrial Management*, 53 (Sept. 1917), 838–45; W. A. Viall, "Employment of Women in Our Industries," *American Machinist*, 48 (May 30, 1918), 909–11; Robert I. Clegg, "Training Women for Record Output," *Iron Age*, 103 (Jan. 1919), 169–74.

11. Maurine Greenwald, "Women, War and Work: The Impact of World War I on Women Workers in the United States" (Ph.D. dissertation, Brown University, 1977), analyzes women's work experiences; see pp. 68–114 for a discussion of women's experiences in railroad machine shops.

12. By late 1916 the switch to munitions work had been so dramatic that traditional employers of women like Bryant Electric and Warner Corset were forced to advertise in local newspapers for women workers to maintain their work force. Remington boasted that nurses and teachers had sought work in their plants because of the excellent wages and working conditions. Fred H. Colvin, "Women in Machine Shops," *American Machinist*, 47 (Sept. 20, 1917), 510. See advertisements in *Bridgeport Sunday Herald*, Sept. 8, 1916.

13. Hewes, *Women as Munitions Workers*, pp. 21–52; Connecticut Bureau of Labor, *The Condition of Wage-earning Women and Girls* (Hartford, 1916), pp. 8–34; "Report on Investigation of Night Workers in Bridgeport," Connecticut Council of Defense, Women's Council, R.G. 30, Box 376, File T62 (Feb.-Apr. 1918), Connecticut State Library.

14. John W. Upp, "The Woman Worker," *ASME Transactions*, 39 (Dec. 1917), 1145–46.

15. Mrs. Edmonde to Connecticut Council of Defense, Jan. 1, 1918, R.G. 30, Box 377, File T62.1, details complaints about dress codes from Bridgeport women workers.

16. Mark Perlman, *The Machinists: A New Study in American Trade Unionism* (Cambridge, Mass., 1961), pp. 23–30. Note that the Bridgeport IAM did not use the term "handyman," but "specialist and operator" as the general designation for various levels of machine workers. See *Machinists' Monthly Journal*, 28 (July, Aug. 1916), 664–67, 732–33, and 30 (Jan. 1918), 84, for a definition of IAM jurisdiction and the admission of women.

17. Zenas F. Potter, "War Boom Towns I—Bridgeport," *Survey*, 35 (Dec.

4, 1915), 237–41; *Machinists' Monthly Journal,* 27 (Apr. 1915), 343, and 28 (Mar. 1916), 261–62; *Bridgeport Post,* July-Sept. 1915, daily issues; *Bridgeport Evening Farmer,* July-Aug. 1915, daily issues.

18. *Bridgeport Post,* Aug. 25, 1915.

19. George Bowen, "The Conquest of Bridgeport," *Machinists' Monthly Journal,* 28 (May 1916), 553–54.

20. M. G. Sayers, "Interview with Industrial Worker Mr. P.," WPA-CT, R.G. 33, Box 134. Lavit, born Samuel Lavitsky, was a Russian Jew whose parents had emigrated to Argentina where he lived until the age of twelve. He then moved to New York City and in 1909 came to Bridgeport, where he settled and married a Bridgeport native. *Bridgeport Post,* Dec. 18, 1958 (obituary).

21. "A. W. Reports," Apr. 20, 26, Sept. 25, 26, 1916. See also *Machinists' Monthly Journal,* 28 (Nov. 1916), 1134. The Scandinavian Lodge was formed because of the success of a recently formed Swedish local of the Carpenters Union and because a few machine shops employed a large number of Swedish machinists. No reason for the formation of the Polish Lodge was given, though its existence suggests the ethnic diversity of the group that the IAM hoped to organize. Sketchy mention of these lodges in IAM statements indicated that membership remained small (under 100) and consisted of skilled machinists, not production workers. No data were available on the ethnic composition of the work force in various plants, but ethnic conflict did not appear as a factor in any sources. Note, though, that in 1910, 75 percent of Bridgeport's population was foreign-born or children of foreign-born, with the largest ethnic groups being Hungarian, Italian, Polish, and Russian. U.S. Army, Military Intelligence Records, Entry 142, Box 1, Feb. 9, 1918, R.G. 165, National Archives, Suitland, Md.; *Thirteenth Census of the United States, Vol. II: Population* (Washington, D.C., 1910), p. 262.

22. "A. W. Reports," July 3, 14, 16, 1916; *Machinists' Monthly Journal,* 29 (June 1917), 524.

23. U.S. Department of Labor, Federal Mediation and Conciliation Service, File 33/567, Aug. 22, 1917, R.G. 280, National Archives, Suitland, Md.

24. *Iron Trade Review,* 61 (Dec. 6, 1917), 1227.

25. Federal Mediation, File 33/519, 33/817; *Bridgeport Evening Farmer,* July 13, Aug. 24, 25, 1917; "Transcript of Munitions Conference," Box 47, K101, R.G. 30, Connecticut State Library.

26. *Bridgeport Labor Leader,* Apr. 4, 1918.

27. *Iron Age,* 101 (Jan. 10, 1918), 174, and 101 (Jan. 17, 1918), 217; Military Intelligence, Entry 142, Box 1, Feb. 9, 1918; *Bridgeport Telegram,* Mar. 30, 1918; *Bridgeport Times,* Feb. 20, Apr. 9, 1918; *Bridgeport Labor Leader,* Feb. 21, May 23, July 7, 1918.

28. Transcript Case 132, pp. 85–86, National War Labor Board, R.G. 2, National Archives, Suitland, Md.; *Bridgeport Post,* June 27, 1918; *Bridgeport Times,* May 6, 9, 13, 1918.

29. *Bridgeport Labor Leader,* May 9, 1918.

30. Transcript Case 132, p. 900, National War Labor Board.

31. "Strong Plea for Permanent Adjustment," *Iron Age*, 102 (Aug. 8, 1918), 132.

32. Particular points in employer testimony and union arguments are in Transcript Case 132, pp. 20–28, 261, 833, National War Labor Board. Also see Military Intelligence, Entry 141, Box 1, July 23, 1918.

33. Banit, "War Machine," pp. 55–68; *Bridgeport Post*, Feb. 10, 11, Mar. 2, June 4, Aug. 16, 1918; Henry M. Wriston, *Report of the Connecticut State Council of Defense* (Hartford, 1919), pp. 70–94; "Springfield and Bridgeport," *New Republic*, 16 (Sept. 14, 1918), 185–86. A copy of the City Council ordinance is in Connecticut Council of Defense, Box 46, File K18.

34. Bing, *Wartime Strikes*, pp. 73–81; National War Labor Board, "Findings in re employers v. employees in munitions and related trades, Bridgeport, Connecticut," Transcript Case 132. For the national IAM view of the Bridgeport situation, see *Machinists' Monthly Journal*, 30 (Aug. 1918), 764–66.

35. *Bridgeport Sunday Herald*, Sept. 1, 1918.

36. National War Labor Board, Transcript Case 132, Box 20.

37. *Sunday Herald*, Sept. 8, 1918.

38. "Investigation of Night Workers," Connecticut Council of Defense.

39. Lavit and his supporters within the IAM, in the wake of the September 1918 defeat, shed their neutral political stance and became openly critical of the government and the national IAM leadership. They formed an American Labor party to run IAM activists in that fall's municipal elections. This attempt rankled the Bridgeport Socialist party, which also ran candidates, and the Central Labor Council, dominated by the Socialist party, refused to endorse the IAM effort. The IAM did poorly, with 2 percent of the vote; the Socialist party received 4 percent. James Weinstein, *The Decline of Socialism in America, 1912–1925* (New York, 1967), p. 222n.

40. National War Labor Board, Case 132, Box 21; *Bridgeport Sunday Herald*, Sept. 15, 1918; *Bridgeport Labor Leader*, Oct. 3, 24, 1918; Military Intelligence, Entry 142, Box 1.

41. *Bridgeport Sunday Herald*, Mar. 30, 1919; *Connecticut Labor Press*, Mar. 29, 1919; "In the Name of Right and Justice," *Suffragist*, 7 (Jan. 25, 1919), 8–9.

42. *Bridgeport Sunday Herald*, July 20, 27, 1919; *Bridgeport Labor Leader*, July 24, 31, 1919.

43. *Bridgeport Sunday Herald*, Aug. 10, 1919.

44. Ibid., July 27, Aug. 3, 31, Sept. 14, 1919; *Connecticut Labor Press*, Apr. 5, June 14, Aug. 23, 30, Oct. 4, 1919; *Machinists' Monthly Journal*, 31 (Sept. 1919), 853, and 31 (Oct. 1919), 953; *Bridgeport Labor Leader*, Sept. 25, 1919; *Progressive Labor News* (Bridgeport), Mar. 18, 1920. Lavit remained in Bridgeport, and in the late 1920s he became active in liberal Republican party circles. He declined a mayoral nomination from the Republicans in 1950. He died in 1958. *Bridgeport Post*, Dec. 18, 1958 (obituary).

PART THREE

FAMILY

Working Men and Women Inside and Outside the Family

Winslow Homer's *Mending the Tears*, Etching, ca. 1891.
Courtesy of The Brooklyn Museum.

CHAPTER 6

The Transformation of Family and Community Culture in Immigrant Neighborhoods, 1900–1940

JUDITH E. SMITH

Family relationships were at the center of the culture of reciprocity that was a characteristic of immigrant communities in the early twentieth century. The primary familial obligation to give and receive assistance was the model for cooperation (and a major source of strain) within extended families, immigrant neighborhoods, and local immigrant institutions.[1] But family relationships were not static; the contextual meaning of *family* was continually evolving. Defining the particular obligations of household members to each other and to households within larger networks of kinship exchange was a constantly shifting process of negotiation, subject to the dictates of regional custom, demographic pressures, and historical change. In late nineteenth-century southern Italy and eastern Europe norms of familial interaction were in flux. Increased economic vulnerability not only drew kin into greater involvement with each other but also undermined the acquisition of resources to stabilize family interests. Immigration accomplished the goal of family preservation through its short-term dissolution; migration placed kin in American cities in new configurations of distance and proximity and, in doing so, redefined the kinds of assistance kin needed and could ask from one another. The social and economic context of life in the United States and the developmental cycle of families and communities in process of settlement renegotiated patterns of dependency and exchange.[2]

Tracing the changes in work, residence, and association of southern Italian and Jewish immigrant families in two Providence, Rhode Island, neighborhoods over two generations through censuses, oral histories, and local records, we can observe the transformation of family relationships and its reverberation through community life. In the early twentieth century Providence's expanding commercial and industrial economy accommodated a range of immigrant economic orientations. Residential expansion, which had moved Irish working-class families to new areas, left Federal Hill tenements available to house arriving Italians, and Smith Hill triple-deckers for eastern European Jewish families.[3] Families consolidated ethnic networks in workplaces and neighborhoods, and for a transitional period an ethic of familial reciprocity extended beyond individual households throughout the community. Boundaries between households were blurred as kin in Providence became neighbors and neighbors and friends from the old country acted like kin. Sharing language and the trauma of relocation made neighbors in immigrant settlements include each other in familial exchanges of assistance; according to personal testimony, neighbors always stood ready to help. Mutual benefit associations formalized broadened patterns of assistance and contributed to an atmosphere that supported the public expression of the values of solidarity and reciprocity. But changes in family life, in the orientation and class composition of the ethnic communities, and in Providence's occupational structure and residential geography meant that by 1940 kin reciprocity was no longer the dominant community ethos. The conditions that nourished the expansion of reciprocity and those that led to its contraction are the subject of this article.

The regions of Europe that would lose a large segment of their population to immigration were diverse in economic structure. What they shared in the closing years of the nineteenth century was the experience of being drawn into more complex market relations. The increased involvement of southern Italian and eastern European Jewish family members in a cash economy made individual family members more vulnerable economically. Subject to these pressures, each family made its own way by combining a variety of different sources of income. Small landholders in the south of Italy joined day laborers in becoming increasingly dependent on the combined labor of all family members. Commercialization of agriculture in other parts of Italy diminished the productivity of the small plots of land in the south. The tradition of partible inheritance and the role of land in marriage settlements increased the fragmentation of landholdings. Even landowning families had to trade some of their labor for wages.[4] The relocation of Jews into small cities and towns in restricted areas of Russia and Poland (the Pale) forced Jewish artisans and traders into intense competition with one another. The introduction of modern industrial tools elsewhere in the northwest provinces of the Russian empire depressed artisan production. Jewish craftsmen and peddlers were displaced as railroads brought factory goods from industrial centers deeper into eastern Europe. Seasonal unemployment and frequent periods of poverty resulted. All during the last part of the nineteenth century, the economic position of the Jews in the Pale deteriorated at the same time that their numbers increased. Jewish families, too, became increasingly dependent on a combination of sources of income.[5]

Families also looked to an enlarged network of kinship ties outside the household for help in dealing with the cash and wage nexus of the new economy. According to the research of Josef Barton in southern Italy, kin ties replaced crumbling village ties during the 1880s, and broadened practices of dowry and donation bound families in circles of assistance. Barton claimed that the increased economic importance of kinship ties was not "preindustrial or traditional" but an innovative response of the rural poor to the new uncertainties of their village economies.[6] Migration forced by settlement laws in eastern Europe may have set a similar process in motion.

The resources of family and kinship networks may have thus become more important because of increasing economic insecurity. But uncertain market relationships also contained the potential to realign family configurations. For example, a study of inheritance patterns in Potenza in Basilicata found that as supplementary resources became more necessary and numerous for families, a shift from inheritance only to sons toward inheritance to both sons and daughters took place.[7]

Orderly marriage arrangements, which preserved and extended family groups through the transmission of property, were particularly vulnerable to economic shifts. Emigration was sometimes directly linked to the disruption of customary marriage provisions, as revealed in a story by novelist Mario Puzo about the migration of his mother from the hills near Naples to New York City: "There had come a time when her father, with stern pity, had told her, his favorite daughter, that she could not hope for bridal linen. The farm was too poor. There were debts. Life promised to be even harder. . . . In that moment she lost all respect for her father, for her home, for her country. A bride without linen was shameful . . . what man would take a woman with the stigma of hopeless poverty?" It was at that moment when her father told her that the family could not afford her bridal linen that Puzo's mother decided to emigrate to America to marry her first husband, a man she barely knew. Many other immigrant women told Women's Bureau investigators that they, too, risked the journey across the ocean for "a chance for girls to work and to marry."[8]

The severe economic constraints on Jewish families in the Pale similarly interfered with customary marriage provisions. For one Jewish family living in a town near Minsk, hard times had meant that a son who had hoped to study to be a rabbi instead earned his living as a tailor, and a daughter who had hoped to be trained as a seamstress worked as a domestic servant. When the son was forced to leave Russia to avoid conscription into the army, the mother who had been living with her son's wife and children realized that they would at some point join him in America, and so the possibility for her daughter to make a good marriage was dim: "Poor Masha . . . what is to become of her? Her chances had been small enough without a dowry. And now, burdened with an aged father and a blind helpless mother, the best she can expect is a middle-aged widower with a half-dozen children." Rather than accept such a situation, the mother sent her daughter to the United States, even though it meant sacrificing her own hopes for security in her dependency. When her son's family left to join him, she and her husband were alone.[9]

Emigration was most commonly a familistic response to the economic and social dislocation in southern Italy and eastern Europe. It was an intentional, self-selecting strategy that had particular appeal in areas dominated by household production. In other areas in central Italy, for example, where improved transportation, expanding markets, and capital-intensive farming had led to some modernization of agriculture, cultivators who worked in large groups in vast estates turned to political and trade union organization to better their condition. Many Italian families initially conceived of emigration as a way of reaching out to distant job opportunities to supplement the family income. Individual economic goals for migration were inextricably connected to survival strategies for family groups. Emigration was for Jewish families a similar attempt to take advantage of less circumscribed economic opportunity.[10]

The bonds of kinship often provided a basis for chain migration linking communities in Europe to communities in the United States. The resources of family and kinship networks were invaluable in facilitating the actual migration process. Cousins wrote to cousins still in Europe, describing what they found in the United States. Family and kin often provided the financial means for migration, and both men and women guided their kin to specific locations, employment, and housing; uncles, sisters, brothers, daughters all wrote to urge other family members to join them in American cities.[11]

Though immigrants were likely to be dependent in these ways on family connections, the experience of migration disrupted family relationships. Many families did not relocate completely, and family members often emigrated at different times. A common separation was that between husband and wife. These separations of varying duration could exacerbate divisions within a family. According to a Sicilian folk song, men had great concern over the conduct of their wives in their absence:

> The wives of the Americans [emigrants]
> Eat and drink like dogs.
> They go to church and pray to God:
> "Send me money, my husband,
> For if you do not send me money,
> I will change your name
> and christen you Pasquale." [cuckold]

In actuality, wives were often anxious to end the separations. One Italian immigrant explained that her husband had made two previous trips to America, but when he wanted to make his third trip, she refused to let him go alone: as she said to him, "Nothing doing, we all go or we all stay." When he argued that they could not afford passage for all to migrate, his wife turned for assistance to her father who was a landowner. He was able to give them a piece of land to sell, and the family made the third and final trip to America together.[12]

Sometimes separations caused by migration grew out of existing tensions in the household. One Jewish immigrant remembered that his parents "did not get along very well. They never agreed." He was a small boy when his father left for America, so he did not understand the roots of the quarrel between his parents. However, he was able to observe the shift in parental authority made possible by his father's absence. Before the father migrated, he was "the boss of the house." It was after the father left for America that "we got the business and mother took care of it." In other families men and women were divided by their response to the opportunity for migration. Varying expectations set one Italian husband and wife against each other. In their daughter's words: "In them days, lots of people was coming over here, and my mother makes up her mind she wants to come here too. My father says, no, I'm all right here, I work on my little farm and I get by pretty good. But you know my mother, she makes up her mind, and she told my father, if you no go, I go, see." The daughter stayed behind with her father while her mother and sister left for America. Parents and children were frequently divided by their willingness or reluctance to uproot themselves. One Italian immigrant tried to persuade his parents to join him and his brother in this country, but they refused the money for the journey. They were both in their sixties, and perhaps they "figure they are too old to come here now." Even knowing they would probably live and die apart from their sons, the parents did not want to leave southern Italy: "My father own his farm and he is satisfied with what he got."[13]

Because marriage meant that men and women were involved in two sets of kin relationships, immigrants often had to choose between them. One Jewish immigrant woman explained the process by which her entire family settled in America and her husband left all of his kin in Russia. Her uncle and oldest brother were the first to leave, and they sent for family members to join them, one by one. At some point, all the men in her family decided to emigrate, planning to send for their families and younger brothers and sisters as soon as possible. Her father, realizing that her whole family would be reunited in America while she was still in Russia, asked her husband to join the group of men. His decision was difficult, as she remembered: "Although my husband did not like his work as a shoemaker, he hesitated about going to America, probably because it would mean leaving behind all of his people." The only one who could make such a hard choice was someone outside the family, and so the husband asked his mother-in-law to speak to the rabbi, and the rabbi advised him to go. In 1914 all of the men in her family and two of her sisters left for America. Frequently immigration meant permanent separation from parents. One Jewish immigrant had lived near her own mother in Russia after her marriage, but emigration meant that she left her mother "as one leaves the dead," for she came to America and her mother died without ever seeing her daughter again.[14] Almost by definition, then, the process of immigration built on ties of kinship and at the same time broke apart family connections.

The ways in which immigration involved both heightened connection with kin and also loss of contact with relatives defined the distinctive shape of kin networks of immigrants in Providence. Because immigration was a family strategy so often facilitated by kin connections, many of the immigrants who came to Providence had relatives there. Sixty-nine percent of the Italian families and 42 percent of the Jewish families in the neighborhoods studied had parents or in-laws, brothers or sisters in Providence.[15] Jewish families, likely to have been separated from kin in eastern Europe by settlement laws, were less likely than Italians to have kin in Providence.

But because of the ways in which immigration separated family members and because of separations already endured by Jews in eastern Europe, kin networks of immigrants were rarely completely reconstituted in Providence (Table 1). Families almost never had both sets of parents or all of their brothers and sisters in Providence. But because of their common needs as strangers in a new land, those families with kin in Providence were quite likely to live with them at some point. Kin networks, which rarely expanded into residence in Europe, did so frequently in Providence.[16] Combination of households or very close proximity between them might have compensated in part for incomplete family groups.

Table 1. Incomplete Kin Networks in Providence
(Date of Arrival to 1915)

Type of Kin Relationships of Heads of Household	Italians	Jews
Immigrant men with parents in Providence	14% (23)	13% (9)
Immigrant women with parents in Providence	30% (48)	14% (10)
Immigrant men with siblings in Providence	39% (63)	22% (16)
Immigrant women with siblings in Providence	40% (64)	19% (14)

Type of Kin Relationships of Immigrants with Kin in Providence	Italians	Jews
Families with siblings and/or siblings-in-law	33% (37)	33% (10)
Families with parents and/or parents-in-law	5% (6)	4% (1)
Families with both siblings and parents	49% (54)	53% (16)
Families with other kin	13% (14)	10% (3)
	100% (111)	100% (30)

Source: Neighborhood data collected from Rhode Island state censuses, city directories, and vital records (in author's possession).

Immigrants were most likely to have siblings in Providence, and brothers and sisters, who would have been extremely unlikely to live under the same roof in southern Italy or in eastern Europe, commonly shared living space. In crises and in ordinary times, living around the corner or on another floor of a triple-decker tenement made it easier for families to offer assistance to one another. Three young Italian immigrant sisters who lived with their husbands in a tenement house in Federal Hill found many ways in which their parallel life situations and the forced intimacy of their crowded housing could work to their advantage, as one of their daughters described: "Then the babies started arriving. The three women would share the housework and motherly duties. . . . The sisters bore their children almost at the same time, and often there was more than one baby crying and fussing. There was so much closeness among the growing family that whenever a small baby began to cry, whatever mother happened to be around, would pick up the child and breast feed it, whether it was hers or not."[17] In this way, women immigrants partic-

ularly benefited from having relatives nearby and may have taken
an active role in encouraging and organizing residential kin networks.[18]

Thus, for immigrant families in the ethnically homogeneous sample neighborhoods, kinship networks were woven through the
neighborhoods. Most of the immigrants with kin in Providence had
relatives living near enough to meet every day to exchange news,
meals, and child care, to travel to work or fraternal association meetings together. Between 1900 and 1935, 71 percent of the Italians
and 53 percent of the Jews with kin in Providence had at least one
relative living at the same address. Ninety-two percent of the Italians
and 87 percent of the Jewish families with kin in Providence were
related to at least one other household within two blocks of where
they lived. Within the Italian neighborhood, neighbors from the
same region were also likely to be kin. Of the 67 percent of the
Italian immigrants in the neighborhood for whom town or region
was recorded, all those from the same town who lived in the same
triple-decker or next door were also related by blood or marriage.

When parents or brothers and sisters were left behind in Europe,
relatives and friends in Providence attempted to substitute for missing family members. Brothers and sisters assumed the responsibility
of absent parents to supervise courtship or finances for younger or
newer immigrants and sometimes stepped in to raise orphaned children. Neighbors from the old country who had already come to
Providence also assumed some of the responsibilities of kin: they
served as a wider circle of assistance for those with only one or two
close relatives to draw on; they provided room and board for those
without family. If boarders were not already relatives, they were often friends from the old country. New neighbors in Providence,
likely to be from the same ethnic group, also provided assistance.
They responded in household emergencies and in times of real
need. A young Italian woman who had only one sister in Providence
depended on her neighbors for help during childbirth: "The neighbors pitched in, and cooked and cleaned for each other at these
times. We Italians say, 'One hand washes the other.' " When her
husband died, again the neighbors came to her assistance: "not with
money, but with companionship, advice (sometimes too much advice), and tending the children. . . . Looking back, I know I
couldn't have survived those first years without my friends and
neighbors."[19] In Providence, then, immigrants compensated for the
disruptions of migration in two ways. Kin became neighbors, and
neighbors acted as kin. The result was to blur the boundaries between households and the distinction between kin and neighbor.

Working conditions in Providence reinforced the development of new connections between households.[20] Families depended on kin for help in finding employment. The economic constraints that Italians and Jews had faced in Europe had made family cooperation a critical strategy for survival, but at the same time the small size of fields in southern Italy and the overcrowded market competition in towns in the Pale had discouraged the formation of work groups larger than one household. But in Providence the recruitment structures of the factories and the entrepreneurial opportunities in the immigrant neighborhoods were amenable to extended family networks at work. The factory foreman's control over hiring made it relatively easy for immigrants to get jobs for one another. Men offered to speak to their foremen for newly arrived brothers, and if there was work, the brother usually got it. Sisters did the same for younger sisters. As immigrants themselves moved into positions with responsibility for hiring, the possibilities were expanded for working with other family members. Although the factories were new work places for southern Italians, and generally larger in scale and more modern in machinery than shops where Jews may have worked in Russia, immigrants made the factories more familiar by working in them with their kin.[21] Over half of the Italian factory workers in the neighborhood sample who had brothers in Providence worked with them in jewelry shops and textile mills (Table 2).

The needs of immigrants for goods and services guaranteed a neighborhood market for artisans and shopkeepers. The artisan tradition in southern Italy and eastern Europe, where fathers taught sons their crafts and passed down the tools of their trades, meant that artisans arriving in Providence with brothers may have shared the same kind of work. These small proprietors also would have had the opportunity to employ brothers or sisters. Half of the Italian barbers, tailors, and shoemakers in the neighborhood who had brothers in Providence worked at the same trade. This was also true for three-fourths of the bakers, watchmakers, and stonecutters. The commercial expertise accumulated by families in Russia meant that small retail proprietors might have also taken up the same line of business as their brothers. Junk dealers, winesellers, poultry dealers, and butchers in the Jewish neighborhood had brothers in the same occupation (Table 2).

The connections among families that ran through neighborhoods and workplaces were articulated on a community-wide basis through the extensive organization of mutual benefit associations in Providence. The principles of mutual support and reciprocal obligation that governed family relations also bound together non-kin in these

Table 2. Kin Connections at Work among Male Italians and Jews in
Providence, 1915–35

	Percentage/Number of Men in Occupation		Percentage/Number of Men in Same Occupation as Brother[a]	
Occupation	Italians	Jews	Italians	Jews
Laborer	19% (30)	0	4% (1)	0
Factory operative	17% (27)	4% (3)	55% (6)	0
Skilled	6% (9)	0	33% (2)	0
Craft, artisan employee	14% (22)	10% (7)	63% (7)	0
Retail employee	11.5% (18)	30% (21)	50% (2)	33% (3)
Craft, artisan self-employed	19% (30)	6% (4)	56% (9)	0
Retail self-employed	11.5% (18)	41% (29)	50% (8)	80% (8)
Professional	2% (3)	9% (6)	0	0
Total	100% (157)	100% (70)		

Source: Neighborhood data collected from Rhode Island state censuses, city directories, and vital records (in author's possession).
[a]That is, of men who have brothers in Providence.

associations. Through the collection of weekly or monthly assessments, which were then paid out as sick and death benefits, mutual benefit associations formalized the obligation normally limited to kin to give assistance, to accept assistance, and to repay assistance rendered. By participating in this kind of exchange, members of mutual benefit societies accepted the responsibility to help people who had helped them.[22]

This form of organization had spread through Europe on the eve of migration as a communal response to the economic and social transformations unsettling village life.[23] Smallholders and artisans enlarged the resources of kinship networks by organizing mutual aid associations. The tradition of such organizations among artisans and small proprietors extended back to the late Middle Ages and early modern period.[24] In the second half of the nineteenth century, changes in the local economy, which undermined ordinary family arrangements, prompted villagers to revitalize and expand this familiar form. In Palermo, Sicily, there were nine such organizations in the 1860s, including groups of fruit vendors, agricultural workers, and master shoemakers. By 1885 there were 106 such societies in Palermo province. Similarly, extensive organizational efforts took root in Potenza, Basilicata, as early as 1870. Emigration affected the membership of these societies in southern Italy, but even as late as 1917 there were still 259 such organizations in the province of Messina, Sicily.[25]

Societies themselves used the metaphor of familial assistance to describe their purpose. A workers' society organized in Villarosa, Sicily, in 1888 explained its goal: "The union and fellowship of all the working classes in order to unite finally into a single family, so that they can reciprocally succor each other materially and morally."[26] These societies engaged in educational self-help activities, organized producer and consumer cooperatives, and provided sick and death benefits for members. Societies often reflected the occupational divisions in the area. In some areas there were two local societies, one for town workers who saw themselves as bound by common entrepreneurial interests, and one for agricultural workers.[27]

In eastern Europe men in the same craft had formed *chevroth* to meet the religious prescription that at least ten adult men must pray and read the Torah together at the beginning and end of each day. Mutual obligations of members began with the collective purchase of Torah scrolls and expanded to include religious duties of staying all night with sick members and of participating in special services for the dead. Because of the increasing economic uncertainty Jews faced in the second half of the nineteenth century, these mutual obligations extended naturally into a collection of dues for the provision of sick and death benefits. As working conditions deteriorated and competition for work intensified, some *chevroth* began to split into separate organizations of master craftsmen and workingmen. In Mogilev, a city in the northwest provinces of the Pale, there were separate *chevroth* for ladies' tailors, carpenters, dyers, and stove builders, and joint *chevroth* for shoemakers, jewelers and watchmakers, tinworkers, roofers, and locksmiths. The workingmen's *chevroth* often acted as unions, negotiating for hours and wages.[28]

Mutual benefit associations also proved to be effective in extending the resources of hard-pressed immigrant families in American cities. In Providence each society drew friends and neighborhoods into wider circles of mutual assistance. Ethnic solidarity within the associations mirrored the interdependency of the family economy.

Fraternal social relations within these organizations echoed the expansive direction and particularly the sibling orientation of immigrant kin networks. As self-generated institutions, mutual benefit associations embodied the familial culture of the immigrant community.

By 1919, 100 Italian and nearly 100 Jewish mutual benefit societies, frequently organized along provincial lines, existed in Providence. Ordinarily the societies made payments to sick or unemployed members, provided burial plots, and paid for the band and other funeral expenses of members and their families. Italian societies sponsored annual feast days in honor of their patron saints. Some groups of Jewish immigrants organized themselves into congregations for religious worship, while groups of tailors, shoemakers, cigarmakers, and junk peddlers established workingmen's associations.[29]

Mutual benefit associations functioned as extensions of kin ties and as a community parallel to kinship networks. Since family-based migration chains were often the underpinnings of village chains,[30] family connections were interwoven with village loyalties in the societies. Evidence from immigrants to various northeastern cities suggested the range of family and family-like affiliations in mutual benefit societies. One immigrant to Boston described the actual overlap of regional, occupational, and family ties in a society to which he belonged:

> It was an association formed by all the people who were [tool] grinders from this area [in Italy]. It was sort of like a trust association where they would meet and have dues and if somebody would lose a husband they would give expenses for the funeral. Also it was like a union because you wouldn't take another person's customers. You would sell customers to another person. Respect for one another, in other words, and since they were all related, it was like a family organization. . . . They used to talk about different peoples' routes, sort of try to patch up disagreements and arguments. . . . When somebody would die, the women would go in and cook in the home and care for the kids and the men are usually the pallbearers at the funeral because they are relatives, too, at the same time.[31]

For a Jewish immigrant to New Haven, mutual benefit members substituted for absent family; he discovered people in his society who had been his playmates in his old village and whose parents had been friends of his parents. He described his association meetings as "like a family gathering." A Jewish immigrant who had come from Lithuania to New Haven without his family felt that his contact with other Lithuanians at mutual benefit society meetings was a "family reunion" of substitute kin.[32]

Rooted in provincial loyalties, mutual benefit associations functioned to sustain regional traditions of Italian folk Catholicism and Jewish orthodoxy. In Providence conflict between eastern European Jews and German Jews or between Polish and Rumanian Jews over the language or ritual of religious services was diffused by the institution of autonomous congregations. Autonomy was not available to southern Italians, whose practice of Catholicism conflicted sharply with the religious principles held by the Irish church hierarchy and the northern Italian priests who headed the Italian language parishes in Providence.[33] Mutual benefit associations played a vital role in keeping alive an immigrant religious culture that provided an alternative to assimilation.

In 1906 mutual benefit societies wrote to the bishop to demand the removal of a priest who refused to acknowledge saints' days rituals. In 1907 several thousand Italians gathered to take the keys from their sexton in an attempt to close their church to protest their priest's opposition to a collection outside the church door for festa fireworks. In 1920 nearly 2,000 women petitioned the bishop for the removal of their priest because he had ignored mutual benefit societies and refused to hold special devotional services. Twelve mutual benefit committees also petitioned the church hierarchy at the same time to demand church leadership more sympathetic to their interests. When seven parishioners were arrested for disrupting a mass by shouting for their priest's resignation, other mutual benefit societies formed a committee of dissenting parishioners to defend the arrested people and to continue demanding acknowledgment of saint worship within the church. Finally in 1922 an acceptable priest was assigned to the parish.[34] In this case, mutual benefit societies defined what kind of Catholic ritual they would accept from the church and provided an organizational form that could be used to mobilize support for their particular practice of Catholicism.

As unskilled workers, many immigrants were excluded from the craft unionism dominant in the period, and for these workers mutual benefit associations provided the only protection against the economic uncertainties of urban and industrial life.[35] In specific instances mutual benefit associations could be mobilized to express class solidarity within the ethnic community. In Providence forty-seven Italian mutual benefit associations joined to organize a parade of more than 2,000 people in support of the 1912 textile strike in Lawrence, Massachusetts, and its imprisoned Italian leaders. According to the newspaper, "Practically every Italian organization [in the city] . . . had turned out." When police disrupted the parade by trying to seize the red flag carried by socialist demonstrators, a riot ensued in which six policemen were injured. The committee representing the mutual benefit associations issued a public statement in which they "laid full blame for the affair on the police."[36]

In the same way that they had settled into distinct neighborhoods, Providence immigrants tended to group themselves in certain trades, partly because of skills or work experience that they brought from the old country, partly because of reliance for their first job on kin and neighbors who had arrived earlier. Tight exclusionary controls exercised by skilled craftsmen combined with the preference of immigrants to work with others of their ethnic group meant that Italians and Jews were unevenly distributed in the city's occupational structure.[37] Because of a sizable concentration within the lowest ranks of the building trades, Italian building laborers were able to mobilize broad-based community support for their strike in 1910. They organized saints'-day type parades in the Italian neighborhoods, with music played by union musicians, followed by open-air meetings. They generated support for the strike by tapping already existing social networks. According to the newspaper: "[The Italian neighborhood] was alive with men, collarless, and in some cases, coatless, who gathered in street corners and discussed the situation. The room used by the strikers as headquarters was packed to its utmost capacity, while scores more gathered [in the street] . . . around the building in which their office is located."[38] The building laborers drew on the mutual benefit tradition, assuming community solidarity and mutuality as they exerted pressure on all Italians to support the strike:

> At a new factory building being built for the Bishop Company, [Italian] strikers interviewed the Italian foreman. The latter, who is gifted with a fine sense of humor, told the interviewers that they might go if they saw fit to a place which is a great deal warmer than Providence is at the present time. He counted without his hosts, however, for the latter simply lifted him off his feet and carried him on their shoulders to a position on the opposite side of the road where they initiated him, willy nilly, into the mysteries of their union. The foreman, Giuseppe by name, found a dollar which he did not need in his pocket, handed it over to the secretary of the union, and signed the roll of the organization. The men gave him three cheers, after which they escorted him to a city-bound car.[39]

The community support on which the strikers were able to draw was a crucial factor in their success.

The tradition of mutual benefit and the implicit assumption of reciprocal obligation also justified the application of collective sanctions against individuals who were seen as taking advantage of community support. When ethnic retailers substantially raised their prices, immigrants viewed such acts as an abandonment of the principles of community justice and particularly as a breach of reciprocity. An increase in the price of necessary commodities was an injury to a customer loyally patronizing his fellow countryman. Neighborhood customers expected special consideration in view of that patronage, and they were outraged when they were offered what they considered to be inflated costs. Jewish women "declared war against the kosher butchers" in 1910, and Italians destroyed the shop of a pasta wholesaler in 1914 to protest high prices. The Italian newspaper articulated the basis for the actions, justifying community claims on the grounds that such people "owe everything to our community."[40]

As the years in Providence turned into decades and immigrants who had arrived carrying babies found themselves the parents of adult men and women, the functions of family networks were altered. As the immigrants themselves aged and as their own children married and settled nearby, the patterns of mutual assistance between brothers and sisters, which had sustained the immigrant generation through the uncertainties of migration and resettlement, were replaced by expectations of aid between parents and married children. Most of the immigrants in the neighborhood sample settled married children in their own building or close by. In 1940, 60 percent of Italian families and 59 percent of Jewish families with married children had a married child living at the same address. Seventy-eight percent of Italian families and 71 percent of Jewish families had married children living within two blocks. With such close relations nearby, immigrants did not need other kin and neighbors as they had earlier. No longer missing members, the family networks of immigrants as they grew older were more likely to be vertical than horizontal, hierarchical rather than fraternal (Tables 3, 4).[41]

The faint boundary between kin and neighbor became more sharply defined as the Italian and Jewish communities spread out from the old ethnic neighborhoods over the city as a whole. This process of residential dispersion meant that kin were not as likely to be neighbors, nor neighbors as likely to be related. By 1940 fewer than half of the Italian families in the neighborhood and one-third of the Jewish families were still living in the areas they had settled as new immigrants. Although the immigrants, who had often left their own parents in Europe, were strikingly successful at settling at least one married child nearby, their other married children spread out over the city. The new residential neighborhoods to which im-

Table 3. Composition of Combined Residence among Italians and Jews in Providence, 1915 and 1940

Kin in Household	Italians 1915	Italians 1940	Jews 1915	Jews 1940
Siblings	51% (20)	8% (5)	40% (4)	8% (2)
Married children	8% (3)	82% (50)	20% (2)	80% (19)
Siblings and parents	18% (7)	5% (3)	30% (3)	0
Parents	15% (6)	0	10% (1)	0
Siblings and married children	0	1.6% (1)	0	8% (2)
Parents and married children	0	1.6% (1)	0	0
Other kin	8% (3)	1.6% (1)	0	4% (1)
Total	100% (39)	100 % (61)	100% (10)	100% (24)

Source: Neighborhood data collected from Rhode Island state censuses, city directories, and vital records (in author's possession.)
Note: Combined residence in 1915 = in same household or at same address; combined residence in 1940 = at same address.

Table 4. Networks among Jewish and Italian Adult Siblings in Providence, 1900–1940

Network Variables	Italians Immigrants	Italians First Generation	Jews Immigrants	Jews First Generation
Joint residence in building	49.3% (38)	20% (13)	58% (11)	24% (8)
Siblings within two blocks	36.3% (28)	43% (28)	32% (6)	30% (10)
Siblings elsewhere in Providence	14.3% (11)	37% (24)	10% (2)	46% (15)
Total number of families with siblings in Providence	100% (77)	100% (65)[a]	100% (19)	100% (33)[a]

Source: Neighborhood data collected from Rhode Island state censuses, city directories, and vital records (in author's possession.)
[a]This is the total number of families with two married children.

migrants and their children moved were less likely to be ethnically homogeneous than the original neighborhoods had been. Families in the new neighborhoods were less likely to have been neighbors in the old country, less likely to share a common past. For many families, residential dispersion continued a process whereby social needs and assistance were more likely to be absorbed within individual families in the interaction between parents and married children than by kin and neighbors. Moving away must have also served as a means of resolving some of the tensions that may have arisen inside kinship networks, given the fragile balance between reciprocity and betrayal. Residential dispersion transformed the community context that had supported and extended kinship networks.

Changing work patterns and shifting forms of voluntary association paralleled these alterations in kin and community life. The disappearance of old occupations and the creation of new ones in the 1920s and 1930s meant that parents could not effectively teach work skills to their children or arrange their employment. Structural economic change determined that the children of immigrants would work at white-collar occupations more often than their parents. In addition, the virtual disappearance of the self-employed craftsman, the decline of Rhode Island's industrial base, and the expansion of the sales and service sector meant that previous ethnic occupational concentrations in Providence were replaced by a broader diffusion of ethnic groups throughout the occupational structure.[42]

The mutual benefit tradition began to weaken by the 1920s and 1930s as the children of the immigrant generation came of age. Reflecting the widening gap between social and occupational experience of the immigrant and American-born generations, different kinds of associations claimed the loyalties of the young people. The children of immigrants preferred to belong to associations aimed at integrating ethnic with American culture rather than maintaining Old World traditions. The new organizations substituted social activities for economic cooperation, assuming a population more diverse in occupation and class than the immigrant generation had been.[43] The American generation preferred alternate forms of insurance developed by the state and corporate sector, whose policies protected individuals rather than families, to the economic benefit plans of the societies. Some mutual benefit associations continued to exist on a diminished scale, but the organizations that were increasingly prominent in the ethnic community were those substituting philanthropic for self-help assistance. No longer would ethnic community organizations represent the concerns of one neighborhood or one trade. Public expressions of ethnic culture and ethnic communal solidarity occurred with much less frequency in the decades of the 1920s and 1930s. By the 1930s mutual benefit associations had lost membership and visibility to citywide ethnic organizations with a varied occupational and cross-class constituency. The decline of these societies meant that the traditions of mutual support, reciprocal obligation, and economic self-help were no longer a dominant presence in community life.

For an important transitional period, family and kinship networks took on new functions, different from what they had been or would become. The expansion of kin networks, and particularly the sibling orientation, was resonant with the fraternal culture of solidarity emanating from the mutual benefit associations. As the repository of shared ethnic regional loyalties, mutual benefit associations facilitated the expression of the religious traditions of their Old World homes as an alternative to the established religious institutions of Providence. Building on ethnic concentrations within certain occupations, mutual benefit associations were sometimes mobilized to express class solidarity within the ethnic community. Ethnic labor organizations built on preexisting community networks, and the public expression of the values of solidarity and reciprocity justified at least two community boycotts.

Immigrant family experience and family values were thus at the core of an expansive reciprocal culture that took its shape amid overlapping networks of kinship and solidarity within workplaces, neighborhoods, and associational life. As immigrants aged, their Providence families expanded, and their neighborhoods dispersed, family networks lost the inclusive, particularly fraternal character they had assumed in earlier years, and the boundaries of family life became more sharply delineated. As the American generation created their own voluntary associations, the resultant waning of mutual benefit societies meant the decline of community institutions that had articulated the familial values of reciprocal assistance. By 1940 the public culture of reciprocity that had permeated immigrant community life had been narrowed to a private ethos of exchange, visible only inside individual families.

NOTES

I want to thank those who have read and criticized the ideas in this article: Donald Bell, Larry Blum, Howard Chudacoff, Maurine Greenwald, Louise Lamphere, Bruce Laurie, Elaine May, Barbara Melosh, Sonya Michel, Christina Simmons, and Jim Smith.

1. Reciprocity as a resource for poor people has been brillantly explored in the contemporary black community by Carol Stack in *All Our Kin: Strategies in a Black Community* (New York, 1974).

2. Recent works that have explored the importance of family networks in the immigration process include: Virginia Yans-McLaughlin, "Patterns of Work and Family Organization: Buffalo's Italians," *Journal of Interdisciplinary History*, 2 (1971), 299–314; Yans-McLaughlin, "A Flexible Tradition: Immigrant Families Confront New Work Experiences," *Journal of Social History*, 7 (1974), 429–45; Yans-McLaughlin, *Family and Community: Italian Immigrants in Buffalo, 1880–1930* (Ithaca, 1978); Tamara K. Hareven, "Family Time and Industrial Time: Family and Work in a Planned Corporation Town, 1900–1924," *Journal of Urban History*, 1 (1975), 365–89; Hareven, "The Laborers of Manchester, New Hampshire, 1912–1922: The Role of Family and Ethnicity in Adjustment to Industrial Life," *Labor History*, 14 (1975), 249–65; Hareven, "The Dynamics of Kin in an Industrial Community," in John Demos and Saranne Boocock, eds., *Turning Points* (Chicago, 1978), pp. S151–82; Hareven, *Family Time and Industrial Time* (Cambridge, 1982); Josef Barton, *Peasants and Strangers: Italians, Roumanians, and Slovaks in an American City, 1890–1950* (Cambridge, Mass., 1975); Barton, "Religion and Cultural Change in Czech Immigrant Communities, 1850–1920," in Randall M. Miller and Thomas D. Marzik, eds., *Immigrants and Religion in Urban America* (Philadelphia, 1977), pp. 3–24; Barton, "Eastern and Southern Europeans," in John Higham, ed., *Ethnic Leadership in America* (Baltimore, 1978), pp. 150–75; John Bodnar, Roger Simon, and Michael Weber, "Migration, Kinship, and Urban Adjustment: Blacks and Poles in Pittsburgh, 1900–1930," *Journal of American History*, 66 (1979), 548–65; Bodnar, Simon, and Weber, *Lives of Their Own: Blacks, Italians, and Poles in Pittsburgh, 1900–1960* (Urbana, 1982).

3. On Providence, see William G. McLoughlin, *Rhode Island: A Bicentennial History* (New York, 1978), pp. 164–94; Kurt Mayer, *Economic Development and Population Growth in Rhode Island* (Providence, 1953); Gary Kulik, introduction, in Kulik and Julia C. Bonham, *Rhode Island: An Inventory of Historic Engineering and Industrial Sites* (Washington, D.C., 1978), pp. 12–16, 21–25; Patrick T. Conley and Paul R. Campbell, *Providence: A Pictorial History* (Norfolk, 1982), pp. 99–178. On the two neighborhoods, see Rhode Island Historical Preservation Commission, *The West Side, Providence*, Statewide Preservation Report P-P-1 (Providence, 1976); Rhode Island Historical Preservation Commission, *Smith Hill, Providence*, Statewide Preservation Report P-P-4 (Providence, 1980).

4. Barton, *Peasants and Strangers*, pp. 27–47; Sydel Silverman, "Agricultural Organization, Social Structure and Values in Italy: Amoral Familism Reconsidered," *American Anthropologist*, 70 (1968), 11–15; J. S. MacDonald, "Agricultural Organization, Migration and Labor Militancy in Rural Italy," *Economic History Review*, 16 (1963), 68–70.

5. I. M. Rubinow, "The Economic Conditions of the Jews in Russia," in U.S. Congress, Senate, *Report of the Immigration Commission: Emigration Conditions in Europe*, 61st Cong., 3d Sess., Senate Document 748 (Washington,

D.C., 1911), pp. 287–334; Ezra Mendelsohn, *Class Struggle in the Pale: The Formative Years of the Jewish Workers' Movement in Tsarist Russia* (Cambridge, 1970), pp. 6–11; Henry Tobias, *The Jewish Bund in Russia from Its Origins to 1905* (Stanford, 1972), pp. 6–10; Marc Lee Raphael, *Jews and Judaism in a Midwestern Community: Columbus, Ohio, 1840–1975* (Columbus, 1979), pp. 96–101.

6. Josef Barton, quoted by David Montgomery, "Comments on Panel on Transfer and Change in the Formation of American Working-Class Culture," Social Science History Association, Ann Arbor, Mich., Oct. 1977. See also Barton, "Religion and Cultural Change," pp. 6–9; Barton, "Eastern and Southern Europeans," p. 154. E. N. Goody's research suggests how an increased incidence of god-parentage might link together kin through their common bonds with children in "Forms of Pro-parenthood: The Sharing and Substitution of Parental Roles," in Jack Goody, ed., *Kinship: Selected Readings* (Baltimore, 1971), p. 337.

7. J. Davis, "An Account of Rules for the Transmission of Property in Pisticci, 1814–1961," in Jean G. Peristiany, ed., *Mediterranean Family Structures* (New York, 1976), pp. 287–303, esp. p. 301.

8. Mario Puzo, *The Fortunate Pilgrim* (1964; reprint, New York, 1973), p. 13; Puzo, "Choosing a Dream: Italians in Hell's Kitchen," in Thomas C. Wheeler, ed., *The Immigrant Experience* (Baltimore, 1973), p. 45; U.S. Department of Labor, Women's Bureau, *The Immigrant Woman and Her Job*, bulletin no. 74 (1930; reprint, New York, 1970), p. 22.

9. Rose Cohen, *Out of the Shadow* (New York, 1918), pp. 29–33, 149, 192–93.

10. MacDonald, "Agricultural Organization," pp. 62, 58–70; Barton, *Peasants and Strangers*, pp. 27, 34–35; Simon Kuznets, "Immigration of Russian Jews to the United States: Background and Structure," *Perspectives in American History*, 9 (1975), 83–93, 100–112; Irving Howe, *The World of Our Fathers* (New York, 1976), pp. 24–29; Raphael, *Jews and Judaism*, pp. 95–99.

11. See John S. MacDonald and Leatrice D. MacDonald, "Chain Migration, Ethnic Neighborhood Formation, and Social Networks," *Milbank Memorial Fund Quarterly*, 42 (1964), 82–97, esp. 89–91; MacDonald and MacDonald, "Urbanization, Ethnic Groups and Social Segmentation," *Social Research*, 29 (1962), 432–48, esp. 439–40, 445–46; Barton, *Peasants and Strangers*, pp. 34–36, 38–40, 47; John Briggs, *An Italian Passage: Immigrants to Three American Cities, 1890–1930* (New Haven, 1978), pp. 75–86; Yans-McLaughlin, *Family and Community*, pp. 57–60. See also Max Horowitz, New Haven, a WPA Federal Writers' Project interview recorded in Connecticut in 1938–40 as part of the national project on ethnic and social life, collected at the University of Connecticut at Storrs as the Peoples of Connecticut Ethnic Heritage Project, Box 58, hereinafter cited as WPA-Conn. The project on ethnic and social life is briefly discussed in Jerre Mangione, *The Dream and the Deal: The Federal Writers' Project, 1935–43* (Boston, 1972), pp. 277–85. I am indebted to William D'Antonio for sharing these materials with me and also to Vaneeta D'Andrea and Laura Schwartz for helping to locate the interviews with Italians and Jews. These immigrants lived in the cities of

Hartford, New Haven, and Bridgeport rather than in Providence, but their experiences were common to many immigrants in eastern commercial and industrial cities. This man was probably interviewed by Rahel Mittelstein in 1939. He was born near Vilna, Russia, in 1868 and came to New York City in 1891. See also Samuel Postol, Bridgeport, WPA-Conn. (interviewed by Edward Reich in 1938; born in Nicolov, near Odessa, Russia, in 1875; to Bridgeport in 1905); Joseph Lazarro, Bridgeport, WPA-Conn., Box 23 (interviewed by Vincent Frazzetta in 1939; born in Naro, Argiento, Italy, in 1866; to Bridgeport in 1920).

12. Charlotte G. Chapman, *Milocca: A Sicilian Village* (1935; reprint, Cambridge, Mass., 1970), p. 108; Marie Zambiello, Bridgeport, WPA-Conn., Box 23 (interviewed by Emil Napolitano in 1939; born in Airola, Benevento, Italy, ca. 1867; to Bridgeport ca. 1903).

13. LR, New Haven, WPA-Conn., Box 58 (interviewed by Rahel Mittelstein in 1939; born in Spinowka near Kiev, Russia, ca. 1899; to New York City in 1924). MP, Bridgeport, WPA-Conn., Box 23 (interviewed by Emil Napolitano; born in Italy ca. 1900; to Providence in 1920); AT, Bridgeport, WPA-Conn., Box 23 (interviewed by William J. Burke in 1940; born in Italy in 1903; to Bridgeport in 1923).

14. KG, New Haven, WPA-Conn., Box 58 (interviewed by Rahel Mittelstein in 1939; born in Orlov, near Pobelov, White Russia, in 1891; to New Haven in 1921); Elizabeth G. Stern, *My Mother and I* (New York, 1922), pp. 155–56.

15. For this study, I traced families through vital statistics and city records from their first arrival in Providence until 1940. Kinship was determined through relationships defined in the 1915 census or as having the same parents as indicated on a marriage license or death certificate. The methods used to identify kinship relations for this study underestimated the actual number of immigrants with kin in Providence because these methods do not identify brothers or sisters of the male and female head of household who did not live in the census household in 1915 or who did not marry or die in Providence between 1880 and 1940; parents of women who did not live with their daughters in 1915 or whose daughters did not marry or die in Providence between 1880 and 1940; the parents of men who did not live with their sons in 1915 or die in Providence between 1880 and 1940; and other kin such as cousins, aunts, uncles, and nephews who did not live in the census household in 1915.

16. See Yans-McLaughlin, *Family and Community*, pp. 63–70. Donna Gabaccia has similarly argued that Sicilians in New York City turned their kin into neighbors, reversing the Sicilian process that had made neighbors the "real kin." See her "Sicilians in Space: Environmental Change and Family Geography," *Journal of Social History*, 16 (Winter 1982), 53–66; Gabaccia, *From Sicily to Elizabeth Street: Housing and Social Change among Italian Immigrants, 1880–1930* (Albany, 1983).

17. Rhode Island Women's Biography Project #400, hereinafter referred to as RIWB. Sharon Strom and several graduate students at the University of Rhode Island developed a women's history questionnaire, which she has

distributed as an assignment in her women's history course every year since 1974. The family histories resulting from this assignment have been collected as part of the RIWB at the University of Rhode Island. Strom gave me access to these materials before they were catalogued and pointed me toward particularly rich family histories. This woman was interviewed by a family member in 1976; she was born in Tova, Province di Piccilli, Italy, in 1894; she came to Providence in 1907.

18. Gabaccia, "Sicilians in Space," p. 59. See also S. Yanagisako, "Women-Centered Kin Networks in Urban Bilateral Kinship," *American Ethnologist, 5* (1977), 207–25.

19. An Italian Immigrant Woman—1920. This interview resulted from a project developed by Priscilla Long and her students at the Continuing Education Division, University of Rhode Island, in 1972. The women's history papers and tapes resulting from this project are collected at the Schlesinger Library, Radcliffe College, hereinafter referred to as the Long Coll. This interview is in Folder 7, Box 175. This woman was interviewed by a family member in 1972; she was born in southern Italy in 1896 and came to Providence ca. 1920.

20. John Bodnar, Roger Simon, and Michael Weber have analyzed the varying opportunities of different urban migrants to build family networks in the steel industry in Pittsburgh. Institutional racism made it difficult for black migrants to arrange employment for their children, a situation that shaped black families and black familial values differently than Polish families, who were very successful at bringing their children into positions in the mills. See Bodnar, Simon, and Weber, "Migration, Kinship, and Urban Adjustment," pp. 548–65; Bodnar, Simon, and Weber, *Lives of Their Own,* pp. 55–68.

21. On the connection between family and work, see George Huganir, "The Hosiery Looper in the Twentieth Century: A Study of Family Occupational Processes and Adaptation to Factory and Community Change, 1900–1950" (Ph.D. dissertation, University of Pennsylvania, 1958); Michael Anderson, *Family Structure in Nineteenth Century Lancashire* (Cambridge, 1971); McLaughlin, "Patterns of Work and Family Organization," pp. 299–324; Yans-McLaughlin, "A Flexible Tradition," pp. 429–45; Yans-McLaughlin, *Family and Community,* chs. 1, 6, 7; Hareven, "Family Time and Industrial Time," pp. 365–89; Hareven, "The Laborers of Manchester," pp. 249–65; Hareven, "The Dynamics of Kin," pp. S151–82; Hareven, *Family Time and Industrial Time,* chs. 5, 6, 9; John Bodnar, "Immigration and Modernization: The Case of Slavic Peasants in Industrial America," *Journal of Social History,* 10 (1976), 44–71; Bodnar, Simon, and Weber, "Migration, Kinship and Urban Adjustment," pp. 548–65; Bodnar, Simon, and Weber, *Lives of Their Own,* chs. 3, 4, 5.

22. On reciprocity, see Marcel Mauss, *The Gift: Forms and Functions of Exchange in Archaic Societies* (1954; reprint, New York, 1976); Alvin Gouldner, *For Sociology: Renewal and Critique in Sociology Today* (London, 1973), pp. 242–47; Stack, *All Our Kin,* chs. 3, 6. See also James D. Smith, "Whatever Else You Might Need: A Study of Reciprocity in the Social Networks of a

Community in Somerville, Massachusetts" (B. A. honors thesis, Harvard University, 1979), pp. 9–13.

23. Briggs, *An Italian Passage*, p. 16–18; Barton, *Peasants and Strangers,* pp. 64–65; Barton, "Eastern and Southern Europeans," pp. 154–55; Edwin Fenton, "Immigrants and Unions, a Case Study: Italians and American Labor, 1870–1920" (Ph.D. dissertation, Harvard University, 1957), pp. 28–29; Rubinow, "Economic Conditions of the Jews," pp. 309–10.

24. Mary Ann Clawson has argued that fraternal institutions were linked historically with an assertion of kinship as a significant social bond in "Brotherhood, Class and Patriarchy: Fraternalism in Europe and America" (Ph.D. dissertation, SUNY Stonybrook, 1980), ch. 1. In the early modern period, religious fraternities were organizations that "embodied the tradition of kinship and communal solidarity." See John Bossy, "The Counter-Reformation and the Peoples of Catholic Europe," *Past and Present,* 47 (1970), 51–70, esp. 59.

25. Briggs, *An Italian Passage*, pp. 17–18; Barton, *Peasants and Strangers,* p. 65; Phyllis Williams, *South Italian Folkways in Europe and America* (1938; reprint, New York, 1969), pp. 187–88.

26. *Statuto della società degli operai di Villarosa* (Castrogiovanni, 1888), quoted in Briggs, *An Italian Passage*, p. 22.

27. Briggs, *An Italian Passage*, pp. 18–36. See also Barton, *Peasants and Strangers,* pp. 66–68.

28. Rubinow, "Economic Conditions of the Jews," pp. 309–10, 322–24.

29. For information on Italian mutual benefit societies in Providence, see "Active Fraternal Life in Little Italy," *Providence Journal,* Dec. 21, 1919, S5, p. 5; and the following articles in the *Providence Evening Bulletin:* "Provincial Societies on the Wane But Still Active," Mar. 4, 1936, p. 15; "Mutual Benefit Prime Aim Organization," Mar. 6, 1936, p. 19; "Italian Provincial Groups Give Way to Nationalism," Mar. 16, 1936, p. 15; "Società Arcese Typical," Mar. 11, 1936, p. 16. For information on Jewish mutual benefit societies in Providence, see "Chartered Organizations," *Rhode Island Jewish Historical Notes,* 2 (1956), 21–78; Manya Kleinburd Baghdadi, "Community and the Providence Jews," *Rhode Island Jewish Historical Notes,* 6 (1971), 56–75, esp. 58.

30. MacDonald and MacDonald, "Urbanization, Ethnic Groups and Social Segmentation," pp. 445–46; MacDonald and MacDonald, "Chain Migration, Ethnic Neighborhood Formation, and Social Networks," pp. 82, 88–91; Yans-McLaughlin, *Family and Community,* pp. 57–60; Briggs, *An Italian Passage,* pp. 72–75.

31. JM, Somerville, Mass., interviewed by James D. Smith in Aug. 1978.

32. CS, New Haven, WPA-Conn., Box 58 (interviewed by Rahel Mittelstein[?] in 1940; born in Taurogin, Lithuania, in 1880; to New York in 1900). Wolfe Baron, New Haven, WPA-Conn., Box 58 (interviewed by Rahel Mittelstein[?] in 1939; born in Leipja, Lettwija [Lithuania], in 1879; to Connecticut in 1899).

33. For information on divisions between German and eastern European Jews, see Rhode Island Historical Preservation Commission, *South Providence*

Statewide Historical Preservation Report, P-P-2 (Providence, 1978), pp. 38–39; Rhode Island Historical Preservation Commission, *Smith Hill*, p. 11. For the appearance of regional congregations, see "Chartered Organizations," pp. 21–65. For information on regional conflict within the Catholic church, see Peter Bardaglio, "Italian Immigrants and the Catholic Church in Providence, Rhode Island, 1890–1930" (B.A. honors thesis, Brown University, 1975). See also Rudolf Vecoli, "Prelates and Peasants: Italian Immigrants and the Catholic Church," *Journal of Social History*, 2 (1969), 217–68; Vecoli, "Cult and Occult in Italian-American Culture: The Persistence of a Religious Heritage," in Miller and Marzik, eds., *Immigrants and Religion in Urban America*, pp. 25–47; Williams, *South Italian Folkways*, pp. 135–45.

34. Letters in the Providence Diocesan Archives, Holy Ghost Church, Correspondence/Documents, 1896–1911, 1887, 1918–21; Rev. Domenico Belliotti File, quoted in Bardaglio, "Italian Immigrants and the Catholic Church," pp. 85–107; and the following articles in the *Providence Journal:* "North End Italians Rise Against Priest," Aug. 26, 1907, p. 1; "Priest's Removal Believed Sought," Oct. 14, 1920, p. 4; "Police Make Seven Arrests at Church," Nov. 8, 1920, p. 3.

35. Stanley Aronowitz, *False Promises: The Shaping of Working-Class Consciousness* (New York, 1973), pp. 151–52.

36. "Paraders Fly Red Flag: Fight Police," *Providence Journal*, Sept. 16, 1912, p. 1.

37. Rhode Island Bureau of Industrial Statistics, *Twenty-Second Annual Report, 1908* (Providence, 1909), pp. 220–21, 224–25; Lester Burrell Shippee, "Some Aspects of the Population of Providence," in *Report of the Commissioner of Labor to the General Assembly for the Years 1916–1919* (Providence, 1920), pp. 227–28, 278.

38. For a general discussion of the struggle for unionization among unskilled Italian building laborers, see Fenton, "Immigrants and Unions," pp. 198–258, esp. pp. 219–57. In Providence, see the following articles in the *Providence Journal:* "1600 Building Laborers in Providence Quit," May 1, 1910, p. 1; "First May Day Celebration in Providence," May 2, 1910, p. 2; "Striking Laborers Fight with the Police," May 5, 1910, p. 1.

39. "Striking Laborers Fight with the Police," *Providence Journal*, May 5, 1910. See also Paul Buhle, "Italian-American Radicals and Labor in Rhode Island, 1905–1930," *Radical History Review*, 17 (1978), 121–51.

40. See the following articles in the *Providence Journal:* "Jewish Women Put Ban on Kosher Meat," June 22, 1910, p. 1; "Jewish Women Here Picket Kosher Shops," June 23, 1910, p. 1; "Federal Hill Mob Wrecks 4 Stores," Aug. 30, 1914, p. 1; "La Revolta!" *L'Ecco*, Sept. 5, 1914. My thanks to Paul Buhle for translating this editorial. These food riots are described in more detail in Judith E. Smith, "Our Own Kind: Family and Community Networks in Providence," *Radical History Review*, 17 (1978), 113–15. For a discussion of Jewish food riots in New York City in 1902, see Herbert Gutman, "Work, Culture and Society in Industrializing America, 1815–1919," in *Work, Culture and Society in Industrializing America: Essays in American Working-Class and Social History* (New York, 1977), pp. 61–63; Howe, *World of Our*

Fathers, pp. 124–25; Paula Hyman, "Immigrant Women and Consumer Protest: New York City Kosher Women's Meat Boycott of 1902," *American Jewish History* 70 (1980), 91–105. Elizabeth Ewen discusses the Jewish food riots in New York City in 1902 and 1917 in *Immigrant Women and the Land of Dollars, 1890–1930* (forthcoming). For an interpretation of food riots in eighteenth-century England, see E. P. Thompson, "The Moral Economy of the English Crowd in the Eighteenth Century," *Past and Present,* 50 (1971), 76–136. For a discussion of women's special relationship to bread riots, see Sheila Rowbotham, *Women, Resistance and Revolution: A History of Women and Revolution in the Modern World* (New York, 1972), pp. 102–4, and Louise A. Tilly and Joan W. Scott, *Women, Work, and Family* (New York, 1978), pp. 55–56; Olwen Hufton, "Women in Revolution, 1789–1796," *Past and Present* 53 (1971), 94–95.

41. John Briggs found this same tendency in the Italian community in Monroe County, New York, which he explained as "characteristic of an aging and increasingly stable community." Briggs, *An Italian Passage,* p. 112.

42. See Alfred DuPont Chandler, "The Beginnings of 'Big Business' in American Industry," in Stanley Katz and Stanley Kutler, eds., *New Perspectives on the American Past, 1877-Present* (Boston, 1969), pp. 3–31; Chandler, *Strategy and Structure* (Cambridge, Mass., 1962), pp. 19–51; Harry Braverman, *Labor and Monopoly Capital* (New York, 1974); Olivier Zunz, *The Changing Face of Inequality: Urbanization, Industrial Development and Immigrants in Detroit, 1880–1920* (Chicago, 1982), p. 8. On Rhode Island in the 1920s and 1930s, see Kulik, introduction, in Kulik and Bonham, *Rhode Island,* pp. 21–25; Mayer, *Economic Development and Population Growth,* pp. 49–59; Robert J. Paulis, "The Changing Rhode Island Industrial Base," *Rhode Island Business Quarterly,* 5 (1969), 1–9.

43. See the following articles in the *Evening Bulletin:* "Provincial Societies on the Wane But Still Active," Mar. 4, 1936, p. 15; "Italian Societies Broaden Membership," Mar. 15, 1936, p. 21; "Italian Provincial Groups Give Way to Nationalism," Mar. 16, 1936, p. 15; Beryl Segal, Providence, interviewed by Paul Buhle in 1977. Jewish family clubs organized in New York City demonstrated a similar historical progression from economic to social orientation. Eighty-one percent of the groups founded between 1908–18 gave equal emphasis to goals of family solidarity and economic aid, but only 53 percent of the clubs founded between 1928–38 gave equal emphasis to economic aid. Almost 40 percent of the clubs founded in the earlier period had burial benefits for members, but this decreased to only 14 percent for the groups founded in the 1920s and only 3 percent of the groups founded in the 1930s. See William E. Mitchell, *Mishpokhe: A Study of New York City Jewish Family Clubs* (The Hague, 1978), pp. 41–47. See also I. E. Rontch, ed., *Jewish Families and Family Circles of New York* (New York, 1939).

PART FOUR

CULTURE

Life-Styles and Practices Outside
the Workshop and Factory

Winslow Homer's *The Morning Bell. Harper's Weekly,* December 13, 1873.

CHAPTER 7

Dams, Fish, and Farmers: The Defense of Public Rights in Eighteenth-Century Rhode Island

GARY KULIK

I

In the late summer of 1839 Henry David Thoreau committed to his notebook a half-dozen lyrical pages on the coming of factories to the New England countryside. It was for him, as for his contemporaries, a familiar subject. Yet he chose to address it in an unconventional way. The occasion was his celebrated journey on the Concord River. He had come upon the Billerica dam, and he began to reflect upon the connections between factory dams and fish. "Salmon, shad and alewives were formerly abundant here," he wrote, "until the dam . . . and the factories at Lowell put an end to their migration hitherward."[1] Dams thwarted the instincts of anadromous fish—salt-water fish that annually spawned in the shallow headwaters of the region's rivers. Moved by their plight, Thoreau imagined a time "a thousand years hence" when "nature will have leveled the Billerica dam, and the factories at Lowell, and the Grass-ground river run clear again."[2] Yet as he further reflected on the ways in which human agency had so fundamentally altered the rhythms of nature, he could imagine a solution independent of nature. "Who knows," he asked, "what may avail a crow-bar against that . . . dam."[3]

Dams troubled not just fish, but farmers, too. New England farmers had long valued fish as an important source of protein, and river fish were free for the taking. Seventeenth-century writers had marveled at the numbers of fish that filled New England's rivers in the spring. Yet the numbers of migratory fish were decreasing—the decline was noticeable as early as the 1770s—and dams were the cause. In addition, dams raised water levels, and some flooded good farm land. All this provoked increasing resentment, and Thoreau gave voice to it when he wrote: "At length it would seem that the interests, not of the fishes only, but of the men of Wayland, of Sudbury, of Concord, demand the leveling of that dam."[4]

It was Thoreau's genius to evoke the passing of an eighteenth-century social order whose values were no longer resonant in his time in a language that seems to ring clearly in twentieth-century ears. More than most, Thoreau understood the costs of technical and economic progress, and the threat that a commercial and industrial order posed to the rural economy of antebellum New England. Yet his reflections on the unequal contest between dams and fish, between factory owners and farmers, had the quality of a personal lament. He gave no indication that he understood that the issue that so vexed him in 1839 had deep historical roots and had once troubled whole communities.

By the time Thoreau wrote, the issue had been essentially decided. The Atlantic salmon would soon disappear from the upper reaches of New England's rivers, not to reappear again until the 1980s, and then only in miniscule numbers. As early as the 1830s, cotton mill owners, the largest users of New England's waterpower, had effectively imposed their claims to the water against all competing users. Morton Horwitz and William Nelson, historians of the law, have analyzed the legal context. Changes in the law of water rights, Horwitz has argued, were at the center of a fundamental reinterpretation of eighteenth-century property law. Traditional definitions of ancient use and permissible injury came to be subordinated to a utilitarian legal calculus whose principal beneficiaries were the cotton mill owners of the early nineteenth century. Both Horwitz and Nelson based their arguments on court cases where mill owners interfered with the individual rights of other riparian proprietors. Both neglected to examine the conflict over fishing rights, which expressed itself, not as a defense of individual property rights, but as a defense of public rights; its arena was typically the legislature rather than the law courts. Yet contests over fishing rights unfolded in ways that confirm Horwitz's and Nelson's interpretations. The claims of unhindered economic development came to outweigh both the customary precepts of property law, discussed by Horwitz and Nelson, and the claims of public rights. The new legal dispensation made it increasingly permissible for large textile mill owners to flood upstream farm land, to disrupt and even injure the operation of smaller mills, sawmills, gristmills, and the like, and to obstruct migratory fish. Mill owners had not always had such license.[5]

For more than a century, New England farmers defended their entitlement to fish—through statute law, through petitions, through law suits, and, at least twice in Massachusetts, through the direct removal of offending dams. For the better part of the eighteenth century, they were successful. The owners of blast furnaces, the first capitalists in the countryside, were also the first to challenge the rights of farmers effectively. They did so most visibly in Rhode Island at mid-century. Cotton mill owners later continued the challenge, even more effectively and with more far-reaching consequences. Farmers, however, were far from passive. They believed that both law and custom were on their side. Fish were important to their economy, not principally as commodities to be bought and sold, but as food for their own consumption. Yet they were defending more than narrow economic interest. They were defending a deeply felt definition of the public good and a sense of the proper balance between public and private rights. The dams of large manufacturers seemed to threaten that balance, and in so doing threatened the independence of farmers. It was no accident that conflict over fishing rights intensified in the late 1760s and early 1770s. Drawing on the intellectual resources of the Whig oppositional tradition, New England farmers saw their rights to fish as emblems of a rural order delicately poised between economic individualism and public virtue.[6]

The growth of economic individualism and the decline of a corporate social order have been principal themes of New England's colonial history since the work of Perry Miller. Over the last fifteen years, a new generation of colonial historians has redefined this declension, largely in the language of modernization theory, and extended Miller's argument to cover not just religious thought but demography, material culture, political ideology, and the law. The work of Kenneth Lockridge, Daniel Scott Smith, James Deetz, and many others has made it more difficult to argue, as Louis Hartz once did, that America was liberal, capitalist, and individualist from its inception. Studies of the pace and extent of social change in early America have thus proliferated. But they constitute, as Michael Zuckerman has wryly argued, an "advancing embarrassment." There is no agreement on the scope, the timing, even the basic units of change. Did a "modern" America emerge in the 1660s, the 1690s, the 1720s, the era of the Revolution, or did important traditional forms persist even later? Are the keys to modernity to be found in the expansion of markets, in the Great Awakening, in the birth rate, in political ideology, in Georgian house forms, in gravestone markings, or in some combination of such, in a synthesis yet unwritten?[7]

In recent years a series of essays on the character of the early American rural economy has given a different form to these questions. At issue are the extent of commercial farming in the eighteenth and early nineteenth centuries and the relationship between the economy of rural America and the consciousness of its farmers. At a deeper level, the argument is over the rise of capitalism: how it should be defined and when it happened.

There are three general arguments. First, commercial farming was widespread in early America, and farmers were economic individualists intent on maximizing profit. This is the inheritance of Hartz, given recent support by Charles Grant and James Lemon. Second, commercial farming opportunities were limited, and subsistence farming was the norm, yet the entrepreneurial instincts of American farmers were only temporarily repressed. This is the position taken a generation ago by Percy Bidwell and John Falconer. Third, the farm economy was based neither on commercial markets nor on household subsistence, but on a combination of subsistence, local barter, communal labor (e.g., house-raising and husking bees), and limited market agriculture. In such an economy, economic individualism was hedged about by considerations of kin, community, and reciprocity. Variants of this argument, inspired by both recent anthropology and British Marxist history, have been advanced by Michael Merrill, James Henretta, and Christopher Clark, among others. Intent on revealing the contours of a precapitalist America, they have reopened a debate important to the understanding of social change in early America. However, they have not made their case in sufficient detail, nor with sufficient attention to time and space, to compel belief.[8]

This article, based on Rhode Island sources, brings new evidence to bear on the eighteenth-century rural economy, the consciousness of farmers, and the rise of capitalism. Definitions are in order. I understand capitalism to mean a system of production based upon wage labor, and as such distinct from that general constellation of economic forces—the growth of commerce, finance, and a market economy—conventionally subsumed under the rubric of commercial revolution. The interior communities of northern and western Rhode Island, where conflict over fishing rights was most pronounced, had economies that were neither capitalist nor strongly commercial. Backcountry farmers were not opposed to the introduction of blast furnaces—more had reservations about cotton mills—but they were insistent that manufacturers respect their rights. It was not simply that farmers had different economic interests, though they did. They were concerned with defending an economy, a polity, and a way of life at odds with the emergence of an industrial and capitalist America. To this extent, the evidence of this article lends support to the perspectives of Merrill, Clark, and company, though it does so by pointing in unexplored directions—to the impact of the American Revolution and of the anticapitalist strands of Country thought on the consciousness of backcountry farmers defending their rights to fish.[9]

II

All contests over water rights in Britain and America turned on questions of law. The social history of water-rights law in Britain remains to be written, but its general outlines are clear. No British subject had the right to obstruct the passage of migratory fish. The principle derived from the common law and had been expressed in the Magna Carta. Parliament reaffirmed it in 1285, again in 1384, three times during the fifteenth century, and again, and emphatically, in 1714 when it prohibited the construction of dams or weirs hindering the passage of salmon on seventeen British rivers. The principle was unambiguous. The public had the right to expect that Britain's stock of salmon, shad, and other anadromous fish would be perpetually replenished by the great spring fish runs. And in a largely agricultural economy that right took precedence over the rights of mill owners to exploit fully Britain's potential water-power.[10]

The legal remedy available to those whose rights were abridged was equally unambiguous. Under the common law, all river obstructions could be defined as public nuisances, which were subject to the summary remedies of the common law and could be removed at will. Appeals to local courts then followed; they did not precede removal. Thus an aggrieved individual had the common-law right to "enter the close of his neighbor, for the purpose of abating or removing the cause of injury."[11] Carefully phrased in the bloodless language of legal prose, the abatement of a public nuisance involved nothing less than the physical destruction of another's property. Those who destroyed their neighbor's dam might well be acting with the law of England on their side.[12]

Yet mill dams were rarely destroyed. England's medieval water mills, most of which ground grain, were too important. Processors of the pre-industrial harvest, many could trace their rights and privileges to the Domesday Book, while others were owned by powerful nobles or religious orders. They were important, however, less as distinct "industrial" enterprises of a type common to the nineteenth century than as integral elements of England's agricultural economy. The common law, itself the product of an overwhelmingly agrarian society, may have subordinated the rights of mill owners to the larger needs of agriculture, but it did not seriously disadvantage the owners of established mills. It did, however, effectively restrain the construction of new mills and the enlargement and intensified use of old mill sites. As long as the characteristic constraints of pre-industrial economies operated to limit mill owners' abilities to expand, the needs of mill owners and the common law remained in harmony. But as opportunities for industrial development increased in the eighteenth century, mill owners and their supporters would seek to modify the common law.[13]

The most direct way to do so was by statute. During the first half of the eighteenth century, Parliament passed 8 Anne c. 3 and 15 George II c. 6, both of which enhanced the legal security of mill owners. No longer would it be an offense to build a dam that obstructed fish, but rather to fail to provide a fish passageway. Moreover, the remedy would no longer be abatement, but a suit at law or a formal complaint to the appropriate political authority. As waterpower became more important, courts and legislatures had to accommodate the claims of mill owners. Yet they tried to do so in ways that acknowledged the public's interest in both water mills and fish.[14]

It was in this context that New Englanders first addressed the issue of competing claims to river use. New England's economy in the early eighteenth century was far less complex than its British counterpart, but the problem of balancing rights to waterpower with rights to fish was even more urgent, for New England needed mills. The work of grain millers, sawyers, and others who employed waterpower was critical to the region's farm economy. Some towns encouraged the construction of new mills through the use of bounties and land grants, while others treated mill dams as they did roads and considered their repair a public duty. Yet these same towns also sought to protect the public's right to fish. As the population of rural New England grew substantially during the first third of the eighteenth century, colonial legislatures found it necessary both to encourage and to regulate the construction of mill dams. They did so by enacting two distinct sets of statutes, the Mill Acts and the Fish Acts.[15]

Rhode Island passed its Mill Act in 1734, modeling it on the colonies' first, the Massachusetts Act of 1713. The Rhode Island act gave owners of water mills the right to build dams and flood upstream farm land "without any Molestation," subject only to the payment of court-assessed damages, in the form of an annual rent to those whose lands were flooded.[16] In effect, the act was a form of eminent domain, sanctioning the enforced loan of privately held land. The Rhode Island act comprised an exclusive remedy, prohibiting any common-law actions, whether for trespass or nuisance. A century later, New England cotton mill owners would interpret the Mill Acts to justify their intensive, private use of the region's water-power. Yet the acts were principally intended neither to free entrepreneurial energy nor to promote extensive economic development, but to draw a proper balance between public and private rights.[17]

The essential rights at stake were the rights of New England towns to attract and support the waterpowered mills necessary to their agricultural economies. To this end, towns were willing to sacrifice small tracts of upstream land. In most cases the loss was inconsequential, for the dams of grain millers and sawyers did not raise water levels substantially. Land was still plentiful, much of it was poor, and New England farmers did not practice a land-intensive agriculture. In cases where valuable land was threatened, however, the calculus of public interest could be quite different. When John Sawin's sawmill in Natick, Massachusetts, flooded good meadowland in 1720, neighboring townsmen ordered it moved to another site. Water mills were important, but they were expected to serve the needs of agriculture. New England towns did not conceive of their mills as independent commercial ventures, but as extensions of their farm economies, and they generally supported only as many as they actually needed. The Mill Acts clearly encouraged the growth of mills, but they provided no license for unhindered economic development.[18]

The encouragement the Mill Acts provided was further balanced by the restrictive character of New England's Fish Acts. Fish were an important source of protein for the region's farmers, and the great spring fish runs came just as stocks of food were running low after the long New England winters. More frequently envoked than the Mill Acts, the Fish Acts protected the rights of the public by regulating the building and operation of mill dams. In the interest of the rural economy, eighteenth-century mills might be allowed to flood upstream land, but they would not be permitted to obstruct the passage of migratory fish.[19]

Consider the laws Rhode Island legislators passed during the first half of the eighteenth century. In 1719, just five years after Britain's comprehensive effort to protect its salmon, the Rhode Island General Assembly approved an act "to preserve and improve the fishing of the [colony's] several rivers . . . and to prevent obstructions from being made to hinder the same."[20] More than one town had complained of dams obstructing the passage of fish—obstructions, in the language of the act, "prejudicial to the Inhabitants of Such Towns and Especially to the poor of the Neighborhood."[21] In response, the

assembly gave each town the power to remove dams and stipulated
that no dams restricting fish could be built without the permission
of the respective town. In 1735 the assembly went much further and
detailed the specific responsibilities of dam owners. It did so within
months of its passage of the Mill Act, attempting to balance encouragement with strict regulation. Under the new act, any mill owner
erecting a dam across water where migratory fish normally passed
had to provide a fishway during the spring runs, specifically from
April 10 to May 20, "annually, forever."[22] Complaints were to be
heard by local justices of the peace. Two deputies from Scituate, a
rural township in west-central Rhode Island, introduced the act to
protect large numbers of herring that customarily found their way
into "Moswansicut and other ponds in the western part of the Colony."[23] Drawing on the act, further regulations were formulated for
some of the more populous parts of southern Rhode Island—for
Point Judith Pond and the "Petaquamscut" River in 1736, for all of
South Kingstown in 1739, and for the Pawcatuck River in the southwest corner of the colony in 1742.[24]

The Fish Acts, and the petitions that led to their passage, expressed the belief of Rhode Island farmers that unregulated mill
dams threatened their right to fish. For mill owners, the colony's
streams were principally a source of power; for most farmers, they
were a source of sustenance. Such differences were bound to produce some measure of disagreement. Yet evidence of explicit conflict
between farmers and mill owners during the first third of the eighteenth century is rare. Grain millers or sawyers may have resented
the Fish Acts and the restrictions they imposed, but they seem to
have accepted them without public opposition.

In at least one instance, a family of mill owners freely accommodated the needs of farmers. In 1714 the Jenckes family of Pawtucket
Falls, proprietors of a forge and sawmill, granted William Arnold
and four others, along with "each and every" inhabitant of Rhode
Island and Massachusetts, the liberty to dig a channel on the west
side of the falls to serve as a fish passage. Pawtucket Falls, the colony's largest waterpower site, was approximately fourteen feet high.
Local residents recalled the sight of salmon struggling over it in a
series of fitful leaps. But smaller fish had no chance. Prior to 1714,
according to Pawtucket Falls' first historian, farmers had taken pains
to smooth the falls' jagged rocks "by battering down the projecting
points, that the fish, in the time of their running, might more easily
ascend."[25] A permanent fishway, however, seemed to offer a better
solution. The construction of Sargeant's Trench, as it came to be
known, was a measure of the importance farmers attached to fish.
Within a generation, though, the trench would become a source of

discord between farmers and mill owners and would remain such for almost a century. Yet it had its origins, not in conflict, but in cooperation.[26]

Conflict between farmers and mill owners in the early eighteenth century was rare for several reasons. Mill owners did not comprise a separate "industrial" interest, for much of what constituted industrial production in the eighteenth century—the grinding of grain, the sawing of wood, the fulling of woolen cloth—was closely tied to agriculture. Farmers and mill owners were thus integral parts of a single and largely undifferentiated economy, and most mill owners did at least some farming. Moreover, the work of mill owners was either seasonal or episodic. For grain millers who worked largely in the fall, or for the proprietors of small sawmills who worked only when work was available, it was no particular hardship to construct a fishway or to open a portion of their dam during the annual fish runs. They might resent having to do so, but it did not threaten their livelihood.[27]

The farmers, grain millers, and sawyers of the Rhode Island interior sought their livelihoods in an economy only tenuously tied to market production. Unlike the fertile coastal lands of southern Rhode Island, home to the pastoral economy of the Narragansett planters, the colony's northern and western lands were poor and unproductive. Backcountry farmers tended small herds of livestock and cultivated few market crops. Most of what they grew they consumed themselves. A few northern Rhode Island farmers raised small amounts of tobacco and flaxseed oil for international markets. Yet the area produced so few provisions for the European or West Indian trade that Providence merchants had to send their agents into central Massachusetts to fill their ships. Local markets were also thin. Providence, the only city of northern Rhode Island, had no market house until 1774 and, like Boston, was a net importer of food. In such an economy the availability of free fish in the countryside was important. And river fish were generally consumed by those who caught them. Such fish were rarely marketed, for backcountry farmers could not compete with the ocean fisheries of the Atlantic coast. The relative absence of a market economy muted tensions over water rights. As long as the economic stakes were low, conflict could be accommodated. But the stakes would not remain low.[28]

III

Conflict over water rights increased in Rhode Island with the introduction of blast furnaces at mid-century. Unlike grist mills and sawmills, furnaces were dependent on wage labor, fully committed to market production, and required continuous amounts of water-power. No other enterprises placed comparable demands on the col-ony's rivers and streams, for furnaces operated around the clock, for months at a time. No other users of waterpower were as concerned with both technical efficiency and profit.[29]

The Furnace Unity provoked the colony's first serious conflict. Owned by two Boston merchants, and located on the Blackstone River about nine miles above Pawtucket Falls, the Unity cast hollow-ware for both local and regional markets as well as cannon and shot used in King George's War. On April 27, 1748, upstream residents claimed before the local justice of the peace that the furnace's dam hindered the passage of fish. The judge agreed and ordered that "the said Dam should be broken and a way made through the same," by April of the following year.[30] The two owners, referring to the plaintiffs as "certain malicious persons," petitioned the General As-sembly in October 1748, asking it to void the court's directive. The owners claimed that saltwater fish were not hindered and that break-ing the dam would not promote the passage of fish and, moreover, would spoil a "useful grist mill now standing in such dam." The owners, however, made no claim for the local utility of the furnace. Their petition was signed by thirty-seven freemen. Even if some of them were furnace workers, it is apparent that local opinion was divided. The General Assembly agreed with the furnace owners and their supporters, its reasoning unknown, and preserved the dam.[31]

Any other solution might have threatened the very existence of the furnace. Not only did blast furnaces have to be run continuously, but they were customarily put in blast in the spring, in the midst of the annual fish runs. New England winters were too severe for pro-longed outdoor work, and winter frosts adversely affected furnace operation. In the fall water was likely to be scarce. And the summer, in the words of one ironmaster, was "too hot for the constitution of the workmen to endure it."[32] Only the spring offered ideal weather and plentiful water. Knowing this, the owners of Furnace Unity had taken no chances. They had drafted a handsome and carefully worded petition and cogently argued their case before the assembly. The stakes were high. Though local opinion was divided, the deci-sion of the local justice of the peace gave notice of a culture that placed a higher value on public and customary rights than on eco-nomic development in the hands of absentee ironmasters. Moreover, such values had been legitimized by local authority. The furnace owners had prevailed only by appealing over the heads of that au-thority, to colony-wide interests apparently more amenable to their influence. Ironmasters would not always be so successful.

Public conflict over fish intensified sharply in the years after 1765, as ironmasters sought exemption from the colony's Fish Acts. Farmers, in response, came to defend their rights with a new sense of urgency—an urgency shaped by the Revolutionary crisis. The intensification of conflict over fish was clearly the product of that extraordinary convergence of economic and ideological change that marked the years from 1765 to 1776.

By the 1760s population growth was pressing against the limits of available economic resources. In the settled portions of New England, land had grown scarce, and so apparently had the numbers of river fish. The Swedish naturalist Peter Kalm, in his travels through New England, reported the claims of Boston-area farmers that fish were in short supply and that mill dams were the cause. Some ironmasters thus appeared to be profiting from their control of an increasingly scarce public resource. The objections of farmers, which at some other time might simply have festered beneath the surface of public life, achieved both voice and legitimacy in the context of the American Revolution.[33]

The growth of a contentious and popularly based politics in the years after 1765 encouraged backcountry farmers to seek redress for their grievances, which struck a louder and more responsive chord than they had a decade earlier. The issues they raised about dams, fish, and water rights had no direct connection to the momentous issues of the Revolution, but they drew upon a common sensibility—the fear of corrupt and arbitrary power. Farmers saw their rights to fish threatened by powerful ironmasters closely tied to the colony's political leadership and intent, so they believed, on turning manifestly public resources to private advantage. In responding to these threats, farmers sought to defend both their specific economic interests and their sense of public virtue, for the public good, as they understood it, demanded that individual economic rights be subordinated to the general will.[34]

Concerns such as these derived their resonance from Anglo-American Country thought, a cluster of ideas about power and liberty, virtue and corruption, private interests and public good, associated with the English Commonwealthmen and widely accessible to colonists during the final third of the eighteenth century. Country thought provided the language of patriot resistance, at its most articulate levels. It was a language of moral regeneration, inspired by classical antiquity, implicitly anticapitalist, and suspicious of wealth, power, and the influence of commerce. Historians are divided about the extent to which the Commonwealth tradition impelled the less articulate—the farmers, mechanics, and laborers of the colonial sea-

board. The evidence from Rhode Island is insufficient, but suggestive. The petitions of the colony's backcountry farmers were the
product of their immediate experience, not an explicit expression of
the Commonwealth tradition. But Country sensibilities lent shape to
that experience, structured its meaning, and legitimized its expression. It was no accident that conflict over fish and conflict over empire overlapped in time and elicited similar fears—the fear of arbitrary power and corrupting influence, the fear that rapacious private
interests might overwhelm a fragile, and traditionally defined, public
good.[35]

Consider the pattern of conflict. In August 1765 Stephen Hopkins, Israel Wilkinson, and Nicholas Brown and his partners petitioned the Rhode Island General Assembly for an exemption to the
Fish Act of 1735. They sought to build an iron furnace on the north
branch of the Pawtuxet River. This was the Hope Furnace, soon to
be the colony's largest and best-known. Its supporters were men of
prominence. Hopkins would later serve as colonial governor. Nicholas Brown's partners were his brothers John, Joseph, and Moses—
the "Browns of Providence Plantations"—one of the colony's wealthiest families. In addition, Moses Brown, who would later play a critical role in the beginnings of the American textile industry, was a
member of the assembly's lower house. That body quickly granted
the company's petition. The upper house initially sought to defer
the issue until meetings of local residents could be held. No record
of such meetings survives, and the upper house eventually con-
curred. But it did so only after stipulating that the furnace owners
construct a fishway whose effectiveness would be judged by three
knowledgeable freemen. If these freemen decided that the fishway
did not work, then the act of 1735 would apply. Despite the furnace
owners' formidable influence, they had not been wholly successful.
The full efficiency of the Hope Furnace had been sacrificed to preserve a customary entitlement to fish. A century later, the first historian of Providence County claimed that this decision, along with
other similar water-rights decisions, "tended greatly to retard the
progress of manufacture."[36] In this case, however, the retardation
was only temporary. Four years later the owners submitted another
petition requesting full exemption from the act of 1735. This time,
with Hopkins himself in the governor's chair, it was granted.[37]

The colony's major furnace owners had succeeded, though not
easily and not without opposition, but smaller mill owners were less
fortunate. Farmers were becoming increasingly prickly about their
rights to fish, and fearful, not just of ironmasters, but of all mill
owners. In May 1766 sixty upcountry farmers in the Pawtuxet Valley

presented a petition to the General Assembly opposing the effort of
Samuel Greene to build a corn mill near Gorton's Pond. The farmers claimed that Greene's proposed mill would block the passage of
fish and, in addition, was unnecessary to the local economy. Their
community already had a corn mill. In June Greene formally applied for an exemption to the colony's Fish Act. The assembly deferred its decision while demanding that Greene, in the interim,
comply with the law. It never again acted on the question, effectively
denying Greene his exemption. Greene had less influence than the
colony's ironmasters, and popular pressure was mounting.[38]

During the same year three other petitions arrived in the assembly
raising new issues and introducing new protagonists. Mill owners
and ironmasters were not the only ones to threaten the rights of
farmers; so did commercial fishermen. In February 1766 thirty-
three farmers near the Pawcatuck River asked the assembly to regulate the use of fishing nets. Some farmers used small nets during
the spring runs to catch as many fish as they could, curing them then
to eat throughout the year. But commercial fishermen, whose presence first became an issue in this period, made extensive use of large
nets, and their actions fundamentally threatened supplies of fish.
Deploying their nets directly downstream of mill dams, they used
the dams as barriers to trap migratory fish. Carefully maneuvering
their boats, they then drove the great spring schools toward their
nets. The petitioners, invoking a "moral economy" of a kind revealed in E. P. Thompson's studies of eighteenth-century England,
claimed that these fishermen then charged an "extravagant price,"
depriving poor families of fish "that Divine Providence had bestowed upon them."[39] They prayed that the assembly outlaw the use
of nets annually from March 1 to June 1, and that it impose a £50
fine on those who failed to open their dams during the spring runs.
In May more than seventy residents of Cranston forwarded a petition to the legislature protesting the "great neglect of timely opening
of mill dams"[40] and demanding stiff penalties for those using nets at
Pawtuxet Falls. In August residents of Westerly and Hopkinton submitted a third petition, asserting that the current laws protecting fish
were ineffective and had thus done "great damage [to] the poor."[41]
They too wanted stiffer laws mandating the opening of dams and
restricting the use of nets. The General Assembly listened and in
February 1767 passed an act prohibiting the use of nets or seines
from March 25 to June 1 on the entire Pawcatuck and a specified
area below Pawtuxet Falls.[42]

The popular pressure of these years was also evident at Pawtucket
Falls on the Blackstone River. By the 1760s the Jenckes family had

dammed Sargeant's Trench and built two anchor shops upon it, converting what had originally been a fishway into a power canal. The rise of shipbuilding in Providence provided the incentive. Upcountry farmers did not immediately protest this abridgment of their rights, but in October 1761 John Dexter of Cumberland and seventeen others requested that the General Assembly authorize a lottery to pay for improvements at the falls. Dexter and his fellow petitioners claimed that a great many fish of "several sorts" entered the river below the falls but could not pass easily upstream. For £1000, Dexter argued, a new fish passage could be constructed to allow fish "that choose fresh water to pass with ease." The assembly granted the request.[43]

Dexter's petition was signed by all of the mill owners then working at the falls—David and Hugh Kennedy, James and Nehemiah Bucklin, and seven members of the Jenckes family. They no doubt believed that supporting a new fishway was far preferable to giving up their rights in Sargeant's Trench—which upcountry farmers might well have insisted upon. Farmers and mill owners at Pawtucket Falls were not yet in conflict, though their interests were clearly beginning to diverge. The new fishway worked, at least for a time. The General Assembly later claimed that the lottery had demonstrated its "public utility," benefiting farmers above the falls—"especially the poorer Sort of People."[44]

By 1773, however, backcountry farmers had come to believe that the fishway did not work, and they convinced the General Assembly to push the issue one critical step further. In August of that year the assembly passed legislation with the ominous title "An act making it lawful to break down and blow up Rocks at Pawtucket Falls to let fish pass up."[45] The traditional common-law remedy for river obstructions had been affirmed by statute. It was now legal "for any person or persons whatsover, at their own proper expense, to blow up or break down any rock or rocks in the falls . . . that obstruct the passage of fish up the said river, the said river being hereby declared a public river."[46] The act was a major victory for northern Rhode Island farmers, clearly asserting the importance attached both to fish and to public rights.

The act was also more than the mill owners at the falls were willing to tolerate. The Jenckeses, the Bucklins, and one Richard Fenner, a miller on the west bank, responded to the assembly at its next session. Asserting that they had been "peaceably and quietly possessed" of their mill privileges for decades and that they had gone to great expense to maintain water mills frequently subject to floods, they did not now want to face the hazards of a new law that would empower anyone "to judge of the propriety of destroying the dams at the Falls."[47] Any person, they claimed, able to "procure a pound of gunpowder, actuated by the worst motives, may at any time in the space of a few hours, blow our interest to the amount of several thousands of dollars to irretrievable destruction."[48] They requested that the law be repealed, and ninety-three freemen who signed their petition agreed with them—their numbers testimony to a growing divisiveness based on diverging economic interests. The assembly did not repeal the law but in June 1774 claimed that it had been "misunderstood" and that "many Disadvantages have happened."[49] The "Disadvantages" were not specified. In response, the assembly formed a committee consisting of Hopkins, Darius Sessions, and Moses Brown—two of whom, as owners of the Hope Furnace, had a direct stake in amending the Fish Acts—to see that the new act was "truely executed." No rocks could be removed unless under their direction.[50]

Yet removal proceeded. Moses Brown later testified that "he directed the blowers where not to blow," as fishways were created on both sides of the falls.[51] The fishways, once again, seemed to work. A later petition asserted that "country" interests had been secured and that fishing continued to prove valuable, "particularly to the poorer inhabitants."[52] The same petition also claimed that the mill privileges had not been damaged, but on this there is contrary evidence. Testifying in a later and unrelated case, one Israel Arnold asserted that the mills lay idle, and the dam unrepaired, for three to four years after the blowing up of the falls.[53]

This victory for the farmers of northern Rhode Island came at the expense, not of the colony's ironmasters—whose efforts to exempt themselves from the Fish Acts had initially provoked conflict—but of a less powerful group of grain millers, blacksmiths, and fullers. This was the first time in Rhode Island's history that farmers and the owners of small mills had seriously contested with each other. In doing so, they revealed the distance that had come to separate their interests.

Now firmly tied to a market economy based upon shipbuilding and commerce, the mill owners of Pawtucket Falls were far less willing to accommodate the needs of farmers than their ancestors had been fifty years earlier. The rise of the port at Providence had made the difference. What had once been a fishway, mutually constructed by farmers and mill owners, was now a power canal. The colony's waterpower increasingly served the needs of an international economy. The economic stakes were higher, and some men had come to believe that the public good now required that customary rights to fish be subordinated to the needs of commerce and manufacturing.[54]

The farmers of the northern Rhode Island backcountry disagreed. Unlike some of their mill-owning neighbors, they had not grown more closely tied to a market economy. And they remained intent on protecting their rights to fish, even if that meant discouraging the full commercial use of the colony's rivers. The ferment of the Revolutionary years had given them at once the voice and the opportunity to reclaim rights once unambiguously theirs. They would continue their efforts to uphold those rights into the nineteenth century. But their power to do so would diminish.[55]

IV

During the 1780s and 1790s growing support for home manufactures increased the importance of waterpower and helped to redefine the nature of public benefit. Rhode Island's General Assembly became less willing to restrict the prerogatives of mill owners, and the rights of farmers to fish gradually came to count for less. Yet conflict over water rights continued, and in one area of the state backcountry farmers did manage to defend their rights to fish.

The Pawcatuck River Valley, located in the southwest on the Connecticut border, had been the locus of sporadic conflict over water rights since the 1760s. Because the river had never been important to the colony's ironmasters, the protaganists did not include the owners of furnaces or forges. They did include farmers, commercial fishermen, and small-scale mill owners. During the 1780s conflict flared. The assembly referred to "great Disturbances," to "Disorders and Breaches of the Peace," and, in response, passed strong legislation in 1785.[56] The new law sharply limited the rights of mill owners, forbidding the operation of any sawmills during the spring runs, from March 20 to June 1, and requiring that the dam nearest the mouth of the Pawcatuck be opened a full fifteen feet during the same period. Acting alone, without powerful local ironmasters whose support they could have enlisted, the river's grain millers and sawyers proved no match for the area's farmers. Commercial fishermen fared better. Previously banned from using nets during the spring runs, they gained the right to use nets two days in the week though only for an hour at a time. Despite growing opposition to the act of 1785, and despite the later emergence of cotton mill owners of the Pawcatuck, wealthier and more powerful than their predecessors, the act remained in force on the river into the 1830s.[57]

Elsewhere in the state, farmers were not as successful. While opposition to dams that restricted fish passage continued, its political effectiveness diminished. On June 4, 1785, sixty-six farmers from Cranston and Warwick petitioned the General Assembly, claiming that dams and nets at Pawtuxet Falls prevented alewives from reaching their spawning grounds. "Before said obstructions," the petitioners asserted, "said fish were taken in great plenty and were of infinite advantage to the Poor and middling sort of people."[58] The farmers defined their fishing privilege in the language of the Declaration of Independence—as an "unalienable right."[59] In August the assembly formed a committee to inspect the falls. Claiming that fish could pass, that nets posed no problem, and that the law of 1735 remained effective, the committee denied the farmers' petition. Less than a year later, the assembly amended the law of 1767, which prohibited the use of nets below the falls during the spring runs, to allow fishermen to use nets four days in the week.[60]

Farmers from Smithfield and Cumberland also found the General Assembly less amenable to their influence. In June 1786, 168 of them, more than had ever previously signed a water-rights petition in Rhode Island, sought the assembly's approval to organize a lottery for excavating a new trench around Pawtucket Falls. The fishway of 1774 had evidently failed. The owners of mill sites on the old trench were willing to allow it as long as their works were not injured. Yet the assembly did not approve the lottery. The area's farmers, acting on their own and with the apparent consent of the mill owners, did make some improvements to the trench and in May 1787 managed to convince the assembly to restrict the use of nets and lines in and near its mouth. It was a minor victory, a pale reflection of what farmers had won fourteen years earlier on the same river.[61]

Conflict over dams, fish, and water rights in Rhode Island took a decisive turn in the 1790s. A dam was destroyed for the first time, new issues emerged, and conflict among mill owners dramatically increased. The new protaganists were the owners of cotton mills. Like blast furnaces, cotton mills were capitalist enterprises, requiring waterpower that was consistently available. Between 1790 and 1820 cotton mills would multiply in number, grow in size, and make unprecedented demands on the rivers and streams of Rhode Island. At one level, cotton mill owners simply took up where the state's economically declining ironmasters left off—demanding that the Fish Acts be amended, or ignored, to suit their interests. At another level, however, they fundamentally redefined the rules of the game.[62]

Again, Pawtucket Falls was at the center of the story. The precipitating incident, however, had nothing to do with the fishing rights of farmers, though the ensuing conflict would have a damaging im-

pact on those rights. The story begins with the Englishman Samuel
Slater, who established the first waterpowered cotton mill in North
America at the falls in 1790. Two years later he and his partners,
financed by Moses Brown, sought to build a new mill. They chose a
site 200 yards above the falls and began work on a new dam in the
summer of 1792. Six to seven feet high, approximately 200 feet in
length, the new dam was arguably the largest yet built in America.
On August 31, Stephan and Eleazar Jenks, blacksmiths, and John
Bucklin, a grain miller, owners of water mill privileges at Pawtucket
Falls, entered Brown's property and, in the language of the subsequent charges, "did . . . utterly subvert, pull down & destroy" the
partially finished dam.[63]

At their trial Bucklin and the two Jenkses claimed that the new
dam was a nuisance, that it diverted "the natural stream" of the river
and "prevented the Water . . . from running to and carrying [their]
Mills in such a manner as it had before run . . . from time imme-
morial."[64] The issue for them was not the rights to fish, but the
rights to the river's flow. Invoking the customary remedy of the
common law, they freely admitted destroying the dam, "as Lawfully
they might."[65]

Rhode Island's eighteenth-century mill owners had, on occasion,
quarreled with each other over water rights, but never to this extent.
The conflict at Pawtucket Falls involved more than competing economic interests. In truth, the obstruction created by the new dam
was only temporary, a product of the building of the dam rather
than of the dam itself. The flow of the river remained the same, and
the same amount of water would soon have been available to the mill
owners at the falls. Why then had a temporary obstruction elicited
such conflict? The Jenkses and Bucklin had long occupied mill sites
at the falls, the former since the 1670s, the latter since the middle of
the eighteenth century. Their trades had been disrupted, however
temporarily, by a new business larger in scale and more demanding
of waterpower than any previous business in the village's history.
The new company was controlled by outsiders—Providence merchants—its most visible representative was an English immigrant,
and it carried with it the taint of English industrialism. There was
prejudice against Slater, according to the village's first historian and
a contemporary of Slater's, because he was English—"prejudice
which lasted some time and attached to everything pertaining to cotton manufacture."[66] Not everyone opposed the new mill, but for
many, cotton mills evoked special fears, of mill owners corrupted by
power and of landless and dependent mill workers powerless to exercise their republican liberties.[67]

After a complex series of trials, Bucklin and the Jenkses won their case. The decision turned not on whether the new dam had a right to stand, but on whether the construction of the dam temporarily impeded the flow of water to the mills below. The court ruled that it did. The cotton mill owners, however, had rebuilt the dam even before the case went to court, and rebuilt twice more, it still stands.[68]

The mill owners at the falls did not acquiesce gracefully in the rebuilding of the dam. Bucklin and the two Jenkses responded by raising their dam two feet. They did so, according to Moses Brown, "with a view . . . to cause backwater to flow upon the wheels above," directly threatening the operation of Slater's mill.[69] But their act also threatened others. By the 1790s Pawtucket Village was a warren of small-scale waterpowered industry. Two anchor forges, three snuff mills, three fulling mills, a clothier's shop, a linseed oil mill, a slitting mill, two machines for cutting nails, and one for cutting screws clustered about the falls and along Sargeant's Trench. A number of mills and shops on the trench were located above the falls, and their owners were no more willing than Brown and Slater to risk injury. They would join with the cotton mill owners to oppose the two-foot addition at Pawtucket Falls.[70]

Others opposed the addition as well, and for familiar reasons. Backcountry farmers saw both dams as threats to their fishing rights, and in November 1792 they so petitioned the General Assembly. The addition to the old dam, they claimed, would make it impossible for fish to pass up river, while the new dam had no fishways at all. The farmers suggested that a committee be appointed with power to remove all obstructions, and the General Assembly complied.[71]

But in February 1793 the assembly reversed itself on one critical point. It redefined the committee's charge and placed the cotton mill dam outside the committee's jurisdiction. Moses Brown's long experience in dealing with the assembly over questions of water rights had proven invaluable. It was an important victory. For the first time in Rhode Island's history, a major water-rights issue had been removed from the political process, insulated from popular pressure. In the strict sense, it did not serve as a precedent, for other cotton mill owners were not as politically adept as Moses Brown. Yet it was a decision that left no doubt where power lay and confirmed the worst fears of those ardently opposed to cotton mills. Brown and Slater had violated the state's Fish Act, but they would never be called to account. No fishways were ever built on the Slater Mill dam.[72]

The committee completed its work in March 1793 by demanding that the two-foot addition at the falls be removed. A month earlier, the mill and shop owners along the trench had drafted their own petition urging the assembly to so decide. The addition, they believed, increased the risk of flood. With its removal, the threat to the Slater Mill and to the works on the trench was eased. The mill owners at the falls had succeeded only in dividing the village. They were the immediate losers, while the cotton mill owners and their allies had triumphed.[73]

The contest they won was different from previous struggles over water rights in Rhode Island. It was both more complex and more intense, and the economic stakes were higher. The General Assembly's decision not only placed the Slater Mill dam above the law but also effectively excluded the interests of backcountry farmers. The conflict at Pawtucket Falls had begun and ended as a conflict among mill owners—riparian proprietors, individual property owners with specific and direct economic interests. Backcountry farmers, defenders not of individual property rights but of larger notions of public right and public virtue, were the real losers. Contests over water rights would continue at Pawtucket Falls for another thirty years, as mill owners quarreled with each other over issues of fair apportionment. But it was a contest in which they were the only players—a contest in which the most powerful among them, the cotton mill owners, would emerge victorious.[74]

The state's Fish Act, as it applied to the Blackstone River, would remain on the books until 1829, though northern Rhode Island farmers would never enforce it again. Their powerlessness to do so had other consequences. With the passage of migratory fish now almost wholly obstructed, it was only a matter of time before commercial fishermen seized their opportunity. In 1804 they and their supporters petitioned the General Assembly to repeal the act of 1787 that restricted the use of nets below the falls. In 1805 the assembly agreed. The fishermen justified their request as beneficial to the public, claiming that they would furnish fish to "indigent people" more cheaply and more regularly than previously while insuring that large numbers of fish were not lost to the community. Since there would be far fewer fish reaching the upper Blackstone, they may have been right. But in associating the public good with the commercial use of fishing nets, their argument reversed long-standing assumptions about what constituted the public good.[75]

Cotton mill owners made the same kind of argument. During the first half of the nineteenth century, they effectively clothed their economic interests in the cloak of public benefit, successfully arguing that their need for waterpower should take precedence, as one of their number sarcastically put it, over "a trifling shad and alewife fishery that does not pay for the grog expended in taking the fish."[76] The rights of individual property owners had come to dwarf older notions of public right. In 1828 the U.S. Circuit Court echoed the trend when it decided that Rhode Islanders could not cross the property of others in order to fish. It was irrelevant that people had been doing so for years. An appeal to customary rights could not justify trespass on private property.[77]

The conflict between farmers and mill owners over fishing rights continued into the nineteenth century—in Rhode Island's Pawcatuck Valley, in Newton, Pembroke, and Weymouth, Massachusetts, and in Shelton, Connecticut. In some places farmers were able to insist upon the maintenance of fishways. But their efforts had little impact. Dams multiplied and grew larger, while fishways proved ineffective. By the middle of the nineteenth century the number of anadromous fish in the rivers of New England had been reduced dramatically, and the Atlantic salmon could no longer be found in its customary spawning grounds.[78]

Yet Thoreau's vision—of clear rivers, of leveled factories, and of the salmon's return—was not wholly a dream. New England's textile mills have been dormant for the last fifty years, the victims not of nature, as Thoreau imagined, but of the international economy. New England's mill dams, with few exceptions, lay idle, no longer generating power. New England's rivers are slowly being converted to recreational uses, and in the last few years Atlantic salmon have found their way, not solely on their own, to the upper reaches of the Connecticut River.[79]

V

Conflict over dams and fishing rights in eighteenth-century Rhode Island was, at heart, a conflict over the coming of industrial capitalism. The annual spring migration of salmon, shad, and alewives furnished the noncommercial farmers of the Rhode Island backcountry with an important source of food. Their rights to fish were protected by both law and custom. Sawyers, grain millers, and other owners of small rural mills, closely linked to local farm economies, easily accommodated those rights. The owners of blast furnaces, the first capitalists in the countryside, could not. Their technology and their capital investment required the intensive use of waterpower. As they sought to alter older patterns of river use, they sought also to alter the laws that protected the fishing rights of farmers. The conflict that furnace owners provoked paralleled the years of crisis leading to the American Revolution.

Farmers defended not just their economy, but their sense of public right and public virtue. They feared not only a loss of fish but also the unrestrained pursuit of private advantage by mill owners. They feared the power of mill owners to impress their will on courts and legislatures. And as events would demonstrate, they had reason. Their fears had no direct connection to the issues of the American Revolution, but they drew upon a common sensibility expressed in Anglo-American Country thought. Country sensibilities lent shape to the experience of farmers and legitimized their concerns. Rhode Island farmers defended their fishing rights most effectively during the years from 1765 to 1772. After the Revolution they continued to defend those rights, upholding an ideal of public virtue that was essentially anticapitalist in its implications. But their power declined. The growing commercial uses of waterpower and, in particular, the rise of cotton mills fundamentally eroded the fishing rights of farmers. The pattern of conflict over dams and fish in eighteenth-century Rhode Island reveals something of the complex and contested nature of the American transition to industrial capitalism.

NOTES

A version of this article was originally published in Jonathan Prude and Steven Hahn, eds., *The Countryside in the Age of Capitalist Transformation: Essays in the Social History of Rural America* (Chapel Hill, 1985).

1. Henry David Thoreau, *A Week on the Concord and Merrimack* (Cambridge, Mass.,1894), p. 39.
2. Ibid., pp. 39–40.
3. Ibid., p. 44.
4. Ibid., p. 45; William Wood, *New England's Prospect* (1634), ed. Alden Vaughan (Amherst, Mass., 1977), p. 56; Thomas Morton, *New England Canaan* (1632), in Charles F. Adams, ed., *Publications of the Prince Society*, 14 (Boston, 1883), p. 222; William Root Bliss, *Colonial Times on Buzzard's Bay* (New York, 1888), pp. 196–99; Peter Kalm, *Travels in North America*, 2d ed. (1772), in John Pinkerton, *A General Collection of the Best and Most Interesting Voyages and Travels in All Parts of the World*, 13 (London, 1812), pp. 470–71; Richard Bayles, *History of Providence County, Rhode Island*, 2 (New York, 1891), p. 235; Howard S. Russell, *A Long, Deep Furrow: Three Centuries of Farming in New England* (Hanover, N.H., 1976), pp. 79, 319; David Starr Jordan and Barton Warren Evermann, *American Food and Game Fishes* (New York, 1904), pp. 105–8; Charles A. Atwood, *Reminiscences of Taunton* (Taunton, Mass., 1880), pp. 5–6.
5. Zadock Thompson, *History of Vermont* (Burlington, Vt., 1842), pp. 128,

140; Morton J. Horwitz, *The Transformation of American Law, 1780–1860* (Cambridge, Mass., 1977), pp. 29–53; Horwitz, "The Transformation in the Conception of Property in American Law, 1780–1860," *University of Chicago Law Review,* 40 (1973), 248–90; William E. Nelson, *The Americanization of the Common Law: The Impact of Legal Change in Massachusetts Society, 1760–1870* (Cambridge, Mass., 1975), pp. 159–65; J. R. Pole, *Paths to the American Past* (New York, 1979), pp. 75–108.

6. On dam-breaking in Massachusetts, see Alonzo Lewis, *The History of Lynn* (Boston, 1844), p. 154; William S. Pattee, *A History of Old Braintree and Quincy* (Quincy, Mass., 1878), pp. 462–64; Charles Francis Adams, *Three Episodes of Massachusetts History,* II (Boston, 1892), pp. 831–34; Edward N. Hartley, *Ironworks on the Saugus* (Norman, Okla., 1957), pp. 262–65.

7. See especially Michael Zuckerman, "The Fabrication of Identity in Colonial America," *William and Mary Quarterly,* 3d ser., 34 (Apr. 1977), 183–214; Kenneth A. Lockridge, "Social Change and the Meaning of the American Revolution," *Journal of Social History,* 6 (Summer 1973), 403–39; Lockridge, *A New England Town: The First Hundred Years, Dedham, Massachusetts, 1636–1736* (New York, 1970); James Deetz, *In Small Things Forgotten* (New York, 1977); Daniel Scott Smith, "Population, Family, and Society in Hingham, Massachusetts, 1635–1880" (Ph.D. dissertation, University of California, Berkeley, 1973). The classic statements are Perry Miller, *The New England Mind: The Seventeenth Century* (New York, 1939); Miller, *The New England Mind: From Colony to Province* (Cambridge, Mass., 1953); and Louis Hartz, *The Liberal Tradition in America* (New York, 1955). A recent newcomer in this old debate is Stephen Innes, *Labor in a New Land: Economy and Society in Seventeenth-Century Springfield* (Princeton, 1983).

8. Charles S. Grant, *Democracy in the Connecticut Frontier Town of Kent* (New York, 1961); James T. Lemon, *The Best Poor Man's Country: A Geographical Study of Early Southeastern Pennsylvania* (Baltimore, 1972); Percy W. Bidwell and John I. Falconer, *History of Agriculture in the Northern United States, 1620–1860* (Washington, D.C., 1925); Michael Merrill, " 'Cash Is Good to Eat': Self-Sufficiency and Exchange in the Rural Economy of the United States," *Radical History Review* 16 (Winter 1977), 42–71; James Henretta, "Families and Farms: *Mentalité* in Pre-Industrial America," *William and Mary Quarterly,* 3d Ser., 35 (Jan. 1978), 3–32; Christopher Clark, "The Household Economy, Market Exchange, and the Rise of Capitalism in the Connecticut River Valley, 1800–1860," *Journal of Social History,* 13 (Winter 1979), 169–89; Robert E. Mutch, "The Cutting Edge: Colonial America and the Debate about the Transition to Capitalism," *Theory and Society,* 9 (Nov. 1980), 847–63.

9. On Country thought, see Bernard Bailyn, *The Ideological Origins of the American Revolution* (Cambridge, Mass., 1967); Gordon Wood, *The Creation of the American Republic, 1776–1787* (Chapel Hill, 1969); J. G. A. Pocock, *The Machiavellian Moment: Florentine Political Thought and the Atlantic Republican Tradition* (Princeton, 1975).

10. Humphrey W. Woolrych, *A Treatise of the Law of Waters,* 2d ed. (London, 1851), p. 195; *Halsbury's Laws of England,* 3d ed., 17 (London, 1956),

pp. 317–18, 343–49; Anthony Netboy, *The Atlantic Salmon: A Vanishing Species?* (London, 1968), pp. 165–85.

11. Joseph K. Angell, *A Treatise on the Common Law in Relation to Water-Courses* (Boston, 1824), pp. 74–75.

12. The King v. Wharton, 12 Mod. 510, 86 Eng. Rep. 1056 (K.B., 1701), cited in T. E. Lauer, "The Common Law Background of the Riparian Doctrine," *Missouri Law Review*, 28 (Winter 1963), 60–107.

13. Woolrych, *Treatise of the Law of Waters*, pp. 85–86, 169; Lauer, "Common Law Background of the Riparian Doctrine"; Netboy, *Atlantic Salmon*, pp. 165–85.

14. Woolrych, *Treatise of the Law of Waters*, pp. 85–86, 169, 195; Netboy, *Atlantic Salmon*, pp. 178–85; Fred S. Thacker, *The Thames Highway*, 1 (London, 1914), pp. 3–4. For general conflict over water rights in Britain, see T. S. Willen, *River Navigation in England, 1600–1750* (London, 1936), pp. 16–51; L. T. C. Rolt, *The Inland Waterways of England* (London, 1950), pp. 15–36; Leslie Syson, *British Water-Mills* (London, 1965), pp. 42–45; John Rodgers, *English Rivers* (London, 1947), pp. 11–17; Christopher Hill, *Reformation to Industrial Revolution* (London, 1967), p. 167; John Sutcliffe, *A Treatise on Canals and Reservoirs* (Rochdale, 1816), p. 246.

15. Horwitz, *Transformation of American Law*, pp. 47–48; Angell, *Treatise on the Common Law*, pp. 124, 507–14; "The Law of Water Privileges," *American Jurist and Law Magazine*, 2 (July 1829), 31–32; "Report of Committee on the Mill," Oct. 6, 1821, Providence City Hall Archives; J. L. Bishop, *A History of American Manufactures*, I (Philadelphia, 1861), pp. 122–32; B. Cowell, *Ancient Documents Relative to the Old Grist Mill* (Providence, 1829).

16. Rhode Island Colony Records, vol. 5 (1729–45), pp. 185–86, Rhode Island State Archives, Providence.

17. Horwitz, *Transformation of American Law*, pp. 47–53.

18. William Biglow, *History of the Town of Natick* (Boston, 1830), pp. 8–9.

19. Bayles, *History of Providence County*, II, 235; Russell, *Long, Deep Furrow*, pp. 79, 319.

20. R.I. Colony Records, vol. 4, p. 221.

21. Ibid.

22. Public Laws of Rhode Island, 1744, pp. 185–87, Rhode Island State Archives, Providence.

23. Cyrus Walker, "A History of Scituate," ms., p. 187, Town Clerk's Office, North Scituate, R.I.

24. Rhode Island Petitions, Vol. 4, p. 3, Rhode Island State Archives; Public Laws of Rhode Island, 1744, pp. 190–91, 254–55, 258.

25. David Benedict, "Reminiscences No. 19," *Pawtucket Gazette & Chronicle*, July 29, 1853; Robert Grieve, *An Illustrated History of Pawtucket, Central Falls, and Vicinity* (Pawtucket, R.I., 1897), pp. 32–44, 104–15.

26. Introductory Deposition, Equity Register, Tyler et al. v. Wilkinson et al., 24 Fed. Case 472, 474 (No. 14,312) C.C.D.R.I., 1827, Federal Record Center, Waltham, Mass.

27. Carl Bridenbaugh, *The Colonial Craftsmen* (New York, 1950), pp. 33–64; Louis C. Hunter, *A History of Industrial Power in the United States, 1780–*

1930, Vol. 1: Waterpower in the Century of the Steam Engine (Charlottesville, 1979), pp. 1–50, 386n.

28. Carl Bridenbaugh, *Fat Mutton and Liberty of Conscience: Society in Rhode Island, 1636–1690* (Providence, 1974); James Hedges, *The Browns of Providence Plantations: the Colonial Years* (Cambridge, Mass., 1952); Lynne Withey, *Urban Growth in Colonial Rhode Island, Newport, and Providence in the Eighteenth Century* (Albany, 1984).

29. Hunter, *History of Industrial Power*, pp. 1, 6, 386n; Arthur Cecil Bining, *Pennsylvania Iron Manufacture in the Eighteenth Century* (Harrisburg, 1938), pp. 55–81.

30. R.I. Petitions, vol. 4, p. 70.

31. Ibid., vol. 7, p. 2; Israel Wilkinson, *A Memoir of the Wilkinson Family in America* (Jacksonville, Ill., 1869), pp. 101–2, 403; Bishop, *History of American Manufactures*, pp. 1, 503.

32. R.I. Petitions, vol. 13, p. 132.

33. Kalm, *Travels in North America*, pp. 470–71.

34. On the general issues, see Lockridge, "Social Change and the Meaning of the American Revolution," pp. 403–39; J. G. A. Pocock, "Virtue and Commerce in the Eighteenth Century," *Journal of Interdisciplinary History*, 3 (1973), 120–34; Edmund S. Morgan, "The Puritan Ethic and the American Revolution," *William and Mary Quarterly*, 3d Ser., 24 (Jan. 1967), 3–43.

35. See Bailyn, *Intellectual Origins of the American Revolution;* Wood, *Creation of the American Republic;* Pocock, *Machiavellian Moment;* Gary B. Nash, *The Urban Crucible: Social Change, Political Consciousness, and the Origins of the American Revolution* (Cambridge, Mass., 1979); John Murrin, "The Great Inversion, or Court versus Country: A Comparison of the Revolution Settlements in England (1688–1721) and America (1776–1816)," in J. G. A. Pocock, ed., *Three British Revolutions, 1641, 1688, 1776* (Princeton, 1980), pp. 368–453.

36. R.I. Petitions, vol. 11, p. 206; Hedges, *Browns of Providence*, pp. 123–54; Mack Thompson, *Moses Brown, Reluctant Reformer* (Chapel Hill, 1962).

37. R.I. Petitions, vol. 13, p. 77.

38. Ibid., vol. 13, part 2, pp. 11, 15, 17.

39. Ibid., p. 10; E. P. Thompson, "The Moral Economy of the English Crowd in the Eighteenth Century," *Past and Present*, 50 (1971), 76–136.

40. R.I. Petitions, vol. 13, part 2, p. 20.

41. Ibid., 41.

42. Acts and Resolutions of the Rhode Island General Assembly, Vol. 11, p. 52, Rhode Island State Archives.

43. Introductory deposition, Tyler et al. v. Wilkinson et al.; R. I. Petitions, vol. 10, p. 176.

44. R.I. Colony Records, vol. 7, pp. 413–14; vol. 9, p. 61.

45. Ibid., vol. 9, p. 61.

46. Ibid.

47. Ibid., vol. 15, p. 105.

48. Ibid.

49. Ibid., vol. 9, p. 118.

50. Deposition of Moses Brown, Jan. 27, 1824, Tyler et al. v. Wilkinson et al.

51. Ibid.

52. R.I. Petitions, vol. 27, p. 83.

53. Deposition of Israel Arnold, Tyler et al. v. Wilkinson et al.

54. See Peter Coleman, *The Transformation of Rhode Island, 1790–1860* (Providence, 1969), pp. 3–25; Sydney V. James, *Colonial Rhode Island* (New York, 1975), pp. 262–66.

55. Evidence on the eighteenth-century economy of northern Rhode Island is drawn from a yet unpublished study of probate records.

56. J. R. Bartlett, ed., *Records of the State of Rhode Island*, X (Providence, 1865), pp. 113–14, 135–39; Frederic Denison, *Westerly and Its Witnesses, 1626–1876* (Providence, 1878), pp. 223–25.

57. Denison, *Westerly*, p. 225.

58. R.I. Petitions, vol. 22, p. 90.

59. Ibid.

60. R.I. Colony Records, vol. 13, pp. 476–78.

61. R.I. Petitions, vol. 27, p. 83; vol. 36, p. 22; introductory deposition, Tyler et al. v. Wilkinson et al.; Grieve, *Illustrated History*, p. 106.

62. Coleman, *Transformation of Rhode Island*, pp. 71–107.

63. Kennedy et al. v. Bucklin et al., Court of Common Pleas, Bristol County, XII, 214–15, 289–91; Bucklin et al. v. Arnold et al., XII, 257; Jenks v. Kennedy, XII, 236–37; all at Bristol County Superior Court, Taunton, Mass.

64. Kennedy et al. v. Bucklin et al.

65. Ibid.

66. David Benedict, *Report of the Centennial Celebration of the 24th of June, 1865, at Pawtucket, of the Incorporation of the Town of North Providence* (Providence, 1865), 87–88.

67. See Drew McCoy, *The Elusive Republic: Political Economy in Jeffersonian America* (Chapel Hill, 1980), pp. 105–19.

68. Deposition of Moses Brown, Tyler et al. v. Wilkinson et al.

69. Ibid.

70. Timothy Dwight, *Travels in New England and New York* (New Haven, 1821), II, 27.

71. R.I. Petitions, vol. 27, p. 83.

72. R.I. Colony Records, vol. 14, pp. 274–75.

73. Bartlett, ed., *Records of the State of Rhode Island*, X, 508; R.I. Petitions, vol. 27, pp. 83, 116.

74. See Tyler et al. v. Wilkinson et al.

75. R.I. Petitions, vol. 36, p. 22.

76. *Pawtucket Chronicle*, Jan. 24, 1829.

77. Smith v. Miller, 5 Mason's Rep., 191. See also Kenyon v. Nichols, R.I. Rep., vol. 1, p. 106.

78. See Denison, *Westerly*, p. 75.; Towns of Stoughton, Sharon, and Canton v. Baker and Vose, 4 Mass. Rep., 552–32 (1808); Commonwealth v. Chapin, 5 Pick., 199 (1826); Francis Jackson, *History of the Early Settlement of*

Newton (Boston, 1854), pp. 107–8; Orra Stone, *History of Massachusetts Industries,* II (Boston, 1930), pp. 1134, 1214–15; Matthew Roth, *Connecticut: An Inventory of Historic Engineering and Industrial Sites* (Washington, D.C., 1981), pp. 33–35.

79. Nelson Bryant, "History Made in Connecticut," *New York Times,* June 14, 1981, p. 108.

CHAPTER 8

Middle-Class Parks and Working-Class Play: The Struggle over Recreational Space in Worcester, Massachusetts, 1870–1910

ROY ROSENZWEIG

"You may take my word for it," landscape architect and horticultur-alist Andrew Jackson Downing wrote of parks in 1848, "they will be better preachers of temperance than temperance societies, better re-finers of national manners than dancing schools and better promot-ers of general good-feeling than any lectures on the philosophy of happiness."[1] This vision of parks as instruments of social uplift and social control has captured the imagination of social reformers for more than a century. Although park advocates have never been mo-tivated solely by a desire to control urban and immigrant workers, social control has been a persistent, and sometimes even dominant, impulse behind their movement. Frederick Law Olmsted, the most distinguished and influential landscape architect of the middle and late nineteenth century, hoped, according to one recent historian, that his pastoral landscapes would "inspire communal feelings among all urban classes, muting resentments over disparities of wealth and fashion."[2]

These motives as well as the overt class bias of park and play-ground advocates have sometimes earned them the disdain and con-descension of historians. "Thus it was," charges the author of a re-cent history of playground reform, "that a movement desiring to release the city's young from the harsher aspects of urban life be-came one which seemed to prepare them to accept their fate uncom-plainingly."[3] But, while social control was certainly an important mo-tivation for many reformers, this analysis distorts history in two ways.[4] First, it tends to reduce social reformers and park advocates to rationally calculating social engineers when actually their motiva-tions were much more complex. Early park reformers, for example,

214

were also sparked by naturalistic visions of society, fears about urban disease, and infatuations with European public gardens as well as by the desire to uplift and quiet the masses. Second, and more important, the social control formula suggests that the object of reform designs—the urban worker—was both inert and totally pliable. It ignores the possibility that workers might have taken an active part in conceiving or advocating parks and assumes that workers uncritically accepted the park programs handed down by an omnipotent ruling class. In an effort to explore the ways in which working people actively shaped their non-working lives, this article focuses on the struggles over recreational space and behavior in one industrial city—Worcester, Massachusetts—in the late nineteenth century.

Neither a commercial port nor a company town, Worcester, with a diversified industrial base, a rapid growth rate, and a large immigrant population, was broadly representative of the manufacturing cities where most American workers made their homes in the late nineteenth century. Worcester's factories turned out a wide range of products from corsets to carpets, but its most important manufacturing activity was concentrated in the metal trades, a rather heterogeneous category that embraced such products as wire, grinding wheels, lathes, and looms. Along with the capitalization of the city's industries, which multiplied about eight times between 1870 and 1910 (from about $8 to $65 million), Worcester's population grew rapidly from 41,000 to 146,000. Generally speaking, the owners of the city's factories came from native American or Yankee backgrounds, while the workers in those factories were predominantly first- or second-generation immigrants. In 1900, for example, native-stock Americans made up only 6 percent of the city's manual laborers. Thus, ethnicity and class loyalties, often analytically counterpoised by historians, were inextricably intertwined in a city such as Worcester. In the late 1870s and 1880s most of these immigrants were Irish. Indeed, perhaps half of the city was of Irish heritage in 1880. By 1900, however, substantial numbers of Swedes and French Canadians had entered the city's neighborhoods and factories. And in the next ten years Worcester began developing sizeable Jewish, Italian, Polish, and Lithuanian communities.[5]

Despite the numerical predominance of the immigrant working class, the city's Yankee upper class officially controlled Worcester's parks, as they did the factories and most major political offices. In the park system, this elite was represented by Edward Winslow Lincoln, the secretary and chairman of the Parks Commission for most of the late nineteenth century. So complete was his control of the commission that his death in 1896 precipitated a total administrative reorganization of the Parks Commission and necessitated, for the first time, the hiring of a full-time park superintendent. A member of a leading Worcester family (his grandfather had been Thomas Jefferson's attorney general and a justice of the Supreme Court, and his father was governor for nine years as well as the city's first mayor), Lincoln spent most of his first forty years seeking a suitable career, first in law and then in journalism. Beginning around 1860, however, he discovered his true vocation in horticulture and devoted most of his subsequent thirty-six years to the Worcester County Horticultural Society and the city's Parks Commission. Lincoln's background and sensibilities placed him closer to the city's old-line "gentry" than to its new manufacturers, but the distinction between the two groups was not always sharp. Lincoln's brother, for example, was president of the Boston and Albany Railroad.[6]

In his elite background, as well as in his career instability and his idiosyncratic personality, Lincoln resembled Frederick Law Olmsted. More important, Lincoln seems also to have shared the conservative social assumptions of Olmsted and such other Gilded Age genteel reformers as Henry Adams and E. L. Godkin, who insisted on a well-ordered and tranquil society based on hierarchy and professional leadership. Parks, in this view, would, in the same way as tariff or civil service reform, promote social cohesion and order. The quiet contemplation of a park's rural scenery, Olmsted believed, would calm the "rough element of the city" and "divert men from unwholesome, vicious, destructive methods and habits of seeking recreation." But Olmsted's elegant vision of public parks—and Lincoln's own, less elaborated view—was not centered on controlling the urban worker. Their primary concern was the middle-class urban dweller, whose frayed nerves and exhausted body could be refreshed and renewed by the contemplation of a carefully crafted landscape.[7]

Initially, at least, Lincoln had scant opportunity to implement this Olmstedian vision of the scenic park, for, upon becoming head of the Parks Commission in 1870, he found he had little to rule. Worcester's parkland consisted of an "unsightly" eight-acre Common and a larger 28-acre tract known as Elm Park. Despite the name, the latter primarily served as "a handy dumping ground for the Highway Department . . . [and] the casual job-wagon or wheel barrow."[8] Such inelegant and inadequate public grounds offended Lincoln's horticultural sensibilities; he found them lacking the beauty of the elaborate European public gardens, fountains, and boulevards that he admired so much. Moreover, such grounds failed to accord with Olmsted's view of parks as instruments of conservative social reform that might defuse social tensions.

Influenced by these aesthetic and moral visions, Lincoln fought for and won the appropriations needed to begin to shape Elm Park into a fair approximation of the Olmstedian contemplative ideal. Gradually, the land was cleared and drained; broad stretches of grass were planted; azaleas, rare trees, and exotic shrubs were artistically arranged; elaborate pools were constructed and arched by intricate wooden bridges.[9]

In pursuit of this ideal, Lincoln sought to banish active uses of Elm Park. Circuses, which had earlier lost their home on the Common, were banned in 1875. Three years later, the soon-to-be-familiar "keep off the grass" signs were given legal sanction.[10] Baseball playing was left undisturbed, but Lincoln hoped that this "dreary amusement" would soon be removed from his cherished Elm Park to specially designated playing fields in "different sections" of the city. Presumably, these fields would be placed closer to the homes of working-class Worcesterites who lived in the southeastern part of the city, not in the more exclusive West Side where Elm Park was located.[11]

This clash between what J. B. Jackson, an environmental historian, calls "two distinct and conflicting definitions of the park"—"the upper-class definition with its emphasis on cultural enlightenment and greater refinement of manners, and a lower-class definition emphasizing fun and games"—continued throughout Lincoln's park regime.[12] His annual park reports provide some guarded hints of this class conflict over park usage. In 1876, for example, he petitioned for police patrol of the Common and Elm Park, declaring "this Commission will exact and enforce that decent behavior from all who frequent the Public Grounds, which is not only seemly in itself but is rightfully expected by the community." Repeated complaints describe correct park behavior as "peaceful," "inoffensive," and "quiet," whereas misbehavior was seen as "rude and boorish," or "disorderly and obscene." The *Worcester Spy* captured Lincoln's notion of proper and genteel park usage when it reported approvingly on Elm Park as a "resort for nurses and fond mamas, the former arrayed in the usual white cap and apron, who have brought out the babies for an airing."[13]

This conflict between different styles of park design and usage climaxed in the 1880s as two contrasting groups asserted new interests. On the one hand, the city's industrialists worked out new, more utilitarian arguments for park development that went beyond the contemplative ideal of Lincoln and the old gentry elite who made up the Parks Commission. They urged additions to the city's parkland for reasons of fire protection, health, civic pride, real estate devel-

opment, paternalism, and social control. On the other hand, a large
and rapidly growing immigrant working class raised its own demands for space suited to its own more active, play-centered park
models. Out of this clash emerged a spatial solution that allowed
both groups a measure of autonomy within which to develop their
own approaches to park usage and play.

In January 1884, 231 members of Worcester's elite, including several ex-mayors and many leading manufacturers, petitioned the City
Council to purchase Newton Hill, a sixty-acre tract adjoining Elm
Park. Their motivation, however, was not primarily aesthetic or recreational. Rather, they saw Newton Hill as an ideal spot for a reservoir that would provide fire protection for their fashionable West
Side homes.[14] Such political muscle could not be easily resisted. But
an unlikely political alliance proved capable of at least temporarily
obstructing the Newton Hill acquisition. On the one hand, fiscal conservatives on the Board of Aldermen opposed any new expenditures
of public funds. On the other hand, representatives of the so-called
lower wards, the immigrant and working-class southeastern section
of the city, threatened to block the purchase in retaliation for the
earlier defeat of their own efforts to secure public parkland for their
constituents.

Residents of the East Side confronted the problem of finding play
space in a city increasingly crowded by thousands of new immigrants. The expansion of the physical city could not keep pace with
such rapid population growth. Before the expansion of streetcar service in the late 1880s and the electrification of the lines beginning in
1891, Worcester workers were sharply limited to their choice of residences.[15] Thus, between 1870 and 1890 the city's population
jumped 206 percent, while its platted area grew only 29 percent.
Consequently, the number of residents per platted acre increased by
more than 50 percent, from 43 to 65.[16]

The effects of this increasing density were felt most strongly on
the working-class East Side: most of the city's new residents—the
immigrants—moved to that section while most of the newly laid-out
areas of the city were on the West Side. Such intensification of land
use and the concurrent increases in property values encouraged the
development and enclosure of vacant land previously used as play
space. Thus, in 1882, the city marshal reported that in the absence
of "public grounds for children and others for play and amusement,
especially in the Southern section of the city . . . boys are driven
from streets and fields, and private lands, by the officers." "Of late,"
the *Worcester Daily Times* added the following year, "a number of
boys have been arrested on the east side for one offense or another

but mostly for reasons that would be obviated if they had a public ground or park in which to play."[17] Although Worcester's East Side never approached the overcrowding of New York's Lower East Side, in the 1880s play space in that district was clearly losing ground to housing and commercial development.

Worcesterites of differing social backgrounds were acutely conscious of the class dimensions of these spatial developments. For its part, the city's elite was determined to prevent working-class encroachment into its West Side precincts. When a single family of French-Canadians, who allegedly "sat around the house and on the front doorstep in their shirtsleeves and smoked white clay pipes," settled on Elm Street in the 1880s, it quickly disturbed "the social serenity of the neighborhood," according to the *Worcester Sunday Telegram*. Soon a "terrible fear" swept "West-side society" in response to a rumor that a "cheap tenement block" filled with "the representatives of all nations" would be erected on the same spot. Only when Philip W. Moen, scion of one of the city's wealthiest families, purchased the property in 1889 did West Siders heave a sigh of relief. "Elm Street Set in Ecstacy: Philip W. Moen Has Removed a Long-Time Nightmare," the *Telegram* headlined its story.[18]

While West Siders fretted about exclusivity, working-class East Siders complained about unequal treatment. James H. Mellen, the Irish and pro-labor editor of the *Worcester Daily Times*, repeatedly accused the city government of favoritism and "deference" toward the "well-to-do people" of the West Side, while it ignored the sewers, streets, and park space of the "workingmen's district." An open sewer, such as that on Worcester's East Side, he noted, "would not be tolerated if it ran through any but a locality inhabited by wage workers." Noting the prevalence of diphtheria and the fear of cholera among the "cooped up" and "huddled together" East Siders, Mellen demanded municipal action: "We want more outside room, we want every inch of space the city can afford us."[19]

In the context of these real and perceived class perceptions of spatial inequality, an indigenous movement developed among residents of the Irish working-class East Side (centered in the Fifth, Southeastern, Ward of the city) to demand public play space. As early as 1879 letter writers to the *Worcester Evening Star*, the city's only pro-labor newspaper, complained about the attention lavished on Elm Park—derisively labeled "Lincoln's Patch"—whereas the more accessible (to the working class) Common was neglected. "One who had to stand" maintained that "the people's seats" had been removed from the Common and placed at Elm Park, which he called a "desolate spot where nobody will use them excepting the crows." Another letter writer, similarly perturbed about unequal treatment and impatient with the shaping of Elm Park into a scenic landscape, lampooned Lincoln as "the Earle of the frog ponds" and the "grandiloquent Earle of model pools." Two years later, the *Worcester Daily Times,* which had replaced the *Star* as the voice of the working-class East Side, joined the chorus of complaints by asking, "If it would not be a good thing if our very able 'park commissioner' gave more of his attention to the common and less of it to the park?"[20]

By the following year, however, East Siders began to demand not just better care of the Common; they also demanded their own park. In 1882 Richard O'Flynn, a leader in Irish temperance and civic organizations, called a meeting at the fire station on Lamartine Street, "with the thought that interest could be aroused for the establishment of public playgrounds." Around the same time, he gathered the signatures of almost 140 neighbors on a petition asking the City Council to acquire a "few acres of land" for "the less favored children." Desiring recreational space more congenial to active use than that of Elm Park, the petitioners declared, "there is no public ground in that vicinity [Fifth Ward] where children or young men can resort, either for health or amusement."[21]

The signers of the O'Flynn petition contrasted sharply with the elite Newton Hill petitioners. Their only real social relation to these leading Worcesterites was as employees. Of the ninety-five signers who could be identified, seventy-five held blue-collar jobs. Even the twenty white-collar signers had little in common with the Newton Hill petitioners: six of them, for example, ran provision or grocery stores and another three kept saloons.[22] Whereas the West Side industrial elite sought a park reservoir, their East Side Irish employees wanted a play space for themselves and their children. Indeed, so strong was the perception of the class basis of Worcester's spatial inequities that the petition drive united normally antagonistic segments of the Irish working-class community. It was one of the few times that Irish temperance crusader O'Flynn joined with the proprietors of the community's working-class saloons. Such classwide support acquires particular significance in a city like Worcester with a traditionally weak labor movement.[23] There, at least, the absence of strong trade unions and of working-class political parties did not mean the absence of class conflict.

Despite this working-class alliance and another major petition, the bill for an East Side park remained stalled in the Board of Aldermen. Finally, however, the city's two Democratic aldermen, prodded by their constituents, the working-class Irish, decided to hold Newton Hill hostage for the Ward Five park. "If the city is not willing to provide a breathing spot for women and children who are forced to live in the thickly settled tenement houses . . . they [East Siders] shall certainly oppose any addition to the already spacious park areas on the west side where every family has its own door yard and children's playground," reported the *Boston Sunday Herald.*[24]

Thus, the political conflict experienced by the Board of Aldermen reflected the deeper class conflict over the provision, design, and use of public space in Worcester. A letter to the *Worcester Sunday Telegram* contrasted the needs of the city's "wealthy" and its "toilers" and left little doubt about the class basis of the struggle for play space in Ward Five:

> Our wealthy citizens live in elegant homes on all the hills of Worcester, they have unrestricted fresh air and perfect sewage, their streets are well cleaned and lighted, the sidewalks are everywhere, and Elm Park, that little dream of beauty, is conveniently near. The toilers live on the lowlands, their houses are close together, the hills restrict the fresh air, huge chimneys pour out volumes of smoke, the marshy places give out offensiveness and poison the air, the canal remains uncovered, the streets are different, the little ones are many. While the families of the rich can go to the mountains or to the sea during the hot months of summer, the families of the workers must remain at home.[25]

The temporary resolution of this class conflict was found in a political compromise: the passage of a new Park Act in 1884 and the development of a comprehensive plan for Worcester parks two years later. Of course, other forces, such as real estate development, social uplift, commercial entertainment, and civic boosterism also fostered this new plan. For example, the city's manufacturing elite increasingly saw parks as a means of uplifting and controlling their work force: a way of "cultivating the love of beauty and order" among people of "small means" and even a stimulus to increasing "the excellence of work done" by the city's work people.[26] Other park enthusiasts were more concerned with the general image of the city than with the output of its workshops. "It will not do," Lincoln wrote, comparing Worcester parks with those in New York and Chicago, "to lag in the rear and fall behind our rivals in the race for supremacy."[27]

While a variety of groups backed the new park plan, its real significance lay in its territorial solution to class conflict over the function and location of Worcester's parks. In effect, if not intent, the Parks Commission opted for a scheme of separate development: the East Side would have its playgrounds, the West Side its scenic parks.

Thus, the 1886 park plan represented a spatial victory for Worcester workers. Of the six parcels recommended by the report, the two located on the working-class East Side were specifically designated as playgrounds rather than public gardens. In these play areas workers would have the space and autonomy to use their leisure time as they pleased.[28] Hence, the enthusiastic working-class support for park reform should not necessarily be seen as an endorsement of the conservative social values of the park reformers. "Even where workingmen made extensive use of the language and concepts of middle-class reformers," David Montgomery writes in another context, "they infused those concepts with a meaning quite different from what the middle class had in mind."[29]

Despite this working-class victory in the conflict over the location and design of Worcester parks, struggles continued over park maintenance and behavior. The "separate but equal" parks faced the same problem as did schools founded under that rubric: in a stratified society separate can never be equal. "Most of the park money," charged labor leaders, "has been expended upon parks where the wage workers and their children are least seen, while in East Park, Crompton Park, and the Commons where the most good would be accomplished, the least money is expended and the least improvements made."[30] Even park enthusiasts admitted that Crompton and East parks were "dumps," and one Republican alderman astutely noted that Worcester had created a system of "class parks."[31] But better maintenance alone could not change this basic inequality, since working-class park users also faced overcrowding. "If you want the use of a baseball diamond at Crompton Park, you must sleep on the ground the night before to secure it," one local resident complained in 1904."[32] Such crowding was largely the structural byproduct of an industrial city in which large numbers of workers huddled in a small area, and smaller numbers of manufacturers and managers resided in more spacious surroundings. Paradoxically, the system of "class parks" meant both autonomy and inequality for Worcester workers.

Moreover, Worcester workers also sought to use parks outside their own neighborhoods. And here the battle over proper park behavior continued unabated. In the East Side parks, working-class park behavior was usually, but not always, condoned or ignored. But particularly in the parks that drew users from all sections and classes of the city, such as the Common, Lake Park, and Green Hill Park, conflict raged over correct park usage and behavior. Since many Worcester industrialists had sold the public on parks on the grounds that they would teach workers "respectable habits" and cultivated manners, they fretted continuously about the obvious persistence of loafing, drinking, and similar habits in these parks. Parks, they feared, were providing a setting for precisely the sort of behavior they were supposed to inhibit.

As the city's most central and visible park space, the Common became the object of repeated middle-class complaints about improper use, particularly by working-class patrons. Generally, these commentators grumbled about "dirty unkempt people," "bums," and "idlers" who "loiter," "loaf," and even "sleep off drunks."[33] The implication was that these offenders against public decency were habitual drunks or transient hoboes. Although a few probably were homeless drunkards, most seem to have been unemployed workers. During the depression of 1893, for example, one labor sympathizer counted more than 400 jobless men on the Common on an average afternoon.[34] Indeed, on at least one occasion, Worcester civic leaders confirmed this picture of the Common's patrons. In 1887 as part of a campaign against the building of a new post office on the Common many prominent citizens proclaimed the Common's importance to "the working class" and "the 'plain people' of Abe Lincoln." "This breathing space in the very centre of the city," proclaimed Senator George Frisbe Hoar, Worcester's most prominent political leader, "is the comfort and luxury of the very poorest of the people; women who can snatch a few moments from work . . . men out of and waiting for work."[35] Perhaps, then, the usual complaints about loafing on the Common simply reflected middle-class blindness to the large-scale, recurrent joblessness of those years. Except when expedient, mid-afternoon relaxation by the unemployed in the city's most visible park space might be defined as unacceptable park behavior, subject to official repression, including the removal of park benches.[36]

Just as idleness was a common experience for nineteenth-century workers, so was drinking an often indispensable part of their popular culture. Not surprisingly, it, too, accompanied them into the parks. Although relatively few users of the Common were drunkards, more moderate drinking and even covert liquor sales could be readily found in that public space.[37] In addition, reunions and outings at the lake, for example, were usually lubricated by ale and beer—often donated by brewers eager to advertise their product.[38] To reduce drinking at the lake, the Board of Aldermen on several occasions refused to issue liquor licenses to lakeside establishments. But the main impact seems to have been to encourage whiskey drinking, since flasks were more easily transported and concealed than beer kegs.[39] Even when liquor selling was banned in Worcester, a heavy traffic in beer and whiskey flourished in the woods along the lake shores.[40]

Naturally, drinking was much more prevalent in the East Side parks, given their proximity to most of the city's saloons. Yet such drinking was less often complained of, in part because middle-class Worcesterites rarely witnessed it. "Crompton Park," noted a newspaper reporter in 1898, "is a place that many people in Worcester have but slight occasion to visit." Consequently, complaints about drinking in East Side parks often emanated from temperance-minded local residents. In 1901, for example, the Reverend James Tuite of St. Anne's Catholic Church urged the Liquor License Commission to restrict the beer sales of a Shrewsbury Street liquor dealer. Otherwise, he feared that the area would be turned into a "place of orgies . . . on account of the proximity to East Park, which has been and will be made a place, both night and day, by men, women, and boys of carousal, and drunkenness to be avoided by all decent people." A sensational crime might also bring notice to East Side park behavior. In 1901 a bloody murder, which began with a barroom fight, culminated with a Crompton Park shooting. A reporter sent to investigate commented on the "dozens of saloons in the vicinity of the park" and the large number of saloon patrons who frequented the park.[41]

Working-class traditions of public and communal leisure as well as the absence of spacious homes and apartments placed working-class drinking in public areas like saloons and parks. Similarly, the lack of privacy in many tenements and three-deckers probably pushed some sexual activities into the public parks. In 1879, for example, the *Worcester Evening Star* reported that a twenty-two-year-old Irish immigrant had become pregnant after a "too intimate" acquaintance with a young man in Elm Park. Some years later the *Labor News* guardedly hinted at similar youthful sexual explorations when it reported that "young people of both sexes" resented the lighting of North Park.[42] Such reports may have only been the tip of the iceberg. In 1902 a New Orleans park official, Edward Baker, told the sixth annual meeting of the American Park and Outdoor Art Association about what he called "immoral uses made of public parks by portions of the public." He acknowledged that some might object to the discussion of such a delicate subject, but he insisted that "among superintendents and other executive officers this subject is not an uncommon topic."[43]

Obviously the parks did not eradicate or reshape deeply embedded behavior patterns. Nor did they Americanize workers—another benefit sometimes promised by enthusiastic park promoters. On the contrary, Worcester parks probably supported existing ethnically based leisure patterns, by providing a convenient location for the outings of ethnic and church organizations. In the early twentieth century, for example, the Chandler Hill and Draper Field sections of East Park seem to have been divided between Swedes and Italians. Chandler Hill, located near the Swedish working-class community of Belmont Hill, was the scene of Swedish temperance rallies.[44] The growing Shrewsbury Street Italian community, on the other hand, dominated the adjoining Draper Field. As recalled by Louis Lomatire, a retired streetcar conductor, it was a "center of activity" for Worcester Italians, with festivals, concerts, fireworks, sledding, skating, and swimming.[45] Green Hill Park offered picnic facilities for a wide array of ethnic groups. However, it was not a place for ethnic intermingling: Worcester immigrant picnickers remained segregated in their own fraternal or church organizations.[46] If the parks ever served as a melting pot, it was a rather volatile one. The custodian of the men's bathhouse at the lake warned against overcrowding in the locker rooms: "You take a fellow from French Hill and double him up with a fair haired [Swedish] boy who lives on Belmont Hill, and there will be a fight right away."[47]

The introduction of parks did not "remake" the Worcester working class in the image desired by industrialists and reformers. Neither did it precipitate a new class solidarity or consciousness. While the struggle to win an East Side park had transcended some of the divisions within the Irish working-class community, the actual use of parks revealed greater antagonisms between ethnic working-class communities. Basically, parks provided a leisure space in which workers expressed and preserved their distinct ethnic cultures. And although these immigrant workers carved out a way of life distinct from that prescribed by the native American middle and upper classes, they rarely united or directly challenged the economic and political dominance of the city's Yankee elite. Thus, the struggle over recreational space suggests both the strengths and weaknesses of Worcester's working class.

The efforts by workers to reshape the designs of park reformers were not confined to Worcester. Although little work has been done on the relationship between workers and parks in other cities, it seems likely that similar conflicts—and resolutions—can be found in other industrial communities. For example, in 1870 Frederick Law Olmsted designed a system of contemplative parks for Buffalo, New York. But, as large numbers of working-class immigrants settled in the vicinity of one of the parks, the complaints of "rowdyism," "vandalism," "disorder," and "improper use of public parks" mounted. Ultimately, the Parks Commission was forced to abandon its efforts to foster park use consistent "with the tasteful embellishment and good housekeeping of the grounds," and to redesign the park in line with working-class usage.[48]

The efforts of reformers to uplift, refine, and control the working class through the provision of parks did not significantly diminish the autonomy Worcester workers exercised over their leisure time and space. On the contrary, workers were able to turn reform efforts to their own advantage and win free space within which to pursue their own conception of leisure activity. Within that unstructured context, working-class communities were able to affirm the distinctive values of the ethnic culture composing them. But given the nature of economic relationships and power in Worcester society, such recreational autonomy existed only within limited boundaries and under substantial constraints. East Side parks never received the appropriations or care lavished on the West Side ones and were, as a result, often poorly maintained and heavily overcrowded. Moreover, although the various attempts to mold working-class recreational behavior were never fully successful, some of these efforts did affect working-class life. Workers could, for example, smuggle liquor to the lake, but that was neither as simple nor as pleasant as purchasing it there. Although not always used, police power stood behind the city's efforts to maintain certain basic middle-class standards of decorum in its parks.

The most fundamental constraint on working-class recreation, however, was work itself. In 1890 the *Worcester Evening Gazette* described in detail how Worcester workers played freely in Institute Park during lunchtime:

> Before the 12:05 whistle blows, the crowd begins to arrive from Washburn and Moen's, the envelope shops, electric light station, and many other establishments north of Lincoln Square. After eating, a good romp is indulged in by the girls, running and racing about, with now and then a scream of laughter when some mishap, a fall perhaps, occurs to one of their number. Some of them wander about in pairs or groups, exchanging girlish confidences, or indulging in good-natured banter with their masculine shop-mates. Occasionally a boat is secured by some gallant youth, who rows a load of laughing maidens about the pond, the envied of their less fortunate friends.
>
> The younger men try a game of base ball or a little general sport, jumping, running, etc., while their elders sit about in the more shaded spots, smoking their pipes. But when the whistles blow previous to 1 o'clock there is a general stampede to the shops and in a few minutes all of those remaining can be counted on one's fingers.[49]

No matter how much autonomy Worcester workers achieved in their leisure space and time, they still had to confront the factory whistle. Its sound returned them to a sphere of life in which power and control resided outside their class.

NOTES

So many people have provided helpful comments on this article that it is impossible to thank all of them by name. I would, however, like to mention Jean-Christophe Agnew, Donald Bell, Betsy Blackmar, Michael Frisch, Deborah Kaplan, Carol Lasser, Bruce Laurie, Warren Leon, Barry Leiwant, Jon Peterson, Chris Rosen, and Stephan Thernstrom. I also thank the Worcester Parks and Recreation Commission for access to its records. An earlier version of this article appeared in *Radical History Review*, 21 (Fall 1979), and subsequently in my book, *Eight Hours for What We Will: Workers and Leisure in an Industrial City* (New York, 1983).

1. Downing, quoted in Jon Alvah Peterson, "The Origins of the Comprehensive City Planning Ideal in the United States, 1840–1911" (Ph.D. dissertation, Harvard University, 1967), p. 76.

2. Geoffrey Blodgett, "Frederick Law Olmsted: Landscape Architecture as Conservative Reform," *Journal of American History*, 62 (Mar. 1976), 878.

3. Lawrence A. Finfer, "Leisure as Social Work in the Urban Community: The Progressive Recreation Movement, 1890–1920" (Ph.D. dissertation, Michigan State University, 1974), pp. 143–44. For even more sweeping indictments, see Joel Spring, "Mass Culture and School Sports," *History of Education Quarterly*, 14 (Winter 1974), 483; Cary Goodman, *Choosing Sides: Playground and Street Life on the Lower East Side* (New York, 1979). For discussions of parks framed in terms of social control, see Paul Boyer, *Urban Masses and Moral Order in America, 1820–1920* (Cambridge, Mass., 1978), pp. 238, 356–7; Galen Cranz, "Changing Roles of Urban Parks: From Pleasure Garden to Open Space," *Landscape*, 22 (Summer 1978), 9.

4. On the use of social-control theory by historians, see William A. Muraskin, "The Social-Control Theory in American History: A Critique," *Journal of Social History*, 9 (Summer 1976), 559–80; Gareth Stedman Jones, "Class Expression versus Social Control? A Critique of Recent Trends in the Social History of 'Leisure,' " *History Workshop*, 4 (Autumn 1977), 163–70.

5. For a more detailed portrait of Worcester's industrial and ethnic history, see Roy Rosenzweig, *Eight Hours for What We Will: Workers and Leisure in an Industrial City, 1870–1920* (New York, 1983), pp. 9–32.

6. Worcester Commission on Shade Trees and Public Grounds, *Annual Report for the Year Ending November 30, 1896* (Worcester, 1897), p. 5; the variously titled annual reports of the Parks Commission are hereafter cited as *Park Report*. *Park Report, 1897*, pp. 3–5; unidentified clipping, Dec. 15,

1896, Clipping File, Worcester Historical Museum; Waldo Lincoln, *History of the Lincoln Family* (Worcester, 1923).

7. Olmsted, quoted in Blodgett, "Frederick Law Olmsted," pp. 872, 877, 878, and Roy Lubove, "Social History and the History of Landscape Architecture," *Journal of Social History*, 8 (Winter 1975), 274. Whether Olmsted was a "conservative" or a "democratic" thinker remains a subject of debate. Compare, for example, the essays by Geoffrey Blodgett and Albert Fein in Bruce Kelly et al., eds., *Arts of the Olmsted Landscape* (New York, 1981). On Olmsted, see Laura Wood Roper, *FLO: A Biography of Frederick Law Olmsted* (Baltimore, 1973); Albert Fein, *Frederick Law Olmsted and the American Environmental Tradition* (New York, 1972).

8. *Worcester Evening Gazette*, Sept. 15, 1870; *Park Report, 1884*, pp. 189–90. On the state of Worcester's parks before Lincoln, see *Park Reports, 1867–70*.

9. See *Park Reports, 1870–85;* James Draper, "The Parks and Playgrounds of Worcester," *Worcester Magazine*, 1 (Apr. 1901), 239.

10. Parks Commission Minutes, Dec. 30, 1874, Jan. 23, 1878, Park Commission Archives, Green Hill Park, Worcester, Mass., hereafter cited as PC Minutes.

11. *Park Report, 1873*, pp. 12–13.

12. John Brinckerhoff Jackson, *American Space* (New York, 1972), pp. 214–15. See also Joseph Kett, *Rites of Passage: Adolescence in America, 1790 to the Present* (New York, 1977), p. 227.

13. *Park Report, 1876*, pp. 9–10; ibid., *1878*, p. 19; ibid., *1880*, p. 10; *Worcester Spy*, Apr. 19, 1885.

14. *Park Report, 1884*, pp. 209–14. See also *Boston Sunday Herald*, June 28, 1884; *Worcester Spy*, July 12, 1884.

15. On Worcester street railways, see Philip Becker, "History of the Streetcar in Worcester, Mass.," manuscript, copy available at American Antiquarian Society, Worcester, Mass.; Helen H. Balk, "The Expansion of Worcester and Its Effect on the Surrounding Towns" (Ph.D. dissertation, Clark University, 1944), pp. 75–81.

16. Robert A. Roberge, "The Three-Decker: Structural Correlate of Worcester's Industrial Revolution" (M.A. thesis, Clark University, 1965), pp. 19–21.

17. *Annual Report of the City Marshal, 1882* (Worcester, 1883), p. 427; *Worcester Daily Times*, July 5, 1887, also May 5, 1883. Paul Faler describes a similar process of "enclosure" of recreational space in early nineteenth-century Lynn, in "Cultural Aspects of the Industrial Revolution: Lynn, Massachusetts, Shoemakers and Industrial Morality, 1826–1860," *Labor History*, 15 (Summer 1974), 384.

18. *Worcester Sunday Telegram*, July 7, 1889.

19. *Worcester Daily Times*, Jan. 25, June 23, Jan. 12, 6, 1885; see also the editorials in the issues of Feb. 17, Mar. 25, Apr. 30, and May 25, 1885. For a similar French-Canadian complaint, see *Le Travailleur*, Oct. 24, 1882.

20. *Worcester Evening Star*, Aug. 5, 7, 1879; *Worcester Daily Times*, Mar. 18, 1881. See also ibid., June 25, July 25, Aug. 1, 14, 1879.

21. George O'Flynn, "Richard O'Flynn—A Founder," *Publications, Worcester Historical Society*, n.s. 2 (Apr. 1936), 55; petition of Richard O'Flynn et al., Aug. 10, 1882, Board of Aldermen Petitions, Board of Aldermen MSS, Worcester City Hall.

22. I identified the occupations of petitioners from the *Worcester Directory*.

23. In 1885, for example, the *Worcester Daily Times* reported that while Lynn "leads the ranks of organized labor" with twelve Knights of Labor assemblies, "Worcester has no labor organization worthy of the name" (June 30, 1885). For more on the problems of Worcester's labor movement and on the relative absence of working-class political parties, see Rosenzweig, *Eight Hours*, pp. 18–26.

24. *Boston Sunday Herald*, June 21, 1884. See similar analysis in ibid., June 28, 1884, and *Worcester Spy*, June 28, 1884. For other petitions, see petitions of Walsh et al., O'Flynn et al., Duggan et al., and Creamer et al., June 23, 1884, Board of Aldermen Petitions. The signers of these petitions were also overwhelmingly Irish and working class, based on listings checked in the *Worcester Directory*.

25. *Worcester Sunday Telegram*, Dec. 28, 1884.

26. *Worcester Evening Gazette*, Sept. 25, 1886.

27. *Park Report, 1879*, p. 23. See Peterson, "Origins of Comprehensive City Planning," pp. 102–3, on parks as part of intercity competition. Of course, working-class agitation did not end with the passage of the 1884 Park Act. The *Worcester Daily Times* kept up with a steady barrage of attacks to insure that the 1886 plan would include adequate provisions for the East Side: see issues of Mar. 31, Apr. 30, May 25, June 23, 30, July 13, 1885, May 1, 7, June 8, 12, July 19, Nov. 30, 1886.

28. It is important to note that middle-class ideas about recreation were also beginning to change around this time. See John Higham, "The Reorientation of American Culture in the 1890's," in *Writing American History* (Bloomington, 1970); Daniel T. Rodgers, *The Work Ethic in Industrial America, 1865–1920* (Chicago, 1978), pp. 94–124; and Rosenzweig, *Eight Hours*, pp. 140–43.

29. David Montgomery, "Trade Union Practice and Syndicalist Theory," paper, 1969. J. F. Roche writes that the two East Side sites were "well adapted for playgrounds" and "bought primarily for playgrounds." "Historical Sketch of the Parks and Playground of Worcester" (M.A. thesis, Clark University, 1910), pp. 12, 13.

30. *Labor News*, June 22, 1907; see also unidentified clipping (1897) in Parks Commission Scrapbooks, Worcester City Hall, hereafter cited as PC Scrapbooks.

31. *Worcester Spy*, undated clipping (probably 1897), unidentified clipping (1897), both in PC Scrapbooks.

32. *Park Report, 1904*, pp. 14–15. See also ibid., *1908*, p. 1044.

33. Removal of park benches was a repeated response to this perception. "Our Common," *Light*, 4 (Nov. 7, 1891), 6; *Worcester Telegram*, July 16, 1895; *Worcester Evening Gazette*, Jan. 13, 1908; *Worcester Sunday Telegram*, July 3, 1910; *Park Report, 1894*, p. 5; ibid., *1914*, p. 835; ibid., *1902*, p. 7.

34. *Worcester Sunday Telegram,* Aug. 5, 1893; this reference was found in the materials developed by the Assumption College Community Studies Program, Worcester, Mass.

35. F. C. Miter to City Council, G. F. Hoar to City Council, both June 22, 1887, Board of Aldermen Petitions. See also *Worcester Daily Times,* June 14, July 1, 2, 5, 1887.

36. Walter Wyckoff, *The Workers: An Experiment in Reality. The West* (New York, 1899), ch. 1, discusses the problems of jobless workers seeking a place to rest. For a general discussion of the Massachusetts unemployed and the relation between joblessness and transiency, see Alexander Keyssar, "Men out of Work" (Ph.D. dissertation, Harvard University, 1977).

37. See, for example, *Worcester Daily Times,* June 22, 1880, May 13, 1886, July 2, 1887.

38. *Worcester Telegram,* undated clipping (ca. 1947) on "Lake Quinsigamond's Great Days," Scrapbook on Lake, Worcester Historical Museum.

39. Ibid., Apr. 30, 1888, May 6, 1889. See also controversy about liquor at the lake in 1877, ibid., Apr. 30, May 1, 1877.

40. See, for example, ibid., July 5, 1890, which reports on heavy July 4th drinking at the lake during a no-license year.

41. Unidentified clipping, Aug. 12, 1898, PC Scrapbooks; *Worcester Telegram,* Apr. 11, May 2, 1901.

42. *Worcester Evening Star,* Aug. 1, 1879; *Labor News,* July 8, 1916.

43. Edward Baker, "Some Abuses of Public Parks," *Sixth Report of the American Park and Outdoor Art Association* (Boston, 1902), p. 25. Baltimore apparently had a "no courting in the parks" rule. *Worcester Telegram,* July 1, 1893. The use of public parks for sexual activity was also noted in the 1911 report on the "social evil" in Chicago. Boyer, *Urban Masses and Moral Order,* p. 207.

44. PC Minutes, May 5, 1913; *Park Report, 1913,* p. 881.

45. Interview with Louis Lomatire, Worcester Bicentennial Oral History Project, Worcester, 1976 (typescript in possession of author). On Italians' use of East Park, see also *Park Report, 1913,* p. 868; PC Minutes, May 5, 1913; *Park Report, 1916,* p. 921; PC Minutes, May 14, 1917; "Cosmopolitan Worcester," *Worcester Magazine,* 18 (Aug. 1915), 180.

46. *Park Report, 1914,* p. 829.

47. *Worcester Telegram,* June 12, 1910.

48. Robert D. Lusiak, "From the Grand Plaza to the Electric City: A Review of the Planning Heritage of Buffalo, N.Y., 1804–1920" (M.S. thesis, State University of New York at Buffalo, 1972), pp. 18–35. For comments on conflicts over parks in other cities, see John F. Kasson, *Amusing the Millions: Coney Island at the Turn of the Century* (New York, 1978), pp. 11–17; Irving Howe, *The World of Our Fathers* (New York, 1976), p. 212; Stephen Hardy, *How Boston Played: Sport, Recreation, and Community, 1865–1919* (Boston, 1982), pp. 65–84.

49. Quoted in *Park Report, 1840,* p. 40.

PART FIVE

POLITICS

Workers, Old Political Forms, New Economic Problems, and Ideologies

Winslow Homer's *Union Meetings in the Open Air. Harper's Weekly,* January 7,
1860. Courtesy of The Smith College Museum of Art.

CHAPTER 9

Unemployment and
the Labor Movement in
Massachusetts, 1870–1916

ALEXANDER KEYSSAR

If the mechanics and laborers of these times could be required to
do less time labor per day, it would extend over a greater length
of time . . . I have so much confidence in this, that I shall certainly look for the remedy for enforced idleness in this direction,
if in any.
—A carpenter, Massachusetts Bureau of Statistics of Labor,
Tenth Annual Report

There should be a law to give a job to every decent man that's out
of work. And another law to keep all them I-talians from comin'
and takin' the bread out of the mouths of honest people.
—cited in Walter Wyckoff, *The Workers: The West*

I

In the Commonwealth of Massachusetts, between the Civil War and
World War I, steady jobs were a rarity for blue-collar workers. During relatively prosperous years, like 1890 or 1900, one out of every
five members of the labor force experienced some unemployment,
and the typical unemployed worker was out of a job for a bit more
than three months. When the economy was less buoyant—a frequent
occurrence—the possibility of obtaining a full year's work became
even more remote: in 1885, a bad but not very bad year, one-third
of the Bay State's productive workers were unemployed, for an average of four months each. During the half century that followed
the Civil War, it is likely that an average of one-fourth of the working class of Massachusetts was unemployed in the course of each
year.

The threat of "involuntary idleness," moreover, was not confined
to specific groups or pools of workers. To be sure, some jobs were
steadier than others, but few blue-collar occupations offered pre-

233

dictably secure employment, and skilled workers, as well as the unskilled and semiskilled, often found themselves "thrown out" of
work. Nor did age, place of birth, or sex provide a ticket to a working-class haven where jobs were abundant and fears of being laid off
merely fanciful. The "reserve army of the unemployed" in Massachusetts—the phrase, in fact, was used by state officials—was composed of native-born recruits as well as immigrants, men as well as
women, new entrants to the labor force alongside experienced
craftsmen in their mid-forties. Different demographic and social
groups did face unemployment rates of varying magnitude, but the
composition of the reserve army shifted from month to month and
from year to year, and few workers in Massachusetts were immune.
In good years and in bad, involuntary idleness—as an experience or
as a threat—affected the large majority of employees who performed manual labor in the Commonwealth.

   Given this record, it is hardly surprising that unemployment was
one of the major concerns of the labor movement that emerged in
Massachusetts during the period. The "insecurity of labor," noted
one contemporary critic, is "the great subconscious element in the
labor problem." Indeed, for workers the issue was not all that "subconscious": the writings of labor leaders and the recorded utterances
of rank-and-file workers were riddled with references to the shortage of jobs. What *is* surprising is the lack of attention to the problem
on the part of historians; neither the efforts of labor to cope with
the irregularity of work nor the impact of unemployment upon the
shape of the labor movement has received systematic scrutiny from
students of labor and working-class history. This article is, in effect,
a preliminary effort to examine those subjects, to explore the ways
in which unemployment challenged and molded the labor movement during the critical decades when organized labor developed
durable institutional forms and strategies. A great deal of evidence
has been telescoped in these pages, and considerable research remains to be done, but the available data certainly suggest that in
Massachusetts, at least, the chronic irregularity of employment may
well have been—to state the argument baldly—*the* decisive influence
upon the labor movement that developed between the 1870s and
World War I.[1]

                                II

Organized labor became a permanent institutional feature of Massachusetts society between the Civil War and World War I. Although
workers' organizations and unions had been formed in the Bay State

as early as the 1820s, these antebellum efforts tended to be short-lived, and the resurgence of labor activity after the Civil War was checked—indeed, devastated—by the long depression of the 1870s. In 1879, according to one contemporary, "trade unionism was without force in Massachusetts." Less than forty years later, in 1915, there were more than 1,400 locals in the Bay State, and a quarter of a million workers were union members. Labor organizations had been built in a wide variety of different industries and had established their presence in all of the cities and many of the towns of the commonwealth. The labor movement was dominated by men and by skilled workers, but some women and some semiskilled operatives—in the boot and shoe industry, for example—had formed viable organizations. This growth of the labor movement represented the triumph of national trade unions, organized along craft lines: fourteen national or international unions accounted for roughly 60 percent of the Bay State's organized workers, and approximately 80 percent of the Commonwealth's unionists were affiliated with the American Federation of Labor.[2]

The most obvious—and well-known—effects of unemployment on this labor movement were restrictive. Despite its remarkable record of growth, the Massachusetts labor movement was hindered in its efforts to build organizations and to attain concrete objectives because of the chronic shortage of jobs in the Commonwealth. The presence of idled men in a trade or in a community meant that those who did hold jobs could be replaced with relative ease: workers were well aware that in most occupations most of the time a labor surplus existed—and that awareness helped to shape their behavior. "The market is glutted and we have seasons of dullness," noted a leather currier in 1879. "Our tasks are increased, and, if we remonstrate, we are told our places can be filled." Clearly, neither cyclical downturns nor chronic, less severe unemployment levels rendered the working class altogether docile and speechless, but the remonstrances of many workers were stifled by the fear that they might end up changing places with the unemployed.[3]

This dynamic was visibly expressed in the cyclical rhythms of trade union growth; although the statistics are imperfect, it appears that the number of local unions and the number of unionists in Massachusetts declined during each downturn in the economy between 1870 and 1916. And even when times were prosperous, semiskilled and unskilled workers had great difficulty forming unions, in part because of the ease with which they could be replaced. Similarly, wage increases were repeatedly foregone and wage cuts were accepted because workers found that their bargaining position had been undercut by the prevalence of unemployment. In Lowell in 1894 the Woollen Spinners Union decided that "it would be better to accept the reduced wages than to be out of employment altogether, which was the only alternative." A few years later the shoemakers of Brockton made the same decision, since many of their colleagues were still "out of employment" despite the upturn in the economy.[4]

Versions of this scenario were played out on innumerable occasions in the course of each year. Cyclical depressions, seasonal slack times, or the chronic availability of pools of labor led workers to refrain from action or to suffer defeat in their efforts to build unions, earn higher wages, work shorter hours, and alter the conditions of work. During the first quarter of 1902, a prosperous year, one out of every eight strikes in the Commonwealth was terminated when new employees were hired "almost immediately." Between 1881 and 1900 roughly one out of every six strikers in the Commonwealth lost his or her job to a new employee. To be sure, strikes were often won despite the condition of the labor market, and losses could sometimes be recouped at more advantageous moments, but there can be little doubt that the shortage of steady jobs in the Commonwealth dampened the militance of the working class and limited the achievements of the labor movement.[5]

Unemployment, thus, was a serious, even critical, problem for individual workers and for labor unions as organizations. Workers whose daily or weekly earnings were already close to the margin (which was the case for most blue-collar employees) could ill afford repeated spells of joblessness, and the organizations that they formed to better their conditions were themselves threatened by unemployment. "A member of the union who is out of work," noted Adolph Strasser in 1883, "is in danger of soon being out of the union." Unemployment meant a decline in dues-paying membership and the threat of workers accepting jobs at reduced wages. The extent of unemployment in the Commonwealth struck at the welfare of workers and jeopardized the progress—at some moments, even the existence—of trade unions. Unemployment was not an issue that the labor movement could ignore.[6]

It was also not an issue that the labor movement could easily solve. As the workers of the Bay State began to construct or reconstruct labor organizations in the aftermath of the depression of the 1870s, they were vividly aware of the evil of unemployment, but that awareness did not in itself suggest a cure. Most important, perhaps, unemployment differed from problems like low wages, bad working conditions, and health hazards in that it did not seem remediable by challenging individual employers. Workers recognized that capitalists were responding to market conditions when they laid men off, and it did not seem to be fruitful to try to create jobs by forcing employers to produce more goods than they could sell. In addition, many workers and their leaders maintained a firm belief in the "lump of labor" theory—the economic notion that there were fixed limits to the quantity of work that an economy could generate. "There can be only about so much work to do any way, and when that is done, business has got to stop," observed a shoemaker in 1879, and his sentiments were echoed throughout the late nineteenth and early twentieth centuries. In effect—and contrary to ideas that have become common in the post-Keynesian mid-twentieth century—the problem of unemployment in a capitalist economy did not appear to be soluble by expanding the amount of work to be performed in the society.[7]

To some workers in the Commonwealth, of course, this was one more reason to do away with capitalism. In the 1870s and 1880s involuntary idleness prompted many workmen to form producers' cooperatives, and in subsequent decades unemployment was frequently cited as an incentive for building a socialist movement. As William B. Adams, a carpenter from West Quincy, concluded in 1895, "There is only one remedy" . . . and that is government control of all means of production and transportation." Accurate as this diagnosis may have been, it did not offer a means of alleviating the problem in the near or foreseeable future. Even during the brief period when socialism was a potent political force in Massachusetts, few residents of the Bay State believed that a socialist United States was just around the corner; and meanwhile unemployment was taking its toll on individual workers and their organizations. The same shortcoming was true of another of the logically possible approaches to unemployment: paying people who were not working, i.e., unemployment insurance. In the political and ideological climate of the late nineteenth century, such an idea was extraordinarily far-fetched. As late as 1908 the governor of Massachusetts blithely referred to the concept as "not only a constitutional impossibility, but a logical absurdity."[8]

Hemmed in by these structural, ideological, and political constraints, the labor movement was left with only two broad strategic approaches to the problem of unemployment: sharing the amount of work available and restricting the supply of labor. Each of these strategies had advantages and disadvantages as well as its own ideological implications and resonance. In a variety of different concrete forms both strategies were employed between 1880 and World War I.

III

The distribution of work to union members was a widespread and traditional activity for local trade unions. The importance of the union as a source of information about jobs varied from one occupation to another—depending most importantly upon the number of employers in the area and the customary length of a term of employment—but most unions maintained some formal mechanism for bringing together available jobs and unemployed workers. The shoe workers of Haverhill, for example, maintained a registration bureau for idled members, and masons and bricklayers used union meetings and a trade journal for the same purposes. Out-of-work listings, in all of their different forms, served both to shorten the idleness of union members and to offer nonmembers an incentive to join the union.[9]

This type of work distribution was essentially painless: no union member had to sacrifice his own job or her own earnings to provide for the employment of a comrade. But when unemployment levels became unusually high, unions also evolved methods of actual work-sharing, of distributing the available work to the largest possible number of union members. The most common mechanism of work-sharing was the prohibition of overtime for any union member as long as other members were unemployed. This prohibition was practiced by a wide variety of different unions, and violations were taken seriously. In 1899, for example, the cotton mule spinners collectively deplored "the working of overtime in the mills of Lowell while there are so many competent operatives out of employment," and they censured those spinners in Lowell who had not protested against the overtime. As the practice of signing written contracts between unions and employers became more common toward the end of the nineteenth century, the distribution of overtime to the unemployed often became a contractual obligation.[10]

In a number of unions this egalitarian principle was extended even further, and in periods of cyclical or seasonal slowdown all work was evenly distributed among the membership. The contracts signed by the Boston local of the brewery workers contained a clause stipulating that "in case of slack business," idle time was to be rotated among the members; similar agreements were put into force by the diemakers of Lynn and the hat- and capmakers of the Hub. When the Boston Protocol was signed in the garment industry, it too provided for the equal distribution of work among all union members, and Boston's tailors followed the same procedure. A less formal, but essentially identical method was for a union, when faced with a slowdown, to demand that the employer put everyone on short time rather than lay off a portion of the work force. Some employers were more sympathetic to this strategy than others, but the demand was very frequently voiced and—as far as one can tell from the available data—often met with success. When jobs became more scarce than usual, workers responded by dividing them up among themselves, often at considerable cost to those workers who might otherwise have continued working full time.[11]

Still another version of work-sharing was the restriction of output. Only occasionally (among printers and plumbers, for example) did unions formally and publicly adopt rules that limited the output or productivity of individual members, but the practice of pace-setting was common. Faced with technological changes, cyclical downturns, or slack seasons, workers frequently chose to slow down the pace of work to preserve jobs. For those who were paid by the day or the hour, this tactic constituted an attempt to increase annual wages; for others, paid by the piece or by the job, the aim was to steady the rhythms of work and to distribute it with some evenness among the members. The threat of unemployment was, of course, not the only cause of "soldiering," but the restriction of output was, in part, a strategic response to the insecurity of jobs in late nineteenth-century America. The plumbers' rule that bicycles could not be used as a means of transportation between jobs—because it was too efficient a means of transportation—emerged from the widespread sense that there was not enough work to go around.[12]

The final method that unions developed for sharing the burden of unemployment was the union-financed unemployment benefit. Labor organizations had sought to offer relief to their unemployed members as early as the 1830s, but it was in the aftermath of the depression of the 1870s that trade unions developed a serious interest in systematic benefit plans—an interest that was heightened by the downturn of the 1890s. Unemployment benefits, of course, were not quite the same as work-sharing, but they did amount to a sharing of income, a redistribution of wages from the employed to the unemployed. The rationale for such plans was compelling: in addition to relieving distress, they would help to keep the unemployed in the union, prevent scabbing, and maintain wage levels. Nonetheless, relatively few unions maintained an out-of-work benefit for any significant period of time. Benefit plans were expensive, and their effectiveness during prolonged depressions, when they were most needed, was sharply limited by the size of union treasuries. More common than systematic plans, perhaps, were temporary assessments upon working members and informal networks through which union members aided one another during periods of high unemployment. Although not permanently institutionalized, these assessments and networks constituted a means through which the employed shared their resources with the unemployed.[13]

The significance of these methods of distributing the burden of unemployment lies less in their achievements than in the values that they expressed. Neither work-sharing nor unemployment benefits could cure involuntary idleness; at best, they could alleviate symptoms—by reducing financial hardship and protecting the union against a loss of membership and a decline in loyalty. Nonetheless, these methods embodied the resolve of the working class and the labor movement to maintain its solidarity in the face of scarcity. Despite the competitive pressures generated by unemployment, workers displayed a repeated and widespread willingness to sacrifice for one another, in the interest of their collective good and their collective institutions. As a strategy for coping with unemployment in late nineteenth-century Massachusetts, work-sharing was built upon a realistic premise of self-reliance and a shrewd assessment of the imperatives of organization; at the same time it reflected the presence of a culture of mutuality that was an important dimension of working-class consciousness.[14]

The attachment of the working class to the value of solidarity, coupled with the evident need for a genuine cure for the unemployment problem, led the labor movement of Massachusetts to focus its energies upon the drive for a shorter work day. Throughout the nineteenth century labor unions had sought to reduce the number of hours in the working week and the working day, but it was only in the final decades of the century that unemployment became a rationale and impetus for the movement for shorter hours. While the drives of the 1830s and the 1860s had stressed the importance of leisure, the maintenance of wage rates, and the demands of citizenship, later efforts claimed that a reduction in hours would have the consequence of distributing work to the unemployed. As a shoemaker observed in 1879, "There is not enough work to last the year round, and work over eight hours a day, or forty-eight hours a week. . . . if there was an eight-hour law, things would be more even." This argument gained currency throughout the labor movement in the 1880s and the 1890s, and by the end of the century the eight-hour day was viewed as the basic remedy for the irregularity of labor, and the persistence of unemployment had become the primary rationale for the eight-hour day. In 1899 the North Adams Central Labor Union concluded that "the only rational solution" to the problem of an "over-crowded labor market" was a shortening of the hours of work.[15]

The felt urgency of the problem of unemployment was reflected in the energy that the labor movement devoted to the cause of shorter hours. Throughout the 1880s and 1890s the eight-hour day was the dominant issue around which trade unions organized. Often led by workers in occupations that were particularly hard hit by the irregularity of work—the building trades and the shoe industry, for example—the drive assumed some of the proportions of a crusade, and the extent of grass-roots activity was remarkable. In the late 1880s and again in the 1890s dozens of meetings were held in the Commonwealth each month; workers throughout the state raised funds, submitted petitions, and went on strike in favor of the eight-hour day. Both the Knights of Labor and the American Federation of Labor backed the drive.[16]

Despite all of this activity, there is no evidence that the movement for shorter hours had any appreciable effect upon the incidence of unemployment in Massachusetts. The drive had its victories, and the hours of labor in many occupations were reduced between 1880 and World War I, but the frequency of unemployment seems to have remained relatively constant. To be sure, it is possible that unemployment rates would have increased had hours not been reduced or that idleness levels would, in fact, have diminished had the eight-hour goal been fully achieved, but neither of these hypothetical arguments could alter the fact that unemployment levels after 1910 were roughly the same as they had been in the 1880s.[17]

The failure of the eight-hour movement to solve the problem of unemployment was, unfortunately, not surprising—since the arguments put forward by eight-hour advocates were seriously flawed. Reducing the number of hours that men worked each day would necessarily succeed in spreading the work only if employees were willing to accept proportional cuts in their daily wages—which was emphatically not what the labor movement had in mind. The trade unionists of Massachusetts wanted a shorter work day with the same daily rates of pay; indeed, many of them argued that workers would produce as much in eight hours as they did in ten. And if so, where would the work for the unemployed come from? The question was skirted, and for decades the arguments in favor of an eight-hour day remained internally contradictory and problematic. Gradually, during the Progressive era, the labor movement faced its quandary and

relinquished the belief that the eight-hour day would solve the problem of unemployment, although the idea died hard and was resus-
citated in the twentieth century.[18]

To the historian, it is not the accomplishments but rather the appeal of the eight-hour movement that commands attention.
Hundreds of thousands of workers in Massachusetts marched under
the eight-hour banner, hoping and believing that shortening the
hours of work would, among other things, eradicate the problem of
unemployment. Those hopes and beliefs seem to have attached
themselves to the movement for a variety of different reasons. The
first was the simplicity and concreteness of the eight-hour remedy:
the drive for shorter hours set forth a tangible and attainable objective that would, if achieved, produce a profound transformation in
the lives of working people. The eight-hour movement was, in its
tone and rhetoric, simultaneously pragmatic and utopian, a curious
but legitimate offspring of the different currents in the labor movement symbolized by the Knights of Labor and the American Federation of Labor. Part of the allure of the eight-hour campaign was its
offer of dramatic results through direct, incremental action.

The appeal of the eight-hour remedy also seems to have been
rooted in its fundamental egalitarianism. Shorter hours would eradicate the threat of unemployment for all workers and increase the
leisure of many; the imbalance between the demand for labor and
the supply of labor would be rectified without imposing a penalty
upon any worker. The problems of an "over-crowded labor market"
could thus be solved while the solidarity of the working class was
maintained. This was work-sharing on a grand scale, and no one's
wages would be cut. Like many of the panaceas that were popular
in late nineteenth-century America, the eight-hour movement led
down alleys that were at least partially blind; at the same time, it
revealed the yearnings and the confusions generated by the rapid
advance of industrial capitalism. The energy and time invested in
the eight-hour movement were testimony to the working class's twin
objectives of obtaining job security while preserving the values of
solidarity and mutuality. The failure—indeed, the perhaps inevitable failure—of this broad-gauged movement to solve the problem of
unemployment was to have an important impact upon the history of
American labor.

IV

Early in the spring of 1894 the Granite Cutters Union of Boston
issued a public protest that contracts for stone-cutting were being

given to men from outside the state "while the granite cutters of Boston were walking the streets in idleness." The union justified its stated desire to take jobs away from out-of-state workers by pointing out that the stone-cutting was being performed in "Sullivan, Maine, where the men own their own farms and do not need the work as much as we do here in Boston." The rationale was revealingly defensive; the granite cutters were evidently sensitive to the need for working-class solidarity and uncomfortable over protecting their own interests at the expense of other workers. Nonetheless, they did their utmost, both in the 1890s and in later years, to compel the hiring of local labor.[19]

The experience of Boston's granite cutters was repeated again and again, in one form or another, in the labor movement of Massachusetts. Despite an authentic attachment to the value of working-class cohesion, labor unions responded to the dilemma of unemployment with competitive as well as cooperative strategies. Work-sharing had its benefits, and the movement for shorter hours might eventually usher in an era of job security, but in the meantime both workers and unions had to be protected against recurrent unemployment. That protection could be achieved, or so it seemed, by restricting the supply of labor, by limiting the number of workers who had access to particular jobs. To achieve those limits, local, state, and national unions adopted policies that were both defensive and exclusionist, designed to maintain the security of some workers by shifting the burden of scarcity onto others. During the final decades of the nineteenth century, these competitive tactics developed alongside more egalitarian and cooperative ones; after the turn of the century, after some of the faith and the steam in the eight-hour movement had ebbed away, they seemed to become the labor movement's primary weapon in the fight against unemployment.[20]

The most overtly political expression of these exclusionist tendencies was the attitude of the labor movement toward immigration and foreign workers. If high unemployment levels were caused by a surplus of labor, it readily followed that immigrants were the source of the surplus and that problem could be remedied by shutting off the migratory stream. For a variety of reasons the labor movement resisted this logic for a number of years, but during the 1890s restrictionist forces began to gather strength, and by 1906 the dominant voices in organized labor were openly and energetically in favor of restricted immigration. The American worker had to be protected— even if it was at the expense of those who had not yet departed from the Old World.[21]

But labor unions alone could not restrict immigration, and the flow of labor into Massachusetts and other states continued unabated until World War I. Individual unions could, however, restrict access into their own occupations, and they strove mightily to do so. The most obvious mechanism for limiting entry into a trade was the fixed ratio of apprentices to journeymen; such ratios were common as early as the 1860s, and their popularity did not diminish later in the century. Carpenters, plumbers, bricklayers, masons, iron molders, printers, machinists, cigarmakers, weavers, and barbers all sought to limit the size of the entry portals into their occupations. As one barber noted, apprenticeship restrictions could prevent "tradesmen clothed with years of experience" from having "to walk the streets of our cities and towns in idleness." As the business community self-righteously pointed out, limiting the number of apprentices narrowed the opportunities of the young, but few tradesmen seem to have been converted by this plea for generational generosity.[22]

The same pressures that yielded limits on the number of apprentices also produced rivalries between workers who belonged to the same trade but lived in different communities. Despite the evident need for national unions and for harmony among the locals that belonged to each national union, workers frequently focused their antagonism upon other workers from other regions. The case of the granite cutters has already been mentioned, and it was not unusual. In 1893 the tailors of Boston held a mass meeting to complain that merchants were sending work to New York, and in the early twentieth century workers in the cigar and clothing industries did the same. This spirit of "home guardism" also shaped the response of local unions to traveling members, to workers who were affiliated with a national union and who sought work in Massachusetts. During the first two decades of the twentieth century, local organizations became increasingly reluctant to honor union cards from outside the state. When a cyclical or seasonal shortage of labor did occur, unions preferred to issue temporary permits to nonmembers rather than encourage unionists from other areas to migrate to Massachusetts, where they might well have chosen to stay even after the demand for labor had slackened.[23]

Similarly, prolonged experience with a shortage of jobs helped to spawn the jurisdictional disputes that created so much animosity between unions, even between unions that belonged to the American Federation of Labor. To be sure, these conflicts between workers who belonged to different but overlapping occupations often had a multitude of causes, but the ferocity with which jurisdictional claims were often pressed was rooted in the need for unions to maximize the amount of work available to their members. The competition between the woodworkers and the carpenters of Boston produced a celebrated and prolonged struggle early in the twentieth century; at the core of it was a shortage of jobs in two trades with notably high unemployment rates. Under the pressure of scarcity, workers and unions abandoned their concern for the welfare of the class as a whole and fought vociferously to protect their own turf.[24]

In effect, all of these strategies were designed to combat unemployment by protecting the interests of an "in" group against the real or perceived rivalry of an "out" group. Needless to say, perhaps, the same forces that produced this internecine warfare also contributed to the labor movement's stance toward unskilled workers and women. Both groups—and they were not totally distinct—did appear to be genuine threats to stable employment in an era of skill dilution and chronically high levels of involuntary idleness. Moreover, both groups, as well as immigrants in certain occupations, appeared to be strategic liabilities, since they could so easily be replaced from the existing pools of unemployed and underemployed labor. Faced with persistent shortages of jobs and battered by periodic severe depressions, the strongest organizations in the labor movement chose not to seek alliances with the weak; instead, they used avowedly competitive means to protect themselves from the consequences of competition. By the beginning of World War I, the generous, if apocalyptic, vision of the eight-hour movement had been obscured by the defensive bulwarks of craft unionism.

V

Unemployment was probably the knottiest and most fundamental problem that the labor movement of Massachusetts confronted during its formative years. On the eve of World War I, after decades of effort to render jobs more secure, the Bay State's labor council still found involuntary idleness to be the "greatest evil" confronting workers, and an official of the typographical union concluded that it was "the most difficult to handle" of all the problems facing trade unionists. A half century of experimentation—marked by confusion, uncertainty, hope, faith, anger, defensiveness, and frustration—had not produced a solution to the problem or even a strategic model for all workers to emulate. To be sure, some working people in some occupations did have steadier jobs in 1915 than they or their counterparts had had in the 1880s, but the societal problem persisted. Only when the United States went to war did there seem to be a shortage of workers, rather than jobs, in the Commonwealth.[25]

Indeed, it is likely that unemployment had a greater effect upon the labor movement than the labor movement had upon unemployment. The irregularity of work in the Bay State created a climate of

scarcity that stifled the growth of unified working-class institutions
and strategies. The working class of Massachusetts was remarkably
heterogeneous in its composition, and, under the pressure of
chronic unemployment, fissures emerged where boundaries had
been latent. Rivalries and antagonisms developed between American
workers and their European counterparts, between men who already belonged to a trade and men who sought to enter one, between the skilled and the unskilled, carpenters and woodworkers,
men and women, residents of Boston and residents of Sullivan,
Maine. The very strategies that the labor movement adopted to fight
against unemployment—strategies that many workers felt were essential to their own survival—served to violate and to fracture the
bonds of solidarity that the labor movement had originally sought to
strengthen. The presence of involuntary idleness stimulated and
reinforced the organization of unions along craft lines and generated conflicts among the crafts. As a result—at least in part—of unemployment, the labor movement of Massachusetts in 1916 was relatively small, composed largely of skilled workers, criss-crossed with
competing factions, and devoted to self-protective goals.

It should be noted, albeit more speculatively, that unemployment
also seems to have had a significant impact upon the internal structure and workings of labor unions, at least in some trades. The
growth of local unions in the late nineteenth and early twentieth
centuries brought into being a network of full-time, paid union officials (business agents or shop collectors) who often wielded great
power in union policy decisions. Their power was enhanced by the
fact that they often controlled access to all available jobs. In occupations with high rates of idleness—like the building trades or the shoe
industry—a worker's livelihood often depended upon his being in
the good graces of the business agent. Thus, the strength of conservative, bureaucratic forces within the labor movement may have
been rooted in the soil of unemployment. A similar conservatism
may also have been produced by the emergence, in some unions, of
formal systems of seniority that governed lay-offs. Seniority provided needed protection for older workers but created a gap between the interests of the old and the young; in addition, it tended
to depersonalize the threat of unemployment for those experienced
workers who were most likely to wield power within the union.[26]

What the labor movement in Massachusetts would have looked
like had there been little unemployment in the Commonwealth is too
hypothetical a question to answer with any precision, but the very
fantasy of a labor movement emerging from a "full employment"
economy suggests the profundity of the effects of unemployment.
Trade unions that did not find job security to be an urgent issue

would have been radically different: energies would have been devoted to other issues, defensive and divisive strategies would have been unnecessary, and different organizational structures would probably have emerged. The labor movement might indeed have been far more able to overcome, rather than accentuate, the economic and social divisions that permeated the working class. Contrary to certain beliefs that commonly inform the study of the American past, it was not the scarcity of labor but rather the scarcity of jobs that determined the shape of the labor movement in Massachusetts and elsewhere. As Selig Perlman noted years ago, American workers did possess a "scarcity consciousness" that originated in the experiences of unemployment that punctuated the lives of most American workers.[27]

Unemployment did not disappear from Massachusetts after World War I. The phenomenon of involuntary idleness was and is endemic to industrial capitalism, and it continues to be a key issue for the working people of the Commonwealth. By the end of the Progressive era, however, the basic outlines of a durable societal response to the problem had begun to emerge. The idea of eliminating unemployment was fading, and strategies for learning to live with the phenomenon were coming to the fore. The labor movement itself played an important role in this evolving political economy, in the acceptance of unemployment as an inherent feature of American capitalism. By 1916 much of the labor movement seemed to have surrendered the goal of solving the problem of unemployment, and, without the support of organized labor, radical proposals designed to guarantee steady jobs for all workers were doomed to political oblivion. In the absence of any such societal guarantees, the labor movement sought to procure and to retain relatively secure jobs for the unionized minority of the labor force: powerful craft unions would protect their own members and preserve their own power. Meanwhile, the inevitable victims of unemployment could have their most severe hardships alleviated by the state—in the form of public works projects or even unemployment insurance.[28] The labor movement that unemployment had helped to shape had begun to put its weight behind structures and policies that implicitly accepted and perhaps insured the perpetuation of the problem.

NOTES

A revised and more lengthy treatment of the relationship between the labor movement and unemployment has appeared as a chapter in my *Out of Work: The First Century of Unemployment in Massachusetts* (New York, 1986).

1. The arguments in this article are based on research that had been completed by the end of 1978: they are stated somewhat tentatively since other sources remain to be consulted and analyzed. Statements regarding the incidence and distribution of unemployment in Massachusetts, throughout, are based on detailed analyses presented in chs. 3–5 of *Out of Work*. John A. Garraty's *Unemployment in History* (New York, 1978) does begin to break the silence of historians on the subject of unemployment, but the book is concerned almost exclusively with the history of ideas about and policy responses to unemployment. The quotation regarding the "subconscious element" is from Louis B. Wehle, cited in Don D. Lescohier, *The Labor Market* (New York, 1919), p. 123.

2. In 1915 trade unionists constituted roughly 15 percent of the entire labor force and 18 percent of all employees in Massachusetts. The proportion of trade union members who were women fluctuated significantly between 1908 and 1916: it never reached as high as 20 percent and was sometimes under 10 percent. See Alexander Keyssar, "Men out of Work" (Ph.D. dissertation, Harvard University, 1977), pp. 57, 60, 430–32. See also Massachusetts Bureau of Statistics of Labor (MBSL), *Forty-seventh Annual Report* (Boston, 1916), part VI, p. 7; MBSL, *Forty-ninth Annual Report* (Boston, 1918), part IV, pp. 9–10; MBSL, *Labor Bulletin #10* (Boston, 1899), pp. 48–55; George E. McNeill, ed., *The Labor Movement* (Milwaukee, 1891), p. 197; Philip S. Foner, *History of the Labor Movement in the United States*, I (New York, 1947), p. 516; Augusta E. Galster, *The Labor Movement in the Shoe Industry* (New York, 1924), pp. 57–60.

3. MBSL, *Tenth Annual Report* (Boston, 1879), p. 133.

4. MBSL, *Twenty-fifth Annual Report* (Boston, 1894), pp. 309ff.; MBSL, *Thirty-ninth Annual Report* (Boston, 1908), pp. 156–57; MBSL, *Forty-second Annual Report* (Boston, 1911), p. 80; MBSL, *Forty-sixth Annual Report* (Boston, 1915), part IX, p. 7; MBSL, *Forty-ninth Annual Report*, part IV, p. 19; *Boston Globe*, Feb. 10, 13, 1894. Although unemployment had an important impact upon both skilled and unskilled workers, the unskilled and semiskilled could be more easily replaced because they could be transferred from one industry or occupation to another.

5. MBSL, *Labor Bulletin # 25* (1903), pp. 42–43; MBSL, *Labor Bulletin #22* (1902), p. 62; MBSL, *Thirty-ninth Annual Report*, pp. 46, 63ff. See Lloyd Ulman, *The Rise of the National Trade Union*, 2d ed. (Cambridge, 1966), pp. 426ff. Existing statistical data make it far easier to detect the impact of cyclical downturns than to measure the impact of chronic unemployment.

6. McNeill, ed., *Labor Movement*, p. 607.

7. MBSL, *Tenth Annual Report*, p. 118.

8. *Report of the Massachusetts Board to Investigate the Subject of the Unemployed*, House Document #50 (Boston, 1895), part V, Appendix H, p. 130; MBSL, *Labor Bulletin # 57* (1908), p. 61.

9. *Report of the Massachusetts Board*, part V, Appendix F, pp. 112–22; MBSL, *Labor Bulletin #28* (1903), p. 207; D. P. Smelser, *Unemployment and American Trade Unions* (Baltimore, 1919), pp. 55ff.

10. Smelser, *Unemployment*, p. 54; MBSL, *Thirtieth Annual Report* (Boston,

1899), pp. 140–41; MBSL, *Thirty-fourth Annual Report* (Boston, 1903), p. 417; MBSL, *Thirty-sixth Annual Report* (Boston, 1905), p. 553; MBSL, *Forty-second Annual Report*, p. 131.

11. MBSL, *Labor Bulletin #33* (1904), p. 252; MBSL, *Labor Bulletin #34* (1904), p. 365; MBSL, *Twenty-fourth Annual Report* (Boston, 1893), p. 281; MBSL, *Forty-second Annual Report*, pp. 230–31; Smelser, *Unemployment*, pp. 113–14.

12. Smelser, *Unemployment*, pp. 45ff.; Ulman, *National Trade Union*, pp. 536ff.; Jacob H. Hollander and George E. Barnett, eds., *Studies in American Trade Unionism* (London, 1906), p. 305ff.

13. Bryce M. Stewart, *Unemployment Benefits in the United States* (New York, 1930), pp. 80–83, 206, 256; MBSL, *Twenty-sixth Annual Report* (Boston, 1895), p. 718; Frank Stockton, *The International Molders Union of North America* (Baltimore, 1921), pp. 23, 67–68; *Report of the Massachusetts Board*, part I, p. xxxvi; *Boston Globe*, Mar. 13, 1909; Smelser, *Unemployment*, pp. 139–44.

14. Regarding the existence of a culture of mutuality and reciprocity within the working class, see Keyssar, *Out of Work*, ch. 6.

15. McNeill, ed., *Labor Movement*, pp. 85, 139, 463, 470–71, 582–83, 596 e, f, g, m, 607; Philip S. Foner, *History of the Labor Movement in the United States*, II, 2d ed. (New York, 1975), pp. 103, 178, 243; David Montgomery, *Beyond Equality* (New York, 1967), p. 237; MBSL, *Tenth Annual Report*, pp. 118, 121; MBSL, *Thirtieth Annual Report*, p. 135; *Boston Globe*, Mar. 12, 1894; *Report of the Massachusetts Board*, part V, Appendix H, pp. 127–30.

16. McNeill, ed., *Labor Movement* pp. 596, 3, f; Foner, *Labor Movement*, II, 103, 178, 181–83, 243; MBSL, *Twenty-fourth Annual Report*, pp. 271ff; MBSL, *Twenty-fifth Annual Report*, pp. 307ff.; MBSL, *Twenty-sixth Annual Report*, pp. 711ff.; MBSL, *Twenty-seventh Annual Report* (Boston, 1896), pp. 309ff.; MBSL, *Twenty-eighth Annual Report* (Boston, 1897), pp. 313ff.

17. MBSL, *Labor Bulletin # 29* (1904), p. 8; MBSL, *Twenty-fifth Annual Report*, p. 308; Springfield Scrapbooks, Springfield (Mass.) Public Library, II, 47; Keyssar, "Men Out of Work," ch. 3.

18. Smelser, *Unemployment*, pp. 50ff. A far more detailed treatment of the rationales for the eight-hour day is presented in *Out of Work*.

19. *Boston Globe*, Apr. 2, 6, 1894; *Proceedings of the Thirtieth Annual Convention, Massachusetts State Branch, American Federation of Labor, September 20–24, 1915* (Boston, n.d.), p. 120.

20. The precise timing, as well as the extent, of this shift in emphasis from cooperative to competitive strategies remains somewhat open to question—and to further research.

21. Constance M. Green, *Holyoke, Massachusetts* (New Haven, 1939), p. 369; *Report of the Massachusetts Board*, part III, pp. 101–2; *Boston Globe*, Mar. 21, 1894; MBSL, *Tenth Annual Report*, p. 136; McNeill, ed., *Labor Movement*, pp. 310–11; John Higham, *Strangers in the Land* (New York, 1974), pp. 48–49, 55, 70–73, 112, 163–64.

22. Montgomery, *Beyond Equality*, p. 147; Green, *Holyoke*, p. 222; McNeill, ed., *Labor Movement*, pp. 135, 183, 200; Stockton, *Molders*, p. 170;

Mark Perlman, *The Machinists* (Cambridge, 1961), p. 247; MBSL, *Eighth Annual Report* (Boston, 1877), p. 19; MBSL, *Twenty-fifth Annual Report*, p. 315; MBSL, *Thirty-seventh Annual Report* (Boston, 1906), pp. 9, 36, 51; MBSL, *Labor Bulletin # 41* (1906), pp. 203–6; Smelser, *Unemployment*, pp. 36–37; Ulman, *National Trade Union*, pp. 310ff.

23. *Boston Globe*, Dec. 28, 1893; Smelser, *Unemployment*, pp. 38ff., 91ff., 108ff.; *Proceedings of the Eighteenth Annual Convention, Massachusetts American Federation of Labor, October 5–8, 1903* (Boston, n.d.), pp. 46–47; *Proceedings of the Twenty-third Annual Convention, Massachusetts American Federation of Labor, October 12–15, 1908* (Boston, n.d.), pp. 10–13; *Thirtieth Annual Convention, Massachusetts AFL*, p. 120.

24. William Haber, *Industrial Relations in the Building Industry* (Cambridge, 1930), pp. 36ff., 40–41, 151–57, 536n; Stockton, *Molders*, pp. 45ff.; Garth Mangum, *The Operating Engineers* (Cambridge, 1964), p. 52; Perlman, *Machinists*, pp. 231–34; Robert A. Christie, *Empire in Wood* (Ithaca, 1956), pp. 107–11; Galster, *Shoe Industry*, pp. 132ff.; Hollander and Barnett, eds., *Studies*, pp. 305ff.; Smelser, *Unemployment*, pp. 41–42; *Eighteenth Annual Convention, Massachusetts AFL*, pp. 64ff.

25. Smelser, *Unemployment*, p. 35; *Proceedings of the Twenty-ninth Annual Convention, Massachusetts American Federation of Labor, September 21–6, 1914* (Boston, n.d.), p. 101.

26. MBSL, *Labor Bulletin # 35* (1905), p. 52; MBSL, *Labor Bulletin # 43* (1906), p. 371; MBSL, *Forty-second Annual Report*, pp. 212, 268; Harry Henig, *The Brotherhood of Railway Clerks* (New York, 1937), p. 273; Perlman, *Machinists*, p. 248; Hollander and Barnett, eds., *Studies*, p. 50; Smelser, *Unemployment*, pp. 58–68, 43ff.; Christie, *Empire*, pp. 12ff., 64, 152.

27. Selig Perlman, *A Theory of the Labor Movement* (1928; reprint New York, 1949). For one of the more precise articulations of the shaping influence of labor scarcity (vis à vis the labor movement), see Ulman, *National Trade Union*, pp. 7–22, 594–604. The argument in this article implicitly raises the question of international comparisons. Statistical comparisons of unemployment levels in different nations are unusually hazardous and perhaps futile, but those who have examined the data for the early twentieth century conclude that idleness levels in the United States were as high or higher than those prevailing in western Europe. For a summary of these studies, see Keyssar, "Men Out of Work," p. 537.

28. *Thirtieth Annual Convention, Massachusetts AFL*, p. 112; *Proceedings of the Thirty-fifth Annual Convention, Massachusetts American Federation of Labor, August 2–6, 1920* (Boston, n.d.), p. 77.

CHAPTER 10

Politics as Social History: A Case Study of Class Conflict and Political Development in Nineteenth-Century New England

LEON FINK

The consolidation of the industrial revolution hit New England small-town society with particular force. An expanding national marketplace coupled with the intensification of agriculture doomed large areas of the countryside to a century of depopulation and demoralization while changes in manufacturing drastically altered the composition and character of the settlements that survived and prospered. In the second half of the nineteenth century a world once ordered by the personalism of book, bar, and magistrate disappeared forever as a society of independent householders gave way to a more complex set of economic dependencies. That the work force for the new mills, quarries, and workshops now derived less from Yankee farms than foreign soil added to the strangeness and abruptness of the arrival of a new age. Finally, the symbolic linchpin of the New England community, the town meeting, also fell by the wayside as more and more industrial towns incorporated and adopted the representative structures of urban government.

Contemporary observers as well as latter-day historians carefully noted the impact of economic "progress" on New England's distinct political and social heritage. Nostalgic late nineteenth-century commentators were apt to regard the urban-industrial transformation of small-town society as "a complete change in the character of the town . . . a change for the worse." In this view a small homogeneous community of freeholders gave way to a "heterogeneous mass of men" "with little knowledge of town traditions and less respect for them." Present-day scholars, of course, have offered a different, almost inverted assessment of New England institutional evolution. Colonial historians have made careful distinctions between village consensus and democratic decision-making, noting the narrow access to power maintained by gentrylike county elites. Likewise, Stephan

Thernstrom, among others, has emphasized the social hierarchy, religious closed-mindedness, and mercantile control exercised in the
early nineteenth-century pre-industrial town. Michael Frisch has argued that real "community"—implying areas of common public concern distinct from private interest—was experienced less in the good
old days than in the very process of modernization or "town-build-
ing."[1]

   Whether mourned as the dying ember of local democracy or
hailed as its true beginning, the displacement of consensual town
meeting politics by the more distant structures of representative government and competing professional political parties appears to
latter-day observers as an inevitable corollary of modernization. In
an inexorable continuum, so it seems, a kaleidoscope of interests replaced the traditional seats of authority; the resulting social dislocation, in turn, bred an anxious "search for order." Finally, stability
was restored by a mixture of institutional and ideological adjustments to a more professional, urban, technocratic, and bureaucratic
society.[2]

   Whatever their unifying value, such assumptions also carry a severe risk of historicism. Process tends to overcome people, forces
replace decisions, and conflicts among contemporaries are reduced
to the tension of accommodating old ways to new circumstances. In
the course of such a progressive *tableau vivant*, popular movements
in particular play only the most minor role. Historical treatment of
the Knights of Labor, whose dramatic rise and fall coincided with
the crucial years of U.S. industrial consolidation, provides an instructive and immediately relevant example. Along the traditional-
modern axis of the modernization yardstick, the Knights fit in either
as a backward-looking remnant of the pre-industrial order or, in a
recent modification, as a transitional expression caught somewhere
in the middle. Either way, this leading working-class movement of
the century figures less as historical subject than as captive to the
assumedly larger social and political currents of the times.[3]

   The political and institutional transformation of the town of Rutland, Vermont, however, offers a markedly different perspective on
the dynamic of urban political development. Here, as throughout
New England, the old consensual town meeting gave way to representative city government under the sway of a socially inclusive two-
party competition. But the timing and significance of this transition
derived neither from a general recognition that it was time for a
change nor from any identifiable modernizing impulse. Rather, institutional change grew out of an intense contest shaking Rutland
and much of the rest of the nation in the 1880s over the exercise of

private power and public authority. The political and governmental reforms engendered by this period of conflict depended both on who was able to reimpose order and what they had to overcome to do so. Throughout these events the presence of the Knights of Labor was of critical historical importance. Given the recent, well-taken injunctions to reunite social with political history, it is hoped that the approach applied in this specific study may prove of more general application as well.[4]

By 1880 a combination of rail and rock had turned the small manufacturing town of Rutland into the state's largest metropolis (population, 12,000) and political center of influence. In the railroad boom of the 1850s jealous rivals Troy and Albany built no fewer than six lines through Rutland seeking connections to the agriculture hinterland and a passage to Canada. (Even Jay Gould lived there for three years and accomplished enough to land his partner in a Vermont jail.) While crossing Rutland County land, the railroads opened the way to the full exploitation of mineral wealth buried beneath them. The largest marble company in the world began to take shape in the early 1870s when lawyer and banker Redfield Proctor entered a fledgling quarrying and finishing industry based in the blue hills surrounding Rutland Village at West Rutland, Sutherland Falls, and Center Rutland (all four settlements lay within the borders of Rutland "town"). By 1880 Proctor's Vermont Marble Company controlled 55 percent of local production, rapidly expanding through technological innovation and vertical integration of marketing, and employed more than 1,000 workers. In 1883 Proctor expanded horizontally as well, getting his rivals to join him temporarily in a marble producers' cartel. The influence of Rutland's leading marble manufacturer was also felt outside the business world. The town of Sutherland Falls was renamed Proctor in the early 1880s, during Redfield Proctor's tenure as governor of Vermont.[5]

In political affairs Rutland was dominated by a group of some thirty to fifty families who administered and adjudicated the public's business. United by deep native American roots (often including or at least claiming illustrious Revolutionary service), farming and/or merchant-banking backgrounds, membership in the less enthusiastic Protestant churches, fraternal connections with the Masons or Elks Club, Civil War officership, a record of philanthropic contributions, and wives active in town benevolent societies and charitable affairs, the leading men of Rutland were nearly all Republican in the most Republican of U.S. states. A rare exception like Democratic attorney L. W. Redington might yet be accepted for being thoroughly "Republican" in his social life. Given the basic homogeneity of local representatives, town politics usually operated at the subparty level of factional rivalry or personal popularity. In 1884, for instance, an identical slate of officers was presented to and approved by both Republican and Democratic caucuses prior to the town meeting. The list, moreover, contained only a single change from the roster of incumbents. By occupational standing, only the top third of the social structure reaching down from capitalists and professionals through self-employed master craftsmen were actively involved in town government. Thus, despite substantial economic growth and development, Rutland town stewards continued to operate in the public realm as if nothing had changed. This political lag was highlighted by the fact that Rutland in the mid-1880s was the largest jurisdiction in the United States still operating under town government.[6]

In 1886, however, things did change dramatically. Beginning in Janurary 1886, Rutland skilled tradesmen and marble workers coalesced under the spreading national umbrella of the Knights of Labor. In and of itself this organizational achievement created the potential for a new political majority. When, in addition, widespread charges of waste and neglect beset the town's incumbent officers in February, the stage was set for a challenge to the lax and honorific tradition of conducting town business. "The time has come when we propose to have a share in the legislation by which we are governed," declared quarryman and West Rutland Master Workman James Gillespie on August 26, 1886, at the town's first workingmen's convention. On September 7, the largest town meeting in Rutland's history elected a full slate of candidates from the United Labor ticket (taking its name from the Henry George movement in New York City), including a state assemblyman and fifteen justices of the peace. Fourteen of the justices identifiable by trade included four marble workers, three carpenters, two laborers, one shoemaker, one clerk, one meat market owner, one country store proprietor, and one small farmer—men who most likely would never have appeared on any other list of nominees for public office. Although their strength was clearly rooted in the 2,000-member local marble labor force, the Rutland Knights derived "from almost every department of work in town."[7]

The Knights saw United Labor government less as a radical transformation than a purification of the public trust. A republican heritage that linked the welfare of the nation to the economic and political independence of the citizenry was extended in the hands of the Gilded Age labor movement into a battle cry against both industrial monopoly and governmental corruption. Rutland labor spokesmen compared their initiative to that of the "horny-handed sons of toil" who had once marched behind Andrew Jackson's assault on "ring rule." Their legislative program, in keeping with their self-image as respectable albeit unrecognized citizens, was in fact quite moderate. At the state level—a plane at which they could in any case expect little influence—they did propose various labor-related reforms, including an employers' liability act, weekly cash payments of wages, free evening schools, and a ten-hour law. Correspondingly, at the local level, they favored expanded appropriations and taxation for roads, schools, and a new town library. Wary of influence-peddling and public debt, the workingmen in their platform simultaneously promised a balanced budget, equitable taxation, and "strict account of all public transactions . . . rendered so as to be perfectly understood." In a period characterized both by unprecedented labor organization and economic downturn for the marble trade, the political arena, while not the point of departure for labor mobilization, must have beckoned to the Knights as a most inviting sphere of influence.[8]

Labor's self-delimited political intentions stood in striking contrast to the revulsion expressed toward the new government by the town's erstwhile political rulers—a feeling summed up in an oblique commentary by the local Republican daily on government by "the vomit of the saloons." The shift in the social locus of power entailed by the workingmen's movement did, in fact, make the 1886 events more than an ordinary succession of the "ins" by the "outs." Indeed, in this context proposals that might in themselves have been accepted as benign took on a more threatening cast. Given Rutland's past, the sudden assertion from below of the right to control public affairs represented a radical political departure.

Widening the chasm between the town's traditional governing elite and the new political forces was the fact that class differences in Rutland were reinforced by a sharp cultural divide. The ranks of capitalists, professionals, merchants, white-collar employees, and farmers occupied men 80 to 90 percent of whom were of native-American background. But Yankee dominance of these upper strata masked the fact that by 1880 immigrants and their sons composed a majority of Rutland's adult male population, two-thirds of the town's wage-earners, and a near monopoly of the lower rungs of manual labor. Most significant, nine out of ten marble workers were of foreign extraction. Six of ten were of Irish background; two of ten were French-Canadians. The rest divided between English-Canadians, Swedes, and native Americans. Among the latter, foremen and supervisors made up the single largest job categories.[9]

The Rutland Knights of Labor, not surprisingly, carried a strong ethnic, and especially Irish-American, character. Local sources estimated that "a majority" of the marble workers joined the Order in 1886, and two of four assemblies within Rutland town were based in the heavily Irish-Catholic marble working community of West Rutland (there were two other assemblies based in other hamlets of the county). The Knights' political efforts signaled a kind of coming of age of the immigrant working-class community. Included on the labor ticket as a candidate for justice of the peace, for instance, was the only French-Canadian name on a list of local officeholders going back ten years. Even more representative of the social turnabout represented by the labor party was the unprecedented slating of the Irish-Catholic James F. Hogan, a clothing storeowner and son of an Irish quarryman, for the state legislature. With utter condescension, Redfield Proctor saluted labor's nomination of "a colored man" for representative.[10]

Under these conditions the prospect of labor rule in Rutland summoned up less a loyal opposition than a counterrevolution. Within days of the town election, Redfield Proctor dusted off plans he had been nursing for some time to rid his business of potential legislative interference and unnecessary taxation by the central government in Rutland town. Through influential contacts at Montpelier, he began a vigorous lobbying effort to divide Proctor from Rutland's political jurisdiction, and he encouraged West Rutland to do likewise. As he put it in private correspondence, in a large town "interests are so mixed and varied that a large part of the voters have little interest in them and never understand them but are led by demagogues and go with the mob." Small-town citizens were less likely to make such mistakes because "the questions are brought right to their doors." In the one-industry village in which only thirty-five homes were independently owned, overwhelming endorsement of a prodivision petition circulated door to door by Redfield's son, Fletcher D. Proctor, tended to prove his point.[11]

The Proctor family picked the opportune moment to push their initiative. Business connections alone helped to corral other marble owners to their side. But Redfield Proctor also figured that labor's electoral success would soften natural commercial opposition in Rutland Village to a move (the division of both Proctor and West Rutland) that would deprive Rutland town of a third of its population and its largest revenue-producing properties. "Fear of foreign rule," Proctor advised his counsel, "had produced a wondrous change in public feeling." While a coalition of eminent elder citizens, independent businessmen, Democrats, and Knights of Labor did organize against the division plans, the *Rutland Herald,* scion of the town's (and much of the state's) older Republican elite, uttered not a word against the proposal. The disposition of the rural-dominated state legislature was apparently never in doubt. "From the fact that the laboring men elected a representative by such an overwhelming vote," reflected a disappointed antidivision spokesman, "they seemed to infer that we were in a state of anarchy down here." One legislator openly advised a group of antidivision Rutland businessmen: "Division is your only salvation. You are in bad shape politically and something must be done for relief." In late November bills sailed smoothly through the legislature approving division for both Proctor and West Rutland.[12]

The basic decision probably surprised no one. But in the final hours of the closing legislative session, the lawmakers tacked on some unadvertised items affecting Rutland citizens. By an amendment to the original town charter, the state withdrew Rutland's right to elect a municipal judge, making it an appointed position. Another hurriedly enacted statute required local trustees to furnish bonds ranging from $1,000 to $5,000 before taking office. Finally, the tenure of the fifteen Rutland justices elected on the 1886 labor ticket was voided on grounds that they could not properly represent the newly created districts. The governor was authorized to appoint interim justices. While the division vote rested on a variety of motivation and justification, the object of the postdivision collateral actions was unmistakable. Presiding (Republican) municipal judge Albert Landon best expressed the combination of humiliation and indignation felt by many Rutland citizens. "The industrial classes have become sufficiently intelligent to undertake to right their wrongs at the ballot box. And this is a mad attempt to wrest that dreaded weapon from their grasp."[13] Forced to choose between political pacification and civic growth, the division forces betrayed fears that underlay the surface exuberance of the Age of Progress. The Rutland Knights of Labor, for their part, had been treated to an elementary lesson in the costs of inexperience among political professionals. It was as if they had sat down to dinner only to discover that the main course had just been removed. Political dismemberment, in itself, however, did not ensure the success of the stratagem. The degree of disruption in labor's political momentum would rest effectively on the specific social and political configurations to emerge in the new jurisdictions of Rutland, West Rutland, and Proctor.

As it happened, three distinct political climates and party alignments arose in the three new governmental units. Precisely because they grew out of the breakdown of an older order of social relationships, politics in the three towns may offer some general clues as to the social content of the political forms that emerged.

A magisterial rule—at once benevolent and arbitrary—quickly settled over the new town of Proctor. In the spring of 1887 the first local town meeting elected Redfield Proctor moderator and proceeded to endorse a company-backed slate by acclamation. For decades to come, the Proctor family, itself a bulwark of the state Republican party, would be able to count on solid, conservative Republican majorities in their town. An apparent absence of working-class organization and activity from 1887 seemed to signal the dispersal of what had always been a relatively weak Knights of Labor presence in Proctor's mills. Effective control of the town's social and political life henceforth emanated from a single center of power.[14]

Proctor family rule combined power with discretion. As early as 1886 the Vermont Marble Company chartered a company cooperative store and an employees' savings bank. While disclaiming direct liability for quarry accidents, it hired the country's first industrial nurse in 1895. Soon a fully equipped hospital was providing free medical care to all Proctor employees. The company also built and funded programs for the local YMCA. Redfield Proctor committed himself to his town and company and tried to ensure that the employees would do likewise. In December 1886, for example, "in these times of labor troubles," he bought back shares of stock from large shareholders to resell them at reduced rates to foremen and salesmen "to bind them all the more closely together." Proctor also worked hard, almost scientifically, at securing a docile labor force. He requested the Cunard Line in 1887 to send 200 to 300 Swedes to the quarrying center: "We want good rugged men and much prefer men from the country rather than such as go from the city." During the same period he took pains to recruit a particular Chicago building contractor known for employing "men who have not got the 8 hour craze and are not controlled by unions." Proctor pointedly did favors for the local clergy and as pointedly expected their loyalty in return. The ambivalent nature of acquiescence in the town of Proctor—rendered in part out of desperation and in part out of gratefulness—explains why the local marble workers paraded in welcome whenever the governor or his son entertained visiting dignitaries and why 3,000 men waited for hours through a severe March snowstorm in 1908 for the Marble King's casket to pass in final review.[15]

The political alignment in Proctor directly reflected its status as a company town. Community in such a town derived not from organic or voluntary ties but from mystique—the artificial attempt to re-create an older set of paternal-deferential social relationships in a new industrial environment. As such, the peculiar social solidarity exhibited there required the continuous and conspicuous exercise of an enlightened despotism. Politically, we might best describe the situation in Proctor as one of *paternalistic consensus,* a state of affairs where the lower classes participate but with little or no autonomy from the will of their employer(s).

Nearly twice the size of Proctor, with a well-organized working-class community owning their own homes and little plots of land, and lacking a single commanding center of political and economic authority, the new town of West Rutland possessed more of both the substance and spirit of democratic self-government. Indeed, evidence suggests that an overwhelming popular majority of West Rutlanders had favored town division. While West Rutland village merchants naturally wished specifically to regulate the excursion trains that carried shoppers away to larger Rutland Village, West Rutland workers shared in more general complaints of town inattention to roads, sidewalks, and other needs of their community. One other factor also probably influenced prodivision sentiment in West Rutland. An Irish political majority would almost certainly accompany political separation of the community. An Irish-American marble worker who had "always lived" in West Rutland had thus spoken approvingly before a legislative committee of attaining "home rule," and two West Rutland Knights of Labor leaders had joined the division forces. Apparently, even disapproving Montpelier legislators fully expected that West Rutland town government "would become more distinctly a working-men's experiment than any other [town] in the state." And at the March 1, 1887, inaugural town meeting, independent labor forces did sweep the field as predicted. But then a new political pattern began to emerge in West Rutland, one at once dominated by the unabashed assertiveness of its Irish working-class constituency and by its limitations. In 1888 a Citizens caucus acquired control of town government, while in national affairs the town took on decidedly Democratic preferences; at least through the mid-1890s local affairs were untroubled by independent labor political agitation.[16]

Several factors seem to have influenced the new town's unexpected political quiescence. The need to establish fiscal solvency was perhaps most important. Division left West Rutland with considerable debts owed to the old town authority, and the new government had immediately issued bonds just to maintain local projects already under way. West Rutland stood on an uncertain economic base in any case as in Proctor practically everyone depended on the health

of the marble industry. From the beginning of their tenure, therefore, West Rutland labor selectmen cooperated with local businessmen and even deferred to the advice of a marble company lawyer.
One of their first acts budgeted public funds for roads requested by
local marble companies. M. W. Cannon, a farmer (and former quarryman), Knights of Labor master workman, and a leader of West
Rutland labor political forces, boasted that "there is no element of
our population that will make greater efforts for the maintenance of
law and order, for the security of person and property and for the
economical administration of town affairs than the workingmen. No
action of the workingmen will ever mar the progress of the new
town."[17]

   If labor's West Rutland representatives displayed a willingness to
work with other local interests, businessmen also accepted the necessity for collaboration. Before the first West Rutland town meeting,
several Knights leaders were offered places on the businessmen's
Citizens ticket. When the Knights refused, other marble workers
were nominated to take their place. Indeed, the 1887 election
amounted almost to a competition in representation from below. In
reaction to the Citizens call for a government of all the talents, the
labor caucus pressed for election of "all nationalities," adding two
French-Canadians (a carriage manufacturer and a marble worker) to
a ticket weighted with Irish marble workers. Looking over the town's
governors in 1887, a visitor noted that West Rutland possessed "the
most common representatives I have run across." By the year's end,
however, the workingmen's politicians appear to have accepted the
political hospitality of town elders. In 1890, for example, Cannon
was elected selectman alongside two other "non-partisan" candidates: one, a marble worker and former United Labor man, the
other, a superintendent of the Sheldon Marble Company. From the
beginning local Democratic politicians showed skill in accommodating to and making use of intraclass political formations in West Rutland. As early as 1886 Democratic businessmen like cigar manufacturer A. H. Abraham and insurance executive W. L. Redington
diplomatically contributed gifts to a Knights of Labor raffle. That
West Rutland was the only site in the county to carry for Grover
Cleveland in 1888 suggested the particular turn that labor's political
strength had taken there.[18]

   West Rutland, in short, displayed political tendencies quite unlike
those of Proctor. A distinct working-class constituency, rooted in
both labor and ethnic communal organization, created the basis for
political pluralism. But it was a most moderate pluralism. The con-
flict-ridden atmosphere of 1886 had given way to a climate of civic

unity under adversity, in which workers identified with the town's commercial welfare, while men of commerce also accommodated to post-1886 political realities. In West Rutland, as in other areas where urban immigrant demography clashed with its surrounding native rural counterpart, the Democratic party provided the warmest welcome for the ethnic working-class voter; still, in local matters partisanship seemed scarcely to matter. West Rutland, by all signs, had entered a period of *democratic consensus,* in which the lower classes remained actively enfranchised on their own behalf (at least relatively free from coercion from above) but nevertheless articulated no independent working-class politics.

In taking stock of the relations between the labor movement and the community power structure that gave rise to such a political juncture, it is important to note that class conciliation in West Rutland took place not in the flush of labor mobilization but during the ebb tide of organized labor strength. As early as mid-1887 employer hostility and intransigence before labor wage demands were reportedly taking a heavy toll in demoralization and loss of membership among area marble workers. While four Knights assemblies, including two based in West Rutland, survived until 1892, they did so with a much attenuated community presence.[19] The collapse of labor leadership and mass discipline (following the national fate of the Knights of Labor) left the movement without confidence in its own future. In less polarized relation to local government, the labor constituency henceforth served as a residual opposition, setting limits rather than clear direction in the public sphere. From another (and not contradictory) perspective we might want to emphasize the conciliationist tendencies within the movement's (again, specifically the Knights') ideology (though this is a subject that must be treated elsewhere). A corollary to the last point would stress the effective blandishments that ideologically flabby American political parties continually have held out to insurgents. And yet, perhaps more important than any of these political deficiencies were the economic limits on labor political autonomy in a small, one-industry town, even a class-conscious and organized one. That such a fledgling community should reach a consensual public *modus operandi* is not surprising. Localism and civic autonomy in the end finally predominated over internal divisions. That a self-consciously working-class party should run such a town, even for a year, is surely the more incongruous idea and remarkable achievement.

While the two new fragment towns, by one rationale or another, settled into a relatively quiet resolution of their internal affairs, the situation in what remained of old Rutland town (roughly two-thirds of the original population) took on an entirely different complexion. If the state legislators had meant to wipe out Rutland labor politics by town division, they failed. Except for the loss of population and taxable property, the only new political factor in Rutland town after 1886 was the added stigma of betrayal attached to many of the town's business leaders; as a result labor politics enjoyed an unusually long and productive life. As in West Rutland, the Rutland United Labor party swept the February 1887 town meeting, then fell off the following year. But the circumstances were quite different. Unlike the situation in the new town to the west, the underlying social tension separating workers from the Yankee elite did not evaporate in old Rutland. Its greater size—Rutland was finally incorporated as a city under mayoral-aldermanic government in 1892—and its more complex economy militated against political manipulation by a few employers. Finally, there was no shortage of confident young Knights willing to challenge the older guardians for control of the community's future. Rutland workingmen thus found it possible to regroup after their first electoral setbacks and to recapture important positions under United Labor and United Workingmen's banners in 1890; they remained a potent independent force through 1892. Even as the numbers behind the Knights dwindled, the constituency that the Order had created endured. When labor finally transferred its strength to the Democratic party, it infused that party with new prospects and with a new character derived from the workingmen's movement.[20]

Rutland's business leaders at first abandoned not only the personalism and informality of older times but retreated from the very framework of partisan loyalty to unite behind the widespread contemporary phenomenon of a non-partisan Citizens party of order. Though the effort initially amounted to little more than dressing up the old ruling Republican faction in new outfits—which got nowhere in 1887—it soon became a more effective counterweight to independent labor politics. Capturing the 1888 town meeting and proclaiming "Rutland Redeemed," the Citizens ticket generally dominated local government until it liquidated itself in 1894. Fear that a loss of business confidence in the town would drive away jobs and investment (a fear seemingly confirmed by the October 1887 announced departure of a local shirt company) no doubt helped the antilabor party. So did two new businessmen's organizations—one a private club, the other a merchants' association—that sought simultaneously to refurbish Rutland's image abroad and to activate "men of education and standing" at home. Though not exactly the association of "Republicans, Democrats, and workingmen joining hands . . . to secure the public good" that it claimed, the Citizens were more than an instrument of middle-class fear and repression. As early as 1888 Rutland Democrats like attorneys J. D. Spellman and T. W. Maloney, who had joined in the antidivision fight and generally enjoyed good relations with organized labor, were taking an active role in the Citizens activities. Unlike the old party caucuses, a mass public meeting ratified the Citizens slate in 1888; in future elections the candidates themselves were nominated at "open" party caucuses.[21]

The more successful the Citizens movement became, however (i.e., the more it resembled a truly democratic consensus), the less well it served its originators' purposes. Bipartisan inclusiveness had proved the key to the Citizens winning ways beginning in 1888 but that approach also risked loss of control over the direction of the movement. As early as the 1888 village election, Citizens leaders were expressing fears that the Knights had infiltrated preliminary meetings and secured nomination of some of their men in Citizens costumes. Two years later, Republican and Democratic businessmen opened what they called a Non-Partisan caucus with a pledge of willingness to select men from all competing parties. The organizers withdrew quickly, however, when workingmen allied with a dissident Democratic faction proposed a genuine "unity" slate. The *Herald* described it most coolly "as a whole not the men who naturally would be selected to conduct the business of any corporation equal in importance and with equal interests at stake to the town of Rutland." Again in 1891 workingmen upset the official slate with a caucus victory for an iron molder for street commissioner. Even if steered through the uncertainties of the caucus, business-endorsed candidates still might face a stiff labor challenge on election day. Both in 1890 and 1891, after achieving partial success within the Non-Partisan slate, workingmen won other positions—and even secured a Georgite tax on unoccupied land—on the strength of their own independent tickets.[22]

The Citizens or Non-Partisan approach thus proved an unhappy compromise with the tidy control that the business elite acting through the Republican party had once exercised over local affairs. As early as 1888, J. D. Spellman had ruffled the feathers of the socially homogeneous Republican inner sanctum with whom he was formally cooperating by publicly protesting the exclusion of a Jewish-*Republican* merchant tailor from the Citizen ticket. By substituting personal popularity and skillful campaigning for party loyalty and social standing, the new system allowed maverick Republicans and ambitious Democrats such unwelcome openings. Republican leaders of the antilabor coalition watched helplessly as their Demo-

cratic partners wooed the opposition forces, steadily enlisting them
under the banner of the minority party. The growing ties between
the Democrats and what was left of the labor movement were apparent in the representation of Vermont's District Assembly 200 at the
1890 Denver Knights of Labor convention by the editor of Rutland's
new Democratic *Evening Telegram*. In the same year the *Herald* de-
precatingly labeled the emerging pattern of electioneering "Spell-
manism."[23]

It was not long, therefore, before the same people who had con-
demned labor's "party politics' in 1886–87 for having "no place" in
local affairs summoned it to active duty. By 1894, two years after
incorporation, the *Herald* had decided that "non-partisan" city government was proving no better than the "old town meeting mobs."
"Narrow ward interests," in the *Herald*'s view, were leading irrespon-
sible Citizens representatives toward unnecessary street and sewer
construction, pushing up both taxes and municipal debt. "A Republican town," the paper advised, "should have Republican government." Indeed, once oft-repeated elegies to New England town democracy had given way to a growing pessimism about local self-
government. The *Herald* argued in 1895 for the appointment of a
professional city engineer and the transfer of "elected committee duties" to "executive [appointed] officers." One could not expect government to improve, this line of logic ran, until the "substantial men
of the city—the men with real interests at stake" took charge. To
protect the city from the vicissitudes of local politics, the Republican
party took structural measures of its own. The party's city committee
tightened local organization in 1895 with the formation of a stable
executive leadership and permanent ward committees. In addition,
the Republicans prepared to operate closed primaries and asserted
the right to remove local delegates who flaunted the city committee's
authority.[24]

With the dissolution of the Citizens ticket, a competitive two-party
system generally reasserted itself over the young city's government.
The Republicans, to be sure, remained the majority party, but they
frequently faced a stiff challenge from the revitalized Democrats.
Heavily working-class Catholic wards Seven and Eight, for example,
transferred their bloc-voting support from independent labor to
Democratic candidates. The same district that in 1887 elected a
United Labor marble worker to the board of selectmen by a vote of
136 to 1 was the single defector in 1904 from Theodore Roosevelt's
sweep of the city. An even more direct link was provided in the
personage of Thomas H. Brown, the Knights' district master work-

man; throughout the 1890s Brown secured nearly automatic claim to the Seventh Ward's Democratic aldermanic seat.[25]

A decade-long political transformation ultimately replaced the clublike atmosphere of old town meeting days with the institutionalization of *two-party pluralism*. The change also roughly coincided with the dissolution of town meeting democracy into the representative structures of city government. If one looked only at the before (say 1885) and after (say 1895), Rutland might indeed fit conventional expectations of political modernization and progressive municipal development. Such a view, however, by attending only to certain external benchmarks and neglecting the impact of class conflict and working-class mobilization would miss the substance of what had happened in Rutland, and why. The social polarization engendered by the Knights of Labor had been responsible for destroying the deferential subparty factionalism in local government. In a period of conflict two opposing formations, each of which saw itself as outside of or above the bounds of partisanship, had fought for political power. Two-party competition became the norm in local politics only *after* and *as a result of* the storm that had preceded it. Rutland, in short, had not passed inexorably along a linear trail of development. Its entire political edifice had been rendered, sundered, and reconstructed in the face of a radical challenge from below.

Conventional views not only tend to take for granted a political pluralism that the Rutland case suggests was the *product* of a historical struggle shifting the social balance of power; they also present an all-too-sanitized picture of two-party pluralism. A final bit of narrative is in order. Rutland Democrats, riding the desperation and bitterness of local workingmen in the depression of the mid-1890s (and calling for work relief programs for the unemployed), elected former Knights of Labor leader, T. H. Brown, mayor of an otherwise Republican-controlled city government in 1896. Panic again spread through the business establishment. The mayor found himself entirely frustrated. All his appointments were blocked, and government came to a near standstill. Halfway through Brown's term, the banker Percival W. Clement, head of the board of trade, warned that the Howe Scale Company, the town's principal manufacturer, might abandon Rutland unless "confidence" were quickly restored. In the same breath Clement declared his willingness to shoulder the responsibility of city executive if called upon. Brown did step down from office, explaining simply that the opposition could not manage "a Republican town."[26]

Given the active enfranchisement of the lower classes, no one po-

litical form, it would seem, was entirely "safe" from popular manipulation. Whatever the forms through which it occurred, a marked
disjuncture in *control* between political and civil society signified, for
some, a social crisis, one that could not be resolved until power had
been reconsolidated on new terms. In this regard it bears reempha-
sizing that the social relocation of power or decision-making as much
as the substance of the decisions involved defined the perceived
threat. In Rutland such a crisis had twice boiled over, once in 1886,
once in 1896. The basic tinder for such a crisis—i.e., the discrepancy
in control between the political and the economic sphere—has accumulated, albeit in different proportions, on many different occasions in American history. The central crisis (and collapse) of southern Reconstruction, the direction (and limitation) of such New Deal
programs as the TVA and WPA, and the recent showdown over a
municipal power company in Cleveland, Ohio, to take three examples, while divorced in all particulars from events in Gilded Age Vermont, share an underlying flashpoint of conflict. If, as in each of
these examples, political power tends to gravitate back toward con-
sonance with private power, such a tendency at once reemphasizes
the intimate connection between the two spheres of authority and
suggests the ultimate reliance of politics on civil organization. A
change or sharp break in the nature of political rule (i.e., the political balance of power) is likely to be sustained only if it is accompanied by a successful revision of the lines of force within civil society.
In the Rutland case the social tremors reflected in the Knights of
Labor toppled one form of elite rule but obviously did not in the
end topple the elite.

But if in conclusion we are ultimately stressing the social sources
of politics rather than the institutional forms, that is not meant to
belittle examination of the forms. In the case of Rutland, after all, it
was the forms of politics (i.e., parties, caucuses, governmental divisions) or more precisely the *transition* within those forms, which
helped to orient us to and define the limits of the movement from
below. The changes in political forms at once reflected and illuminated the complex tensions of the local social reality. The Rutland
story provides only one (rather, only three) examples of intimate
interaction between working-class social history and the development of American political institutions. It is true, I suppose, that
known situations of labor upheaval would prove the most fertile
ground for further explorations along these lines. The period of the
Great Upheaval, at least, is replete with distinct but related examples. But I think that quite different periods may be susceptible to
similar analysis. A recent examination of Boston's incorporation in

the 1820s, for instance, refers to the breakdown of a "deferential pattern of politics. . . . No longer able to agree among themselves, the members of the upper class found it increasingly difficult, as one of them delicately phrased it, 'to manage that class which is acted upon.' " The point of collapse of any existing political form or arrangement may, in fact, be a good place for the social historian to dig in. Giovanni Sartori, a political sociologist, has asserted provocatively, "Whenever conflict means what it says, parties fall into disrepute." Any scholar who chooses to explore this axiom may find the connection between political and social history inextricable.[27]

NOTES

I am grateful to Donald M. Scott for his searching comments on the manuscript and to Lewis Perry for exercising better judgment than I wanted to admit. An earlier version of this article appeared in *Social History*, 7 (Jan. 1982).

1. Charles Francis Adams, *Three Episodes of Massachusetts History*, 2 vols. (Cambridge, Mass., 1892) II, 965–74; John Gould, *New England Town Meeting: Safeguard of Democracy* (Brattleboro, 1940), pp. 59–60; see, e.g., John M. Murrin, "Review Essay," *History and Theory*, 11 (May 1972), 226–76; Stephan Thernstrom, *Poverty and Progress: Social Mobility in a Nineteenth-Century City* (New York, 1970); Michael H. Frisch, *Town into City: Springfield, Massachusetts, and the Meaning of Community, 1840–1880* (Cambridge, Mass., 1972).

2. For illustrative application of modernization theory, see Robert H. Wiebe, *The Search for Order, 1877–1920* (New York, 1967); Samuel P. Hays, *The Response to Industrialism, 1885–1914* (Chicago, 1957); and Richard D. Brown, *Modernization: The Transformation of American Life, 1600–1865* (New York, 1976).

3. Gerald N. Grob, *Workers and Utopia: A Study of Ideological Conflict in the American Labor Movement, 1865–1900* (Chicago, 1969): Michael J. Cassity, "Modernization and Social Crisis: The Knights of Labor and a Midwest Community, 1885–1886," *Journal of American History*, 66 (June 1979), 41–61.

4. For further elaboration of these themes, see Leon Fink, *Workingmen's Democracy:The Knights of Labor and American Politics* (Urbana, 1983).

5. H. P. Smith and W. S. Rann, *History of Rutland County, Vermont* (Syracuse, 1886), pp. 170, 158–59, 161–62; Edward Chase Kirkland, *Men, Cities, and Transportation: A Study in New England History, 1820–1900*, 2 vols. (Cambridge, Mass., 1948), I, 166–67, 229–30; Jim Shaughnessy, *The Rutland Road* (Berkeley, 1964), pp. 358, 471; U.S. Tenth Census, 1880, *Statistics of the Population*, 1 (Washington, D.C., 1883), p. 355; *Rutland County Gazetteer and Business Directory* (Syracuse, 1881); U.S. Tenth Census, 1880, *Report on the*

Building Stones of the U.S. and Statistics of the Quarry Industry, 10 (Washington 1885), pp. 109–11; Walter H. Crockett, *Vermont: The Green Mountain State,* 5 vols. (New York, 1921), IV, 98–99; Paul A. Gopaul, "A History of the Vermont Marble Company," (manuscript, St. Michael's College, Winooski, Vt., 1954), pp. 42, 47.

6. Hiram Carleton, *Genealogical and Family History of the State of Vermont* (New York, 1903), pp. 406–7; *Book of Biographies: Biographical Sketches of Leading Citizens of Rutland County, Vermont* (Buffalo, 1899), pp. 113–15; Rutland city directories, 1884–85, 1889–90; Smith and Rann, *History of Rutland County; Rutland Herald,* 1880–86. On the dominance of the Republican party, see John D. Buenker, "The Politics of Resistance: The Rural-Based Yankee Republican Machines of Connecticut and Rhode Island," *New England Quarterly,* 47 (June, 1974), 212–37.

7. *Rutland Herald,* Jan. 29, Sept. 8, 1886.

8. Ibid., Aug. 27, 1886.

9. Ibid., Feb. 26, 1887; Manuscript Tenth Census, 1880, Rutland County, Vt.

10. Jonathon Garlock and N. C. Builder, "Knights of Labor Data Bank: Users' Manual and Index to Local Assemblies" (manuscript, University of Rochester, N.Y., 1973); *Rutland Herald,* Sept. 2, 1886.

11. Redfield Proctor to William P. Dillingham, Sept. 14, 1886, Proctor Family Papers, Proctor Free Library, Vt.; *Rutland Herald,* Nov. 1, 3, 1886; "Division of Rutland, Argument of Remonstrators before Committee in Representatives Hall, Nov. 9, 1886," Proctoriana Collection, Vermont State Library, Montpelier.

12. Proctor to Dillingham, Sept. 14, 1886, Proctor Family Papers; *Rutland Herald,* Nov. 4, 1886. Insurance agent L. H. Granger typified middle-class antidivision sentiment in his fear of the power of a man like Proctor. To Granger, twin dangers threatened republican government; one involved "the anarchists who seek to destroy, the other, greater because insidious— the encroachments of great corporations, which seek to control and pervert our political institutions, until we shall live only in their shadow." *Rutland Herald,* Oct. 30, Nov. 20, 1886; *Burlington Free Press,* Nov. 20, 1886.

13. *John Swinton's Paper,* Dec. 5, 1886; *Rutland Herald,* Dec. 7, 1886.

14. *Rutland Herald,* Mar. 2, 1887.

15. David C. Gale, *Proctor: The Story of a Marble Town* (Brattleboro, 1922), p. 213; Redfield Proctor to Elizabeth H. Arnot, Dec. 24, 1888, to Emil Oelbermann, Jan. 1, 1887, to Francis B. Riggs, Jan. 5, 1887, to The Cunard Line, Nov. 15, 1887, to F. R. Brainerd, July 8, 1887, to Rev. J. C. McLaughlin, Mar. 12, 1886, Proctor Family Papers; Crockett, *Vermont,* IV, 394–95. As late as 1975, Anna McLaughlin, the senior librarian at the Proctor Free Library, recalled how "Miss Emily," Redfield's daughter, used to place new pairs of shoes in front of the workers' doors at Christmas; McLaughlin herself had once been sent to a Boston hospital for a checkup at the wish and expense of the Proctor family. Conversation with Anna McLaughlin in October 1975 at the Proctor Free Library, reconfirmed by telephone, Dec. 13, 1976.

16. *Rutland Herald,* Oct. 23, 1886, Mar. 2, Nov. 18, 1887, Mar. 29, 1888.

17. Minutes of the Selectmen, Oct. 22, Nov. 1, 1887, West Rutland town archives; *Rutland Herald,* Feb. 28, 1887.

18. *Rutland Herald,* Feb. 28, 1887; Annual Reports of the Board of Officers, West Rutland town archives; *Rutland Herald,* Oct. 22, 1886, Nov. 7, 1888.

19. T. H. Brown to Terence V. Powderly, June 20, 1887, Terence V. Powderly Papers, Catholic University, Washington, D.C.

20. Postdivision Rutland retained sections of the Vermont Marble Company, a few smaller marble concerns, the Howe Scale Company works, several foundries and machine shops, wood-working establishments, two shirt factories, railroad shops, printshops, and binderies. By 1890 Rutland town's population stood at 11,760, compared to West Rutland (3,680), Proctor (1,758), and the village of Rutland Center (786).

21. On Citizens tickets, see Zane L. Miller, *Boss Cox's Cincinnati: Urban Politics in the Progressive Era* (New York, 1968), pp. 88–89; Cassity, "Modernization," p. 57; and Cliff Kuhn, " 'Democratic Confusion': Working-class Politics in 1880s Atlanta" (paper, 1980, University of North Carolina at Chapel Hill).

22. *Rutland Herald,* Mar. 27, 1888, Mar. 3, 4, 1890, Mar. 13, 1891.

23. Ibid., Mar. 27, 1888, Mar. 3, 1890; Knights of Labor, "Proceedings of the General Assembly, 1890," Powderly papers.

24. *Rutland Herald,* Jan. 23, 1894, Jan. 29, 30, 1895.

25. Separated by railroad yards from the rest of the town, wards Seven and Eight included St. Peter's Roman Catholic Church, parish, and convent house, and both the Irish-Catholic and French-Catholic cemeteries. Ibid., Jan. 21, 1888, Mar. 14, 1892, Mar. 2, Nov. 9, 1904.

26. Ibid., Feb. 19, Mar. 4, 1896, Feb. 10, 15, Mar. 3, 1897.

27. Robert A. McCaughey, "From Town to City: Boston in the 1820's," *Political Science Quarterly,* 88 (June 1973), 191–213; Giovanni Sartori, *Parties and Party Systems: A Framework for Analysis* (Cambridge, 1976), p. 16.

CHAPTER 11

Italian-American Radicals and Labor in Rhode Island, 1905–30

PAUL BUHLE

Within recent years the Italians have through force of character
taken a place in the front ranks of the revolutionary movement
which is so rapidly developing throughout the world. Especially is
this true in the United States and Canada. . . . The working class
of America is indebted to the Italians and have cause to congrat-
ulate themselves that these people have come to this country in
such large numbers bringing with them the heritage of centuries
of civilization: the traditions, culture and refinement of a great
nation, all of which will contribute to enrich the blood of the new
race that is being born in America. The Italians have no deep-
rooted racial prejudice. They readily mingle with other people,
imbueing their surroundings with their native tenderness as well
as force of character.

—William D. Haywood, *Il Proletario,* May 3, 1913

Come, O May, and entertain the oppressed with the virile fanfare
of the Ideal; these are the ones, don't you see, who did not listen
to the fraternal voice that tried to lead them away from a slow
death, who have no rest from backbreaking work and are damned
to be modern slaves.

Come, O May, and in the powerful chorus of robust voices
which calls you, may the downtrodden, may the weak of today
hear clearly the bell that you ring to call them together; come, O
May, harbinger of peace, of justice, of love and make each slave a
free man.

—Carlo Tresca, "Vieni, O Maggio!" *Il Proletario,* May 1, 1906

I

The history of new immigrants in the American labor movement
and of their influence on the American social landscape remains,
with few exceptions, little known and less understood. The institutional character of labor history, the biases against non-English language materials, and the primitive state (and predominantly conservative character) of community and family studies have obstructed
an intimate examination of immigrants in the labor movement below

the level of union victories or defeats and political alignment with one major party or the other. Mainstream American historians, sharing a common preoccupation with success, have meanwhile brushed aside those dissident movements such as anarchism, syndicalism, and revolutionary socialism that deeply touched and helped to shape the new immigrant communities. Studies of American society have thus ignored a great wave of class organization and ideological development that occurred in the second decade of the twentieth century when these new immigrants threatened the established system of class, ethnic, and religious privilege. Even so acute an analyst of current industrial life as Stanley Aronowitz simply reiterates old myths: "Italian and Polish peasants provided a perfect labor force for an industrial system that demanded complete subordination of the worker. . . . These workers were imbued with the inevitability of social domination. . . . It was precisely the old (feudal) code of obligation that attracted Eastern and Southern European immigrants to the unions."[1] Such statements reflect an inability to perceive the complex relation of militance and apparent apathy, resistance and passivity, coexisting in the same community and indeed within the same individual.

Perhaps most evidently, historians have failed to grasp the complex interactions of class and ethnicity within the ethnic community—divided against itself by class fissures but united at some points in a rough solidarity against the outside world. Joseph Stipanovich's study of south Slavs suggests that in the crucial period of the teens, the Left not only took shape within the peculiar parameters of the ethnic community, but also exerted a wide influence upon the success of the group and the modes of Americanization finally taken. We cannot, he warns, measure the radicals' success or failure by the yardstick of American labor or socialism alone: English-language socialists and craft union radicals looked for the most part to existing political structures and AFL craft unions that they hoped to transform. Immigrant radicals looked first to their communities, participating in the industrial union movements and class-conscious economic cooperatives foremost. Conservative ethnic forces, divided between the preservation of their Old World prerogatives and their hopes for amicable relations with the American business community, were momentarily thrown on the defensive. The communities at large took a middle position, supporting unions when they promised success and also defending ethnic victims of repression. To a great extent, the forced patriotism of World War I and even more the postwar rollback of industrial unions isolated the Left once more.[2]

Nineteenth-century Italian radicalism had developed as the ragged edge of the European socialist movements. In the Po Valley and the northern industrial cities, socialism struck roots between periods of illegality and reprieve. The near-medieval attitudes held toward workers by landowners, clergy, and the rising bourgeoisie provoked a recurrently violent response—demonstrations, strikes, and riots tinged with a millenarian ideology. Stable working-class organizations assumed a community-wide orientation, the *camere* and their institutions, the *Casa del Popolo,* reaching out from organized workers toward all those with radical sympathies. As political socialism and trade unionism developed, they retained many of the characteristics of a semianarchist organization: a minority bent on revolution through the general strike; a violent, inexorable opposition to the church; and impatience with the parliamentary maneuvering of socialist leaders. Repeatedly disrupted by internal dissension and state repression, Italian socialists never achieved a tightly controlled mass party. By the same token, they remained on the revolutionary fringe of the world socialist movement.

The distinctive character of southern Italian radicalism grew out of extreme economic and cultural "backwardness." Overpopulation, heavy taxation, poor land, and inadequate markets for agricultural produce pushed the level of suffering beyond toleration. As in the Iberian peninsula, such conditions and the savagery of the landowners (along with their clerical supporters) promoted anarchism rather than labor socialism. Hunger riots, landowners' leagues, rural *fasci,* and other forms of "primitive rebellion" flared up repeatedly and were repressed with great bloodshed. The main activists in these riots, the *contadini* (agricultural workers), combined an unabashed hatred for the rich with elements of fatalism. Confined by the hundreds or thousands to poverty within the "rural cities," by and large illiterate, they remained loyal to the traditions of family unity, village provincialism, and "superstition" (as opposed to institutionalized religion). As a result, the socialists made few inroads into the south. And it was this region that provided the bulk of immigrants to the United States.[3]

Radicals among the emigrant *contadini* operated under special handicaps. All but a small proportion of the immigrants lacked the urban sophistication, skills, and national or ethnic self-identity that enabled Germans and Jews to establish a strong Left within their communities around trade unions and political issues. The Old World peasant rebellion lost its essential meaning. But newer forms of exploitation called out for an aggressive response. Slowly, with painfully uneven results, radical émigrés turned resentment against the ethnic *prominenti,* businessmen, landlords, and professionals whose client relationship with the American elite impelled them to serve as middlemen for a systematic discrimination.

The initial Italian-American protests against miserable wages and conditions and against racism were a conglomeration of Old and New World means and logic. Émigré intellectuals, often fleeing arrest or deprived of their means of living because of their political activities, took the lead with a thin fringe of skilled and semiskilled workers. Wherever possible, they established a framework for systematic agitation, creating their own organizations or joining American left-wing bodies, publishing newspapers, and instituting an American *Casa del Popolo*. In times of relative apathy, these groups did little more than to create an enclave of free thought. During strikes or community protests they channeled hostility against the American system of discrimination and exploitation into an active attack upon the Italian-American "parasites" who preyed upon their own people. Foremost among these, they identified a most American figure, the *padrone*—banker, politician, or employment agent—who extended the entrenched familialism into the functions of economic broker between the English-speaking employer and the Italian-American worker. By and large the *padrone* exploited the immigrant's plight, introducing the raw Italian as a strikebreaker, the miserably housed and paid employee who drove down existing wages, the boom-and-bust worker who went from long hours of beastly labor to long months of idleness. By attacking the *padrone*, radicals could draw the class lines in their own community, dispute the sway of the *prominenti*, and appeal for the unification of all workers across ethnic lines.[4]

Among the various old and new immigrant communities, Italian-American radicalism had several distinct characteristics. Ideologically, it was more deeply and consistently touched with anarchism than any other segment of the working-class movement in America. Anarchist newspapers like *Cronaca Sovversiva* (The Subversive Chronicle) and its editor Luigi Galleani rapidly assumed a towering presence among the radicalized Italian-American workers. The Galleanistas, as the members of the most extreme wing of the movement were known, foreswore permanent organization, defended individual violence against tyrants, and continually called for general strikes and insurrectionary labor uprisings. This anarchism colored most of the Italian-American radical spectrum. Its nearest political relative, syndicalism, preached the union as the basis of the new, decentralized order and dismissed electoral politics. Political socialism proved a weak competitor to those tendencies until well into the 1910s. The single important political organization, the Italian Social-

ist Federation (FSI), remained outside the American socialist movement, dominated by the syndicalists' loyalty to the Industrial Workers of the World (IWW) as the true movement destined to make the
revolution. Even when political socialists and more moderate unions
gained ascendency in Italian-American radicalism, by 1920, they remained open to the leadership of quasi-anarchists and the inspiration of the general strike.[5]

This emboldened Italian radicalism was as much the result of internal weakness as ideological fortitude. High rates of illiteracy precluded the patient mass education that American socialist periodicals
attempted. The disproportionately male character of immigration
along with the forced geographic mobility of the unskilled worker
discouraged community formation and undercut the founding of
radical neighborhood networks. The traditional sex-segregation of
Italian social life and indifference toward the education of women
greatly impeded the kind of contributions radical women made to
Finnish, Slavic, and Jewish socialist movements in the United States,
rooting radicalism in day-to-day family practices.[6] The Italian-American movement tended more than its counterparts among other ethnic groups to be an ephemeral force, scattered among a handful of
trades and neighborhoods, crisis-oriented rather than well organized
and evolutionary.

Such weaknesses did not negate the movement's significance. The
cadre of FSI members, newspaper subscribers, and consistently active sympathizers remained small in proportion to the population.
But this minority undertook the monumental task of community
and factory organization with unexcelled vigor. Carlo Tresca, who
had defied death and community disapproval by attacking the Black
Hand societies and the clergy, stirred crowds to revolt with a few
roaring phrases. Arturo Giovannitti, simultaneously a leading union
agitator and the foremost American radical poet, personally demonstrated the inspirational character that Italian-American revolutionaries so proudly possessed. The Italian radical press spread the
slogans of the day with exemplary style and gusto. Italian-American
radicals might fall into disastrous quarrels, pay too little attention to
organizational details, and fail to maintain so much as a publication
schedule, but their little flame of inspiration illuminated vast reaches
of political territory.

II

Industrial conditions and the specific character of the Italian-American population in Rhode Island underlined both the need for im-

migrant self-defense and the difficulty of an aggressive posture vis-
à-vis the ruling economic authorities. By the second decade of the
century, the state displayed all the contradictions of a New England
manufacturing center in transition from industrial leadership to relative backwater. Although the relocation of textile mills in the South
had scarcely begun to reduce gross production of cottons and wools,
Rhode Island's share of the national market diminished. The specter
of cheap competition further induced managers to drive wages
lower and intensify sweated labor. Still, the urban compactness of
the state and the diversification of industry held the proportion of
industrial workers in the population to a remarkable 20 percent. Machine shops, preparing for the expansion for war manufacture, expanded the pool of semiskilled labor as did the "junk" jewelry industry, rubbermaking, electrical parts, and other minor industries.
Regressive manufacturing techniques—piecework and homework—
found new life among the new immigrants and particularly Italians,
where families waged a collective battle against the margins of poverty. Female labor, nearly twice the national average of 20 percent
in manufactures, carried the stigma of low wages and poor conditions, Italian-, Irish-, and Polish-American women providing New
England textiles their last reservoir of low-paid labor.[7]

The first state Bureau of Labor study of population groups by
origin, published in 1915, officially designated the Italian-born and
Italian-stock population—some 55,000 in the state, with more than
85 percent in and around Providence—as the lowest-paid population group in the state, with the least likelihood to seek redress
through any formal political mechanism. Over half surveyed averaged $10 a week or less. Along with the Irish, they constituted more
than 80 percent of the unskilled category "laborers," and held the
bottom rungs in the jewelry, machine parts, and textile industries.
Comparable only to the less numerous French-Canadians and Por-
tuguese, Rhode Island Italians had a staggering illiteracy rate of
some 30 percent; compared to their nearest equivalent in population
size—the Irish—naturalized Italians voted only in small numbers, 20
percent to the Irish's 71 percent. Prone to both seasonal and long-
term unemployment, unlikely to return home to Italy, without political power or the industrial leverage of skilled positions, Italian-
Americans were an especially vulnerable group.[8]

Italian-American radicals devised a variety of ways to meet their
needs. Along a continuum with considerable overlap were absolute
anarchists who scandalized the neighborhoods by their priest-bait-
ing, industrial syndicalists interested foremost in union organization,
and political socialists working toward an integrated political move-

ment. These political variations reflected the very real divisions in the Italian-American community in terms of background, political skills, and intellectual finesse.

Italian-American stone workers in Westerly, at the southwestern tip of Rhode Island, offered a model in exotic radicalism. A highly skilled and relatively well-paid minority within an Italian population of 1,500 or so, they espoused the white-hot anarchism of Galleani. After leading an insurrectionary strike and riot in Paterson, New Jersey, in 1902, Galleani had fled to Lynn, Massachusetts, where Carrarese anarchists had gathered following an unsuccessful rebellion in the 1890s. Galleani was a frequent visitor to Westerly, his bombastic denunciation of capitalism all too evidently a thin disguise for the radicals' isolation. The granite-cutters viewed older community members as "ambitious . . . cretins," ignorant and afraid of the ideas of liberty and fraternity. "Subversives, canaille, thieves, freebooters and bad ones" (as they mimicked the local attacks upon them), they harassed *padroni* in the quarries, local priests, and city officials, all of whom they envisioned as one reactionary mass.[9] Their spirit emerged most clearly in their picnics and outings where they heard speeches cursing the oppressors and raised funds for *Cronaca Sovversiva* and *Il Proletario,* the official FSI organ. Despite their sincerity they made few converts, and by World War I had ceased to be an important factor in the statewide movement.[10]

The movement in Providence, Pawtucket, and to a lesser extent Woonsocket was both more vital and more complex. The Italian-American constituency was overwhelmingly from southern Italy, with little political background or negotiable skill. Scattered tradesmen could be found, however, among the tailors and construction workers, a thin stratum of free thinkers among artisans and professionals. In the metropolitan environment radicals could attract a minor neighborhood following, call in agitators from New York and Boston, and create institutions and local publications. Galleanista anarchism remained strong, especially at historic junctures when the revolutionary minority of the Italian-American community felt most hopelessly isolated and most thoroughly determined to make a revolutionary sentiment heard. Where the gap between propaganda and actual organizing narrowed, more cautious and strategic-minded elements held sway.

By 1905 FSI adherents in Rhode Island had recommenced the strategic debates held in contemporary European radical movements. An agreement on a rather vague combination of propaganda and revolutionary unionism remained abstract for the local scene. The radicals attracted the most attention through their espousal of free thought, freely trading insults with the clergy. One comrade launched *Il Libero Pensiero* (Free Thought) to open up questions of faith to scientific scrutiny. Radicals flaunted the religious consecration of marriage by staging civil ceremonies, "free love" unions "without the dirty water" the priests sprinkled on. Apart from such forays, socialists and anarchists tended essentially to create a radical world within a conservative one, replacing orthodox ceremonies with their own. Holidays such as the celebration of the Paris Commune substituted for Epiphany or Easter. Summer outings took on a special character when sympathetic women, presumably family members, could be seen in joyful dances, red ribbons in their caps to show their loyalties, and when comrades from all parts of the Old Country, Tuscans and Sicilians, Romans and Neapolitans, drank and sang together with ceremonial unity.[11]

Luigi Nimini, the leading Rhode Island émigré intellectual, was a natural leader for the small radical movement. Reared in a comfortable Verona family, Nimini had grown radical in the university, turned socialist in the 1890s, suffered political persecution, and departed for the United States. In Providence he published his own monthly newspaper, *Ragione Nuova* (New Reason) as an organ of free thought and socialism; it later became the official national journal of the American Socialist Labor party.[12] Nimini founded and led a Karl Marx circle, dedicated to propagating uncompromising political socialism—unlike the ambiguous reformism of the mainstream American Socialist party—and joined the Socialist Labor party (SLP). When Nimini challenged the SLP's narrowness, he and his paper were disowned. But Nimini accomplished several more important objectives in Rhode Island. Because he believed so deeply in free thought, he was able to gain the loyalty of local anarchists, syndicalists, and socialists across factional lines, and present the community with the Left's own *prominenti*. Because he upheld a political strategy rather than mere anarchist resistance, Nimini greatly advanced radical influence on local institutions and customs. Besides attacking reactionary priests and staging grand public debates between the infamous Galleani and local intellectual-religious figures, Nimini also threw his energy into local reform activities from fundraising for the victims of the 1909 Calabrian earthquake to publicity for the Political Refugees' Defense League. He carried radical agitation from the street corner to mainstream political banquets. Most of all, Nimini nurtured the vision and practice of industrial unionism. Through continuous propaganda and personal leadership of early IWW locals, Nimini helped focus the attention of Italian-American radicals on practical bread-and butter agitation.[13]

By the time he died in 1912, Nimini had laid the groundwork for the second stage of Italian-American radicalism in Rhode Island. As elsewhere, the movement had failed to take hold through purely ideological means. To succeed, the Italian-American Left had to attach its polemical thrust to a physical presence that promised immediate betterment for ordinary laborers. This activity promised to accomplish two great objectives: to give a class interpretation to the instinctive resentment Italian-Americans felt and to bring together supporters of labor and radicalism across ethnic lines. The difficulties involved were correspondingly great. The radicals might prove too weak or too inept to overcome the opposition of conservative Italian-American leaders. And whatever their exertions, the radicals might be unable to mobilize illiterate, politically powerless, unskilled laborers against a mighty industrial-political complex.

III

The national strike wave in the years 1909–13 electrified a stagnant American labor movement and allowed the new immigrants to take center stage for the first time. As Isaac Hourwich remarked in his pioneering study of labor and immigration, the claims made about new immigrant labor's passivity and apparent acceptance of miserable conditions had never been accurate. Before the recession of 1903 flooded the job market with superfluous labor, Italians and eastern Europeans on the East Coast had already staged dramatic strikes and demonstrated a community staying power rare among the Irish and English workers and one all but unknown since the strike wave of the 1880s.[14] Following an outbreak at the Pressed Steel Car Company in McKees' Rocks, Pennsylvania, in 1909, a nationwide pattern of mass strikes developed in the heavily capitalized industries—steel, rubber, and auto—along with textiles and the needle trades. With few exceptions, AFL unions remained unwilling or unable to organize the new immigrant groups; frequently craft union officials denounced the strikers.

In Rhode Island as elsewhere in the industrial East, Italians proved the key ethnic sector and the IWW the central organizational mechanism. Through an aggressive industrial program that reconciled the practical and the ideal—the building of the union to replace the political state—Italian-American radicals sought to reverse in one sweep their isolation and powerlessness. The IWW readily became the vehicle for Italian-American hopes, the Lawrence, Massachusetts, textile strike of 1912 proof of what the Wobblies might do for New England workers. By appealing to all workers regardless of sex, color, or ethnicity, the IWW gave voice to the vision that Italian-American radicals longed to hear from American labor: "non lotta di razza, ma di classe" (not race, but class). Italian-American Wobblies threw themselves into major organizing drives among shoemakers, hotel workers, barbers, piano workers, and textile workers, while seeking to displace AFL unions with "one big union" among building tradesmen, stone workers, and others.[15] The Lawrence conflict gave drama and substance to this organizational flurry. Touched off by a wage cut due to the passage of a state law that limited the work week to fifty-four hours, the strike embraced 10,000 employees of diverse ethnic backgrounds, with Italians more numerous than any other single group. "Big Bill" Haywood, joined by Elizabeth Gurley Flynn, her companion Carlo Tresca, poet-agitator Arturo Giovannitti, and the "boy" orator Joe Ettor, plunged into activity while Socialist party women spirited the strikers' children to other cities for safekeeping, and the English-language radical press raised funds. Local Italian-American militants echoed Giovannitti's editorial cry in *Il Proletario* that the IWW *was the revolution*, while more moderate supporters reflected that a coalition of radicals had made possible a giant step forward by the unskilled and foreign-born.[16]

Support for the Lawrence strike surpassed previous Italian-American radical agitation in Rhode Island. "The moment has arrived, the hour has come," *Il Proletario*'s Rhode Island correspondent appealed to state readers, "your comrades have shown the way through their struggle and sacrifice."[17] FSI militants and anarchists held meetings in February affirming solidarity for the strikers, condemning the AFL efforts to settle the conflict on company terms, demanding the release of political prisoners, and raising funds for the strike. During the next months new sections of the FSI and IWW appeared in Pawtucket and Woonsocket. Demanding freedom for Ettor and Giovannitti, Pawtucket syndicalists called for unity among all Italian political and fraternal organizations, utilizing a Social and Dramatic Club to raise money and elevate spirits through a series of performances. Galleani went on the stump in Westerly, denouncing the "cossacks" in typically bombastic terms, winning an enthusiastic response that he had not enjoyed there in years.[18]

Support for Ettor and Giovannitti, now symbols of outraged Italian-American citizenry, continued to swell over the summer in two decisive directions. First, despite the continuing attacks by the Catholic church hierarchy and Italian business leaders against the IWW, organizers found audiences more curious and receptive, and workers were willing to risk their jobs by union membership. Second, the

Socialist party, scorned by all but a few Rhode Island Italian-Americans, lent its enthusiastic support for a united labor defense. In the first significant joint action between Rhode Island English-language socialists and the FSI, a grand parade was planned for September. As thousands marched under red flags to Infantry Hall, overflow crowds had to be turned away. En route, Italian-Americans gained yet another experience in special oppression. In what the local socialist paper called "an attempt to arouse race prejudice," police chose to attack Italians marching through Federal Hill and to seize the red flag. Against these divisive tactics, one-time state legislator and Socialist party leader James P. Reid declared, "The unjust incarceration of Ettor and Giovannitti [will] be the incident that will weld together all the forces of the proletariat against the common enemy, the capitalist class, for their accomplishment of their common ideal [in] the abolition of the wage system" as the Lawrence strike had shown the way to industrial unionism.[19]

These events foreshadowed the first round of mass strikes in Rhode Island during the teens, the most important since the textile and streetcar workers' conflicts of 1902, the earliest in which the new immigrants in the textile industry took part. Although the IWW was unable to carry through on its plans of leadership for most strikes, it spearheaded and dramatized the conflicts. Socialist party activists, though small in number, played a key agitational role in the English-language public and among trade unions. The existence of this coalition permitted Italian-American radicals to proliferate, to seek the consolidation of their ranks in a public breakthrough so long in coming.

Economic and social conditions in the state underlined the ripeness of the industrial scene for a decisive intervention. Although new immigration to the state continued at record levels, most particularly among Italians, the national prosperity in 1912–13 gave the "green" laborers adequate opportunities for work and stimulated greater demands by the employed. Rhode Island workers sought equality with their counterparts elsewhere. And inflation, which was to decimate family incomes during the war years, had already begun to erode family budgets, evoking a call for a larger share of the booming textile profits.

The state labor movement had so far proved unequal to the task of organizing its workers. By the end of 1912, only workers in the building trades, streetcar drivers, brewery workers, and employees in minor trades, such as typographers, had any semblance of sturdy organization. Scarcely 10 percent of the dominant textile industry was organized, after eighty years of sporadic agitation. The IWW, with its proclaimed program of "one big union," had likewise been unable to secure a foothold.

In early 1913 the Esmond mill in North Providence, adjoining Greystone, where an independent mill union had been formed during a successful strike a month before, became the prime site of state IWW activity. Mostly Italian and disproportionately female, the Esmond employees had demanded a 20 percent raise and the rehiring of several IWW members. In the early days of the strike mass meetings were held every day, and deputy sheriffs intimidated the strikers. The Olneyville IWW local provided key leadership, aided by the New England locals of the National Industrial Union of Textile Workers (NIUTW). The socialist *Labor Advocate* could rightly proclaim the conflict "the first strike in Rhode Island that has been under the supervision of the new school of Industrial Unionism."[20] Ethnic differences prompted Italians to form their own special branch of the IWW, but did not otherwise hinder unity. As more than 300 strikers enrolled in the Wobblies and the mill capitulated, a local unionist boasted: "The tea kettle has arrived, also the oven. We are going in for 9 o'clock breakfasts, a good hot dinner, also afternoon tea. What do you think of that, you guys at [neighboring] Centredale and Georgiaville? We'll show you how to make a mill a pleasure to work in. . . . We are wanting a good sized barn or cottage to turn into a club-house. Then we are going to start a cooperative society on working men's lines—no profits, no working expenses, goods at cost price to all members."[21]

The success at Esmond helped inspire a wave of cotton and wool strikes in Pawtucket, South Kingston, Centredale, Thornton, Warren, Woonsocket, Berkley, and Olneyville, as well as work stoppages among Italian laborers and road workers across the state, craft carpenters, teamsters, bricklayers, and unskilled workers of virtually every ethnic and occupational variety. In most cases the strikers were able to gain some immediate objectives—no reduction in pay from the statutory reduction of the work week—or actual wage increases, better housing, and an end to "padroning" (as it was called), the job favoritism practices by the minor bosses. Understaffed at a time of national strain upon IWW resources, denounced in press and pulpit as an illegitimate, immoral organization that served merely as a front for atheistic socialism, the Wobblies intervened successfully in only a few places. These served, however, in tactics and drama, to highlight the character and limits of the strike wave.[22]

In Pawtucket weavers at the Hope Webbing mill struck against a corrupt padroning system and the company's refusal to post a consistent price list for piecework. The strikers, half Italian, met in an

Italian hall to request that the IWW help organize them and formulate their demands. The critical problem of the strike was to
bring out the 500 workers in other parts of the plant, mostly girls in
the finishing and warping rooms. The IWW adopted a two-part
strategy: mass picketing at the factory gates and visits to the homes
of nonstrikers. So successful was this effort that more than 400 enrolled in the IWW, as strikers accepted management concessions.[23]

In Peacedale, at the rural, southern end of the state, IWW organizers initiated the state's first "Free Speech Fight," as local and outside speakers faced mass arrest to dramatize the right to open labor
agitation. Displacing the small craft following of the United Textile
Workers, the IWW convened large-scale public meetings until these
were banned by authorities and briefly led two walkouts for higher
wages, fairer treatment in company housing, and nondiscrimination
against IWW members.[24]

The most dramatic IWW conflict pitted Providence tailors against
the combined hostility of the Catholic church, the foremost newspapers, and AFL unions in the state. The International Ladies Garment Workers Union had just won recognition in New York; Boston
tailors struck in sympathy in January 1913, with 5,000 local garment
workers leaving their jobs. In Providence more than 300 members
swelled and transformed the formerly small IWW local, drawing
Jews, Italians, and scattered others together. At the end of March
the IWW sought to win a comprehensive victory in the department
stores and finishing shops, over 1,000 workers avowing to hold fast
for a single contract. Mass meetings, reputedly held in Italian until
younger seamstresses demanded Yiddish and English, ended in the
tailors' expulsion from their rented hall. Plans for a mass parade
were presented to obdurate police, who refused to issue a permit
and rushed in to break up a demonstration of IWW supporters on
Federal Hill.[25]

The newspapers damned the IWW as a "socialistic organization."
Father Bove, the leading prelate and a long-time enemy of radicals
on Federal Hill, issued statements disavowing the IWW's purported
"violence and disregard for the laws of God and properly constituted authority." Local leaders of several important unions, including the Italian-American business agent of the Building Trades Laborers, poured abuse on the strike, the state AFL president warning
members, "You must be either for or against the IWW." General
secretary of the International Ladies Garment Workers Union, John
Dyche, made a special trip to Providence to protect the ladies' tailors
from interference, to warn against the IWW, and to urge members
to "join a reputable union."[26] AFL officials thanked the reactionary

Providence Journal for its aid in fighting "the menace to the peace of a community." And the *Labor Advocate* rightly concluded, "Never before in the history of the labor movement in this city has any organization of working men and women been more bitterly assailed, and never has a struggle for better conditions been more vigorously opposed than in the present instance."[27]

Such pressures proved too great for the state IWW. In Esmond, at the Hope Webbing Works, at the Queen Dyeing Company in Providence, and the giant Brown & Sharpe machine complex (where the IWW had begun agitation), management weeded out the "troublemakers" and intimidated other workers into accepting nonunion status. At Peacedale, United Textile Worker president John Golden (best known for his attempt to "settle" the Lawrence strike over the head of the IWW) sought to renew the industrial peace by pressuring striking weavers to resign publicly from their jobs and by holding rump meetings of "loyal" unionists ready to return to work while the IWW conclaves were hounded by the police.[28]

The IWW adventure in Rhode Island gave way to reaction. Galloping inflation practically negated wage advances. Woolen operatives reported a particularly savage increase of the workpace. And management, after uprooting the IWW, acted against other troublesome unions. Thus the B.B. & R. Knight firm, with more than 8,000 workers, employed the ultimate weapon against a 1914 strike. Rather than give in to the 200 mule spinners, owners replaced the mules with ring frames run by children, destroying the state's most important spinners' local, which had roots going back to the 1880s.[29]

IV

The core of Italian-American radicalism had not been destroyed, nor had labor grown permanently quiescent. The wartime expansion of production and a simultaneously growing self-consciousness among Italian-Americans generally broadened the possibilities for labor success. Although they remained on the edges of their communities, Italian-American radicals drew a wide following among residents in the period of high excitement during 1912–14. Community members turned out in the hundreds to hear Joe Ettor in late 1912, and again in 1914 to protest the Ludlow Massacre. When Rhode Island Governor Aram Pothier called openly for wage reductions to keep local mills competitive, the Italians participated in a protest meeting described as "one of the largest ever held in Olneyville." Meanwhile, the FSI and the anarchists erected clubhouses in Providence and Pawtucket, the *Casa Proletaria* as in the Old Country intending to win workers and community members away "from their patriotic and religious sentiments," and to provide a meeting hall with a center for leisurely entertainment.[30]

Continuing unemployment, skyrocketing prices, and the specter of a European war from which American profiteers were amassing fortunes deepened Italian-American resentment in 1914 and provided radicals with unprecedented legitimacy. By late August 1914 syndicalists and socialists had sponsored demonstrations in Providence to protest prices and to demand state government relief. A community-wide committee broadened the agitation, as *L'Eco* reported, against "hunger, unemployment and systematic discrimination in America." Activists passed circulars through the neighborhood, urging residents to attend a mass meeting. Following a rally, crowds sacked the offending stores. The following day's events are described variously as "the worst riot in the annals of the city," and (by socialists) as the "most awe-inspiring demonstration . . . that has ever taken place in the history of Providence."[31]

Whatever their lack of political experience in American society or lack of strategic acumen, Providence Italian-Americans had in large numbers demonstrated an unwillingness to tolerate the worst humiliations of their position. As a socialist eyewitness wrote: "Not possessing the sluggish nature of natives, these fathers, mothers and children of action, angered by the insulting and evading tactics of the Governor and Mayor shown by their faking investigations, took the bit in their teeth. . . . Hunger knows no law, and the sight of loved ones and children wasting away for the lack of the poorest sustenance while polite thieves like the managers of the Atlantic Mills are swelling in luxury, will produce more and better fruit."[32]

Events in the following years pointed to a growing self-consciousness through a blending of ethnic and class awareness.

And yet radicals were never able to consolidate these energies into a political movement. English-language socialists headlined their account of the protest rallies following the rioting, "Italian Workers to Seek Redress on Election Day."[33] This encapsulated the difficulty socialists experienced in relating to the new immigrants, especially the Italians. An electoral strategy had no more appeal now than earlier, even while Italians seemed determined to fight for their prerogatives. Italian-American syndicalists and anarchists did no better with their insurrectionary appeals to war resistance and their avantgarde attacks upon American (or Italian) patriotism. While these appeals stirred sympathy and individual response, the trajectory of the new immigrant movement lay in the direction of labor seeking higher wages and better conditions, not in ideological slogans and party-building.

Although Rhode Island textile profits hit a new high in 1919, the specter of southern competition and the option of shifting work from region to region bolstered the owners' determination to resist unionization. The depressed character of the economy and soaring unemployment in 1914 deprived Rhode Island workers somewhat of the sellers' market enjoyed by labor in war-related production elsewhere. Nevertheless, Rhode Island labor demonstrated an unprecedented volatility during the war years. While profits soared, wage demands stalked inflation, and maximum hours in key industries dipped under fifty-four for the first time, settling at a historic forty-eight-hour week for much of the mill population. The earlier labor offensive, broken by economic downturn and concerted employer resistance, reasserted itself in ever-wider circles between 1915 and 1919. As David Montgomery has suggested, the cooperation of skilled and unskilled workers, an unprecedented solidarity of various ethnic groups, made this forward leap possible.[34]

By 1915 the first stage of this development had already altered the character of Rhode Island labor's situation. Following the lead of machinists in Bridgeport, Connecticut, who had struck citywide in the summer for an eight-hour day, Providence machinists demanded the same of Brown & Sharpe, now prospering under war orders. When 100 men were fired for union activities, 5,000 strikers poured out, later parading through the streets, running in and out of the plant, shouting "Eight Hours." Underlining the importance of this event, as the *Labor Advocate* noted, was the "awakening it has caused among all classes of labor, organized and unorganized."[35] Indeed, most of the "machinists," outside the top grade of skilled worker, were recent immigrants, especially Italians. Iron foundry workers in Providence also joined in a sympathetic strike, and unions across the state increased their membership overnight.[36]

The most remarkable aspect of this outpouring was the sanction it received from normally timid official trade union leaders, and the shifting ideological framework that the strike leaders sought to create. Attacking charges that the strike was a "German Plot," International Association of Machinists' leaders proclaimed their constituents "loyal American citizens . . . striking for a larger measure of industrial freedom."[37] The state metal trades council's short-lived paper, the *Labor World*, proclaimed: "The country is talking national preparedness. The Church is talking spiritual preparedness. And the one thing that should receive the most consideration is neglected

by those who it would benefit most, and that is industrial preparedness."[38] Far from implying any hesitation to make demands against
the "public interest," the appeal for industrial democracy became a
battle cry for those like the executive member of IAM who threatened to pull out every metal worker in the state to gain eight hours
and then "fight until every girl in the city of Providence is working
only eight hours a day."[39]

In the years 1915 to 1919 the number of strikes and the size of
union membership rose impressively. From the metal trades to the
traditional low-wage industries—jewelry and textiles—unionized
workers gained increased wages and shorter hours, which also benefited those who remained outside organized labor. Most of the sites
of earlier IWW agitation—Hope Webbing, Brown & Sharpe, and
Queen Dyeing—continued to be centers of strike activity, but now
without direct IWW involvement. Textile workers, teamsters, and
brewery workers at various times threatened sanctions or staged
sympathy actions to ban "hot" (scab-produced) items from production and to enforce local demands. Amid an atmosphere that must
have reminded old-timers of the Knights of Labor drive in the
1880s, Rhode Island labor appeared to be coming of age.[40]

The advance applied more perhaps to Italian-Americans than to
any other single nationality. A rising self-consciousness briefly embraced unionization on the one side, progressive community activity
and public opinion on the other. In Natick operatives at the giant
B.B. & R. Knight mill walked out in 1918 to protest ethnic slurs and
mistreatment.[41] Such overt actions were rare. But the identification
between labor's advance and the Italian-American's right to share
the fruits of democracy grew obvious even to the middle-class press.
In 1919 several Rhode Island branches of the Sons of Italy, a fraternal lodge, gained broad coverage in L'Eco for demands that Italian-
Americans receive fair treatment from employers.[42] The same paper
complained that what Americans needed was labor unity, the spirit
of the IWW infused with that of the practical AFL. This was a far
step from the trepidations of the early teens and marked a vaguely
defined but crucial shift in the balance of forces among Italian-
Americans.[43]

Nevertheless, unions of unskilled workers remained fragile, unable to coordinate labor's strengths in any systematic fashion; the
result was that they were thereby subject to the worst of company
counteroffensives. The labor defeats in the jewelry and textile industries demonstrated this vulnerability. A maverick AFL union, the
International Jewelry Workers, had spread out to Rhode Island's
junk jewelry center to follow the trade running from New York City

shops organized through the cooperation of Jewish socialists and Italian syndicalists. Relatively small and regionally limited, the jewelry workers' union was yet a spirited expression of the time, free-minded enough to print essays by Tolstoy and Kropotkin alongside organizational reports in its journal even while engaged in a desperate struggle for existence. The jewelry workers' key conflict in Rhode Island pitted 800 employees of Ostby & Barton's, one of the largest jewelry firms in the nation, against a pool of jewelry employers, labor spies, and a press filled with smears of "radicalism" and "anarchy." Despite a vigorous effort, jewelry workers were beaten, their membership in Rhode Island reduced to a scattered few. Likewise in the great textile conflict of the summer of 1918 mass picketing and parades seemingly presaged a long-awaited union breakthrough. John Golden, United Textile Worker president, urged moderation, warning workers that all strike funds would have to be raised inside the state and beseeching them to trust in his negotiations with the War Labor Board to settle the crisis. As the strike sagged and collapsed of its own weight, the promise of industrial unionization faded away once more.[44]

The leadership that Italian-American radicals gave to trade union work and the orchestration of community and fraternal support in New York, Chicago, and Lynn scarcely existed in Rhode Island by the late teens. At best, the remnants of other IWW locals, like the tailors, found their way into the broader union movement through "amalgamation"; at worst, as among the hotel workers or mill operatives inspired to resist by Wobbly oratory, organization seemed to vanish.[45] The radicals had been unable to make the turn away from an old ultra-radicalism to a more calculated politics. An itinerant organizer for the Amalgamated Clothing Workers complained in 1919 that nearly everywhere in New England the same was true.[46] The continuing isolation of the self-styled revolutionary vanguard led to a sense of absolute distance from the majority, who followed the orders of the factory owner and the admonitions of the priest. The limitations of such uncompromising spirit upon a strategic outlook grew more painfully obvious as the years advanced. While labor in Rhode Island moved ahead largely without the leadership of the anarchists and syndicalists, government agents seized upon the open antiwar stance of radicals to persecute, imprison, and deport them. As Rhode Island syndicalists faced the jailing of their national IWW leaders, anarchists looked on in horror at the suppression of *Cronaca Sovversiva,* including the jailing and deporting of many subscribers and of Galleani himself.[47] Conscientious radicals could not fail to resist the world slaughter, but many had left themselves open to repression by severing too hastily the links of potential support from the ethnic and labor communities. The Italian-American revolutionaries' moral strength had been their strategic weakness: they could not, would not abandon their feverish dreams for a paler reality.

V

A full consideration of this explosive era's aftermath in the 1920s and the implications for Italian-American labor and ethnic radicalism in Rhode Island is beyond the scope of this article. Yet the outline is revealing as a somber epilogue, a lesson in the cultural isolation of radicals and the defeat of labor by overwhelming forces, the tipping of the balance in a community away from a progressive inclination. This shift took place in a context of increasing antiunionism and nativism. A massive and prolonged textile strike in 1922, against reductions in pay and extension of hours to prewar standards, brought the radical Amalgamated Textile Workers union to the center of the conflict, along with the familiar craft-oriented United Textile Workers. Lost after six months, the strike may properly be regarded as one of what David Montgomery calls the "desperate battles" of the retrenchment period.[48] But the intensity of the campaign—the mass rallies, the dances, and even a baseball league—among thousands of workers previously unorganized suggests also a synthesis of IWW-like inspiration and practical "mainstream" unionism. The ethnic origins of the strike and the extraordinary tenacity and willingness of Italian-Americans to work with other groups offer perhaps the best evidence that Rhode Island Italian-Americans had joined those in New York, Pennsylvania, Illinois, and elsewhere in linking the fate of their people with the success of labor.

This successful mobilization came too late and offered too little in an era dominated by the open shop rollback of wartime union gains, a racism and nativism dramatized by the Ku Klux Klan's revival, and the successful isolation of radicals from most centers of power. Italian-Americans in Rhode Island and elsewhere also faced their own special problems in Benito Mussolini's seizure of Italian state power. Fascism, with some of its tangled roots in the radical movement, spoke to a vicarious nationalistic pride among not only the business classes, but also among wider sectors of the population hurt by discrimination and poverty. While other important ethnic groups (Jews, Hungarians, and Finns) felt the forward pull of the Russian Revolution, Italian-Americans endured the steady erosion of their hard-won gains by the power of organized bullies. Thus the direction of the Sons of Italy, once mobilized in support of the Italian-American labor movement, fell increasingly under right-wing influence.[49]

For a brief historical moment, the Italian-American Left in Providence and elsewhere experienced an Indian summer. The reactionary turn in American culture had, perhaps, the effect of enlivening a self-conscious avant-garde for the last time. New fraternal centers, like the Matteotti Club (named after the Italian socialist deputy assassinated by the Fascists in 1924) in Cranston, flourished as social and recreational institutions. New local associations, like the *Gruppo Autonomo* and *Gruppo di Anarchisti*, associated themselves with a new generation of Italian-American radical newspapers, Carlo Tresca's popular *Il Martello* and the Galleanista *Adunata dei Refrattari*. The 1922 strike briefly widened the pool of radical recruits, most especially for those drawn to Communism rather than to anarchism. While the Italian-American Communists nationally began a short-lived daily newspaper, *Il Lavoratore*, in Chicago, the Rhode Island faithful launched "Language Federation" branches of the Communist movement in Providence, Pawtucket, and Woonsocket. Communist, syndicalist, unaffiliated radical, all but the most extreme anarchists joined together in anti-Fascist activities: building local support for tours by Tresca and others, fighting a backstairs struggle against the advancing Right in the Sons of Italy, and proclaiming a positive, progressive Italian identity through the Risorgimento Club.[50]

These activities had an essential function in counterbalancing the pressure of the Right. Indeed, the presence of a democratic anti-Fascism in Providence through World War II owed its existence to radicals. But the institutional base for a leftward ethnic orientation eroded rapidly. Their events well-attended on picnic days, the Italian-American radicals had less and less of a political function outside anti-Fascism. Their movement disappeared by degrees, through the retirement and death of old comrades and the indifference of the newer generations.

The last important struggle to reach outside the Italian-American community and to make demands in the name of Italian-Americans as a whole suggests both the essential nature of the 1920s radical movement and its limitations. Radicals in Providence had begun a community support for Nicola Sacco and Bartolomeo Vanzetti as early as 1920, professors as well as proletarians drawn to the podium in the prisoners' defense. As the case reached its final stages, the agitation accelerated. Perhaps most novel in this activity was the role of the theatrical troupes, notably the Providence-based Spartacus Filodramatica, which toured the state raising funds and demanding justice for the two victims. Support from the labor movement, elicited by such figures as Luigi Nardella and James P. Reid, helped erect a wide basis of support by bringing many non-Italians (and

non-radicals) into the defense. The major lesson urged by the Left,
however, thrust home the impact of the Sacco-Vanzetti case for millions of Italian-Americans: the case was not one of simple justice,
but rather resistance to armed discrimination, the murder of two
noble figures as scapegoats for all that conservative Anglo-Saxon
America despised but could not destroy outright. In the final
months of appeals Italian-American sentiment ran higher than for
any other political issue in memory. When tens of thousands gathered on the Dexter Training Ground in Providence a few days prior
to the execution, representatives of the Right and the Center, fraternal and religious groups spoke in the prisoners' defense, but the
initiative and the responsibility fell to the Left, which had seen
through the fight from the beginning. Broken hopes in the wake of
Il Martello's call for a political general strike, the final futility of a
mammoth demonstration on the Boston Common (for which Rhode
Islanders scheduled special trains), the hopelessness of appeal by
even leading American intellectuals—with these, one might say, the
great cause of the 1920s Left faded, an expectation in, American
democratic processes disappointed Italian-American labor would
never experience again.[51]

Even by the 1920s political reality had bypassed Italian-American
anarchism and syndicalism. Each new generation defines its own
needs by the world immediately around it, and the broad participation of Italian-Americans in Rhode Island and elsewhere in the CIO
and subsequent labor movements required no such ideology. The
early Italian radicals had contributed most to labor's development as
a background force, ancestors rather than mentors. And yet something had been lost with the failure of labor and radicalism in the
1910s. The revolutionary Italian-Americans even more than the native-born Wobblies carried the nineteenth-century romantic vision—
a pure dream of mass participation in every aspect of life, an auto-
didact culture in which learning suggested enlightenment rather
than intellectual drudgery, the expectation that social controls over
people's lives would produce an *absolute* negation in liberatory energy—into a disillusioned twentieth century. Perhaps this earlier
radicalism has no place in a world where most choices seem good
only in reference to worse alternatives. Then again, perhaps a Pawtucket syndicalist from 1913 has something to say that has not yet
clearly been heard: out of the humblest sources, the materials for
revolt may be assembled; the problem is to invest the familiar symbols of freedom with an intensity so extraordinary that a leap can be
made from the "objectively necessary" to the possible. Not so long
ago, in a small ethnic ghetto of a small state, there were people who
knew it could be done.

NOTES

I thank Professor Rudolph Vecoli, dean of Italian-American radical history, and David Montgomery for helpful, sympathetic comments on an early draft of this essay. Judy Smith provided much guidance throughout, and Sue Benson, James Celenza, Mark Naison, Gary Kornblith, and Ted Burrows, among others, also made helpful criticisms and suggestions. An earlier version of this article appeared in *Radical History Review*, 17 (1978).

1. Stanley Aronowitz, *False Promises: The Shaping of American Working Class Consciousness* (New York, 1973), pp. 164–65.

2. Joseph Stipanovich, "Immigrant Workers and Immigrant Intellectuals in Progressive America: A History of the Yugoslav Socialist Federation, 1900–1918" (Ph.D. dissertation, University of Minnesota, 1978), preface.

3. See, e.g., Richard Hostetter, *The Italian Socialist Movement*, I (Princeton, 1958); the brief but incisive treatment in Gwyn A. Williams, *Proletarian Order* (London, 1975), ch. 1; and Rudolph J. Vecoli, "*Contadini* in Chicago," in Herbert Gutman and Gregory Kealey, eds., *Many Pasts*, II (Englewood Cliffs, 1973).

4. The outstanding work in the field of Italian-American radicalism and labor, Edwin Fenton's "Immigrants and Unions, a Case Study: Italians and American Labor, 1870–1920" (Ph.D. dissertation, Harvard University, 1957), contains much valuable information and insight, but treats the role of radicals in a traditional manner, as an ephemeral influence upon labor bound cheerfully toward consensus. See ch. 1 on the early years. Rudolph Vecoli, "Italian-American Workers, 1880–1920: *Padrone* Slaves or Primitive Rebels," unpublished essay, considers the same subject from a more dynamic standpoint.

5. Rudolph Vecoli, "Luigi Galleani: Knight Errant of Anarchism," unpublished essay.

6. Few studies exist on this vital aspect. See Mari Jo Buhle's *Women and American Socialism, 1870–1920* (Urbana, 1981), pp. 298–99.

7. This is summarized best in Susan Jaffee, "Ethnic Working-Class Protest: The Textile Strike of 1922 in Rhode Island" (Honors thesis, Brown University, 1974), ch. 1.

8. *Report of the Commission of Labor Made to the General Assembly for the Years 1916–1919* (Providence, 1921), pp. 214–28.

9. Vecoli, "Luigi Galleani"; "Westerly," Sept. 17, 1905, "Westerly, R.I.," July 30, 1905, both in *Il Proletario* (New York), hereafter referred to as *Il P*.

10. "Westerly," in *Il P* for the following dates: Sept. 3, 1905, Mar. 18, 25, Nov. 19, 1906, Apr. 21, 1907.

11. "Providence, R.I.," in *Il P* for the following dates: Jan. 29, May 21, June 4, Dec. 10, 1905, Jan. 28, Mar. 11, 1906, Sept. 1, Oct. 20, 1907. "Fra Libri e Giornali," ibid., Apr. 22, 1906.

12. "A Quelli che se ne vanno," *Cronaca Sovversiva* (Barre, Vt.), Oct. 12, 1912, hereafter referred to as *CS*. "Luigi Nimini," *Il P*, Oct. 19, 1912.

13. "L'errore dei socialisti nel trattare la questione religiosa," *CS*, Sept.

18, 1909; and the following items in *Ragione Nuova* (Providence): "La Ragione Nuova," Jan. 31, 1909; "Teatralia e Chiesa," Apr. 30, 1909; "Providence, R.I., L'Epilogo," and "Diversi methodi ma unico intento," May 31, 1909; "Providence, R.I.," June 30, 1909; "I.W.W. Local N. 530, Tessitori Italiani," "Unione Sarti Italiani," and "Industrial Workers of the World," Sept. 30, 1909; "Providence, R.I., Banchetto," Dec. 31, 1909; "Organizzazione or Unione?," "Propaganda," and "Per Il Columbus Day," Aug. 15, 1910.

14. Isaac Hourwich, *Immigration and Labor,* 2d ed. (New York, 1910), pp. 380, 393.

15. "Non lotte di razza, ma di classe," *Il P,* June 4, 1909; Fenton "Immigrants and Labor," p. 186.

16. "Le Insurrezioni della fame nel Mass.," *Il P,* Mar. 22, 1912; "L'IWW e la rivoluzione," ibid., Sept. 6, 1913.

17. "Providence, R.I.: Grande Agitazione Operaia," ibid., Jan. 25, 1913.

18. The following items in ibid.: "Da Pawtucket," Mar. 1, 1912; "Per i Prigionieri," May 1, 1912; "Movimento Operaio," May 11, 1912; "Da Pawtucket," June 1, 1912; "Da Pawtucket," June 8, 1912; and "Westerly, R.I.," *CS,* June 8, 1912.

19. "Sciopero in Vista," and "Providence, R.I.," *Il P,* Feb. 9, 1912; "Intense Enthusiasm at Protest Meeting," and "Police Interference Cause of Disorder," *Labor Advocate* (Providence), Sept. 22, 1912, hereafter referred to as *LA.*

20. The following items in *Il P:* "Sciopero di Tessitori," Jan. 18, 1913; "Providence, R.I.," Jan. 25, 1913; "Providence, R.I.," Feb. 1, 1913. "Strike at Esmond," *Solidarity* (Chicago), Jan. 25, 1913; "Prospects Brighten for Strike at Esmond Mill," *LA,* Jan. 19, 1913; "Broken Promises Cause Walkout Again at Esmond," *LA,* Mar. 2, 1913.

21. "Notes from Esmond," *LA,* Mar. 23, 1913.

22. "Strikes and Lockouts in Rhode Island in 1913," in *Twenty-Seventh Annual Report of Industrial Statistics* (Providence, 1914.) Also see "Hamlet Strikers Win Complete Victory," *LA,* July 27, 1912, and "Jewelry Workers Rebel at Thirteen Hour Day," ibid., Sept. 28, 1913.

23. "Strikers at Hope Webbing Stand Firm," *LA,* Feb. 9, 1913; and the following items from the *Providence Journal:* "Pawtucket," Feb. 4, 1913; "Pawtucket," Feb. 6, 1913; "Strikers Picket Pawtucket Mills," Feb. 8, 1913; "Pawtucket," Apr. 3, 1913.

24. "Complete Tie-up at Peacedale Mill," *LA,* Mar. 23, 1913; "Peacedale Mills Still Tied up in Big Strike," ibid., Mar. 30, 1913.

25. See the following items from *Providence Journal:* "Hub Tailors Join Garment Union," Feb. 4, 1913; "IWW Organizers Strike Move Weak," Apr. 1, 1913; "Permit to Parade Refused the IWW," Apr. 3, 1913. Also see the following items from *LA:* "Tailors Union Rapidly Adding New Members," Jan. 26, 1913; "Garment Workers Form Strong Union," Mar. 9, 1913; "Striking Tailors Battling Against Tremendous Odds," and "Garment Workers Waging a Magnificent Fight," Apr. 6, 1913.

26. See the following items from *Providence Journal:* "IWW Holds Up Lo-

cal Merchants," Mar. 30, 1913; "Labor Union Heads Denounce IWW," Apr. 1, 1913; "Union Leader Here to Assist Tailors," Apr. 4, 1913; "Labor Men Score Methods of IWW," and "Priest Warns Against IWW," Apr. 7, 1913.

27. "The Garment Workers Strike," *LA*, Apr. 6, 1913.

28. "Pawtucket," *Providence Journal*, Apr. 3, 1913. See also the following items from *LA:* "Correspondence: A Word from Peacedale," Apr. 13, 1913; "Esmond Worker Explains 'Repudiation' Story," Apr. 30, 1913; "Brown and Sharpe Plan to Weed Out 'Undesireables,' " July 27, 1913.

29. See the following items from *LA:* "Mule Spinners Strike in Knight Mills Broken," Aug. 1, 1914; "Men Displaced by Women at Sayles Bleachery," Aug. 8, 1914; "Big Wage Cut Causes Strike in Pawtucket," Nov. 28, 1914; "Shannock Weavers Strike," Dec. 19, 1914.

30. See the following items from *LA:* "Ettor Given Royal Welcome," Dec. 22, 1912; "Textile Workers Will Fight Wage Reduction," Nov. 30, 1913; "Italian Workers Hold Protest Meeting on Colorado Massacre," June 27, 1914; see also "Pawtucket, R.I." *Il P*, July 6, 1912; "Da Pawtucket, R.I.: L'Inaugurazione della Casa Proletaria," ibid., Dec. 7, 1912.

31. "La Rivolta! . . ." *L'Eco* (Providence), Sept. 5, 1914. "Italian Workers on Federal Hill Have Big Protest Meeting," *Providence Journal*, Aug. 29, 1914; "18 Hurt in Riot on Federal Hill," ibid., Aug. 31, 1914. "Organized Protest Brings Merchants to Their Senses," *LA*, Sept. 5, 1914.

32. "Correspondence: The Cause of the Food Riot," *LA*, Sept. 5, 1914.

33. "Italian Workers to Seek Redress on Election Day," *LA*, Sept. 12, 1914; "Olneyville," *Providence Journal*, Sept. 8, 1914.

34. David Montgomery, "The 'New Unionism,' and the Transformation of Workers' Consciousness in America, 1909–22," *Journal of Social History*, 7 (Summer 1974), 519.

35. "The Eight Hour Day!" *LA*, Aug. 28, 1915; "Brown & Sharpe Employees Strike," *Providence Journal*, Sept. 21, 1915; "Second Bridgeport Here, Says Preble," ibid., Sept. 23, 1915.

36. "Brown & Sharpe Employees," *LA*, Sept. 25, 1915.

37. "Brown and Sharpe Have 3208 at Work," *Providence Journal*, Sept. 22, 1915; "Brown and Sharpe Will Fight to End," ibid., Sept. 24, 1915.

38. "Providence Labor Forward," *Labor World* (Providence and Woonsocket), Dec. 4, 1915.

39. "Second Bridgeport Here, Says Preble," *Providence Journal*, Sept. 23, 1915.

40. See, e.g., "Lo Sciopero di Providence," *CS*, Apr. 15, 1916; and the commissioner of labor's yearly reports on strikes, *Report of the Commission of Labor . . . 1916–1919*, pp. 125–205.

41. Ibid., p. 176

42. "La Protesta del Grande Concilio," *L'Eco*, May 22, 1919.

43. "La Unione, e gli operai," ibid., July 24, 1919.

44. The following items from *Jewelry Workers Monthly Bulletin* (New York): "Help to Win the Strike in Ostby and Barton's Shop, Providence, R.I.," May 1917; "Reports," Nov.-Dec. 1917; "Report of Local No. 8 in Providence, R.I.," Mar. 1918; "Badge and Emblem Makers' Meeting in Providence,

R.I.," Nov. 1922. See also *Report of the Commissioner of Labor . . . 1916–1919*, pp. 179–83.

45. "Fra i panettieri di Providence, R.I.," *Il P*, Oct. 6, 1917; and "Hotel Workers Union Formed," *LA*, Feb. 2, 1913; "Joseph J. Ettor Talks to Textile Workers," ibid., Apr. 24, 1915.

46. G. Vaoente, "Se l'esperienza valesse a qualche cosa . . .," *Il Lavoro* (New York), Sept. 27, 1919.

47. Vecoli, "Luigi Galleani."

48. Montgomery, " 'New Unionism,' " p. 517.

49. Interviews with Luigi Nardella, Cranston, R.I., Fall 1977.

50. Interviews with Luigi Nardella and Thomas Longo, Cranston, R.I., Fall 1977; see the following items from *Il Martello* (New York): "I tessitori scioperanti del Rhode Island," May 13, 1922; "L'operaio filosofo," June 17, 1922; "Il Gruppo Autonomo," Aug. 1, 1925; "RI—Altre a farabutti dell'O.Fd.I.," Aug. 28, 1926; "Abbasso il Fascismo," Dec. 28, 1926; "Nel Ordine Figli d'Italia," Sept. 24, 1927; "La Nostra attività Antifascista," Feb. 4, 1928; "Da Providence, RI," July 13, 1929. And see the following from *Il Lavoratore* (Chicago): "Providence, R.I.," Aug. 20, 1924; Woonsocket, R.I.," Sept. 22, 1924; "Providence, R.I.," June 3, 1925; "Da Providence, R.I.," June 14, 1925; "Providence, R.I.," June 27, 1925.

51. From the discussion at Sacco-Vanzetti Commemoration Meeting, Rhode Island Labor History Forum, Cranston, Sept. 1977, and "Comunicazione," *Adunata dei Refrattari* (New York), Apr. 11, 1925; "Corrispondenza," ibid., June 18, 1927.

Notes on Contributors

DONALD H. BELL is a member of the department of history at Tufts University, Medford, Massachusetts, where he teaches modern European history and comparative labor history. His publications include *Sesto San Giovanni: Workers, Culture, and Politics in an Italian Industrial Town, 1880–1922* (Rutgers University Press; in translation, Il Mulino Press) and articles and reviews in *Social History* and the *American Historical Review*, among other journals.

DAVID BENSMAN is a member of the department of labor studies education at the Graduate School of Education, Rutgers University, New Brunswick, New Jersey. He is the author of *The Practice of Solidarity: American Hat Finishers in the Nineteenth Century* (University of Illinois Press) and *Shattered Dreams* (McGraw-Hill, forthcoming).

CECELIA BUCKI is a doctoral candidate at the University of Pittsburgh, where she is studying worker organization and political action in Connecticut, 1920–40. She has participated in numerous public history projects in Connecticut and recently created the Connecticut Labor Archives at the University of Connecticut.

PAUL BUHLE is director of the Oral History of the American Left, Tamiment Library, New York University, and is oral historian of Rhode Island labor for the Rhode Island Historical Society, Providence. His publications include *A Concise History of Woman Suffrage*, co-edited with Mari Jo Buhle (University of Illinois Press), *A History of Rhode Island Working People*, co-edited with Scott Molloy and Gail Sansbury (Providence, Institute for Labor Studies), and *Working for Democracy: American Workers from the Revolution to the Present*, co-edited with Alan Dawley (University of Illinois Press).

LEON FINK is a member of the department of history at the University of North Carolina at Chapel Hill. His publications include *Workingmen's Democracy: The Knights of Labor and American Politics* (University of Illinois Press) and articles in *Social History* and *Southern Changes*. He and Brian Greenberg are working on a study tentatively entitled "Awakening in the Quiet Zone: The History of a Hospital Worker's Union."

The late HERBERT G. GUTMAN was Distinguished Professor of History at the Graduate Center, City University of New York. His publications included *Slavery and the Numbers Game: A Critique of Time on the Cross, The Black Family in Slavery and Freedom, 1750–1925,* and *Work, Culture and Society in Industrializing America.*

ALEXANDER KEYSSAR is presently a research fellow at the Russell Sage Foundation, New York, and has taught at the Massachusetts Institute of Technology and Brandeis University. His book, *Out of Work: The First Century of Unemployment in Massachusetts, 1870–1916,* was published by Cambridge University Press in 1986.

CAROL LASSER is a member of the department of history at Oberlin College, Ohio. Her book, *Friends and Sisters: Letters between Lucy Stone and Antoinette Brown Blackwell, 1846–93* (co-edited with Marlene Merrill), is forthcoming from the University of Illinois Press.

JONATHAN PRUDE is a member of the department of history at Emory University, Atlanta. His publications include *The Coming of the Industrial Order: Town and Factory Life in Rural Massachusetts, 1810–1860* (Cambridge University Press), *The Countryside in the Age of Capitalist Transformation: Essays in the Social History of Rural America* (with Steven Hahn, coeditor), and essays and reviews in *Labor History, Journal of American History,* and *New Republic.*

ROY ROZENSWEIG is a member of the department of history and director of the oral history program at George Mason University, Fairfax, Virginia. He is the author of *Eight Hours for What We Will: Workers and Leisure in an Industrial City, 1870–1920* (Cambridge University Press), the co-editor of *Experiments in History Teaching,* and the co-producer of a historical documentary film, *Mission Hill and the Miracle of Boston.*

JUDITH E. SMITH is a member of the department of history at Boston College, Newton, Massachusetts. Her book, *Family Connections: A History of Italian and Jewish Immigrant Lives in Providence, Rhode Island, 1900–1940,* was published in 1985 by the State University of New York Press.

ALFRED F. YOUNG is a member of the department of history at Northern Illinois University, DeKalb. He is the author of *The Democratic Republicans of New York* (University of North Carolina Press) and editor of two volumes in the series Explorations in the History of American Radicalism: *The American Revolution* and *Dissent* (both Northern Illinois University Press). His book on the workingmen of Revolutionary Boston is forthcoming.

Books in the series *The Working Class in American History*

A Generation of Boomers: The Pattern of Railroad Labor Conflict
in Nineteenth-Century America
SHELTON STROMQUIST

The New England Working Class and the New Labor History
EDITED BY HERBERT G. GUTMAN AND DONALD H. BELL

Barons of Labor: The San Francisco Building Trades and Union Power
in the Progressive Era
MICHAEL KAZIN

Once a Cigar Maker: Men, Women, and Work Culture in
American Cigar Factories, 1900-1919
PATRICIA COOPER